Earthbodies

Earthbodies

Rediscovering Our Planetary Senses

Glen A. Mazis

State University of New York Press

Published by
State University of New York Press, Albany

© 2002 State University of New York

Printed in the United States of America

For information, address State University of New York Press,
90 State Street, Suite 700, Albany, NY 12207

Production by Marilyn P. Semerad
Marketing by Fran Keneston

Library of Congress Cataloging-in-Publication Data

Mazis, Glen A., 1951-
    Earthbodies : rediscovering our planetary senses / Glen A. Mazis.
      p. cm.
    Includes bibliographical references and index.
    ISBN 0-7914-5417-7 (alk. paper)—ISBN 0-7914-5418-5 (pbk. : alk. paper)
    1. Body, Human (Philosophy) 2. Ethics. I. Title: Earth bodies. II. Title.
BJ1695 .M39 2002
128—dc21
                                       2001049423

10 9 8 7 6 5 4 3 2 1

Contents

Acknowledgments

Deborah Tangen has been an inspiration and a helper. My mother, Charlotte Mazis, taught me the love of language and has always believed in me. Judith Johnson encouraged me to undertake this project. Catherine Keller, as always, has provided so many stimulating dialogues about topics essential to this book. Jason Starr, Marion Winnick, and Crispin Sartwell have made wonderful critics and supporters. Bruce Wilshire has added many insights about our shared loves and philosophical concerns. Bill and Connie Mahar, Donna Wilshire, Ed Casey, Pat Johnson, John Neill, Joan Kuenz, and so many of my students have given me so much support and love. As befitting the spirit of the human animal dialogue of this book, Bhakti, the "Zen Chihuahua," is due innumerable thanks for her calm, buoyant support throughout the writing process. Penn State Harrisburg was kind enough to grant me a year's sabbatical to work on the manuscript. My new colleagues at Soka University have helped me in the homestretch especially David and Stella Chappell, Peter Sanchez, and Kathleen Adams. Without Dr. Michael Choti, Dr. Daniel Drachman, and the good folks at Johns Hopkins, this earthbody wouldn't be around to finish this book: thanks! Finally, I must thank Jane Bunker: she is the kind of enthusiastic, supportive editor that every author hopes to find. Use of the reproduction of Henri Mattise, "The Dance II," on the cover is with permission of ©2001 Succession H. Matisse, Paris/Artist Rights Society (ARS), New York/and Bridgeman Art Library International, New York.

Introduction

This book is written from a concern for the planet. It is written for all the sensitive living beings and quieter non-living beings who are this planet's flesh. It is written in the faith that philosophy doesn't have to be an arcane endeavor, abstracted from the world and dealing with scholastic problems only scholars would care about. Philosophy should be written in a way that all citizens can encounter as a wake-up call. Philosophy should be the kind of thing that allows people to change their lives. We should not be self-defeatingly driven to professionals and experts to deal with problems we try to manage that are the result of misunderstanding what human beings are and misperceiving our relationship with the natural and social world. This happens because these core questions are never really examined, since philosophy has not made itself available to our neighbors. Philosophy can and should speak in understandable, even if unusual, ways. Philosophy should speak to the heart and not just to abstract intellects. Philosophy should be a work of imagination, fun, and excitement, dreaming new possible worlds by transforming the one we have always loved.

There is a lot wrong with our planet that does require the help of experts among others, from the ecological crisis to people slaughtering each other in wars of hate to the breakdown of the community fabric, etc., but I am concerned with a philosophical disability that is widespread. If we look at ourselves, others, and the natural world in a way that denies ourselves the abilities we have as embodied beings and distorts the nature of reality, then any solutions we devise to help us personally or collectively are doomed to failure or at least to short-lived makeshift success. I believe that there has been a fundamental misunderstanding of what our bodies are in relation to the rest of the planet in the dominant Western culture for the last two and half millennia. If we were to understand who we are as embodied beings, I believe the ecological crisis would appear in a new light and the animosities among peoples who are different might become welcomed instead of feared. The experts deal with symptoms and these symptoms must be addressed, but we also need to get at the root of our disconnection from the planet.

Inspired by the work of the French philosopher Merleau-Ponty and phenomenology to describe the rich ambiguity of how we experience being caught up in the world and in other people by hearkening to how we are bodies in ongoing flux—bodies that feel, sense, intuit, remember, dream, fantasize, and get caught up in emotions and passions—I have written as scholar for decades from a viewpoint at odds with the mainstream rational, detached, and compartmentalized philosophy of the profession. In this work, I seek to articulate these more scholarly insights in a way that dispenses with jargon and academic borders to engage the reader viscerally and directly with their experience. "Earthbodies" is a term I've coined to describe the way in which we have no body as a thing or substance. Embodiment is an ongoing process that never ceases. We are processes and not things. Our processes have driving rhythms that can give the illusion that they are just solid, stable blocks of being. However, like all processes that are open to other unfolding processes, they are fragile equilibria that can suddenly veer off into illness or death or disintegration of our personal or collective existences. We as individuals or as collectives can stay within a rhythm for such a long time we are deluded that we subsist as this identity, and then suddenly we shift into a new universe. Suddenly, the robust person struggles to use his or her limbs or the nation that had been a model of cooperation degenerates into terror and genocide or the perfectly conforming functionary becomes an outlaw or a homeless person or loses their mind. Then, we suddenly notice, perhaps, that all people, all things, all creatures are in a flux that incorporates myriad energies from disparate beings.

I also believe that concepts mean nothing without being presented in the concrete circumstances which gives them vitality and importance. Discussing how in a film one of Anne Rice's vampires can be worried or how it is that adolescent boys are drawn into school shootings or how Koko, the gorilla who has been taught English, gets on-line to explain death are not mere examples of ideas or concepts. Rather, the concept is empty without its specific circumstances in which it takes on full significance. Philosophical and cultural studies are not separable, if we are to achieve real self-understanding and creativity in dealing with our world's challenges—the goals of philosophy.

Although I have mentioned a philosopher and a way of thinking that helped inspire me, I refuse to think in the straightjacket of any orthodoxy. I find postmodern philosophy fascinating, as well as American philosophy, ancient Greek philosophy, Taoism, Buddhism, radical feminists, enlightenment rationalists, social contract theorists, depth psychologists, raving suicidal Romantics, scientists and filmmakers. I hope that I have succeeded in betraying loyalties to any particular school of thought I admire, for I find such allegiances ridiculous. The idea is think about our lives with any lively, stimulating interlocutor who comes along.

This book speaks from a contemporary American context. The problems it points to are configured in different ways in the collisions with race, class, and gender. Scientific studies that generate data about ecological parameters or about brain physiology and other issues are essential to considering questions related to this work. However, this book doesn't delve far into these realms. Although the

American context, perhaps unfortunately, is becoming more global, cultural differences are key to many issues raised here. Again, these are carefully articulated by others. I myself have written about the gender issues related to this book. Others have written eloquently on race and class. Instead of these dimensions being examined, this book focuses on some phenomena like industrial clock time and on attitudes like the sentimentality surrounding the current uses of the Internet that have widespread currency. The focus of this book is on the underlying philosophy—the sense of reality—at the heart of our misappropriation of the planet, our violence towards ourselves and other species, and our self-defeating ways of being defended from the open avenues of embodiment. It is an attempt to redefine embodiment in terms that could offer us fuller, more cooperative, and creative lives. Hopefully, this meditation can provoke a questioning of the common sense of cultural assumptions that are threatening to become global ones, so that embodiment can be appreciated as a radical resource of interconnection that has gone wanting for millennia.

Chapter One

The Earthly Dance of Interconnection

Moving Earth and Flowing Flesh

At any moment, you are much more than you probably imagine yourself to be, since you are an earthbody. An earthbody isn't "yours," it's the world's. Despite cultural biases, you don't "have" this body. You are part of a dynamic process that we might call "earthbodying," if we weren't so used to referring to ourselves with nouns. Earthbodies are sensual, perceptual and feeling conductors through which richer meaning flows than we can grasp intellectually. The world to which I referred is also not properly a noun, but more a verb, a process, too. The currents moving through these bodies are dynamic processes. Both the unfolding of the world and our bodies happens within a sensual richness that weaves diverse energies. We build machines that monitor all sorts of physical inputs and often believe this is a model of what our perceiving bodies tell us. Our senses, however, are not mere sensors. The senses infiltrate and are infiltrated by each perceptual experience saturated with layers and layers of significance. While you have been reading this first paragraph, the imagined image of a robed Socrates speaking a few thousand years ago, the shifting of the clouds overhead, or the expanse of a night sky, the collapse of a city in an earthquake, or of a building under the implosive impact of a highjacked jetliner, the memory of a relative who spoke to you of strange thoughts, the longing for a distant love might have been part of the interconnected reverberations of the words for you. Many of these layers of sense are personal to you and but many are shared by the conjurings of my words and the sense of the objects to which I refer. Many of the primary meanings of even seemingly unrelated terms, however, are the senses of things taught to to you by natural beings, whether of flow from water, solidity from rock, flight from birds. Words enmeshed speak a meshing world. No expressions are simple or static.

We shape the world since it is indeterminate and fluctuating as it flows forth. The world shapes us since we are indeterminate and fluctuating as we flow forth. We are only a node in a vast field of energies and meanings. Perceiving is an art. We take in the world more or less gracefully, more or less expressively, and more or less sensitively. There is a minimum we gain through perception in order to function in an environment. However, there is an unreachable maximum that our body gleans and dreams from the world. This book will explore our bodies as a place of enlacement among varied forces, some in our control, some not. There are no bodies for us without the other bodies with which we're interwoven. There are no bodies without the world of which they are a resonance. These ongoing currents comprise earthbodies.

In our modern sophistication, we believe that we know that our experience of motion is relative to a frame of reference. We are smug in the knowledge that although the earth rotates at great speed, we can't feel it, given that everything is moving at the same speed. Our intellectual constructions afford us a taken for granted security that allows us to discount other strange feelings. Yet, experience is richer and less stable than the apparent rational lawfulness of existence, if we pay attention to nuances. The abstract and general notion never fully fits the particular, except insofar as vital parts of its identity are discounted. Cultures, personal rites of passage, and even moments of a lively spirit alter our sense of things radically, let alone altered states of experience in illness, in war, during catastrophes, in moments of ecstasy, in inspiration, or love. After my neighborhood has fallen beneath bombs or I am rescued from drowning by the bravery of a swimmer plunging into the icy river or I see a Van Gogh painting, something may shift in the meaning of the world. The everyday experience fluctuates just as much, if we hearken to it. The power of the words you are reading, if they move you, very much funnel a deep and enlivening movement of the total earth through your being. The pouring rain, the blowing branches, the speeding cars, the soaring birds, the jostling crowds don't stand against an utterly still backdrop and stable foundation. All this movement infuses the world and draws from the world. The world rocks, and rolls. It is a high meditative art to experience absolute quiet, stillness and stability. Without this effort, and even within it, we are always impelled by myriad trajectories crisscrossing through us from the world.

Earthbodies are of a flesh that moves with this movement of the world. Earthbodies insinuate themselves into this larger rhythm in order to be alive and add back to the larger mix their own distinctive rhythms. The image on the cover of this book is meant to represent a key notion about earthbodies. It is Matisse's famous painting, The Dance. As the women swirl around, forming a circle moving over the earth, the earth itself can be seen to be both a stage and yet itself a swirling circle; their steps, their motion, and their hearts echo and resonate to the motion of the circling earth beneath them, and yet are grounded—balanced—in the plane of this motion. Whether Matisse intended it or not, this image can be seen to say something about the nature of bodies in all cultures and natural settings on this globe, although always inflected differently given the locale: there is no living creature, that is unmoved by what goes on around them. This sentient responsiveness only occurs because flesh of all kinds are moving vectors within the world in a kind of circulation among things that is their real body. The marrow of things is fluid and always becoming within and through everything else as fluid.

We "are moved"—feel, think, and desire—because the whirling, spinning dance of the earth moves through the body. Its kinetic energy and centrifugal force are central to our sense of existence. The fact that gravity is the outcome of a never-ending movement is easily understandable in rational terms. However, in the depths and nuances of our earthbodies, we live the force of meanings that are logically at odds with each other. In our bones is both stillness and motion, security and restlessness. On an immediate level, we feel as though the earth is still. On a deeper level, we feel held by an embracing earth. It actively holds onto us, giving us the weight to walk, work, and love. This earth is not just inert, but a protector actively engaged with us. We also feel spun around as part of a movement of vitality. We have the feeling that life on this planet is irrepressibly lively, full of motion, since it resonates to a deeper sense of each person as part of a larger movement, a whirl, a dance whose rhythm is spun by the earth itself. The earth is also playmate. This is the ultimate source of our motivation.

This may sound fantastic to you because we have been taught to close our bodies, lock our knees, and brace ourselves for life and its tasks in such a way in our modern Western technological society that we fail to experience the pull, the tides, of the earth's motion which stream through us. The seas are not the only tidal regions on the earth, the land tides are more subtle, and it requires an adjustment in our sensibilities—a fine tuning—to catch onto their movements and rhythms, but they are there. To open ourselves to this motion would require many changes in the ways we currently conceive ourselves, since these "normal" ideas are powerful tidal barriers which contain our natural movement and feelings of kinship with the deeper motion around us. If the jetties created by our identities as responsible adults in modern society were to be dismantled, vitality and new realms of meaning could be gained from joining these subtle yet swelling tides.

This motion of the Earth is not just "physical" motion. It's not merely about static entities moving through a static and empty space. That is one way to see the world. The motion of the earth, like the motion of the dancers under the sky, is about a movement of identities and within identities. Motion in its fullest sense is a continual transformation that occurs within and among everything. There are areas of rest, where things can remain more stable if we carve out a controlled area in order to get certain things done. That doesn't stop the underlying vitality of everything on the planet from entering an intercourse that gives rise to new forms, meanings, relationships, feelings, dreams, atmospheres, directions, expressions, shapes, possibilities, and even histories (yes, we can see how the past always changes, too!). If we can reveal the dance of the planet, we will see where the earth's motion is material, but equally ideational, emotional, imaginative, spiritual, linguistic, communal, and natural. Each of these traditional dimensions is caught up in a host of other dimensions and "belongs" not to us, but to the infusing significance of the planet.

To see how it is that we are part of a dance with others, whether with our fellow human beings or with other types of beings, requires that we challenge the first barrier of our conceptual tradition: what seems logical or "the commonsensical." Our understanding of what is logical or reasonable has long determined how we think. We rely on "solid logic." Matisse's painting is not only a beautiful work of art but is also a powerful lesson about another logic. The lesson is contained in the structure of the dance. Within this canvas is portrayed the more open logic of the relation of lives and even inanimate beings on this planet in their rhythmic being. Matisse's painted scene evokes the sense of the women dancing, circling, and being caught up in the swirling magic of the dance. Each woman follows her own steps, her own inner urgings, and the spirit of the moment as it feels to her uniquely. Yet, each is part of the spinning circular motion of the whole group.

At points, the circle of dancing women is not literally closed—hands have spread apart for this particular instant—yet fingers will find fingers again in the next moment and reclasp. Even isolated at this instant, however, the circle is unbroken because its shape, its form, is not comprised of an outline—a literally unbroken line—but rather is powerfully drawn by the vector of the interconnecting flow. The rhythm moving among the women also catches the power emanating from the earth and sky that asks to be rejoined. It offers itself by being sketched out among the women in a movement among them that flows and binds. Each woman is both separate in her own heartfelt celebration of her body and each is brought into unity with the swirling presence of all the women with the earth and sky.

This image of the dancing, celebratory women can teach us what it means to have a human body in a way that all the anatomical drawings will never begin to reveal. We have mistakenly understood our bodies through anatomy for several centuries, yet this gives us a distorted understanding of the body as fixed, the body as dead, in order to fathom its life. We can only understand the alive body through its liveliness, only understand the body's deepest life through the life of the planet, which opens us up to our earthbodies.

One reason that the image in Matisse's painting can lead us to a sense of our earthbodies is that it contains both a lesson in another logic and in the sense of relationship possible for moving, expressive human beings. We need to have a sense of these relationships and this other logic before we can even begin to sense the kind of bodies we are. The logic taught by these swirling women is not to be found in traditional texts of logic. Philosophers from Aristotle on have focused on *assertions* made about things and people as the locus of truth and logic. They tell us that the earth itself says nothing and "has" no truth. Only when things become "objects of predication" have they been seen to be involved in truth and logic. "Predication" as defined by philosophy, is the act of saying something about the relation of an isolated object in terms of another isolated object or property. It is seen as our crowning achievement as human beings. It gives us an analytical power that eventually leads us to be able to split atomic particles and send spaceships into the cosmos.

Yet, predication of this sort splits the event—the dance—into subject and object—into the dancer and the dance—a potentially dangerous doubling and splitting of reality that thinkers as diverse as Yeats and Nietzsche have noted with disgust. The starting point for our traditional logic is to observe entities seen in the denuded state of having been removed from the spell of the dance, once the circling sense of existence has been vaporized by a quantitative reckoning, and once the linking through rhythm has been dispersed. Then, the dynamic quality of all things is to be reestablished rationally as "accidents" which befall things through "external relations." The flow and the relatedness of Matisse's dancing women, however, is neither "external" nor "accidental": it is the heart of their being at this moment and essential to their sense of themselves and the world. This alternative logic will emerge only by exploring the sense of the body awakened to the vitality lodged within the rhythm that interconnects all living and nonliving beings into a type of song and poem, a story of an inexhaustible, never-ending odyssey. This other logic unlocks many other potential relationships for this earthbody on this planet.

Logic may well seem a silly thing to worry about in the face of global violence, governments out of touch with citizens, alienations from massive bureaucratic institutions, and the dying out of parts of the natural world. Yet, much frustration, lack of vitality, increasing anxiety, and spiritual dislocation comes from a short-circuit in the way we see ourselves. The flaw in logic concerns the way we think about our bodies and their relationship to world and to others, and is at the heart of why we don't know ourselves. It is this lack of knowing, of feeling ourselves in this other way, as earthbodies, that leads to these current problems.

Sometimes we think we have created so many machines that they are crowding us out. Their presence and that of their by-products have come to take over the space which we humans, animals, and the natural world needed to thrive. However, the problem is not that our machines have pushed us aside, but rather the problem is that *we have ourselves become machines*. We take ourselves and make our bodies into machines by what we do to our senses and imaginations. Once our rhythm in an intertwined dance with others is broken and our place in a spiral with the planet lost, we are left to create a new relationship as a cog in a larger engineered scheme of existence. The vitality and moving interconnections appear only to those who can sense and imagine in a dancing way. The machine doesn't feel the fluid motion, the rhythm, and belonging with others and can't move in sync with it. Insofar as we fail to sense and feel these rhythms, we are machines stuck in a larger machine.

As we will explore in this book, the power of the mind as integrated within the body is greater than we usually believe. Even though we tend to overvalue the mind's worth in other silly ways as an independent power, we still don't seem to realize that the body/mind (as the Zen Buddhists call it) can create new realities. It does so, not out of itself, but in how it allows the transformation of the planet and other beings with which we can interweave in their identity. Through our attitudes, which are partly ideas, partly emotions, imagination, etc., we can allow changes in our experience. We can change the look, even the overall appearance, and the sense of things around us. We invented the machine, not as a separate tool, but as what we were to become and what our planet was to become—a factory containing more factories within it. Machines are separate from their environment in the sense that they are not in relation with them: machines grind in a certain direction that is their function. This is what makes them machines, this unswerving following of a set path of operation and function. Even self-regulating ones have set options. As humans tend to become separate from interrelation with their environment, self-contained, and unswervingly functioning in set directions, we become another variety of machine. After we ourselves have become machines in so much of our daily life, then we hunger to create other machines to reinforce our set purposes, to thrill us with their efficiency, to keep us company. We like to have them join in our work as manageable partners, because we have entered their realm of efficiency, unswervingness, and indifference. Of course, the lust for the machine life and the actual proliferation of machines gives rise to other problems.

Exactly how we are machines can only be understood bit by bit. The first clue, however, is in looking at the dancing logic of Matisse's women and contrasting it with the common sense logic of a pervasive sense of rationality, the logic of yes or no, of true and false, of one or zero—the binary logic of the machine and the computer. We have become so accustomed to this logic that we are unaware of its sinister power. If our "objective" logic starts with the basic assumption that each entity has the property of being itself versus everything else in time and space, then it implies to us that out of these separate entities collected on the surface of the earth and throughout the cosmos, we must be the ones to articulate their relationships. These other "helpless" beings (driven by necessities external to them) are seen as locked in an indifference to each other, isolated from each other, and compelled into random, mechanical, and meaningless collisions with each other. We are the one thing from this vast collection that can stand back and measure all the others. Doing this, we believe we are the only truly free beings. We believe ourselves to be self-determining in a world locked in slavery to deterministic chains of cause and effect. This sense of our unique "human dignity" is the basis of much of our Western spirituality, religion, and moral thinking.

However, if there is a dancing connection of which we are already part and can witness, then we are breaking up this set of relations of which all beings are a part in order to step back and tear things apart and then put them back together according to ideas we deem sensible. We assume that the world is just a jumble, a chaos, because it doesn't seem to naturally fit our traditional logical categories. However, we might be missing the proper identities of the other beings in the world around us that are forged fragilely in the rhythm of dance, in the fluidity of transformations of which we are a small part. Not only that, but we may have other identities as part of this dance that we lose sight of when we break off its rhythm and disconnect. Not only that, but the answers we believe we arrive at independently from our special vantage point may have been insights first given to us by being part of the dance and interchange with our partners. Even worse, for all the human clarity we obtain from isolating ourselves and speaking from that vantage point, we may be losing some of the insight, meaning, and wisdom we had as dancers being infiltrated with different kinds of felt communications—ones which might still resonate in our earthbodies when we learn to listen and feel them. If we are tearing things apart in our misguided effort to see them better, this is a mean trick to impose on the planet and to play on ourselves. This is why we may call logic either "nurturing" or "diabolical", depending on whether it is the logic of the earth and sky or the logic of a certain kind of sorcery that calls itself "pure objectivity," but may not be what it seems.

Dancing versus Diabolical Logic

The logic with the sober face of "pure rationality" hides a diabolical grin. This latent intent is masked, however, by the platitudes that make up "common sense." The "cardinal rule" of this logic—the "law of non-contradiction"—says that "*a* is *a*" and correlatively that "*a* is not *b*." What could be more simple? What could be any more obviously true—*objectively* true? To put this in more concrete terms, I could say the first rule shows me that I am I—or that Popeye the sailor man is Popeye the sailor man, as he proudly sings. The second rule can remind me that I am not Popeye but rather that I am me, or that I am me and not that tree outside my window. This is the obvious sense that is at the heart of *binary* logic: yes or no, *a* or *b*, true or false. Psychologically, this is very reassuring, because our identity seems clear and distinct, given and identifiable. Whether personally or politically, I can think of my own interest and my own identity without worrying about how much I am caught up in your identity, whether as my friend or spouse or as a member of another ethnic, economic, or national group. I just am whomever I am, no matter what happens to you or to that group, and I am free to treat others in whatever way seems best or right to me.

It is the either/or—two value—system that drives our computers, becoming more and more the law of our world and the way we think about ourselves and life on this planet. We are told that we couldn't think or make sense of the world or communicate without these simple logical rules. Although this is true in some aspects of our lives to some extent, it is also true that we couldn't even feel who we are or what is our connection to the environment or what is our connection to other people without the counterbalancing ever-present *logic of inclusive ambiguity and depth*. If who I am is ambiguously tied up with all the beings around me, objects, creatures, and other people, then my identity and my welfare is enmeshed inextricably with theirs. It is not merely a matter of my choice as to how I choose to think or act towards others, because whatever I do changes who they are and who I am as part of a linked being with them. This *logic of care*[1] among beings precedes overt recognition and decisions about how to act towards other entities, creatures, or people. It is that force in life which is overwhelmingly compelling, but we ignore both its presence and its meaning. It is because of this logic of inclusive ambiguity that we first find ourselves always fascinated by the world around us, concerned enough about anything even to notice it, to want to do things to have an impact on the world and to obtain things from the world. Since we ourselves are caught up in the world, our identity, our flow of existence only moves through the world, from the world, and back through us; we are focused always on that world. From the baby's first very unfocused stare that is nevertheless utterly captivated, taken with the world around it, sinking into an intensity of watching this play it feels drawn to enter, *because it starts to feel there is its life*. It is only because of this logic of inclusive ambiguity that we feel any urges, desires, or motivations to join and participate in the world. That is me—the world.

There was a film made in 1986, called *Silent Running,* about the fate of the last forest and natural ecosystems. It is not about the last forests and natural ecosystems on the planet, because in the film, they are no longer here, on Earth. They have been preserved within encased biospheres and sent into space until the earth can be detoxified enough that they might be brought back to flourish again on the planet. In a sense the biospheres are the last seeds of renewal for a sterile earth. One scientist, Freeman Lowell (played with an intense desperation by Bruce Dern), is fighting to make others see the importance of the existence of these plants and animals. The viewer senses that he is fighting a losing battle on behalf of their survival. The inhabitants of the earth who initially wanted to save the wildlife and animals have come to see themselves as beings who are self-sufficient and can do fine outside a connection to nature. Freeman's crewmates can't taste any difference between synthetic rations and the tasty meals that he cooks—an effort that just seems a bother for nothing. The peace of the brooks, the beauty of the flowers, the quiet of the small animals scurrying about the forest find no echoes, no resonance, in their rhythms, in their sense of being, or in their emotions. They see Freeman's soaring as he watches a bird soar or his own sense of blossoming with life and vitality as his plants and flowers blossom, but they just "don't get it." Their logic, their constructed world of barriers and distances from other such beings who have their own rhythms, rather than those the engineers have constructed along their own specifications for machines or the social engineers have designed for their human entertainment, is so great they can't experience what Freeman experiences. What is he talking about and feeling? They make fun of him and feel he is a fool. The crew, besides Freeman, is bored and has to spend its time gambling or racing their electric cars to try to fill their feelings of emptiness. They do not feel as though they are missing some essential part of their lives and have forgotten what these other beings meant to them. They cease to care about the fate of the last trees, plants, and animals, and don't want to invest time or effort in the project of preserving and restoring them to the planet. This is a perfectly logical and understandable position in a cost/benefit analysis under the sway of the diabolical logic that considers all entities as discrete. However, by contrast, within a logic of inclusive ambiguity, these supposed benefits makes no sense, since they miss a deeper issue.

In the binary system of thinking there is me and you, or me and it: we are juxtaposed as separable identities. As long as we are separable in space and time we are distinct entities. There may be external links which connect us—chains of cause and effect, like the fact that I need to take in air or water for the chemical reactions which go on inside me and sustain my functioning, but any element that can bring about that functioning can be substituted, obtained in some other way, and used for this purpose. It does not speak to me, it is not of me, and who I am and what my life means is not comprised by its identity. If we think this way, we may think that we have enjoyed these other beings—trees, animals, flowers, or whatever—but that they were just "out there" in a space with us, external to us, that there was "us and them." In the film, it is interesting that when the orders come from Earth to abandon the project, the command is to destroy the biodomes with nuclear explosions. Why destroy these last trees, plants, flowers, animals, streams? Doesn't this betray an unconscious recognition? A recognition that in abandoning the other creatures of the planet and our tie to them a violence is already being committed? Is it that to, cut them off from us is to cut off part of us, and to let them remain—even light years away drifting in space—would be to allow a vital part of ourselves to drift with a tie still to us, even though unacknowledged as such? There would still be drifting in space a claim upon us, a voice from within us, needing a response? That would be painful, would be a burden—the burden of the repressed that still haunts us on some level. So, instead make the violence overt and try to obliterate that part of ourselves that we can't deal with, can't fit into neat schemes of efficiency and consumption—Nuke them! declares the space agency. It is not surprising that from this point on, *Silent Running* degenerates into a blood-bath because the original distancing of humans from nature was a violent gesture, now fully consummated. Is our current relationship to nature that much different: for many, might not the voices of the natural world be light years away?

If we have so little connection to natural beings, then we can just substitute other enjoyable objects for them and still derive the same satisfaction from these substitutes. Why we could even just create artificial dogs or orchids that were holographic or biomechanical, if we wanted to be nostalgic about the particular kind of enjoyment they had provided us! Although, strictly speaking, most who use this logic define "pleasure" (and most aspects of reality) quantitatively, so whatever gives *as much* pleasure is substitutable without any discrimination among different and possibly irreplaceable qualities of pleasures. This is a utilitarian outcome based on diabolical logic.

This fantasy is pursued in Philip K. Dick's novel, *Do Androids Dream of Electric Sheep?* Simulated mechanical entities substitute for the animal, insect, and plant worlds, after they have died off. The people living in this twenty-first–century world work their whole lives to save enough money to at least afford an "electric animal," which can give them some simulation of the companionship they used to have from real animals. It wasn't until most of the species of animate beings had become extinct that people realized that without the other creatures in the web of life they lacked a sense of belonging with the planet—a sense of soaring in the sky, of gliding on the winds, of romping across the fields, of bleating, of nuzzling, of boring into things, of propelling underwater, and a myriad of other sensations shared with what the Native American peoples called "the brothers and sisters of the fourlegs, the crawling world, and the flying world." The Native American names recognized the kinship of all creatures in a world of many dimensions. Later, we will look more closely at how animals and other living beings are part of our bodies and the sinew of the earth.

Decker, the main character of the novel, comes to hate his electric sheep because it doesn't awake in him these same feelings, because these feelings were responses engendered by communicative relationships with these other beings, even though he, like others, hadn't noticed this at the time. Decker, suddenly realized one day that electric sheep or other biomechanical animals "had no ability to appreciate

the existence of another"(*ES*, 37). In appreciating the existence of the other, there is
an openness to the other, a felt relationship set up between beings of differing
species, and a recognition in the eyes, in the nostrils, in the ears, in the fears, the
affections or dislikes, and in the excitements of the other creature. Then I see myself
and feel myself through the rabbit's scampering away or in the dog's contentedly
rubbing up against my thigh as it naps beside me on the couch. With this opening
up of dimensions of mutuality among beings, the dancing logic of blurred boundaries and identities unfolds. There has to be a meeting—an encounter—among
beings who have their own place within existence; then the creatures, including the
human ones, get to venture out through the lines of connections among creatures
to wander in other spaces, whether for the instant soaring above in the air as the
bird flies overhead or feeling the airy playfulness in their chirping as they swoop
around one another friskily. If we identify or create other creatures to be just enslaved
functionaries of the human ego, we lose our ability to expand ourselves through
these other creaturely realms in the flow of our kindred flesh with them.

The circle of the dance in which there is overlap of awareness and shared being
in the open, earthbody logic, had been lost in this projected fictional future. Instead
the rational logic of manipulating all entities, even other living ones, as if they were
merely discrete units that can be utilized for certain functions, dominates. Decker is
alone in his world as he realizes that there is a level of his own being that had been
intertwined with the life of these animals, even if logically it didn't make sense. Now,
electric equivalents of animals that make the same noises or move the same way or
behave similarly give only a display of what the animals were. Being surrounded by
them allows his fellow citizens to *project* sentiments upon these simulations. Sentiments are generalized ideas of certain emotional states, but do not arise in response
to a unique situation. With these android animals, there is no relationship, no deeper
reciprocity, only the illusion of what had been an encounter with another. Instead,
there is a programmed propulsive display, but this offers no mutuality or reciprocal
relationship coming from these electronic creatures. The sheep will wag its tail not
because it is glad to spot its human companion, but according to the inexorable grinding along of its self-propelled program. In thinking about this determinate display
versus the free play of two beings responding to each other, Decker realizes his electric sheep is merely an example of what he calls "the tyranny of the object" and is disgusted by it (*ES*, 37).[2] It is a tyranny because it just pushes along indifferently, using
repetition as a poor substitute for responsiveness and creativity. The interaction it
invites is also only a mechanical repetition of a set number of events. To truly *encounter*
another being is to retain the possibility of being surprised by them and of being called
upon to be in some way different than one is accustomed to be. If it is a true meeting,
either of the two may be thrown off its habitual response to be taken to some new
possible interaction: the formerly vicious dog or horse suddenly responds to the
gentle voice and touch of the person and expresses friendliness, or the formerly
distrusting and cruel person is touched by the horse's nuzzle or the dog's wiggle
and suddenly smiles and melts into affection. This is why the symbol of the dance
is so appropriate: each step calls for responding to others and the environment. The

dance calls for each participant to be creative and to improvise the rhythm in a unfolding life to which all contribute in their own way.

Even in the presence of the quietest of our interlocutors in nature or of the most ethereal dancing partners, one still can be called to account and be given the chance to transform. A temper tantrum exploding in the hushed presence of a grove of redwood trees can suddenly be interrupted by the dawning sense of one's irrationality, pettiness, and impatience—maybe even intolerance—in the face of these mute presences whose towering quiet calm can be overwhelming, if heeded. Or, perhaps, one starts to cry with the pain of a personal loss in love or friendship on the beach. The ocean waves answer with their tales in their crashing, sighing, roaring rhythm about endless loss and gain being accepted with strength and the determination to endure. Feeling, seeing, and hearing this ocean song may change the tears into an accepting smile or nod of acceptance to flowing with change. It certainly has engendered this response for countless people throughout global history. For another example, many people struggling with their sorrows, anxieties, or ego concerns have found an inner peace suggested to them by the solid rocks placed in the sand in the eloquent Japanese Zen gardens, just as the rocks and stones sitting massively within an imposing mountain range whisper to the hiker or climber to resonate to their stillness, calm, and balance.

Whether in the dialogue with these quietest fellow beings around us or with our dog's licking of our face, while we sob in depression about the daily cares of consumer life we find ourselves brought back to more important and life-affirming feelings. We slip from our self-containment into a tide that flows from the supposed "other" beings around us all the time. Certainly, the worst conclusion of the either/or mentality of the diabolical logic is that often people even seem to have no experience that they are only a human being as caught up within the circulation of human feelings that washes among us all, from our smallest family circles to the largest global web. Yet, even the person most rigidly circumscribed in their function and conformist feelings can be shaken out of this role by even a quiet unwavering glance from another person, as when the dying Christmas in Faulkner's *Light in August* defeats the lynch mob by the intensity of his glare back at their blind hatred. They feel their objectification of him as a merely hated thing overcome by his regard:

> For a long moment he looked up at them with peaceful and unfathomable and unbearable eyes. Then his face, body, all seemed to collapse . . .the man seemed to rise into their memories forever and ever. They are not to lose it, in whatever peaceful valleys, beside whatever and placid streams of old age, in the mirroring face of whatever children they will contemplate old disasters and newer hopes. *It will be there, musing, quiet, steadfast, not fading and not particularly threatful, but of itself alone serene, of itself alone triumphant.*[3]

The last look from Christmas as he dies from their brutality has pierced them in a way never to be undone, as described by Faulkner. This passage is so powerful that it is quoted at even greater length by Sartre in *Being and Nothingness* (it is his italicizing of the last sentence that I repeat here), when he is trying to describe the power of the look of another person. Even these characters, locked into themselves and not experiencing any connection to their victim, can be shaken. However, all of us all of the time are called out beyond ourselves, but like the lynch mob in this passage—who didn't encounter this man as a man until this climactic instant—we may not see the other person's or the other being's appeal to us when we are locked into ourselves.

The encounter with all levels of beings calls us to match our rhythms to larger ones or divergent ones. If attended to, the rhythm of encounter helps keep us from being trapped within a world in which we have not only treated all other beings as mere objects to be used, but in so doing have become trapped ourselves as merely a bounded, separated, and functioning object. Philip K. Dick suggests this when Decker becomes confused in chasing androids because he realizes most people have become androids themselves; they are just well-functioning mechanisms.

Addicted to Self-Laceration

There is a problematic ethics that corresponds to the diabolical logic. In the logic of discrete entities to be approached from a distance and exploited for their use, we are led ethically to a utilitarian concern about "the environment": since we are "tied" to the world through chains of cause and effect, for our own well-being we should be concerned that we preserve those beings which are the causes of the effects that we need for the quality of our lives. For example, if we need oxygen to survive, to power our metabolic processes necessary for maintaining our own bio-chemistry, then we should be concerned with the demise of the rain forests because they might be essential in providing oxygen to the rest of the biosphere. However, this reasoning also presumes that if we could find other comparable sources of oxy-gen that would allow our continued, comparable functioning, then this would be equally suitable. If we could find a new chemical reaction that would be cheap and efficient, and not produce other unwanted side-products, then these oxygen creat-ing and releasing manufacturing processes could substitute for this aspect of rain forests (there would be other functions too for which we would have to find equiv-alents). In an ethics of utility, there is nothing wrong with this. It is a matter of managing functions and attaining desired results.

However, this logic, and its resulting reasoning and ethics, dictates a certain sense of who we are. It is assumed that we are separable beings: that our minds are not different minds because they had barking, nuzzling moments of dogs become part of their own makeup; that our imaginations were not colored by the purple iris or white daisies outside our door that opened new creative possibilities; or that our capacity to remember was not lined with the soft light, bracing smell, and springy feel of pine trees that gave our memories new recesses and nuances. It assumes that our imaginations can still take the same flights without perhaps the crystalline visions of stars and deep night above us, or of myriad species of elaborately colored birds flitting about (or at least somewhere to which we can journey and experience the encounter), or that human patience is not interconnected with the slow gaits of tortoises or the way in which a stalking lion or fox can wait silently and stealthily for its prey. As separable, each being has its own set of functions. It is a matter of manipulating from the outside the ways we can ensure the functioning that we desire. If the process entails that different beings intermingle and are transformed in who they are through their new interrelation, this is undetectable in utilitarian assessments. If we are like the women in Matisse's painting who become inseparable from the dance, changed by being part of it, this doesn't compute in utilitarian calculations.

What if the sweetness of the mountain air, or the dank richness of the early morning sea breeze on the dock, or the bracing smoky smell of logs on the fire on a cold, wintry night, allowed us to breath as fully alive beings who have a sense of meaningfully being located on this planet with myriad enriching qualities that infiltrate who we are? So, we can feel like we are buoyantly arising like mountains or flowing like oceans or fecund like the woods. Perhaps experiencing myriad qualities is as essential to the sense of "breathing in life" as breathing is for furnishing materials for oxidation? Perhaps the human mind can think certain thoughts or the human imagination can cast forth certain images or the human feeling can sense certain nuances of significance or the human passions can be drawn in certain compelling directions—or even the physical functioning can contribute to our sense of well-being—because they have drawn meaning and vitality from our being a part of other beings?

For a diabolical logic, this sounds like lunacy. We are what we are—*a* is *a*, a person is a person, and not a tree, flower, or bird. For this logic, our functioning is our functioning. We can think, feel, experience emotions, remember, imagine, intuit, and can be trained, engineered, and maintained by numerous strategies in these functions as long as we take care of ourselves. It is our doing. The founder of logic in our Western tradition is usually seen as Aristotle, who first proposed the rules of syllogistic logic,[4] outlined a system of classification to separate all the plants and animals in their distinctive species and class, and also offered what came to be the most famous traditional definition of human being as "the rational animal." Furthermore, rationality was seen to be a separate faculty of the soul—different from perceiving or moving or feeling emotion or imagining, etc. This kind of thinking has become our "common sense." We feel we are special and different as thinking beings. We believe that we have all these separate functions that some scientists even hope to "localize" as operations of different aspects of the mind tied to separable physical sites in the brain. So we see ourselves "thinking" like an automobile "moves." We see ourselves thinking as a higher-order combination of subordinate operations like sensing, as the automobile moves because of the sum of component functions like the spark plugs firing and valves opening and closing. This makes logical sense.

But what if we're giving ourselves too much credit? We could be seen to be arrogantly blind to the *interdependence* of all of our functioning within the functioning of the world and its myriad aspects. Do *we* really think? Where do our thoughts come from? Was Cezanne just crazy or was he rather sensitive to an interplay through his open body—his waiting hand, mind, and spirit—when he stated that he no longer had the feeling that he was painting Mont Sainte-Victoire, but rather felt that the mountain was painting itself through him? Most cultures have felt that the earth speaks, that the wind speaks, the sun, moon, stars whisper to us, that animals, whether lion or deer or soaring birds bring us messages or at least are the living bearers of certain senses about the world that we can then come to recognize and put into human speech. It is interesting that the philosopher who currently has the largest public following in the United States, Richard Rorty, starts a recent book, *Solidarity, Irony, and Contingency*, with the statement that "only man speaks."[5] For us, this seems obvious. For many peoples, this would seem crazy—the statement of a crazed group of people who could not sense what was around them. It isn't accidental that Rorty's conclusions lead to a sense that all we can do is express irony about the fact that we can't really share our experience or know the world, and that the only thing we have in common is the experience of pain. This is what a Native American wise person would predict about a culture that thinks everything else is silent and dead, and they are alone and have to function from within themselves, self-propelled, and isolated. How can people who see the world in this way be left with anything other than the basic experience of pain, skepticism, and isolation?

To say that we are the thinking animals, as if thinking were some property, some performance that was solely our doing, is to claim that we are self-contained and self-sufficient in our functioning once certain external needs have been met. This way of thought led Descartes to solidify this idea even further with his declaration, "I think, therefore I am." This has been taken as the bare bones of truth and self-identity for centuries for Western culture, to the extent that we now declare a person dead when there is no evident brain activity, when we seem sure that no thinking is occurring. It is interesting then to ponder the words of a miner who was interviewed by a health department official I knew about the miner's claim about his "black-lung" disease. He spoke about the experience of having been trapped by a mine cave-in. He was pinned in a very small space with no light. After lying there for days, he confessed that although he knew that he was still thinking, he was no longer sure if he existed, if he still was alive, or if he was still the person he had been. His situation was drastically different than that of Descartes, who was sitting by the fire, at leisure for once in his life, wearing his dressing gown, and overlooking the city below him. Doesn't thinking give us a security about our existence because of the context in which it occurs? Thinking thoughts is a different kind of guarantee of certainty, selfhood, having a foundation in life, when sitting in a comfy apartment than it is when lying in the dark at the bottom of a collapsed coal shaft. Is it a self-generated activity or one that arises from a certain environment within a set of relations? Perhaps human functioning and human characteristics move in certain ways or to certain degrees or with certain directions given the context. In a logic of discrete entities—of "yes or no" properties— there is not room for "more or less," or for other entities somehow also being part of our activity, or expressing something about *themselves* in our thoughts, in our painting, or in this text.

Of course, once we have unleashed the cutting diabolic logic upon the world, like all other diabolical creations, it doesn't just stop at some arbitrary point. So, in considering the power of this logic to cut off a deeper link with the natural environment, we invoked the specter of the oppositional logic of "us" versus "them," but this logic doesn't stop there. Why even keep the "we" or "us" human beings? If all entities are discrete beings, then I am I and you are you, and the sense of "we" or "us" as enlaced in who we are together is also gone. Not only can I substitute for flowers or hedgehogs or oaks some other being that would function in the same way, I can substitute for you too any other entity that could function in a comparable way. Human beings become objects for one another and somehow the other people's feelings are not part of my feelings, the other's thoughts are not part of my thoughts. The fantasy of replacing troublesome partners with a robot or an android is appealing to many.

However, as we look out on others as obstacles or tools or even alluring objects to be possessed or collected or enjoyed, then we are using logical robot eyes like the mechanisms portrayed in *Westworld* or the original *Terminator* movie. In both these movies the director properly conveyed the sense that if there were humanoid machines, they would be confronted by the natural world, by animals, and even other humans as "sensory inputs" to be deciphered in their rational significance. The scene encountered would not *involve* the robot as part of it, as somehow being absorbed into and a part of its emerging meaning, the robot would in a distant and detached way survey the input logically and have to *decide* its meaning and import. We see in the movie that each of the robot's perceptions shows up in its internal input screen as a spectacle of different possible, logically alternative meanings. For example, if the robot "sees" a man standing by a tree in front of it, a series of possible interpretations is generated at the bottom of the screen, say, for example, (1) potential enemy concealing a weapon, (2) a possible source of information when tortured or threatened, (3) a diversionary focus of interest distracting your attention, (4) an object inessential to achieving the mission, (5) a potential hostage to be used for bargaining, etc. The machine then keeps scanning and reasoning, until it decides on the logical explanation that seems to fit the most facts. Although this example focuses on the warlike interests of these two robots, the same type of vision could scan other "people objects" as possible buyers for a product, possible alluring sexual objects, possible suppliers of some service, possible votes in the upcoming election, and so on, in more everyday projects that color our vision. Notice, how the other person becomes meaningful mainly in light of how they fit into achieving a goal. We would have no immediate connection among us other than as objects of utility.

Of course, all of us experience this robot vision of others at times, and probably could approach chronically this level of distance and being cut off from an ambiguously inclusive identity with others insofar as we allow the constant brainwashing of society to carry us along as mere functionaries and consumers. Then, the way all beings, and certainly other people, immediately speak to our senses, emotions, imaginations, and intuitions in a way that is "under the skin" is lost in the alienating attitudes we assume and promote. The palpable interconnectedness starts to seem to be fantastic and unreal.

This is how we become machines at the price of our humanity. The most frightening example of this is how humans become the killing machines we call "serial killers." These people report feeling a great distance from the experience around them, as if they are watching themselves and others from afar. However, even these people can't maintain indefinitely this life like the robots we described, because eventually this extreme detachment causes overwhelming anguish. They kill in an attempt to rejoin this reality that has become so distant that it seems unreachable. In killing, they get to experience the feelings of others: the horror and pain of their victims that becomes so palpable, so charged, it can jump the gap they've erected from others. So, at least there is still a sense something is missing, something that they are trying desperately to regain. Their detachment motivates and allows for their horrific actions. Another extreme example is the behavior of the SS troops in World War II: those troops assigned to mass slaughter, such as machine-gunning Jewish victims all day, had to be given alcohol constantly. This allowed them to numb the natural feelings of connection we all feel to other human and living beings that tears at our own feelings, because in killing others we are killing part of us. To keep sustaining such violation the SS troops had to have a means to block out these feelings.

The most chilling aspect of how this diabolical logic leads us to confront the world as separable from our own being and thus distant from our selves is not the extremes to which some people's psyches are pushed, but rather the overall attitude of our society. In the book *Ceremony*, author Leslie Marmon Silko describes our modern American consumerist society as a "destroyer," one which destroys "the feeling that people have for each other." She says the nature of the destruction is to "gut human beings while they are still breathing, to hold the heart still beating so that the victim will never feel anything again. When they finish, you watch yourself from a distance and you can't even cry."[6] The knife that performs this surgery is the cutting blade of diabolic logic: me versus you; us versus them; us versus it; my plans versus my feelings. It rationally divides and opposes that which is one. Silko comments that when destroyers surround us, and "the sensations of living" have been silenced, then "only destruction is capable of arousing a sensation, the remains of something alive in them." Our society as a whole may be approaching some milder form of the syndrome that plagues serial killers, when only violent sensations inflicted on others make them feel anything. Maybe only the suffering we cause others allows us as a society to break through our detachment and feel ourselves to be a part of the world around us.

The name "diabolical" logic is appropriate, given the older meanings of this term for being devilish. The Greek roots go back to references of slander, of denying or distorting something about someone that is manifest. The power to negate the palpable seems a most devilish power. Perhaps this logic denies what we feel in our bones, in our hearts, in our troubled dreams at night, and in fervent poetical visions of beauty: that we are connected, are not so separable from those people, animals, living beings, and things around us. In a brilliant scene in *The Brothers Karamazov*, Dostoyevsky has Ivan,—the tortured Karamazov brother who wants to believe in something life affirming, but can't find it amidst the atrocities of this world,—confront the devil. It turns out that the devil is not a bad fellow. He is just the "spirit of negation." He denies, cuts off what could go together, and is that skeptical power that makes us lose ourselves. From this humble movement of separation comes much horror.

Throughout *The Brothers Karamazov*, characters feel compelled to deny their feelings and their sense of belonging. Dostoyevsky parallels this theme with that of self-laceration. Characters cut themselves. This is the final cut of the diabolical logic—the one we perform on ourselves, also on our own inner worlds. When Descartes says he is only his thinking, he also says I am not my body, I am not my senses, I am not my emotions, I am not my fantasies, etc. He cuts himself off from these dimensions of who he is and from any sense that his being is a being shared with other people, creatures, or things. This really is no different from the old man Karamazov's "buffoonery"—when he takes pleasure in denigrating and violating everything he is. Then he glories in this debasement. He is distancing himself from his body-self caught up with others in sensual and passionate life. This becomes an object of derision. As mere object, it is not he any longer. Nor is it different from Sonia's declaration that she will no longer be the vulnerable human being who is wracked with the pains and passions of being caught up in connection with other human beings. Sonia slams the door on her hand—keeping her pain internal and private. She has slammed closed the way to others and of others to her.

Given the either/or logic, we choose something at the price of relinquishing other aspects of reality, including, if necessary, our own reality. We cover this with the cynical resignation that "you can't have everything." Why this self-lacerating gloom? Why deny ourselves what we are within the circle of the dance? Perhaps *we need to be everything*, at least to some degree, because everything within us and without us dances with everything else in assuming its full vitality and reality.

Earthbody Sense

To argue that our culture has long been missing a vital part of its own reality, that it has inflicted upon itself the damage of the diabolical logic, may seem counter-intuitive. We just said that perhaps we are denying that other humans, other living beings, and even inanimate beings are somehow a part of us, are present in the workings of our minds, our imaginations, our memories, our artistry, and in all our creative involvements with the world. They are ourselves as part of these processes. If that is the case, then how could it be that so many people do not experience this? They would adamantly claim their thinking and their feeling was solely their own doing and that their being a person was not tied up with the existence of mountains or trees or fish. They might admit that the existence or non-existence of other beings affects their well-being "from the outside," as a matter of "external interactions," but not that they would somehow lose a part of who they are without these other beings.

This declaration of self-subsistence assumes that the world is defined by certain tangible boundaries—ones that can be quantified and ordered by this either/or logic. It is felt that this is tied to seeing things as they are "objectively," as being materialistic in a straightforward way, taking the physical aspect of things as what can be counted (upon) as real. I would claim, however, that such logic is neither straightforward nor materialistic. Such a person would, of course, have answered to Cezanne that he was indeed crazy, that he is a person, a painter, and the mountain is a mountain, as anyone can see, and that only people paint paintings and not mountains. They might grant that Cezanne could feel as if the mountain were helping him paint, because humans can "make up" or imagine all sorts of things, but that what is real is easily provable and not just about what people think. It is a brute fact, one that can be held, and one that holds up against all kinds of opposition.

This is an interesting prejudice: that the firm—that which resists all kinds of attacks on it—is somehow what is real. However, there is no reason not to assert that what is very fragile, what is perhaps only fleeting and intermittent, is no less real. If we see that *the degree of meaning and vitality that something adds to our existence and our understanding might be the more appropriate standard of what is real*, this opens us up to a different realm of experience and a different logic. Let's see what this means in terms of our relation to the other beings on the earth and within our own psyches.

For the moment, let's assume that the ways in which other beings speak to us, the ways in which other beings take part in our own processes of understanding and expressing the world around us are very fragile, fleeting, and subtle. An experience may be very fragile and yet be the most palpable and dominant reality in any particular situation. For example, experiencing love between people or hate or excitement or boredom may be very fragile: a few words, a few actions, might transform a situation in a way that will never be recovered after those wonderful or horrible words are spoken or after the person or people do this or that. For example, in Arthur Miller's play, *All My Sons*, after the protagonist's son has discovered that his father did knowingly send defective aircraft parts overseas to the troops during the war, he will never respect his father or feel the same love for him that he had felt during his entire life in such a palpable way. It often happens that one incident or one misspoken phrase turns a political leader who has the faith of the people behind him into a distrusted also-ran; or a sports team is lifted by a play or even just a spirited gesture and suddenly finds the rhythm and the touch—beautiful, palpable, and even overwhelming to behold and experience, but ever so fragile. *Much of what is most real is most fragile*. It is most "real" in being palpable, meaningful, and dictating the kind of experience we have, whether with our friends, spouses, children, jobs, community, etc.

The only reason for defining the reality of the earth and its objects, beings, events, and relations exclusively in terms of how they can be seized and sized up in the common dimension of "brute thereness," merely as physicalistic masses that resist other masses, is to try to make the world the most permanent, controllable, and stable place it can be. It is the attempt to gain control and shield oneself from change, from disappointment, and from the need to keep transforming oneself in time to the dance of the beings all around one. So, we can see a rock as just inertly there, a heavy, unmoving mass, or see a waterfall as just a certain mass of water molecules being displaced in space, or we can even see our neighbor as "really" just three-quarters water, with tissues, bone, genetic material, and capable of certain functions. Or instead, as earthbodies, we could feel the stone whispering messages to us about being grounded and calm, heavy with taking to heart the stories around one, or the waterfall speaking of vitality and the peace of speeding along in a caress with the ground, or see in our neighbor's face the expressions of hundreds of people who have helped him or her be able to speak and to have joy, and also to be the recipient of the wonder of colors and sounds and loving kindness. These voices are not determinate, do not provide controllable identities, but rather they wander and have wide ranges of meaning and are indirect.

Like much of the world, in order to exist and thrive, the indirect voices, the silent gestures, and the playing expressions of the myriad beings, relations, and events require cooperation. So much of human and other life requires constant, delicate, and exhaustive cooperation, but we fail to notice it, except when suddenly someone causes great havoc and pain by not cooperating. To write this sentence took countless people: to create the language I'm using to express myself, to manufacture the computer I'm using (and all its components, the processes that made the components, the knowledge that led to all these processes and objects, etc.) or to generate the electricity I'm also using. Certainly, in some rather direct way, there are billions of beings who helped create the materials, the forces, the knowledge I'm using at this moment, from mitochondria in my cells that took up residence with other microscopic creatures to form those "cells" (which are communities) so "I" (another community) live, to the myriad creatures who created the oxygen I breathe, and to those that made the computer or even the myriad things that were included in the manufacturing—or even just the paint on the keyboard letters I'm striking, etc. However, again, even this sort of reasoning is focusing on the "physical," even if it is an attempt to see the wider sense of "cause and effect" relations. We still must also realize that these creatures, things, and events also have myriad meanings that were conveyed and converged in this moment of communication. There are so many aspects of what the world and dimensions of ourselves have come to mean that enter into every moment of life. They are not human creations from nothingness (only God could do that), despite our powerful history of articulation. We have also learned from myriad voices of the earth—from flowers, rocks, and birds. We can at any moment slow down, attend to nuances, and to the layers and webs of meaning. Then, we would start listening to what Bachelard called "the murmuring among things."

We can also choose not to hear any of these voices: then the world is just made up of physical masses in motion that collide with each other in certain generalizable ways. To hear these voices requires a different sort of ear than the ones we have cultivated by thinking that we humans are exclusively the "speaking animals." First, we would have to be willing to take the hands of all these beings and events and enter the circle of the dance, as we see the women doing in Matisse's dance. This means that we have to be open to their gestures, to hearken to them, to try to find ways to connect to them, and finally to find ways to pick up and join into their rhythms. This requires both ceasing certain ways of relating to the world that are habitual for us and cultivating others that are new for the mainstream of our culture, but known in many other cultures, by artists and by other people who have discovered their earthbodies. (They, too, tend not to be heard by our bustling culture.)

First, we would have to cease encountering objects, events, creatures, and even other people within the habitual grid of determinate categories. Ordinarily, the object perceived is always a "whatever"—whether a "mountain" or a "waterfall" or "an old man in a home for the aged"—an object experienced as a certain type, usually also containing a value judgment of political, social, or economic import. Then we don't have to encounter the particularity of the object of our experience or even of ourselves in the midst of having the experience. However, there are those among us, even among those raised in the Western Cartesian culture, who listen and sense differently. Rather than dismissing Mont Sainte-Victoire as just another mountain, Cezanne opened himself to another sort of sensual and spiritual experience—a sensually spiritual experience—by painting it over and over again for a decade. Steiglitz did the same through taking photographs of the same tree for fifty years. These artists were making obvious that one never really does know another being, despite the fact that we assume we do when we feel one tree is like any other tree or one dog is like any other dog or one friend is like any other friend. Instead, the artist knows that it takes great time, effort, and openness, cultivated gradually, to start to truly "hear," "see," or "feel" more of the inexhaustibility of possible communication with any other being. Only gradually, when one is open to the flow of the process of seeing or hearing or experiencing emotion or imagining, does one register just that particularly distinctive hue or just that unusual curve there or just that particular quality of quietness in the object or just that particular grace in that gesture of another living being—as well as only gradually do I experience in the process that, oh yes, I am such a creature who can distinguish the hush of slowing and quieting down from the hush of expectant waiting or who can feel the difference between the quiet joy of wonder from the moving joy of triumph, and that these are my emerging and possible sensitivities.

The recognition of the unending richness of the "simple, everyday" stuff of experience is one of the key dimensions of *ceremonial experience*. In our current American culture we tend to confuse ceremony with certain uniform, repeated, institutionalized, and public acts of social conformity. In some senses, ceremony has even come to indicate formalities that have become utterly meaningless— actions performed with no thought or particular intention other than sticking to proper form: "mere ceremony." Yet, the deepest sense of ceremony is to mark the sacred, to indicate one is open to the messages of a larger, deeper sense of life and to give it reverence. In our culture, the sense of the sacred has usually been taken to be found in opposition to the earth and our bodies. However, if we return to being earthbodies, we will discover a different sense of the sacred and of the place of the ceremonial in our lives.

If we return to our earthbodies, it might be possible to live our entire lives in a ceremonial fashion. The ceremony marks this particular place, time, and interaction as full of meaning and full of the power to awaken us and that to which we relate. To be ceremonial is to commit oneself to paying unwavering attention out of a sense of gratitude and wonder that just this particular time and coming together of beings is occurring and should be honored. The honoring is initiated merely by fully participating in the possible dance of the beings assembled at the moment. This kind of fully being there in grateful and aware attention is the opposite of the categorical way of relation that says to itself, "oh yes, that is a tree, a flower, a worker, a child," or whatever else, and passes by or uses the information to get on with functioning efficiently in the midst of these other beings.

Paying attention in this way is not a matter of will, but rather of giving oneself up to the situation in which one finds oneself, as the women in Matisse's rendering of the dance have given themselves up to the spirit of the rhythm shared among them and with the earth and sky. This giving oneself up allows these other beings to infiltrate the flow that enters one's body from the larger situation. It allows these rhythms and pulsings to sing out more loudly by having quieted down all the ongoing demands, strategizing, and commenting that ordinarily proceeds within ourselves. This internal noise normally blocks out our hearing the quiet, but powerfully insistent other voices of the world. If we were internally quiet, the green of the leaf of the plant, the face of the old woman on the street, or the sound of the creek running by the house might slip us away to somewhere else, at least for an instant.

Yet we resist even entertaining the current of images, the feelings, the memories, and all the swirlings of our immediate "inner" responses to the world. In our cultural context, such attention would feel "foolish" or "frivolous." We have to stay in control of ourselves, because if we become fluid, joining with the world as a flow of feelings, imaginings, ideas, etc., we become unpredictable, transformable, and desirous of kinship with the myriad beings of the world and of the significance from being in relation with them, instead of staying in our functioning mazes of routine and dispassion. The roots of "silly" actually mean happiness and innocence, but it now has taken on connotations of "weak-mindedness" and "lacking good sense," given the prejudices of diabolical logic and rigid rationality, which seek to keep us distant and well controlled in our thinking and relating to the world.

To be able to hear the voices of the world requires us to come back to our fullest participation in the dance with all these other beings around us, which further means to give ourselves up, to relinquish hold on ourselves, to lose ourselves to all the echoes—the reverberations—these things or other living creatures or people cause to sound within our various depths. The failure to allow this letting go— what the Zen Buddhists call "the dropping of the will"—of the dancers within us is one of the major reasons so many people just don't experience that the world does speak to us. We fell impelled to remain within our ego images of ourselves, in charge of things and our minds, our conduct, and even our imaginings. Yet, within each perception, even the most simple one, there dwells many emotions, many possible imaginative images and creations, many memories, personal and impersonal, that can echo only if allowed to encounter our bodies, our senses, and our fullness of faculties as sounding boards, as resonating tuning forks, or as the tightly stretched receptive skin of a drum.

These possible imaginings, feelings, or rememberings found within the simplest patch of color, sound, or texture or the most complicated web of visual or tactile patterns contain many ideas, many connections to others, many intuitions, and all of them are wanting to dance with the others in such a way that each becomes bound up in the others' rhythms. They find each other through the openness of the paths that run through our earthbodies. Our five senses, our remembering, imagining, speaking, thinking, intuiting, expressive, and gesturing powers can be allowed to dance with each other like Matisse's women. Then it can happen that we are open to the meanings suggested by the rock face of the mountain or the night sky or the smile of that person or the swoop of the bird over our head. Then a rock can speak to us about possible tranquility and feeling centered through the image it engenders in us or through the solidity of its mass beneath our body rested upon it. This is not passivity. It is an openness that takes great focus and energy, but rewards us with the return flow of energy from the myriad beings around us.

The first level of the body, our rich earthbody, is the level of the senses. It is here, in a return to the stirrings within our bodies, that we must start to open our capacities to relate to other beings. At this level, artists have allowed us to experience the way in which the five senses always dance with one another like Matisse's women, when we see the sounds and smells in a painted scene or hear the height of the notes or the texture of the sounds within the symphony or see the silence around a sculpture. Whether it's hearing the waves crash and the wind howl in Turner's *Slave Ship*, or feeling the soaring, upward, insistent motion in Beethoven's final movement of the *Ninth Symphony*, or hearing the peaceful hush around the sculpture of the Buddha in meditation, each sense is both its own world (such as the world of blue or the world of heat), and also dances over and spills into the others— just like the women dancing, each unique but also inseparable from the others in the moving rhythm of the whirl. So it is always the case that the senses play with each other and register more than just sensor screens, but we do not often tune into these dimensions. The dropping of the will to be taken over by the stirrings of the body is about coming back to what was already there for us, but unacknowledged and unappreciated.

However, the intertwining of meaning is also not just present among the varied senses but also among the differing ways to apprehend. In the perception of blue, one can feel emotionally a certain coolness, imagine a certain water world or remember a certain piece of clothing a loved wore on a certain occasion, or conceive a certain iciness of character, etc. Each sense and each way of having beings appear, whether in emotion, memory, intuition, thought, imagination, etc., can be a way of joining up with the others and taking over their rhythms in a journey. To become open to this process, we must relax our indomitable control and open ourselves to any eddy of current or any tracing of paths in new directions that our bodies always allow us as the sounding board of the world. It is as though *each object of perception given to our body is a magic doorway* that can be entered and slowly explored to allow myriad other meanings to come forward. The earth's objects are rich in being linked in the earth's flow in changing, branching ways. Each of us has our unique ability to launch out on differing currents, if we dare let go and float in the world's senses. No definite result is ever predictable, since this flow is a dance of separate dancers who may or may not join this particular spin together. Without joining, however, certainly the rhythm of a new dance will not begin.

Another aspect of opening earthbody sense is to be surprised by whom within us the rock or the blueness or the flowing water addresses. None of us has allowed ourselves to meet all our inner dancers, living to differing degrees under the rule of the diabolical logic. With its common sense, we cut ourselves off from the dancers in us who respond to different voices. Not only are there distinctive corners within the senses and faculties of apprehension, but also there are myriad selves within. The rock may speak to our stony determined self who endured various trials, while the soaring bird overhead may link up with the soaring spirit in us that wants to leave its boring perch of a job and fly towards greater skies of fulfillment; the shuffling homeless man may speak to our self that wants to lie down and feel the despair into which modern life has backed us. Under the sway of our rational logic these are irrational feelings. In fact, they are not too silly to demand our attention, but rather too dangerous. To give these many selves a chance to register their resonating voices, to feel the spring in their steps, means we will experience their power. This will transform who we are. The movement to embracing one's earthbody is a movement away from stifling certain dimensions of oneself and a halt to disowning the selves that don't seem optimally functional or accommodating to a strict rational plan of behavior. It is a coming to awareness of the richness inside us all as mirroring the richness of the world about us. Instead of living impoverished in our experience of the outer world, like people of the day of the living dead, and correlatively having no sense of our inner richness, the earthbody allows all these currents to flow and add to the depth of the path we have chosen.

Ceremonial Awareness

In everyday life, on levels of which we are not usually aware, our bodies as earthbodies pick up and enter rhythms around us—whether it be the slowly simmering torpidity of the humid, summer heat wave, the quick, jerky, and hurrying pace of the people rushing to work, selling papers and coffee, rushing for trains and buses, the slow hovering, fluttering, and almost prancing of the swarm of butterflies that have gathered around the bush next to the bench, the coolness of the blue walls or the shrieking moving-in-tension of the screeching subway brakes. Also, sometimes during the most mundane tasks, our earthbodies gain energy, and motivation, and suddenly take new directions through modulating rhythms to fit others around us or to play off those others in creative ways, say in drinking in the crispness of the beautifully laid out and colored sheets my co-worker just produced and placed in front of me or the crispness of the air this morning or the melodic, rolling humming of the woman kneading the dough at the bakery at which I stopped. What happens is that in the richness of the sensual, emotional, and intelligible world around us there is a call to levels of our awareness to join in with other ways of being and other selves. We are continually called to come out to play with the world. When we are in the flow with what we are doing, this opening to other rhythms just happens, as I pick up on the design flow and its rhythm embodied in the shapes, materials, and spatial relations of the engine on which I'm working or on the conceptual turns of the new idea in the book I'm reading as it draws me through its unfolding words. The shifts that take me over, infusing through my body, may be very minor, unnoticed shifts, as when I plant a flowering plant in the garden. The beautiful pink blossoms, the rich scent of the moist soil, and the protesting tension of the stem call me to lose my impatient, productive, adult self, and be more sensitive to the stem's bending-but-resisting announcement of its fragility. I am being asked to slow down and dig deeper into the soil, to let myself get dirty, let myself play with the mud and the digging in the spirit of the young boy I once was and still am when I let myself be. The luminous pink hue attempts to arrest me in a call for a slower, more appreciative, and sensitive planting. This may be one moment of a minor act, but it is these calls that can change us in their cumulative effect, if needed.

This is where ceremony begins. These currents are the structures of ceremonial awareness. There are rhythms, flows of meaning, ways of relating, and manners of experiencing that we or our elders or founders in various traditions have identified as augmenting our sense of well-being, our sense of expressing our abilities, and our wonder or joy or love for our fellow creatures, or as giving us purpose. Ceremonies have been created to highlight these aspects of the flows and rhythms that tug at our earthbodies and to allow us to be moved by them more poignantly. These important rhythms, sense flows, and streams of meaning can pass by unnoticed. Yet, it is also true that opportunities for joining these streams of significance and felt belonging are present everywhere in the most mundane tasks and their sense is always present. If we were all perfectly enlightened, utterly spiritually creative constantly, ceremonies would be superfluous, or rather, all life and each action and each perception of anything would have become naturally ceremonial—an ongoing ceremony of appreciation and fullness of meaning. However, we are not so perfectly developed.

The reference to this deeply felt, revitalizing power of ceremonial awareness may jar on modern ears, because for so many so-called advanced societies ceremony has become the opposite. It is defined in American dictionaries as indicating adherence to formalities, occasions which call for formal, conventional means of conduct, gestures that are intrinsically meaningless but express the conventional forms of society. This indeed does describe what has become of the place in much of contemporary industrialized society that had been occupied within other societies by ceremony. The root words of ceremony refer back to sacred rites, to a kind of care (*cura*), to a recognition of something beyond the human sphere of commerce (sacred, *sacer*), and to a kind of order of which we find ourselves a part (the same reason why in ari*th*metic—the *arith*mos of the Greeks—*rit* [of rite] is present to indicate an underlying order). However, in many of the so-called developed societies of the globe, we have become self-enclosed, caught within bureaucracies, and the scramble to fit into driven economies, and even within the hyper-paced diversions of "free time," such that society's conventions are omnipresent and behavior regimented, lacking the room for discovery and spontaneity. To have an encounter with an "underlying order" of the planet that embraces us, and may include our rhythms and productions, but still encompasses them in its wider rhythms, seems impossible to many most of the time. Yet, ceremony in its truest sense, its original inspiration, is an awakening from the daily round that can hypnotize. It is a way to come back to our senses, our emotions, our intuitions, our imaginations, our deepest memories as part of a community, and even our dreams: to let go into the levels of earthbodies that open up to the deeper flow of the planet. Yet, like other forms of community and discovery, ceremony has become degraded by being integrated into modern (or postmodern) society, in which much of each person's activity is involved in the social, economic, and political manipulations of the day in order to survive in the rat race.

Ceremony, when it moves us most deeply into wonder, into purpose, into rhythms which revitalize and open meaning, connects to the deepest flowing meanings of the earth itself as they resonate in our earthbodies. So, although we could construct a ceremony that would augment the frantic rush hour feeling that our bodies take on unconsciously, it would not augment our perceptual, emotional, and spiritual capacities; it would instead only intensify the disconnected and harried emotional, intellectual, and spiritual constriction we experience in living like we are over-working mechanisms. That is why, for example, we find so many religious, spiritual, philosophical, psychological, and communal ceremonies of differing cultures and time periods that attune their participants to the rhythmic, burbling, flowing, dissolving, melding, shape-shifting, cleansing, calming, clarifying, and opening qualities of moving water. This is because, as Feuerbach aptly put it, "water itself is holy," as are the elemental dimensions of the planet. Their indirect voices express to us in the qualities we perceive in them messages about the widest contexts of life and its deepest interlocking rhythms. They help us break out of the petty and self-absorbed circles of meanings we create in our daily tasks, and also social and cultural small-mindedness. With opened capacities, and as fully engaged, we drink in deeper meaning and well-being.

Ceremony is the highlighting of our experience of deeper shared rhythms, the augmenting of opportunities, the setting of the mood, and the helping us to let go of our will to allow us to be able to make those shifts, those joinings, with other rhythms we haven't experienced. The bringing together of a greater number of possible selves to apprehension is an ability that is present in us all always, but it can be augmented by special places and special actions whose aim is to create, with others, a distinctive spell that allows these rhythms to carry us in a shared energy and within an intensified reverberating resonance. This is one of the key ways of allowing ourselves to hear the indirect voices of the other beings of the planet, whether the voices of the more self-contained ones like rocks, or of the midrange interactive ones, like the Chihuahua at my feet, or of those that continually turn to others to interact, the humans. The ceremonies of many cultures, the myths, the poetry, the spell of various arts, and many ways of meditation are ways of allowing other voices to be heard. The experiences they open may be fleeting and they may be very subtle, but they are so real that they might change a person's life, even though only experienced for a few instants.

Ceremonial awareness summons these selves and this dance of our powers of apprehension that are usually lost in our everyday bustle. For the moment, it changes our bodies from vehicles employed to achieve tasks to sensitive tuning forks picking up other rhythms, resonating, and humming with, and repeating in our own movement what others are saying to us. To start with an example from our own culture, let's think for a moment of the wedding as an authentic ceremony—not as a legality or a social function, but as a way of awakening to new dimensions of meaning. If it is successful on this level, then the two people of the couple will not only come to experience on that day emotions of profound joy, love, gratitude, hopefulness, and wonder. They will also see images of myriad other couples who have so joined or images of old age together, or remember when they first opened to one another or think ideas of commitment and eternity; if it is a certain religion that joins the couple, they will then feel the gratitude, solemnity (this couple) and sacredness of the divine source of their union. In the ceremony, these feelings and images join with a long history of other couples, other instances of love and loyalty that have infused the tradition with its flow and warmth.

However, these feelings and images imperceptibly flow into yet deeper currents of planetary pairing: ongoing care and concern within couples of all sorts, from a bird returning to its mate at the nest with twigs or worms to bears together in the forest. Yet, the current is wider, in even more far-reaching resonances. Even the most specific religious or secular enactment, with its own unique tradition and meaning, draws upon and enters other image and meaning flows that go beyond references to other creatures, to references about inanimate objects or more fundamental properties of the physical world (such as how even earth and sky seem to call out for each other in union, as articulated in so many myths, or as how water flows, transforms, cleanses, etc., or even how modern science describes the going together of electrons and protons). The feeling the ceremony evokes also draws on even the broadest elements of tangible reality itself, like light and dark or soft and hard that also seem to join in complementarity and union despite differences, as specifically symbolized by the Tao in the Taoist tradition.

If the wedding ceremony has "come off" well, as does a dance that has caught harmony, grace, and energy, then all these subtle feeling flows will be moving through the earthbodies of the participants. This transforms the way the couple experiences each other at that ceremonial moment—a transformation which hopefully they can rekindle at least partially at later moments in their life together or at least remember in its impact at the ceremonial moment in coming years and decades. The differing apprehensions contained in the feelings, in the rushing images, in the sense of awe of the moment begins by augmenting the beholding in perception of the other partner of the couple. The other person's features, their palpable character and personality, and their ways of being who they are—the invoked sensual presence—washes over the other partner and the participants, but the flow originates within the experience of the beloved person and dances among all these other rhythms of image, meaning, and feeling. If the ceremony is working, they display a startling beauty and a depth of feeling that can be felt by all attending. After the play with all these images, feelings, intuitions, memories, etc., that are the power of the marriage ceremony evoked in its words, costumes, special place, decorations, and community, they spiral back into the perception of the beloved person to enhance it with an added intensity and significance. This is ceremonial awareness. This is its transforming and augmenting power.

Ceremonies are a shifting of our inner psychic arrangement. To enter a ceremony in the "right spirit"—in the spirit of sincerity, playfulness, and openness of feeling—means to let go of the inner psychic structure that one relies upon for everyday identity and stability, at least for the time of the ceremony. If one lets go and allows a process to gather its spell, then a playing occurs not only with the world, others, and all these different flows of sense "out there," but also an inward dynamism is born. A dance inside oneself and with the past becomes augmented by our shared letting go with others, and the dancing among our extended bodies opens hearts and minds and spirals back within our deepest psyches and viscera. Ceremonies involve different gestures, postures, and appeals to the senses, because they open up differing, resonating levels of apprehension within earth-bodies. For example, in a ceremony we don't speak abstractly of union, but rather we hold hands or dance or embrace. Other cultures don't speak of kinship with deer or kangaroos, they dance out kangaroo postures and gestures. Psychically, as Huizinga points out,[7] in such a ceremony, the dancers are no longer who they were before the ceremony: they don't pretend to be the kangaroo, while still being who they usually are, they *are* the kangaroo at the moment—not in some trivial physical sense, but as a way of being, a way of moving, a way of feeling, a way of experiencing, a way of dreaming, or in other words, as a flow of experiences. All we ever "are," really, is such a flow of experience. Our earthbodies, connected to the dance of the planet, its dreams, feelings, imaginings, intuitions, and rhythms reveal this to us—our flowing being. The ceremony presents the risk and the opportunity to let go and enter more wholeheartedly and more intensely a heightened stirring of psyche in a larger flow.

Partially, the ceremonial is a risk to allow oneself to become more taken up in the visceralness of the body—but as earthbody, where flesh is not mine, but of the planet's of which I am part. The depth and power of the ceremonial dislocation are grounded in the density, the earthiness, and the thickness of being played out by our earthbodies' visceralness. If I feel myself the kangaroo, it is not in a mental representation, but in the particular hopping, dancing movement of my feet, the blood rushing through my veins, the new vision through my eyes, the particular feeling in my stomach, in the way the particular drumbeat and foot movement of the others kinaesthetically moves through and resonates with my body movements. Or, at the funeral, the unyielding finality of death is not just a thought, but is in the shiny, hard surface of the coffin. The gloom is palpable in the black dress of those present. The tearing at our love is felt in the back of our throats in the keening noises we make. The departing is felt in the body's kinaesthetic sense as the coffin is lowered, withdrawing from the tactile, visual field into the darkness of the grave's hole. The return to the soil is felt in the soft, loamy handful of dirt which we throw onto the coffin. The indifference of how life continues despite any individual's passing is heard in the thuds of the soil on the coffin lid. The together-ness in grief is felt in the mourners' huddling together shoulder to shoulder. Our hope is in the colorful, vibrant faces of the flowers with which we decorate the graveside. Our bodies are gripped and held in sensual ways which are our emotions and our spirits speaking a deeper language than that available through words or thoughts. The images stay and resound in the tides of our earthbodies—rippling over us in the days to come, and sometimes in strange moments for the rest of our lives. Their multiple references to smell, to tones, to sounds, to textures, to kinaesthetic feel-ings, to touch, etc., stay within our earthbodies as a different kind of sinew; they make possible different kinds of movements resonant with those muscular sinews make possible: movements of the spirit, the heart, and the imagination.

The ceremonial spell summons new interplays of our emotion and fantasy or of our ideas and intuitions, or of selves undiscovered as yet interacting with older selves. These new combinations of powers well up from our breathing, from our moving, from our taking in of symbols of color or smell or gesture—from the body open to its awakened awareness of being part of larger flows, of being earthbody. By contrast, when we have allowed our ceremonies to become formalities, we go through the mechanical motions of disconnected bodies. Then, we have failed to remember the magnetism of shared symbol, ritual, and heartfelt letting go of our social selves into deeper realms.

Other cultures, such as the Native American, have remained closer to the power of the ceremonial to awaken their lives to more meaning. For them, it is not only a few occasions in their lives that take on ceremonial dimensions as it is for many Americans (even these few moments are often sacrificed in our consumerist American culture). Within Native American tribal culture, there is an attempt to integrate the ceremonial dimension into daily life, whether in the way the sun is greeted or in the way one encounters the animals in the environment. Within a culture that realizes the ongoing importance of ceremony, there is the ability to retain a dimension of experience that is fragile in that it can be lost—a dimension that opens for us as earthbodies. As Paula Gunn Allen explains in her book, *The Sacred Hoop*:

> The purpose of the ceremony is to integrate: to fuse the individual with his or her fellows, the community of people and that of other kingdoms . . . . A raising or expansion of individual consciousness naturally accompanies this process. The person sheds the isolated, individual personality and is restored to conscious har-mony with the universe.[8]

Ceremonies allow the celebrants to feel their renewed and heightened sense of connectedness with all other beings. Awareness is intensified and broadened. The kinship that brings people together is not human-centered, as it has been in the long Eurocentric tradition, but rather is a way of being with the earth, of being integrated in the dance of all beings. As Allen continues, "Entities other than the human participants are present at ceremonial enactments, and the ceremony is composed for their participation as well as for that of the human beings who are there" (*SH*, 63). The spell of the ceremony is one that changes perception and places people within a philosophical framework at odds with Western tradition, but at the heart of the Native American differing tribal cultures, as well as many other cultures: that our bodies open us to the flow of beings that constantly interchange with one another and give one another meaning and vitality.

Paula Gunn Allen states that despite great differences in ritual and symbol, all tribes have a sense of the "magicalness" of existence—that existence is not mechanical and comprised of separate parts, but rather dances in interweaving connection—because there is an appreciation of "an enduring sense of the fluidity and malleability, or creative flux, of things". (*SH*, 68) The long Western tradition from Plato onwards sees the world as composed of inanimate and separable substances, "but the tribal person perceives things not as inert but as viable and alive" (*SH*, 69). This shift in perception and in the sense of the nature of existence as interconnected and alive comes not just from another intellectual perspective, but from a ceremonial experience of the body, the earthbody. As Allen says of the spell cast by the ceremony, by the chanting, the repetition, the enactments, the dancing: "Soon breath, heartbeat, thought, emotion, and word are one. The repetition integrates or fuses, allowing thought and word to coalesce into one rhythmic whole" (*SH*, 63). As we have explored, it is only in such a letting go into the body's wider powers of allowing movement and thinking, imagining and seeing, feeling and breathing—and the whole range of faculties to interweave and be highlighted in their dance—that an openness to this flow occurs and supplants the possible diabolical rational logic of either/or, one versus the other.

Western philosophy and culture have been dominated for thousands of years by the strange idea that to understand reality is to "capture" it in some mental representation or formula, rather than opening oneself up to its palpable experience. Other cultures have realized that the way of understanding reality is a matter of making its experience wider, deeper, more intense, open to sharing, and multi-voiced. This experience is not from within us, but *the understanding is held in the material world around us*, which is not inert and silent, but speaks to our earthbodies on many levels, if we hearken. The beings that hold such wisdom within their very makeup are to be joined in handclasp, in dance like Matisse's women, by finding an emotional attunement to their aliveness. As Lame Deer, the Lakota shaman articulates it:

> We Indians live in a world of symbol and images where the spiritual and the commonplace are one. To you symbols are just words, spoken or written in a book. To

us they are a part of nature, part of ourselves, even little insects like ants and grasshoppers. We try to understand them not with the head but with the heart, and we need no more than a hint to give us the meaning. (*SH*, 69)

To move with the rhythm of the drum, to sing, to look at the sky, to be quiet with grasshoppers, and to utter words are the interweaving actions that open a deeper knowing as part of the sense of ceremony. The ceremony marks the opening of all levels of the engaged human beings with the comparable levels of the beings of the world, animate and inanimate.

It is only in this unity of experience, of which mind and body, reason and emotion, imagination and articulation, self and other, human and non-human, etc., are a part that *the dancing unity* of the world can reveal itself. It is a danced unity because it is one where both uniqueness and belonging are at an intensified pitch. This necessary synchronization of ways of knowing and what is revealed is no different than the case which we Westerners take for granted as the norm. The world as broken up into pieces to be rationally manipulated or logically dissected only reveals itself to a certain distancing, cutting, and controlling logic and way of being. So, too, the dancing world is revealed only to a dancing logic. The earthbody unity highlighted in ceremony is not "projected," is not just a "feeling" or a "fantasy," but instead is located outside of the world-view of binary logic:

> Symbols in American Indian systems are not symbolic in the usual sense of the word. The words articulate reality—not 'psychological' or imagined reality, not emotive reality captured metaphorically in an attempt to fuse thought and feeling, but that reality where thought and feeling are one, where speaker and listener are one, where sound and sense are one. (*SH*, 71)

To come back to who we are as embodied beings of a stuff that is not inert, but shared in interplay, in flux, with all other beings, means both to let go as one does when swept up in ceremony, but also to allow a different sense of reality emerge. Both feed each other: letting go and the sense of all beings as one tribal dance. Without one, there is not the other. With one, the other grows. Again, the same has always been true for the cycle within which the West has circled: to rely upon diabolic logic is to experience the world as opposed to one and within one. The cycle then continues as experiencing the world as a split between a knowing subject and other things or persons; this gives rise to recourse to a disembodied and binary logic to make sense of these alien or oppositional presences.

To turn to a very different cultural perspective that attempts to articulate a similar idea, we could turn to the famous Vietnamese Buddhist teacher and peaceworker, Thich Nhat Hahn. Hahn has tried to articulate how each bodily gesture, each sensory perception, each way we are moved by the world around us is an opportunity to enter and experience the dance of the beings around us. If we can quiet the consumerist and egoistically oriented obsessions that dizzy our minds and take us away from the experience of our body in the environment then we can achieve what Hahn calls the "miracle of mindfulness." To achieve this is to enter our lives as one ongoing ceremony in which everything calls out to us to celebrate each moment as unique and each being's existence as connected and valuable. It is what Hahn calls opening the awareness of the "interbeing" of all things. For Hahn, then each step can be a way "to enter the world of reality":

> I like to walk alone on country paths, rice plants and wild grasses on both sides, putting each foot down on the earth in mindfulness, knowing that I walk on the wondrous earth. In such moments, existence is a miraculous and mysterious reality. People usually consider walking on the water or in thin air a miracle. But I think the real miracle is not to walk either on water or in thin air, but to walk on earth. Every day we are engaged in a miracle which we don't even recognize: a blue sky, white clouds, green leaves, the black curious eyes of a child—our own two eyes. All is a miracle.[9]

For Hahn, we live in what we've been pointing to as "ceremonial time"—the time in which each moment contains all of time in a palpable way—a slow time in which there is always "enough time," because it is the right time, the only time, for every thing to come forward and enter the dance of moving with all things celebrating all that exists.

This first meditation on the nature of earthbody might be summed up by saying there is a logic captured by Matisse's painting that can be called "not one, not two."[10] It is neither a matter of shattering the world with cutting oppositions nor of saying that really everything is just one thing—whether really atoms or all one Supreme Being. This logic allows how in rhythm, in movement, in interchange, in flux, in folding over, in attunement, and as described in myriad other images, there is both a uniqueness to each being and also a joining that stays moving "between" all beings in their rhythmic linkage. This being within rhythm is both fragile and palpable. Not one, not two . . .

This kind of logic has its home, however, not in the mental realm of pure reason, but by opening our seemingly limited bodies to the indefinite expanse they have as part of their extended life in the world's material realm. Within this larger flow among things, bodies come to embrace, caress, resonate, harmonize, and find innumerable ways of interweaving themselves, keeping their own solidity within a felt kinship among beings of the material world. Matter is not dead and inert in this experience, but rather it is rich, thick, dynamic, it offers the way each being can encounter others. Openness comes from a way of holding ourselves as carved into the heft of material being that calls for supplement by others. Matter as our mater, mother, gives birth to possibilities of linkage: our hands allow us to caress and express affection to each other or to a horse or to our cat or even to a stone as we rub its smooth wonderful surface; the substance of our childhood home—its bricks and wood, walls and porches—holds the memories that are not "in our head," but discovered in the interaction of our heart with this place we haven't seen for twenty years; or the material substantiality of even a piece of cloth with various colors in a definite pattern can express the hopes, shared memories, fantasies, values, and dreams of a people in their flag or banner; and so all the properties of material beings in being sensible to other material beings are able to express meanings. We have thought of matter in a hostile way, as opposed to us and as comprising walls of separation, but each bit of the material world is a gateway for traveling mentally, emotionally, imaginatively, etc.. It is a way of connecting up beings, so they can interweave with each other. It is this sense that was represented to Paula Gunn Allen by her mother, who described the beings of the world as linked in "the sacred hoop." A grasshopper or a dandelion was to be treated with as much respect as the most noteworthy human as part of the sacred hoop, because it, too, had lessons to teach and wisdom to impart.

Earthbodies are part of this pattern of interconnecting material beings that contain myriad levels of expressing, knowing, and communicating among themselves and within their dance together. With the logic of inclusive ambiguity our body opens us to in indefinite and inexhaustible connection with the world. From this flow, as earthbodies, we are endowed with meaning for which we should share our gratitude, as Paula Gunn Allen so articulately expresses: "I am especially fortunate because the wind and the sky, the trees and the rocks, and the sticks and the stars are usually in a teaching mood, so when I need an answer to some dilemma, I can generally get one. For which I must say thank you to them all" (*SH*, 7). If we come to abandon our limiting, isolated sense of the body as really being just a mechanism or an animated corpse, then we would not feel stuck in a specific location, nor as if we must think and dream and make ourselves vital or else become inert. If we rather experience ourselves as open earthbodies, then we will experience that all beings always have more to say to us and give to us, depending on how we listen to, touch, or dance with them.

Chapter Two

Earthbody Dimensions

We Are Time

Certainly some alien life form, if it were to arrive on our planet unobserved, would be quite perplexed by our Western beliefs about our planet and ourselves. Rather than seeing the richness of matter and the earth as that which holds meaning for us, speaks for us, and remembers us, we see matter as dumb, inert, that which separates ourselves, and ultimately threatens us mortally, either by direct confrontation or by indirectly "wearing out" our bodies. We think this way, despite the origin of the word "matter" in "mater," our Mother, that common body with the planet that nourishes, sustains, and informs us. As we explored in the last chapter, the ways the richness and the openness of matter link us with a vital dance can be invalidated by an unrelenting demand to master the world and frustration at being part of the flowing and constantly changing material world.

However, these attitudes are even less bizarre than those that center on time and its "passing." Time is seen as something that is again separate from us—another "dimension" of reality—that we are "caught within" and that constantly both eludes us and is pushing us to our "end." The alien observing these attitudes might hypothesize that this group of humans needs to cast the planet's enriching dimensions and even its own body as a threatening, separate force in order to feel some thrill, some challenge, or some motivation born of adversarial desperation. Yet, even this strange scenario doesn't account for this century's more bizarre relationship with time.

Clock time, digitized time, electronic time, supersonic time, hyper-time: the race is on to always find more time, to get more done with less time used. Early in this century, T.S. Eliot wrote, "HURRY UP, IT'S TIME. HURRY UP IT'S TIME!" in *The Waste Land*. It signaled that not only had our eating, drinking, breathing, and sensing being on this planet become so rushed, according to regimented time schedules, but so had our embraces, our words, and our actions—such that they all became empty motions performed mechanically. Now, our time-sense has become so hyper-digitized that we obsess over gaining even infinitesimal fractions of seconds. Waiting even a second longer for a computer to process information may now seem unbearable to many of us. As the mechanized pace of production gains ascendancy in setting up many of life's rhythms—and now the electronically paced processing of information speeds up even more the overall pace of daily life—we lose sense of where time was located. It becomes more and more an externalized force pervading life. Lost is how time may have moved differently and how time moved with us as part of it, like part of a tide arising from our communion with the earth. Time becomes increasing the adversary we feel it to be. Time as our theater stage offered to us for our life's play seems unimaginable. Time as a gift of being invited into relationship with others that is both caring and enabling is a bewildering notion to most. Yet, many cultures and eras have seen time as the inviting open world stage.

A shift in time-sense follows the shift from losing the body to ascendancy of the mental as the locus of identity, as the locus of identifying what the world is about, and as the dominant way of understanding the meaning of existence. The mental representation of things is a way of withdrawing from being caught up in their rhythms and in the density of their mass. Bodies enter into relation with the matter of the world and work with them. Mentally, I can make a decision to terminate or change my relationship with a friend or loved one in an instant. Mentally, I can suddenly envision a house of magnificent design. I can mentally decide that I will learn to play the piano or tennis in a moment's resolution. However, to transform the relationship, build the house or a city, or learn to play the piano or tennis is an engaged bodily, material relationship that will involve us in a long, slow process.

Furthermore, to have this process maintain its direction will require that we commit ourselves to an interaction with the world that may never be fulfilled; we may remain always "on the way" to where we want to go. Let's consider a few, minor examples of this aspect of the dimension of time all around us—the time of the body, the time of our earthbodies as caught up in myriad rhythms with all the beings with whom they are in a continuous flow. I make a simple decision to lose ten pounds or to learn to drum a certain beat. Either will require that I faithfully pour my endeavors into a process that will move at its own pace, slower than any progression my restless mind vainly tries to summon forth. The first task will be a time of learning about the needs of my body and the impact of various activities and nourishments on the community of my organs and psychophysical processes. The latter task will cause me to enter the building sense of differing patterns comprising varied rhythms and to develop new movements and strengths in my hands, wrists, and sinews, and also to explore possibilities of leather hides in different temperatures and humidities. The time of the body and the time of the earth is a slow time, since it is a thick, rich time. *The time contained within and among the things of the earth, where matter is their marrow, is the power of working with many other beings, of finding resonances with their differing rhythms, and ways of meshing in their unfolding steps of development and change. Time as this emergent timing brings us all together to some place other than the beginning.*

This sense of time differs from a time "from above" into which everything is placed coercively. Rather, all beings—living and non-living—emanate time by exhaling its atmosphere and generating together its characteristic movement. Time's atmosphere is with us constantly as our sense of where we are in the processes with which we are involved, just as we constantly have some sense of where we are located within our environment. For example, part of my awareness that we are speaking is the implicitly accompanying sense that we are well into our conversation. Similarly, I have the sense in washing the dishes that I have been working on them for too long. The movement I experience is how I must join up with, encounter, and respond to the unfolding of the events, things, and processes that comprise the event or action of which I am part. As the food remnants slide off the dish or the water fills the sink or your last surprised phrase resounds or the car ahead swerves or the wind blows, lines of movement emerge. Each moment is patterned within the dance with all other beings to summon my sense of where things are now temporally insofar as we have become enmeshed.

Part of the heritage of Western culture and its philosophy has been to portray human beings as helpless before a host of forces that stand in opposition to us. These forces can only be dealt with by taking them on in heroic confrontation. Time certainly has been cast as such a monster. Time is portrayed as something "outside" and "beyond" us; and we are helpless before its "relentless march"—as if it were some invading force, rather than a cooperative or communal creation we have continually chosen to enter. Time's first voice is always the murmur of possibilities, not only about the future, but also about the present and past. Yet, the Greek mythic representation of time is as an adversary embodied in the image of Chronos—the root of our word for time, used in terms like "chronograph." Chronos devoured his children, just as we see time devouring our lives. Not only that, but Chronos ate his children out of fear that they would usurp him. He wanted to control the fate of the cosmos and keep his power. As embodied in Chronos, time itself wants to remain eternal, static, yet this is a contradiction. It is a key to our ambivalent relationship with time. We tend to see Western culture as being optimistic, as giving motivation for making "unending progress," but this is only in terms of *taking on* the world and trying *to remake it* to fit our needs better. We want to be in control and create the future we feel is right based on our present grasp of things. Our so-called optimism in the face of "the challenge of life"—of human existence itself—is based on a prior negative view of time, in its mysterious transforming power, as alien and as an adversary of inevitable crushing, grinding force. We are called upon to meet this force in a heroic battle, as indeed Chronos's son Zeus was forced to do.

A pervasive flaw in many of our mythic images and philosophies is to project evil and confrontation onto other parts of existence, rather than seeing ourselves and our part in shaping reality. Perhaps we are the enemy, and not time or nature or aging or chaos. Perhaps we are time itself, at least as part of the dance that times itself out in the particular rhythm and pattern. If time appears relentless and cruel to us, as running out on us as the popular hourglass image portrays it, perhaps we have helped to shape it this way. Perhaps our own cruelty and violence have contributed to our sense that time is cruel to us. Certainly, everything in existence, as many indigenous cultures have realized in their myths, has both cruel and kind, mirthful and mournful, and constructive and destructive aspects. So there may be aspects of time as the fabric of the world that are unrelenting and grinding, but perhaps we have a part, a responsibility, in drawing both time's traditional and current faces as so menacing. Rather than feeling helpless before the "passing of time," maybe we need to relearn how we can participate in time's flow in an aware and empowered fashion. We have learned to feel helpless and cut off from the flow of forces which comprise our earthbodies, which are currents in wider streams in which we tend to feel ourselves imprisoned. Certainly, no one individual can make time itself or be in charge of time, but again there may be a fertile middle ground between being in charge of existence and being victims of larger, alien forces—as being partners, participants, in a communal effort. This is another instance in which we hurt ourselves with our binary or diabolical logic: seeing ourselves either having to be in charge or helpless may seem the two choices, rather than recognizing an ambiguous strong pull on us by the concert of the Earth's other beings, of which we are a part and are able to influence and play out in varied rhythms.

We have a saying that "life is a matter of timing" and this simple sounding dictum actually has profound associations. It is not only a matter of circumstance or of pacing oneself to be ready for opportune moments, as the two most common applications of this saying seem to indicate, but it could be seen that existence is as much about coming together cooperatively in various ways as much as life is a "passing." *Time doesn't "move" at all without timing, as correlatively timing itself isn't possible without ongoing transformations that could mesh.* As humans, it is our lives passing, our aging, and our moving towards death that captures our attention most compellingly. Yet, we would not age, would not "run" toward death without billions of "timings," of coming together in various dances, various interacting relations— whether of parts of our cells or their chemical constituents or parts of the environment and our organisms. Of course, neither would we live without billions of sorts of timings occurring "all the time": there is a pulse, a rhythm given by the background of a planet full of myriad other timings which give it a relentless beat, but we have to enter its patternings through our own timing in order to experience this. It is a two-sided game of existence and being alive: what brings pain and destruction is the same marrow of events that brings joy and building—a tide of risky potential joinings. When meshed, the ongoing transformations of time are full and enabling, not relentless and destructive.

We have been focusing on how a body works or how a person expresses themselves and/or acts, but it seems more obvious that within the social realm the "happenings," whether of political events, friendships, raising children, performing a job, etc., are about timing. In this realm, besides the basic coming together of all parts of the interactive environment, organic and inorganic, the gestures of the human realm must come together in synchronization, in rhythm, and interchange for the occurrence to "unfold" as meshing together sensibly or "move forward through time," as we ordinary say it. If the constant "fitting together" didn't happen, the "moving forward" wouldn't happen either. There would be no coming together, no dance, and so no real movement. Everything would meet at colliding angles, at nonsensical juxtapositions, instead of "moving"—which means having a "step" or unfolding pattern, which can be seen as the sense of a "succession." Without timing, as the coming together of the dance resulting from the meeting of its participants, all would be "frozen" or "suspended," as out of touch or like a "jingling" of a cacophony of noise. Time is the coordinated connecting of all beings, each of whom is just this unfolding process.

We know this, but assume that the "timing," which we recognize must be brought about, is completely independent from the flow or passing of time, which we feel is unremitting. However, this makes no sense. The quality of the coming together, the richness or poverty of the "timings"—the making contact in relationship—helps determine the nature of the flow or the "passing," and vice versa. If the pace is always fast, the flow of time speedy, the "timings"—the sense or depth of relating within the interchanges of the dance steps together—becomes shallow and poor. What we haven't allowed ourselves to see is that if the timings are poor, then the speed, the cruelty, and the relentless pressure of time's flow increases. We don't see this because we don't want to see our responsibility for this—as if time has its own speed apart from any human participation. As part of not seeing our role with other beings in timing time, we also don't experience our earthbodies and their temporally magic power of finding time.

If, as we started to explore in the past chapter, among the various tribes Native American cultures retained a deeper sense of earthbody as way of entering a flow with all beings, we would expect them despite all their differences—to have a sense of time similar to that we're describing. For Paula Gunn Allen, born of a Keres Pueblo, it is the shared sense of the "ceremonial motion" of time that is most different for Native Americans from the people who came here from Europe, who are dominated by linear, mechanical clock-time. She believes that "Chronological organization also supports allied Western beliefs that the individual is separate from God, that life is an isolated business, and that the person who controls events around him is a hero" (*SH*, 149). Time as passing externally and unidirectionally creates this sense of separation and the need to fight back, which Allen sees as having been used in the West to implant an "industrial time sense" in its populations. This manipulates them into being good producers: "The idea that everything has a starting point and an ending point accurately reflects the process by which industry produces goods." However powerfully this may work to give us motivation and a structure within which to be productive in this industrial sense, it also gives people a sense of identity and reality that rips apart the fabric of earthbodies:

> That understanding, which includes a strong belief in individualism as well as the belief that time operates external to the internal workings of human and other beings, contrasts sharply with a ceremonial time sense that assumes the individual as a moving event shaped by and shaping human and nonhuman surroundings. (*SH*, 149)

In ceremonial experience, there is the palpable sense that we are of time, helping to fashion the rhythms with which dances among beings—people, creatures of all sorts, and all things.

If there is no deeply lived connection with the world—living one's body as a container, a separate inner place barricaded from threatening outer places and externally related to other people, creatures, and things—then we just move "through" reality as our cars seem to race through the landscape. We would be untouched and disconnected. Then "inner" time would be the sense of this "moving through" in comparison the movement of the whole in which we are contained. Time is so constructed by our representations to be the ultimate "super-vehicle" moving through the empty, yawning space of eternity, and we are the resigned losers in this drag race who are left behind by time. Actually, the image is more of a never-ending marathon in which we know that we ultimately can't keep pace with time, because it will relentlessly keep to its pace after we falter. Time as popularly represented is about our ongoing disconnection with the world and our helplessness faced with its rhythms.

Instead, however, we could, as earthbodies feeling inwardly the connectedness to all things—the moving through them and their moving through us even if we are physically still—feel instead the richness of all timings that brings a fullness of relationship among things, people, and creatures. Time is the opening doorway, the stage, and the interlocking of rhythms that is the emergence of dance from what otherwise would just be empty, disparate motions. Time is that timing of motions as gestures—as each being's expression that ends up finding itself encircled, responded to, and prolonged in the mirroring gestures of all these other beings that together form a graceful dance, like the women in the moving, prancing circle. Time is this power of the world to be a "uni-verse," whose roots literally mean to be of "one" "turning"—again like the turning and turning of Matisse's women of the dance across the meeting of earth and sky. Time is this timing—turning—which in its realm becomes a grace, a beautiful going together that we call "dance."

It is an easily recognized fact that time passes much differently in different situations within our personal lives—there is the agonizingly slow time of boredom, of waiting for dreaded or eagerly anticipated events, and the swiftly flowing time of being creatively involved by making music, writing poetry or building something, or of being fascinated by discovering new places, events, or people. I'd like to suggest, however, that we see instead that there are different times, many sorts of times, and these are not just a matter of pace. In our usual way of seeing things there can only be the one time above and beyond us, whose only property is to move—from the past to the future. Since this is the only property we give to time as this thing in which we're caught, this dimension, pace is the only difference we can attribute to time. Of course, however, even this difference can't really be attributed to time given our world-view, in which time is seen as indifferent to the existence and experience of every being "within it." Time must be eternally the same, keeping its own unvarying and thus heartless pace. So given the feeling of variously moving times, we instead deny that our experiences could reveal something about the world and its coming together and say these are merely "subjective" feelings about time, not indicative of "time itself." However, if time is the result of timings, of the interactions of all beings and their experience within the dance among all different beings, then there are many more properties of time and many different times, just as there are many dances. It also means that time could fail to happen sometimes or happen in a very minimal sense, just as sometimes the dance fails to "come off." It also means the opposite of the "common sense" notion that no one is responsible for time: instead all beings would contribute to time's coming forth.

Right now, we are largely insensitive to the depth of time's experience in our lives or even its genuine occurrence, because we are so caught up with this one image of clock-time we have created to relieve us of the responsibility for taking part heartfully in the shared interaction of the planet. The cost of not taking responsibility is to have installed this mean and relentless Wizard of Oz, Chronos, to rule our experience with crushing authority and beyond our reach. If we could face this responsibility for the times of our lives in embracing our earthbodies and learn to distinguish our times as the Eskimo learns the distinction among scores of different "snows" (round, pebbly flakes, softly falling lacy flakes, etc.), then we could start to talk about different possibilities of how time might be. For example, we might be able to distinguish a slowly embracing, fully present, richly sensed time versus the slow, empty, grindingly disconnected time in the way we had taken up our bodies at that moment. We might find we could pause and take on means of finding other attunements with the world in which there would be many kinds of time. Ultimately, we would begin to feel some part in establishing the gift of time our returning to the earthbodies could create in concert with others, creatures and things, in ever-shifting rhythms and through all sorts of connections. Then these kinds of connections and rhythms could be celebrated and cultivated, or in other words, we would have ceremonies of presences of all different sorts, differing timings, and bringing of beings into these shared rhythms, which is the province of ritual and ceremony.

We could also then feel more sensitively and take seriously our experiences of "bad times" and experience our ability to shift the way time occurs. The "slow" time of boredom is really the "emptiness" of time or, as Kierkegaard put it, the "nothingness" that can "dizzily" permeate time. Rather than connection, a dancing among beings, there is some radical disconnection among people's experience and with the other parts of the situation such that there is a ripped, frayed, jangling sense of missing co-presence; they've all sunk away and we are just all inertly side by side with no felt electricity of connection among us. It's not "slow" time as much as outside the flow of time, out of the swim, at all kinds of angles to the meetings with things and others that engenders absorbing timing. It's a sense of disturbed flow: there is not a captivated rhythm that brings things, people, and beings together. It is as though, at that moment we were lost in an alley parallel to the time of everything else that still meets everything else—dances—at that moment. What we call "slow" time or time that "drags" in boredom or anxiety or other disconcertingly disconnected times is a time that lacks the pace, the pacing, of the flow of rhythmic interplay, but it is more short-circuited, turbulent, frayed, lurching, sputtering, or grating than "slow time," which would be a time that still flows but does so with leisure, with expanse, and with the timing of even more opportunity for connection. That is time that we almost don't know anymore in our disconnected world—a time we'll turn to at the end of this section.

Similarly, the supposed "fast" time of racing through so many tasks and demands that our current compulsively productive clock-time often demands, is actually more about a harried time, a time in which there is such a confusion of interactions that none has been given the time—allowed the timing—to pick up shared rhythms, but there is much stomping upon one another's feet, whether our own or other people's or those of inanimate beings. In lives in which we are forced back into our heads, scrambling to "get by" but not really there and engaged, or "turned off" and just "moving through," days and years can end and there can have been "no time" for these persons, because there was no timing occurring, no meeting and gaining a shared rhythm and interaction, no dance. If we live in a world which has constructed too much of our ongoing situations as either boring or harried, for example, it is a correct intuition when we feel that we have had no time, that we've been robbed of our time and wonder where it has gone. Both are similar times, even though they feel like opposites. One is the frantic juxtaposition of disconnected aspects of our world and experience and the frustrated frantic attempt to create connection, to "get it together," by the speed of juxtaposition. However, no matter how quickly one aligns things or crams them together, the rhythm of dance is not born of these collisions. Rather, it takes time, it takes a timing among the beings to emerge, to catch on, so there can be an entry into each other's flow that is coming into rhythm together.

We're so concerned about the speed of time because of our obsession with clock-time, with the image of time as a moving race towards the future, and with seeing time as external to us. It leaves us little to say about it except this way to qualify its only remaining sense—the sense of moving. This sense of moving though is only a misplaced suggestion of the moving among things, between beings, that comprises timing and time, rather than the time that would move past us. Movement, at any rate, would be a misleading way to consider time: the examples we've discussed show that actually what is more at issue is the fullness of time, its richness, and its quality as bringing together in meaningful interaction. So, when we speak of the hours having "flown past" when we were absorbed in a stimulating task or an uplifting conversation or a thrilling experience of something or with somebody, what we really mean is that time was present, was full, was rich—that the timing, the joining of rhythms, the opening and flowing into each other of different beings, was superb. Then, suddenly, we feel that we have the time we need for our lives, or rather that we are the time of our lives, which is true. Coming back to the Native American sense of time, with these ideas in mind, we can see how there has been an understanding of time which doesn't make sense from the perspective of time as clock—as linear, authoritarian dimension over our lives. In contrast, the Native American sense of time centers on the fullness of time as earthbodies dancing with things, creatures, and people:

Ultimately, Indian time is a concept based on a sense of propriety, on a ritual understanding of order and harmony. For an Indian, if being on time means being out of harmony with self and ritual, the Indian will be 'late.' The right timing for a tribal Indian is still the time when he or she is in balance with the flow of the four rivers of life. That is, Indian time rests on a perception of individuals as part of an entire gestalt in which fittingness is not a matter of how gear teeth mesh with each other but rather how the person meshes with the revolving of the seasons, the land, and the mythic reality that shapes all life into significance. (*SH*, 154)

Time as described here by Paula Gunn Allen is about coming to meet all the beckoning streams that could flow into our lives, especially those that come from the natural environment, which is not some abstract "Nature" but is shaped by myth and culture sensitively. Clock-time will always be secondary in achieving this fullness of time life can offer.

There are some images that extend this sense of time, at least for me. Time does not appear as some abstract character in Native American mythology, but there are images I find suggestive of this dance of timing, of these meetings across the horizons of the world, and of recognizing how the world can go together gracefully, which is this fuller sense of time. It is interesting to consider globally that in most cultures there are myths of human origin, myths of the sun, wind, water, earth, war, love, most animals, and so on, but few about how time came to be or what time's life is about. I believe this is because time is already there, in the ways all these other elements and creatures find each other in each particular myth's sense of timing. Time is not a character of many myths because it is what is among all mythic characters: it is nowhere specific, because it is everywhere. This sense of timing within each world, within each culture's images and traditions, permeates its poetics, its sensibilities, and the emphases of its dramas. This is why the faces and shapes of time are so difficult to identify and understand, not because it is an inaccessible other dimension, but because it is everywhere in our world.

There are several tales, from the Native American tribes who lived where California now is, that resonate with the images we've been discussing. In the Yurok notion of the world, there was a balance within the world maintained by those called beyond the sky's rim, beyond the horizon of the world, those who followed the waters to the Land-Beyond-the-World, and undertook to give themselves over to the World Renewal dances. The tales describe the sense of aliveness and harmony of such dancing and its necessity for the world's timing: "to keep this balance, the people must dance the World Renewal dances, bringing their feet down strong and hard on the earth. If they are careless about this, it tips up and if it tips more than a very little, there are strange and terrible misplacements."[1] The world calls for our participation in its dance in its farthest and deepest reaches or else things, creatures, and people lose their places. To enter this dance is fun, but it also takes the courage to go beyond the normal realm of daily tasks and an intense vitality.

A Wintu tale tells of a village that found itself drawn into "dance madness," which "sometimes happens when many people are gathered together for dancing and singing and feasting" and "one or another of those that are dancing does not stop when the others stop, does not eat or sleep or rest, but goes on dancing and dancing" (*IW*, 77). In a village on the Swift Creek, the coming into womanhood of Nomtaimet, a beautiful daughter of one of the village families, was being feasted and celebrated. As the days went on, more and more of the people, from the oldest to the youngest, joined the circle dance. Even after the feasting ended on the tenth day, the singing and dancing didn't cease. They all went dance mad. As the tale continues, the village dances its way across the world, managing to eat and do what they had to do to keep alive, but always dancing. They dance through the turning of the seasons. When their clothes wear out, they dance for the rest of their dancing trip with no clothes at all, except for fresh body and face paint. Their main desire is to keep dancing. Finally, they have danced through the world and danced through the cycle of the seasons. Then "the dancers were home, and the dance madness was no longer on them. It had lasted through all the moons and seasons and had carried them around the world" (*IW*, 84). To become dance mad is to lose the worries of the day-to-day life, to give oneself up to celebration that all are present here together, young and old people, women and men coming into their prime, the rivers singing and flowing, the succulent creatures of the earth giving up their bodies to one another to nourish the whole.

A culture and people who don't have some dimension of their existence that is dance mad is instead chained within the linear cause and effect of industrial clock-time, of functioning as machines in a fixed line of societally defined productivity. Part of us needs to have danced all over the world, to have permeated all the cycles of the world's timing, in order to be in time, to be fully present in the dance with other beings. As the tale rightly claims, then we will have found our sense of home, of place, and belonging.

The tale of Umai is another tale of mythic vision from the Yurok that speaks of how we can see this earth and feel the connection of our earthbody as part of it. Umai was a young, beautiful, lonely, and restless girl of the Woge, the first people in the world. As Umai would stand on the riverbank by her home on the far edge of the world, she would look out to the edge of the Downriver Ocean where the sun would set and wait for the little silver flash right after the setting of the sun that would form "a brief crescent of light no thicker than the crescent of a fingernail along the horizon line" (*IW*, 91). This brightness called to Umai and she traveled across the waves to the horizon and to the edge of the world. Here, she discovered that the thin crescent of light was actually not a narrow crescent, but a waving, moving something with a center of living brightness. She then traveled further until she reached the Land-Beyond-the-World, where she found that the shining was really coming from the shore because a young girl, Laksis, Shining One, stood there waving. Laksis had always come down to the shore at sunset to wave at the Earth, just as Umai had always looked out to the world's horizon to see the shining. Of course, between such shining spirits there could only be warmth. The two girls walked and talked as friends. Umai returned to her home on the other side of the world. However, she had gained something: ". . . each evening at sunset, she goes to the riverbank and she and Laksis face each other across the width of the world, and Laksis, Shining One, signals to her friend from behind the moving sky. You may see her for yourself after the sun has set—a silver streak where the sky meets ocean" (*IW*, 95). This is the ultimate dance step in the timing sense of time, one that doesn't require a literal dance. It is a certain movement or prancing of the heart: to look out into the world and its greatest reach and to feel its shining aliveness and know in your heart that it is a smiling back of a facing being. It is to know of a moving energy, in whatever form, that is kin, is sister, and is friend in a signaling of welcome, appreciation, and openness to feeling close despite whatever distances intervene.

This is what time really is—that shining forth, the meeting across spatial distances, that depth of encounter, that graceful mirroring of all beings in timing together, resonating and resounding with each other's intoned sense. The continuity of time is connection, forged among the beings of the earth. It speaks and flows through our earthbodies, when we become at home with our bodies as part of all the environments about us: earth, sky, land, and creatures, but now also buildings, pieces of iron and wood, and even our machines insofar as we craft them to join up with this timing. To achieve timing, we need to craft our technological creations as gifts of a larger flow with the earth that within their functioning are designed to turn back in salute, in greeting, in echoing these older and larger rhythms in every way possible that we can devise when devising tools. If we can't build into our creations this sense of connection and relation to the larger earth context, then it a self-enclosing tool that should not be built, unless we are willing to give up our earthbodies and the earth—which is not a viable choice as soon as one has for a time allowed oneself to experience these larger rhythms. The fullness of time is so delicious and nourishing to the sense of meaning that humans crave it, as much as they need oxygen, that it cannot be ignored, at least not without suffering.

Within the Buddhist perspective time is not something external to us as some other dimension. We are time, says Dogen, the famous Zen master of thirteenth-century Japan. "All is time," he explains, and "all time is now." If timing is really what time is about, the way in which all interrelates with each other, shiningly, encountering each other—then of course that conversation is now, to be entered, to be listened to. The Buddhists tell fables of the past lives of Siddhartha, the Buddha of sixth century B.C. One of the most famous tales is how he is chased by a tiger to the edge of a cliff and leaps over the edge. In the act of falling, he reaches out and grabs onto a branch that is growing out of the cliff-face. As he dangles from the branch, he notices that at the bottom of the cliff awaits another hungry tiger. However, as he is suspended, hanging onto the branch, he notices a strawberry growing there beside the branch. He reaches out to pluck the strawberry and puts it in his mouth. Its succulent juices hit his tongue and he smiles widely. For the Buddhists, this is time. Not the tigers chasing us from behind, nor those lurking ahead of us. Time is the fullness of encountering the richness, the nourishment, that all parts of the world are for each other when approached in open relation.

If we cling to our dishonest notion of time as clock-time, as the relentless march of something supersensible, ineffable or metaphysical, before whom we are helpless, then we cannot come back to earthbodies. As victims of a time projected away from our own being and responsibility, we shatter the fragile relationship with all aspects of our world, whose magic glow must be carefully tended. We feel condemned to passivity. Yet, we are timing our lives away, but in a disconnecting time, projected as all powerful "Father Time," who devours our lives, as Chronos ate his children.

A full, rich, and engaging time has the right timing: various people or beings have come together in a meaningful interchange and merged rhythms. Other times have the quality of empty or dead time despite having the same number of events occurring, in these times there has been a disconnection, a going by or through that has not brought different beings into contact or rhythm. So, it might be better to talk of degrees of emptiness, fullness, and pace in regard to time and learn that we are a part of time's timing and flow. Then we could see that there is more to being "time-ful" as open, as attentive to rhythms, and as more artful in the ways of connecting with the world and others in their becoming. To merely take up space doesn't guarantee being in time. It is about joining the dance.

Sensing Enters the Earth

If time is about timing as a joining of offered relationships, the usual way of being a body and of being "in" time must overlook constant offers for joining in fulfillment that are simply not seen or felt or experienced in any way. In the everyday sense of time, it seems that everything is racing by in a disconnected way, at a distance from each other, scrambling not to collide, and engaged in competing with others. It then seems up to us—that humans alone can impose meaning and order onto this cascade of indifferent events that comprise the universe or that humans alone can get inklings of a higher order beyond this confusion. However, if the deeper time of earthbodies is always with us, as a deeper background, like the deeper booming sound of a drumbeat which is heard as sounding the voice of the earth (as it is in many cultural traditions), then we are also aware on some level of a solicitation from the world. In the everyday way of being caught up with our tasks, what we fail to feel is the way in which the entranceways to these myriad avenues of relationship with the world are always present in our bodies and tugging at us, asking for attention. Of course, a more self-destructive possibility is that because we are aware of these constant offers and what they mean for us, we want to flee from them or even ambivalently want to destroy them and the parts of ourselves that are part of them. Instead of taking these journeys, caught up in the distanced world of competing, racing fragments, the body can be driven around like our beloved automobiles or captained like a ship, as Descartes put it, or employed like a "vehicle for our minds to ride around on," as Steve Martin put it in *The Man with Two Brains*—as indifferent to these subtle callings as are the sheet metal and steel of our cars.

If in this commuter way of living our bodies, we pay attention to the sensuality of our bodies, we tend to do so only as another way of confronting or pursuing the world or others as separated from us. Feeling the distance from things from within our automobile bodies, we decide to "take in" objects or people in a sensual way as a hedonistic indulgence. In other words, feeling a hunger from the emptiness of this disconnected life, this "taking in" is another form of consuming the world and people as precious commodities. We seek to bridge the gap we feel between our bodies as self-contained vehicles and the passing parade of other bodies of the living and non-living varieties. This supposed "gratifying" of the body doesn't bring us back to our open bodies that are part of the circulation among all things nor to the earth as joined in the dance of the opened or shared rhythm, but rather keeps us at the distance of the closed and impoverished body as cut off from things.

In this pursuit of so-called sensual gratification—be it gazing at beautiful objects or people or stuffing food treats down our gullets—the distanced body is now given a few morsels. Through this gratification by "sending out" for things or people, it captures a distant reflection of their sensual richness. It is not surprising that this "gratification" doesn't quell the hunger we feel. The emptiness of being cut off from the only fullness that is ours naturally, as a sensitive human body that is part of this extended interplay through the other beings of the earth, can't be filled by disconnected objects or experience. Once this flow has been cut off, it is as though our blood supply has been cut. Then the flow of meaning and energy that comes through all other beings to us to inspire us with thought, feeling, motivation, and other psychic needs can only reach us through deeper levels of circulation we might not have been able to damn up completely and from these sporadic transfusions we take in by "venturing out" to the "outside."

The emptiness of this separation is a void, as untraversable as the furthest reaches of space if we must "send out" on expeditions from our inner self to capture prizes. The urge for food or sex or money inspired by this inner void always craves more, and we find a society of food, sex, money, consumption, and power addicts. As we ingest these essential aspects of life as if they were all drugs, we don't even really experience the nuances, the dimensions, and the different qualities of what they are. So, what we do "take in" is damaged in the level of energy, meaning, and inspiration it can provide us, like the food we eat after damaging its nutritive and aesthetic content through overcooking and technological processing. The sensory possibilities announced in the caring, appreciative, and sensitive experience allowed by a more fully open relationship to our senses goes unnoticed. We are out of touch with the emotional, imaginative, and intuitive sensual "elongations" (in the sense of lengthening our sense of self beyond previous boundaries) of experiencing as an attuned body that moves us into different rhythms.

What could happen distinctively if we were to live the body as earthbodies is the opening of a sensuality within perceiving that is felt as a call from all corners of the earth. It is a call felt deep within the body's comprehension to enter into constant play of sense, emotion, and fantasy that is lodged within all sensation. From the most visceral to the most outwardly extended perception, there is a layer of meaning that speaks of the connections of all bodies—animate and inanimate—in a particular glow and vitality that is a reflection of the world's deep life. When we let go into our bodies, into our viscera as reflecting swirls of energy, we can start to feel different currents pulling us outside our normal boundaries. When we let go into the fullness of our senses, there is a multiplication of possibilities of different ways to imagine, feel, dream, breathe, touch, sense, and remember different streams of meaning of the world. When a sensation is allowed to wash over us in such a way that we give up resistance and enter a tide of its impulsion, we are taken to theater stages on which are playing worlds of circulating meanings and whispering voices that are the communications of what the Taoists called the "ten thousand things." An example of such an instant is when the narrator of Proust's *Remembrance of Things Past* encounters an expanse of hawthorn hedges along the path his family calls "the Meseglise way" or "Swann's way" in their walks around the town of Combray in France:

> I found the whole path throbbing with the fragrance of hawthorn-blossom. The hedge resembled a series of chapels, whose walls were no longer visible under the mountains of flowers that were heaped upon their altars; while beneath them the sun cast a checkered light upon the ground, as though it had just passed through a stained-glass window; and their scent swept over me, as unctuous, circumscribed in its range as though I had been standing before the Lady-altar, and the flowers, themselves adorned also, held out each its little bunch of glittering stamens with an absent-minded air, delicate radiating veins in the flamboyant style like those which, in the church, framed the stairway to the rood-loft or the mullions of the windows and blossomed out into the fleshy whiteness of strawberry-flowers. . . . But it was in vain that I lingered beside the hawthorns—inhaling, trying to fix in my mind (which did not know what do with it), losing and recapturing their invisible and unchanging odour, absorbing myself in their rhythm which disposed their flowers here and there with a light-heartedness of youth and at intervals as unexpected as certain intervals in music—they went on offering me the same charm in inexhaustible profusion, but without letting me delve any more deeply, like those melodies which one can play a hundred times in succession without coming any nearer to their secret.[2]

The narrator is transported to a church-like space, with dappled lights of stained glass, and into a realm of other linked objects like incense and musical melodies, which moves him beyond the capacity of rational thought to a different sense of youthfulness or lightheartedness. This movement is one that happens within the realm of emotion, intuition, image, and memory, which are layers within the sensory character of the experience. It is not "physical movement" through space—but rather what Merleau-Ponty called a "movement by vibration." The movement circles within its own spell and doesn't let the intellectual narrator go to his "deeper" thought, but rather keeps him within the profusion of the sensual body. Perception is a magic carpet, if opened up to fully and sensitively, that can take us into realms of space and time that dazzle and speak to us in tongues that are incantatory. They tell us things felt all over within the flows of our body and understood in this bodily way—which can be enlarged upon by artistic rendering, by stumbling forth in original uses of languages, by actively imagining and other means of gaining a creative focus. However, since this kind of understanding can't be parroted back to others in stock phrases, given our society's prejudices, we tend to discount it and even shut it out. This movement by vibration, humming within and among all things, is an ever-swirling mass of currents that can be followed here or there. Earthbodies are mobile bodies, movements within the heart of matter which constantly find new connections, new flows to be followed, offered from the dance among colors, shapes, lines, shimmerings, lighting, sounds, rhythms, tones, smells, textures, pressures, tastes, etc., and within all the myriad facets of the perceived.

One can traverse galaxies sitting and just looking at a leaf or stone, if one allows the perceptual richness to grab all the dimensions of "being moved"—whether emotionally, imaginatively, memorially, etc.—through these sensually open passages, these rivers of flowing senses. Proust's narrator has allowed himself to "moved by vibration" through places remembered, through feelings of piety and vitality, through hues of color and fragrant perfumes, by opening to the movement by vibration in the perception in full sensual richness of the hawthorns. In Willa Cather's *Death Comes to the Archbishop*, the archbishop, Father Jean, awakens in his Sante Fe mission, to the chiming of the Ave Maria bell. He feels as if his body is awakening in Rome within the spell of the bell's pealing. Then an instant later he feels as if the bell's "Eastern tone" has transported him to Jerusalem, even though he has never been there literally. As he lies in bed for a moment, he thinks about this power of the sensual—sounds, smells, and colors—to carry a person to different places:

> Keeping his eyes closed, he cherished for a moment, this sudden, pervasive sense of the East. Once before he had been carried out of the body thus to a place far away. It happened in a street in New Orleans. He had turned a corner and come upon an old woman with a basket of yellow flowers; sprays of yellow sending out a honey-sweet perfume. Mimosa—but before he could think of the name he was overcome by a feeling of place, was dropped, cassock and all, into a garden in the south of France where he had been sent one winter in his childhood to recover from an illness. And now this silvery bell note had carried him farther and faster than sound could travel.[3]

Father Jean, being a product of our culture's diabolical logic and thereby sensing that the body as a entity separated from its surroundings, explains his experience of being moved though the world to different locations as having "been carried out of my body." Yet, he also describes his experience in these places as one in which he is experiencing sights, smells, and other perceptual currents. What is less misleading to say about these kind of experiences and brings us back to the power of the body is to realize that as a dancer among powerful currents of the world, these sensual streams are *extended body experiences*. They are not "out-of-body experiences" but diving deeply "into body" experiences. We flow with the body's powers as unfolding fields of energies caught up with so many other energy and meaning currents within colors, sounds, smells, etc. The opposite of our "common sense" and its expressions are true: for once Father Jean is not "leaving his body behind," but instead really entering the sensory and sensual richness that can transport us, "move us," in so many enriching directions!

Proust's narrator also brings to our attention the reason why this power is often fled from or not experienced. For all of us raised in a long tradition of "standing one's ground" in a clearly definable and locatable reality, such constant journeyings offered by the material reality of the world in its perceptual glory may be experienced as vertiginous. Proust's narrator feels the foreboding of the vibratory, moving power of things, of sensual richness, and seeks an anchoring answer intellectually to stop this swirl. He wants to "delve more deeply" to find firmer ground, but it is an art to let these flows follow their course through the surfaces of the world and into and through one's earthbody. The world's sensual surfaces have an even richer meaning and message through their intensity and crisscrossing than the traditional call to "penetrate" to the "depth" of things. It is an understanding of resonance. Yet, if we really let go into the power of these experiences—and do not let the foreboding that the narrator briefly has that his mind can't get the answer to the riddle of what the richness of the sensory world is communicating through his senses at this moment—the meaning circulating through matter can give us other understandings of ourselves and the world.

As a matter of fact, the narrator does dismiss this foreboding. His experience with the hawthorns continues, shifting to a hedge of pink flowers, who "had chosen precisely one of those colors of some edible and delicious thing." Looking at this even more vivid tint, the narrator states, "And indeed I felt at once, as I had felt with the white blossom, but with even greater wonderment, that it was in no artificial manner, by no device of human fabrication, that the festal intention of these flowers was revealed, but that it was Nature herself who had spontaneously expressed it. . ."(*RTP*, 152). From this moment on, a certain kind of happiness that has no definite word to express it, that the church and its incense had been able to begin to suggest, will always be conveyed to this person by the presence, and later the image, the echoes in all his senses, and other remembrances of these hawthorns. For the narrator, a certain feeling, a certain psychological state, and a condition in life centering on an upspringing, pungent, and refreshing happiness will be understood and then later represented by "Swann's way" or the "the Meseglise way"— the path through the landscape of his childhood that is now also a psychic path.

This new face an object comes to wear, or rather the deeper expression in its face, which suddenly we can see, comes to embody a kernel of meaning that will always be held there for us by that object and which can be rediscovered when experienced again. Some more rational ideas are more fully held within our consciousness, but many of the most vital meanings of the world are held by objects or people or landscapes or events and the meanings can only be reopened by finding the associated objects again in the world. The expression of these other faces in objects, events, and people joins the other expressions that most of the things in our world hold out to us, greeting us like our neighbors. Some objects or landscapes come to embody key significances in our life, just as the faces of certain central people in our lives do; a certain peace may be embodied for someone by a lapping, sparkling lake in the Adirondack mountains of New York, or a similar peace may be embodied for someone else in the many sights, sounds, smells, and textures experienced during a certain day of lying in the grass when they were a teenager struck with wonder and awareness. Matter is not dead and senseless, if heeded. Yes, like all communication, someone who wants to engage in dialogue must bring their own significance to the encounter and they must really hearken to the other. That is the meaning of the "ten thousand things" of the Tao: all these qualities that give life meaning, whether love, hate, awe, kindness, and all their variations and nuances are found not in some abstract, ethereal realm, but in the concrete presence of the qualities of objects, events, creatures, and people that face us—the "ten thousand things."

For Tayo, the protagonist of Leslie Marmon Silko's novel, *Ceremony* (and whose story will become important to follow later in this book), the mountains are one part of the landscape which embody a dimension of meaning and connection with others and to the flow of life that has almost been beat out of him by his experiences fighting against the Japanese in World War II, his lifelong brutalization as a "half-breed" (part Laguna Pueblo, part white), and by the desperate state of those on the reservation. Tayo's brother Rocky is dead; Tayo carried him as he died from his wounds during a long forced march after being captured by the Japanese in the Philippines. His Uncle Josiah is also dead—his only supportive fatherly presence during his life. Tayo is struggling with the hatred and oppression left his generation on the reservation after the war. It is the sight of the mountains during his long odyssey from his hell that presents him with something powerful that has been kept for him by those hills:

> The dreams had been terror at loss, at something lost forever; but nothing was lost; all was retained between the sky and the earth, and within himself. He had lost nothing. The snow-covered mountain remained, without regard to ownership or the white ranchers who thought they possessed it. They logged the trees, they killed the deer, bear, and mountain lions, they built their fences high; but the mountain was far greater than any of these things. The mountain outdistanced their destruction, just as love outdistanced death. The mountain could not be lost to them, because it was in their bones; Josiah and Rocky were not far away. They were close; they had always been close. And he loved them as he had always loved them, the feeling passing over as strong as it had ever been. They loved him that way; he could still feel the love they had for him. (*C*, 221-222)

The mountain's face still remains, watching Tayo and waiting for him to return its glance. When he does, he sees that it expresses all the love he thought he had lost, the love of the earth for its people and creatures, the love of those who have loved him deeply, and even his own love that he thought had dried up. It's there, that circuit of feeling, and he re-enters its flow.

When we allow our bodies to let go and enter the eddies of the rhythmic flow among beings present distinctively within each perception, then we start to feel the dances among all beings. Whether it is the way our body comes to meet the blue of the sky or the glistening of the ocean wave curling into itself or the hushed brown of the bark of the old tree outside our door, or even within the clenched tense energy moving around in our own stomachs, we could find offers from the world to all the avenues of our marvelous abilities to register and echo, transmute and communicate, with these voices of the world around us. We will have to explore that nature of these pathways leading from our earthbodies in and through the world around us, which will require us to look at perception and understand it in a different way than we normally do. For most of us most of the time, perception just furnishes information about the physical nature of the environment, things, and people around us or apprehended through "sense organ" instruments, but is not the opening up of these magical pathways to wandering around within unexplored dimensions of the world and others. We think of magic only as the object of superstitious beliefs or perhaps as something that would be supernatural. We will see the world of earthbodies is magical. The most natural dimension of existence for earthbodies is magic. We fight desperately to wall it out from our experience. However, before we see how perception is something much different from the earthbody perspective, we need to understand how and why from the "common sense" perspective of "Western culture" it seems so opposite: that matter is dead, that things are inert, that the body is itself a dumb mechanism, that the earthly is not the spiritual, that things and people are discrete and separate objects, and that we have to work to forge any connections among people, with things, and among the differing dimensions of the world.

The necessity to be logical and think about both ourselves and the earth in a mechanical way has been presented to us from Plato through the Enlightenment to our present postmodern technological intoxication as the means to gain a certain manipulative power over the earth and its material basis. However, other cultures present us with paradigms that work with the material environment more cooperatively, less invasively, to achieve similar goals. Plato, as the most influential early philosophical thinker of this tradition presented his readers with the argument that the gaining of knowledge could only be achieved by tearing our bodies away from the fabric of the earth. The question arises whether Plato and the Greeks really sought power: the power over things that can come from outright confrontation with parts of our existence as if they were adversaries to be controlled and defeated. Politically, Plato's Athens was an imperial power that treated other cities as resources to be subdued and plundered. Culturally, the cult of heroism was blossoming, which envisioned masculine dominance over life as a way of achieving glory that made life worth living.

However, an even deeper issue for Plato and the Greeks was using this sense of power and glory to solve a spiritual anguish as to how they were to confront death, which seemed to them the greatest evil. Their religious and metaphysical vision had moved away from accepting death as part of the earth's cycle to seeing it with horror. An early and chilling expression of this feeling is provided by Homer's *Odyssey* when the shade of Achilles in Hades speaks to Odysseus and his fellow Greeks from beyond the grave: "its better to be the most miserable slave in life, than a king in death." If we look at the classical foundations of philosophy as we know it, this love of "wisdom" may well be a twenty-five hundred–year tradition of fearful flight. In so fleeing, we cut a natural tie: the life-sustaining circulation between us and the earth and all its creatures, including among ourselves. Seeking dominating power rather than cultivating kinship signals the desperate shift away from being vulnerable to dialogue and relationship with others to trying to stave off feared disaster by staying in charge. However, despite this earthly payoff, it may be the flight from the dreaded specter of death that is the real issue. It may be that this underlying fear and flight from death, which is really a flight from the fullness of life, has added a particular undertone of hysteria to the supposedly rational and sober progress of Western thinking and philosophizing. Once this fear is felt, it is easy to hear it behind the seeming rational judgments of our philosophers, psychologists, religious and spiritual leaders, which makes their attempt at control over themselves and the planet a desperate effort.

The kinship with the creatures and things of the earth is equally a belonging to the cycles of change, of birth and death, and these cycles themselves were embraced by many cultures as sacred and as giving meaning to individual lives by rejoining them to a larger interchange of energies. However, to the heroic Greeks of the classical age as represented by Plato, it seemed that to remain part of the fabric of the earth damaged one's identity if coming into being and passing away was seen as part of the natural cycle of things on earth. This common fate and transitoriness seemed to deny the heroic ego its glory: the human self would be on the same level as the rest of the earth (and not above it) and its renown would not be eternal but only fleeting. For Plato, this seemed a terrible indignity; he must attempt to transcend to a higher plane of existence, one that left his body behind. So, for him, those who loved the body could not be wise, and finding ourselves on this earth, "lovers of learning understand that philosophy taking possession of their soul in this state, gently encourages it and tries to free it, by showing that surveying through the eyes is full of deceit, and so is perception through the ears and the other senses."[4] Statements like this help inaugurate a few-thousand-year-long Western tradition of despising the body and distrusting perception—the human, and more than human, way of communing with the world and each other.

Instead of being considered as ways to enter other beings and find more meaning, the senses are seen as necessary evils, to be *used* distantly and with caution, as if they were poisonous: "she [wisdom] persuades the soul to withdraw from these, except so far as it is necessary to use them and exhorts itself to collect itself and gather itself into itself, and to trust nothing at all but itself (*PI*, 487 [83B])." With this paranoid stance towards all of earthly existence, the soul of humans is instructed to enclose itself within itself, as in a cocoon, to be able to make good its escape. The price of not being caught by death is that people will not really be here while they are alive: their bodies will become just vessels for their spirits. Notice, this is a plan, one that perhaps is somewhat achievable, but highly perverse. Turning against ourselves, denying some aspect of ourselves that is most excellent, and even taking satisfaction from watching what is valuable perish, is perverse—it occurs when we leave the rich offers of the planet to amaze us streaming within our body unanswered.

For Plato, "it follows that anyone who is confident about his death is foolish in his confidence unless he can show that his soul is actually immortal and imperishable," or otherwise "it is necessary that he who is about to die must always fear for his soul lest at the moment of separation from the body it may perish" (*Pl*, 492 [88A]). Rather than admit this possibility and give credence to this fear, Plato insisted that we must have a discrete human essence to our being—a soul—the seat of our intelligence and spirit, which was not really of the earth and the body. He had to insist that "our soul existed before coming to the body just as the essence exists which has the name of 'real being'" (*Pl*, 496–97) [92D]) in order to insure that having always existing imperishably, who we are, each of us individually, will always continue. Plato urged us to see that our true being is always something beyond the "infinite mud and slime wherever there is any earth, things worth nothing" (*Pl*, 513 [109C]). For this slimy realm threatens us, if we allow it to really infiltrate our true being, and insofar as we are enmeshed in it at all, we are degraded. In Plato's famous cautionary parable, the "myth of the cave," our being caught up in the senses, in our emotions, in the rich imagistic proliferation of the imagination, in the intoxication of sexuality and sensuality, is represented as like being chained in the dark of a cave, in a line with our fellow prisoners captive to a shadow play, mistaking the shadows for objects in their true substantial existence. The tale of being chained by our own fascination with this earthly dumb show is told in order to convince us that the naturally felt appeal of perception, imagination, and sensuality is something that is really ghastly.

Plato very insightfully sees that each perception is like *a nail* that drives through our body and binds us to the earth and to its life of images and emotions: "Because each pleasure and pain seem to have a nail, and nails the soul to the body and pins it on and makes it bodily, and so it thinks the same things are true which the body says are true" (*Pl*, 488 [83D]). It is insightful, because it show Plato's psychological acuity to realize that emotion and perception are what connect us to the earth; they are the powers that enmesh us in the earth's rhythms. He also realizes that for most of us love is not an abstract idea but is found in the face of my beloved or that beauty is to be found in that breathtaking statue which connects us to earthly objects. However, what this means to Plato is that *perception itself crucifies us, since it nails us to the greatest cross, that of the earth itself*: "for this earth and the stones and all the places here are corrupted and corroded" (*Pl*, 513 [89C]). To be joined with the body of the earth, like being crucified by enemies, is to suffer a slow, tortured death, since to be swept up in the flow of this slimy, polluted stream of earthly life is an inexorable moving towards death, wracked by the torture of ever-changing passions on the authority of the false powers of the senses.

Because of this threat of being reduced to a level of change and mortality shared with the rest of nature (and even matter, which "dies" from its present form to assume others), Plato sees the most fulfilling and virtuous life as one which "dies to" the body—which learns to turn away from that mixed power of the senses, the emotions, and the imagination in perception. This had led the Western tradition to continually "turn inward" for security and to feel as though there is an "inner reality" of soul or self that is sacrosanct and provides the one certainty that each person brings with them into this life and can strive to know in order to become a better person. If such statements were not dressed up in lofty language and the veneration of thousands of years of history, we would undoubtedly call such sentiments schizoid.

Plato's doctrines dominate Western culture, and are central to the way early Christianity becomes established in the official Christian philosophy calling for the transcendence of the bodily and earthly realm, as Saint Augustine admits in his *Confessions*. He credits reading Plato with allowing him to finally see Christianity's message, that he then spreads, about the impoverishment of the earthly realm, materiality, and the body. However, this belief of Western philosophy in the disembodied self comes to its clearest expression in Descartes' seventeenth-century "Meditations on First Philosophy." Coming at the time of the secular and scientific break with the preceding dominance of church thought, Descartes' "Meditations" helps preserve and intensify the insistence on the rejection of the body, but now in secular terms of taking control and developing the rational will. Instead of seeing the body as threatened with enmeshment in a sinful world, Descartes stresses that the body would lead the mind into error and misjudgment that would threaten its detached, purely rational, and quantifiable grasp over nature and the material world. If in the rising scientific and technological command to reengineer the world, knowledge is power, then the body, emotion, sensuality, intuition, imagination, and other irrational forces are weaknesses that limit the person's control and efficiency.

In the "Meditations," Descartes laments his inability to know who he is or to find perfectly certain knowledge about the world. He laments that in the course of his life he's learned that anything that the senses tell him may deceive him, and so should be valued no better than something that is false, since the senses and all related to them and the body would never give him the absolute certainty he desires. He can only be certain that he is "not more than a thing which thinks, that is to say a mind or a soul, an understanding or a reason."[5] His body, the sensual world, and even his perception of other people not only can't be trusted, but Descartes doesn't even want to consider them part of his own being: "There is certainly within us a certain passive faculty of perception...the faculty resides in some substance different from me" (*WD*, 191). This realm of the body, its senses and its feelings, can't be trusted except insofar as whatever they might tell him in their irrational way can be transformed by his mind into clear and distinct thoughts about these objects—hopefully into ideas that are quantifiable. Otherwise, he can't be sure that he may not be "deceived," since what we experience emotionally, sensually, imaginative, intuitively, and recollectively can change, is indeterminately ambiguous, and is not absolutely guaranteed to be eternally true in the way that "one and one are two" is true and can be trusted.

It seems obvious that this is a rather paranoid stance, yet this man and these ideas are considered to be, respectively, the "father of modern philosophy" and the "foundation" of modern Western culture. On one level, the appeal is obvious, since the conclusion is that only the quantifiable, the mathematical, can be accepted as true, which fits well with the agenda of the industrial and scientific revolutions to reduce the world to that which can be manipulated, engineered, and made to produce profits. However, on another level, there must be some further appeal to the psyche of the West to continue this war on embodiment, since it has survived through Greek, Christian, and now scientific and humanism revolutions in values and thinking as one of the only constants. Other aspects of Cartesianism can be left for other kinds of critical rejoinders, but the question to be faced for us is why should human beings, if they are at heart earthbodies, be drawn so continually to take such pains to deny the reality of this bodily dance among the beings of the planet?

Certainly, the desire to escape the threat of death by being above the earthly realm of creatures and objects that dissolve and take new forms is powerful, and perhaps powerful enough to explain this attraction to the idea of being a disembodied self or soul. However, what makes this belief even more powerful is that it satisfies the opposite response to the fear of death simultaneously: if we are drawn to recognize the power of death, and rather than deny its triumph over us, we seek to join with its complete mastery over our fate, then we would be led to the same attempt to strike out at what is most vital and involving—our earthbodies. If we deny our earthbodies, if we sever our links to the earthly dance that runs through all the matter around us and through all other creatures, we have taken on the most lethal power of death and made it our own. We are then living death. When we sever our earthly lives as being part of a larger circuit and as played out by an all-embracing rhythm of myriad conductors, we have grabbed an illusion of personal control. By being cut off or dead to our extended earthbodies, it seems that retreating from the body is the way to stop the process of dissolution that aging presents to us. Aging is overwhelming because we know that it is the result of all material beings, through their interactions, gradually working their way back from the separation of their unique form towards rejoining the larger dance and taking on new forms. But rather than having defeated the combined power of all the world's beings' interaction with our body, by retreating from its openness and dialogue with the material world, we have only succeeded in killing its vitality prematurely, losing the preciousness of life that we didn't want to relinquish.

In hardening our bodies to the enmeshments of the world offered in every sensory solicitation, we manage to become dead while still being alive in some very real sense. The appeal of movies and novels about the various "undead" creatures, like *Nosferatu, Invasion of the Body Snatchers*, or the countless retellings of the Dracula myth, is the thrill of being dead, of no longer being alive, while still being present in the space of the earthly realm, but not its time. The desire of all the ghouls, the pod-people, or the vampires, is to be left alone so they can feed on life without having to be part of the interrelation that feeds it back. They represent the dream to walk this "physical space" but be out of time, be eternal, but not in some heavenly realm, but right here on earth, yet somehow unreachable—to be an intruder who not only profits from the earth, but masters all its vulnerabilities, discovered in each of the sense's deeper felt meanings as they elicit our passions, our responsiveness, and our care. In the Francis Ford Coppola's film, *Bram Stoker's Dracula*, a recent retelling of the myth, the opening makes it very explicit that it is the excruciating and unfair death of his wife and the maddening pain he feels about it that drives Dracula to his fate of joining the undead. He feels crushed by death in being deprived of what he loves and enraged by those who wield death's power on earth, so he embraces death in life. This aspect of the vampire fantasy becomes clearer in the more recent film *Interview with a Vampire*, which shows at length what the "life" of being the "undead" is like: endless emptiness and boredom, as one can't be touched by others and by life. To achieve the eternal life as being cut off from the rhythms of the earth or, in other words, to be "undead," has often been portrayed as the goal of life in our cultural tradition from Plato onwards—thereby negating the threat of death over life—but it turns out to be a poor joke: one defeats death only by joining its ranks and having killed one's true life and vitality.

This idea of wanting to get beyond the hurt and pain of life (whose root meanings hearken back to the idea of being impacted by all the other beings that exist and being caught up in this larger web of beings to whom we owe our lives[6]) was articulated by Freud as the "death instinct." Insofar as part of us wants eternal peace, wants no bother from any other people, creatures, or even objects of any sort, insofar as we want an end to frustrations, failures, and longings, we want to be like we imagine a rock to be: inert, unmoved, and unmoving—dead, even though we've seen that this is not even the truth of the rock as part of the dance of the planet. So, this death or peace we imagine doesn't really exist on this planet, except as we can block out the feeling of vitality and interchange of meaning that flows through all things. It is an "ideal state," the despairing truth of the realm of "pure being" that Plato imagined as beyond the slime and pollution of this earthly realm, as have so many others following in his fear. What seems so shining is actually a horror. How strange that what horrifies, like these ghouls, vampires, and zombies, is really the secret of many of our desires.

There is a power in examining popular films in order to understand aspects of the way we look at ourselves and the world. There is something analogous to looking at films while examining our contemporary culture in looking at the plays of the ancient Greeks or the myths of indigenous cultures. Not only are films one of our most popular mass communication forms, but they excite and fascinate us in ways that reveal our cultural fantasies. To view the popular film is one of the few places that vast numbers of our citizens come together and engage in an experience much like "dreaming together"—as might be implied by a deeper reading of the way in which Hollywood itself is known as the "dream factory." Like our dreams, the film as it has been constructed by writers, directors, actors, actresses, and editors, and shaped by its geographical setting, culminates in an expression of not only these people's but also many of our own unconscious ideas, feelings, and desires. As the audiences let go in the dark, gripped by the scenes on the screen, feeling in a very bodily and emotional way, there are subtle recognitions and responses that add to the unfolding meaning of what the images and actions say.

The meanings that really grip us are often not the straightforward message they seem to portray, but like the actions in a dream seem to have many layers of meaning, many of which we are not aware at first. The simultaneity of the address to many of our senses, emotions, imaginations, and kinetic feelings in an environment in which we feel enveloped opens for us these many levels of apprehension and expression. The thrill of the vampire movie is partly the thrill of not just projecting ourselves into this mythical identity, but on another, less conscious level, the greater thrill of recognizing and glamorizing ourselves as part of the population of the undead. We have had to hide from ourselves our identities as the vampire creatures we are. Now, we can come out and play for a while with this dimension of our culture and glorify it as incredibly powerful.

We are ambivalent about the vampire, at once rooting for him or her to take power over these other mortals and mortality itself, but we also can't wait until someone drives a silver stake through the vampire's heart. This is because we are so ambivalent that we are vampires, at least for much of our lives. We ambivalently want to escape from life's pains in its enmeshment with all other living beings. Even though this deprives us of much of life's wonder and vitality, it does afford a power,—the power of detached manipulation over others, the environment, and even ourselves. Part of us thrills to that power, even as it drains the lifeblood out of our existence. However, the starved voices inside us that long to feel the energy, the meaning, and the joy of being part of the interconnected dance of the planet scream out against this vampire life and its violence that is ultimately against ourselves, as well as against all other beings in cutting them off. So, there is the horrified part of us that longs for someone to drive a silver stake through our deadened, disconnected hearts and end this nightmare of being the undead. This is the voice of our denied earthbodies that is also thrilled when the vampire on the silver screen falls.

There are even more sinister levels at work here in this dynamic of death and life. There is a joy in killing that is also part of the overall horror of these films that we will turn to in the next chapter—a turning of a natural erotic drive into something wicked—that we will address once we have an earthbody understanding of the erotic. First, we will move on from seeing how earthbodies not only offer us an extended life as part of a flowing planetary vitality, but also how within the perceptual experience we are offered a deeper and broader erotic dimension to our lives than we have allowed ourselves for the past thousands of years. Then we will see how this kind of eros can turn to its destructive side, too.

To conclude this consideration of how the Western tradition has often been a turning against the dimension of earthbodies, seeking to cut off the ties to a rich sensuality, to a joy in being caught up in the environment and each other as animal beings, we must say that in some very real sense, it has been a suicidal tradition. We have been asked to kill our larger lives as part of the planet. We have not been a culture of life, but rather a culture of death in the way we've understood our bodies. Christianity is an example of how we can quickly turn the power of life inherent in earthbodies into a suicide pact. Jesus preached the power of the *incarnation* and how divinity was here on earth as he was the "son of God." From this, we could have realized, and dedicated ourselves to experiencing, how our bodies and the whole realm of incarnation, the flesh of the world itself, is interconnected across species and even categories of being, and how this being interwoven is holy, is divine. In this sense, we should all experience ourselves as the sons and daughters of God. Quickly, however, this message was transformed into one of despising the body, and the materiality of the earth: "this life" was condemned as something to be left behind as not our proper home and destination. The joy of the natural cycle of life and death and that of being caught up in everything else of the earth was lost. The sense of incarnation as honoring flesh and the earth was distorted.

By contrast, the price of taking full joy in our earthbodies and the planetary flow of vitality is to embrace our deaths as only another part of a larger rhythm of change and interchange. It also means that humans are wonderful in their way, but not absolutely different in kind or worth—just another wonderful link in a planetary or cosmic circle of dancers.

Eroticism Truly

We tend to think of our modern culture as "advanced," as if we had "progressed" beyond the understanding and capabilities of ancient cultures. The Western technological culture especially seems to believe its scientific and technical productions have brought humankind closer to realizing its potential. Most of us realize that in our personal lives, when we focus on cultivating certain abilities, our making choices means that other potentials will go undeveloped or remain undiscovered, and even that some previous accomplishments will atrophy and become lost to our repertoire as the cost of these new endeavors. Culturally, we seem to lack this humility to realize that we have a "style" or character or, in other words, that we are good at certain things, poor at others, and have completely forgotten some aspects of life. Our greatest pride is that we can achieve technological feats such as sending a manned flight to the moon or imaging the flow of circulation within the brain or creating computer chips capable of incredible numbers of operations in microseconds. We may not all identify these activities as most valuable, but we do tend as a culture to see this as the prime evidence of our "progress." However, somewhere in our collective psyche we know this is a lie and that it does not make us more "advanced," just wonderfully skillful in certain technological areas. Popular culture, from the enormously popular film of the past decade, *E. T.*—in which the space creature lies dying, surrounded with acres of technological machinery trying vainly to revive him through technical means, when all it needs is affection, love, and belonging—to constant warnings that our gadgets are not the crowning glory of existence in themselves, emerges from this other sense we have. Yet, we succeed in discounting these other feelings as being "sentimental" and not the objective measure of our status. It is still difficult for us to see how in some very fundamental ways, we are becoming very dumb, almost helpless in our ignorance of basic dimensions of existence, and unaware of our disconnection with many aspects of life.

One dimension of life on this planet that we seem to have no understanding about is the erotic dimension. All our popular words, ideas, and behaviors concerning eroticism fail to even approach true eroticism. This is in spite of the fact that this is a very erotic planet. Earthbodies are erotically charged, open, and expressive in each of the structures in which they function. Yet, we seem determined to destroy these gifts offered to us, even while we plaster the planet with representations of a supposed eroticism that moves against this powerful tide of the earth and its beings. Most of what we label as "erotic" is actually anti-erotic. The thousands of years of turning against the materiality of the world, its sensual richness, its ability to engender these feelings, intuitions, and imaginary productions if we would let go and be taken up by the earth's energies, have also made it impossible for us to feel the true eroticism of this world. It has made us ignorant lovers, dampened the electric charge the planet tries to send through us, and made us look in the wrong places and in the wrong manner for erotic excitement, pleasure, and nourishment.

Our definitions of the erotic and our understanding of this realm refer back to sex as the source of this energy, pleasure, and significance. Sex and sexuality are supposed to be obvious to us as the source of their own meaning and excitement. It is a "primitive" "force" or "drive." To call something a drive or force that is indefinable means just that we are ignorant about its nature. We have just wandered so far from the proper context of this phenomenon, that we can't describe its meaning. Yet, somewhere deep within the more vital currents of our own bodies, we know sex is not a blind force nor is it "primitive"—at least in its full possibility. Sexuality in its fullest sense doesn't "drag us down" to some "lower level," but "raises up" or makes more acute dimension of sensibility and expressiveness.

However, sex, as our culture represents it, is profoundly anti-erotic, as are the body and the earth. Sex is defined as, and often made the object of obsession as, the meeting and interpenetration of genital organs. The body is a biomechanical mechanism and container that extends as far as our skin and blocks us from the rest of the world, including others. The earth is made of inert stuff, which is mute, senseless, and the passive plaything of mechanical chains of cause and effect. In this "true" and "objective" accounting of reality, there is no dance together of body and earth currents. In terms of rhythmic unity, attractions, shared energy, fire, meaning, joyous overrunning, richness, sweetness, sensitive mirroring, and all the other attributes that we will see properly belong to the erotic, there is none in these genital juxtapositions, rubbing bodily containers, and surrounding dead matter. However, it is this making sex, the body, and the earth unerotic that causes us paradoxically to cast them as so powerful in the role of blind, relentless, and compulsive forces of our pseudo-sense of eroticism. Within recesses of our being, we know we have lost something vital. Its lack is painful and compelling.

Living in a cultural and historical context in which the body is seen as "prison house" of the flesh, part of the polluted and meaningless slime of the earth, it is inexplicable how we experience the body and certain of its parts as having such a pull on our energies, aspirations, and even dreams. Given the context of our understanding of our "higher" natures—our moral, loving, and spiritual side—as "beyond" the mere body, eroticism as stemming from sex, the sex organs and the "irrational" systems of the body is felt to be an overcoming of this human dimension by other forces, by the animal within us, as if our humanity were swept away in thrall to another nature. We picture ourselves as divided beings: spiritual, moral, and loving selves situated atop a volcano of "drives" or "devils" or combustibles. These are seen as magical or irrational or biomechanical forces that get us from "below," since we've left no room for eroticism in our "higher selves." Yet, we will see another way of looking at eroticism can see it as quite sensible, rational, and at the heart of our most noble humanity.

This sense of disconnection, of not knowing ourselves in this most intimate and expressive impulsion of energy, passion, and vitality, leads to a childish sense that "I can't help it," as if we are swept away—like some child's excuse of how he or she was taken over by forces which really did "the bad thing." Eroticism as this other force combating with us becomes something "depraved," or at least embarrassing. It is not part of our public, openly communicated and acknowledged sense of selfhood, except by those who seek to rebel by publicly identifying with the erotic just because it is seen as inappropriate to the shared sense of pride of self—like Anais Nin or Madonna. Yet, if eroticism is a powerful, vital, and electric energy bringing the earth's beings into greater intimacy and interchange, shouldn't it be seen as a high achievement—one that requires intelligence, open-heartedness, and expressive sensitivity?

Of course, the other avenue our Western tradition has taken is to glorify the erotic as being quite different from how we think we experience it. This stance claims that the erotic is actually the passion of our "higher" selves. Since this perspective claims that human dignity comes from our disembodied spirit, only such a "higher calling" would not compromise our dignity. Rather than being about the body's power and meaning, such a gripping force must be about the "spirit" beyond the body. This shows how crazy we can get in turning against who we are: the most palpable bodily celebration about being a body is made into something anti-body! Plato decided this was the solution to his worry how eros could come from the body to so overwhelm the rest of the human being. He decided that it couldn't be that our higher selves could be so swayed by a depraved source. He declared that we were confused at first when we believed we desired other bodies. Actually, the erotic drive is towards the source of beauty, goodness, and truth in the eternal spiritual realm. We, in our ignorance, misread the excitements we feel in our bodies about other beautiful bodies. This is only a lesson from our higher spirit that we need to look outside ourselves for something else to seek in order to be satisfied. For Plato, appealing bodies are only an inadequate representation for something eternal and purely spiritual that we seek to join and so transcend our enmeshment in the slimy earth. For Plato, part of eros is this natural tendency to be drawn ever higher, away from our initial feeling that eros is about sex and the body.

It is not surprising that the Judeo-Christian tradition, very much at one with Platonic thought in many ways, also took eroticism to be, in its truest nature, the calling of spirit towards both God and an immaterial eternal realm. As the longing for unity with the Godhead or as the return to our eternal spiritual and disembodied home, as Aquinas put it, this also has affinities with the Hindu path towards reunion with Brahman after achieving "release" (*moksha*) from the chains of the cycle of rebirth as a fleshly creature. The striking feature of all these ways of attempting to rescue eroticism as something leading to the "higher" nature and instructing us that we can transcend our delights in color, tastes, the beauty of other people's bodies, the excitement of sexuality and our sense of belonging with the earthly, is that they preserve the same basic analysis of eroticism as irrational force, as well as the same valuation of the earth, body, and the material world as "lower" or less worthy realms. This is the same approach taken by those who indulge in extreme forms of eroticism in our alienated culture, indulging in promiscuous sexual acts in a detached manner because they, too, claim it has no intrinsic meaning, is just a blind satisfaction, and should be disconnected from love and "sentimental" appraisals.

The structural dynamics of Platonic or Judeo-Christian eros is the same as the Freudian definition of eros: the desire to combine and achieve a greater sense of unity. For those who see eroticism as some irrational drive, it is a matter of irrational bodies coupling together to overcome their incompleteness. For those who spiritualize eros, it is the drive towards uniting with a higher and more pure ground of being, rather than staying separate and abandoned in the flesh. As Augustine expressed it in his *Confessions*, God's worst possible punishment would not be some kind of suffering inflicted on the sinful, but the withdrawal from the sinner so that he or she could no longer hear the calling to something higher and ultimately satisfying. With either the secular version of irrational drives or the metaphysical version of longing for a better realm, both approaches see the erotic as aiming at a deliverance from the basic pain and gnawing dissatisfaction of being a separate, unique individual on this earthly plane. However, this pessimistic view of eroticism can be contrasted with an eroticism that would be part of the recognition and celebration of our status as freestanding, unique dancers able to join with other earthly beings through certain sensory means. The erotic would be the highlighted and intensified sense of appreciation of a separateness that can play with others in the back and forth of not being one, but not being wholly separate either in the dancing, earthbody logic of surfaces and depths of our bodies. The logic of inclusive ambiguity is not a dry rational one, but rather we play it out among ourselves and especially within the visceral surfaces and depths of our earthbodies.

Both the religious and secular psychological portrayals of the erotic define desire as the drive to overcome incompleteness, and its satisfaction would overcome our sense of separateness. Both are responding to a crisis they themselves have caused with their view of reality. In the dualism of mind versus body, of spirit versus soul, or of individual versus individual, there is a pain of missing something. This missing of something, however, is caused by the dissociation of the person from his body as pure spirit or of the person from the palpable perceptual feelings of belonging with all others in an embodied spiritual kinship. Making spirit and bodies self-enclosed and self-subsistent realms causes pain through fracturing people's extended being though others. The desire to overcome this pain is misleadingly articulated as the origin of eros, instead of seeing it as the result of distorting it.

For both dualistic approaches, the value they give the body and the eros is the same: it is meaningless in itself. For the hedonistic materialist, the Freudian, or the bioscientific materialist, eros is the drive for bodies to unite. For them, there seems to be no logical reason to limit a promiscuity of so-called erotic indulgence, since satisfaction relieves the sex "drive." Since eros as means to relieve an irrational tension in bringing together sex organs has no greater meaning, why not discharge these tensions as much as random luck allows? In a parallel valuation, for the metaphysical approach, there is a need to transcend these indulgences: since these erotic acts are meaningless in themselves, it makes no sense to pursue them, instead using one's effort to achieve eternally valuable goals. If sex could be abandoned and instead spiritual acts pursued that offer the person the chance to achieve the real satisfaction they crave, eros shouldn't be wasted on these lower and tarnishing forms. Both perspectives devalue the body and the intrinsic meaningfulness and grace of eroticism. This way of defining eroticism, which both share, as seeking union and as being just a "merely physical" event, leaves the erotic as either something to be indulged or as something to be transcended, but neither captures the heart of human meaning and identity that can be manifested through the erotic dimension.

Both these approaches also easily lead to a psychological overlay of eros with the drive to *possess* the other. If eros is about the urgency to not feel separate and isolated, either in a visceral sense or in a spiritual sense, and the bodily experience itself in sex that is identified with eros is of no consequence other than as a means to overcome physical distance or launch the spirit in motion towards a higher goal, then the erotic becomes defined by its goal. We will see how the erotic should be defined in terms of a unfolding process, focusing on all the nuances of the erotic encounter. However, once the erotic drive is seen to be about achieving goals, then it is easy to see it not only as a vehicle for physical release or a starting point for the spirit, but also as continuing the species or for overcoming the insecurity of either physical or spiritual aloneness experienced as psychological loneliness.

Given our alienation from our sense of ourselves as earthbodies, this problem of feeling psychological loneliness is acute. Rather than the earthbody's openness to rhythmic interconnection, as symbolized by "dance madness" in the Wintu tale, we feel cut off from other humans, living creatures, and the material objects of the world. For the transcending spiritualist, this isolation is the distance from God that can be overcome with the true eros of returning to God's possession. However, our society's indulgence in and obsession with the so-called erotic comes from our materialist sense of being trapped within confining bodies that are part of the materialistic milieu. Feeling this isolation, the erotic offers a way out of this anxiety and insecurity. To capture the regard of the other through ensnaring their body with my body in such a way that their admiration overwhelms them, is experienced as a troubling need, a compelling want coursing through the flesh that makes me start to feel viscerally my own value through the eyes of the other and overcome my alienation through the force of the other's desire. Jean-Paul Sartre's analysis of this dynamic in *Being and Nothingness* is the most famous articulation of how through the erotic seduction of the other person, one can offer oneself as an object of regard for another consciousness which becomes "fascinated" by it while under the "troubled spell" of erotic excitement.

Given our dualistic framework, we can't help but experience sexual interplay as another's mere body reacting to my body, since our bodies are those merely fleshly vehicles of consciousness. That is why Sartre says that in erotic experience, we must make the other's body into a *snare* for their consciousness. Seeing our minds as separate from our bodies, in desire we try to break down the other so that the other's body absorbs their consciousness like a "blotter absorbs ink" (to use Sartre's image). The fact that we have separated ourselves from our bodies gives us this isolation and insecurity, but it also gives us a way to catch others' insecure floating consciousnesses by enslaving them in desire for our bodies. In this game, they are either ensnared or free from being compelled by our desirability. It is the diabolical either/or for high stakes. If they slip out of our trap, the insecurity will return that we don't really *possess* their bodies through ours. It is an "all or nothing" risk, that can always break down, if the other's consciousness suddenly looks at me as not driven by desire, but as looking on from the distance of a cool, judging consciousness. Within this cultural context, erotic experience means possessing the other through the vehicle of sex, which is a competition to gain security from the partner, and whose spell becomes broken when the sexual tension is released. It is tragic, or perhaps self-destructive, that this sense of the erotic colors much of our society's experience of sexuality. Its logic leads to a pervading sense of frustration and even violence, since it is the drive to gain an impossible security from an insecure situation. It is an attempt to be in our bodies and not hover distantly over ourselves as detached consciousnesses through securing the compulsion of our partners to be driven in their need for our bodies by becoming ourselves enslaved to our partner's bodies. The game starts in painful detachment of mind and body and can only end there, too, after "the thrill is gone."

This sense of the erotic helps explain the success of our contemporary society in offering the constant temptation to people to promote packaging themselves in ways that would be irresistible to erotic partners. We become obsessed with the fantasy of gaining this allure. It is obsessive, because our sense of reality is at stake. Having lost the real flow of the planet in denying our earthbodies, we want the feel of the real back and its connectedness. The female breasts displayed on the film screen or at the topless bar, the male butts revealed on the jeans ad at the bus stop or at the Olympics, are seen as the unleashing of the power of the erotic to capture the desire of the others. Yet, whatever magnetism still operates on the tawdry setting of a red-light district display of flesh is a very distant cousin of the true power of the erotic, as much as a bargain with God to win tomorrow's lottery would be a distant distortion of the true nature of prayer and its power, or sharing a ride to work with someone is a far cry from the intimacy and commitment of friendship. Given this sense of our body as biomechanical entity or separate mass of matter ending at the skin boundary, frustration is pervasively felt by many of the closest loving couples to generate this sense of eros in their partners. Sex is the source of an eros that becomes generated between bodies of certain aesthetic features and released through certain physical interactions. As such a dimension, the erotic itself would be a mechanical, isolating force that flashes a temporary, blind connection between people for irrational and superficial causes. This is a rather distorted and trivializing sense of the erotic. That it is so pervasive in our culture creates much suffering, exploitation, and violation, but also helps keep hidden the possibilities inherent in our earthbodies, in the ways of many other cultures and time periods, and in many other relationships which could gain depth and excitement from a recognition of how they could be infused with the erotic.

As a first step toward describing a very different sense of the erotic, I'd like to begin with an experience that seems very distant from our normally considered sense of the erotic. Then, we can fill in this sense through the example of perhaps the oldest surviving written account of a sexual encounter. This ancient document opens up dimensions of eros other than those our contemporary American culture would embrace. The first experience belongs to Loren Eiseley, who was a naturalist and anthropologist with a gift for writing and a love for the planet in all its sensory aspects. Such a love, I propose, was actually a sparking erotic sensibility. Prior to the incident he describes, Eiseley was out wandering "in the course of some scientific investigations" in the area of the upper Platte River on the high plains as the river flows from the Rockies. He headed towards Missouri. He was in a section of the riverbed that is wide and shallow and becomes dispersed in a "series of streamlets flowing erratically over great sand and gravel fans." Eiseley describes how among the indefinite shorelines here, there are shifting islands and quicksand. After ten miles of hiking on a hot day, Eiseley made his way through the dunes and a thicket of willows into the shallows of the river. He took off his clothes to splash around in the cooling water. He began to feel the water beckoning to him to stretch out in its body and be gently carried along by its current. However, ever since a near-drowning accident in childhood, he was afraid of bodies of water. Eiseley felt hesitant to launch out even in this knee-deep region of the river, since it was treacherous with holes and quicksand. People had drowned in this area.

Eiseley had the spirit, though, that found such urgings of the landscape irresistible, so after standing in the water for a moment considering the lure, he launched out. As Eiseley enters this experience, he is entering *the truest sense of the erotic*. I say "truest" in the sense that there is a "truth" of earthbodies insofar as experience can transform us, give greater meaning to our lives, reveal to us sensitivities we didn't even know we had, and through those sensitivities allow an understanding by kinship to be kindled with other beings:

> Then I lay back in the floating position that left my face to the sky and shoved off. The sky wheeled over me. For an instant, as I bobbed on the main channel, I had the sensation of sliding down the vast tilted face of the continent. It was then

that I felt the cold needles of the alpine springs at my fingertips, and the warmth of the Gulf pulling me southward. Moving with me, leaving its taste upon my mouth and spouting under me in dancing springs of sand, was the immense body of the continent itself, flowing like the river was flowing, grain by grain, mountain by mountain, down to the sea. I was streaming over ancient riverbeds thrust aloft where giant reptiles had once sported; I was wearing down the face of time and trundling cloud-wreathed ranges into oblivion. I touched my margins with the delicacy of a crayfish's antennae, and felt great fishes glide about their work.

I drifted by the stranded timber cut by beaver in mountain fastness; I slid over shallows that had buried the broken axles of prairie schooners and the mired bones of mammoth. I was streaming alive through the hot and working ferment of the sun, or oozing secretively through shady thickets. I *was* water and the unspeakable alchemies that gestate and take shape in water, the slimy jellies that under the enormous magnification of the sun writhe and whip upward as great barbeled fish mouths, or sink industriously back into the murk out of which they arose. Turtle and fish and the pinpoint chirpings of individual frogs are all watery projections, concentrations—as man himself is a concentration—of that indescribable and liquid brew which is compounded in various proportions of salt and sun and time. It has appearances, but at its heart lies water, and as I was finally edged against a sand bar and dropped like any log, I tottered as I rose. I knew once more the body's revolt against emergence into the harsh and unsupporting air, its reluctance to break contact with that mother element which still, at this late point in time, shelters and brings into being nine tenths of everything alive.[7]

Eiseley's experience starts with a "launching out" from not just the banks of the river, but from his normally consolidated boundaries of the self. He lets go *into* his body as a tide of sensory and meaningful currents into the larger world of kindred sensory currents. All renewing erotic experience is such a "letting drop" of the normal ego, as the Buddhists might say, by opening to the way in which the body always streams beyond any limited definitions we have of our identity and circumscribing concerns. The body is itself a river as truly erotic: always flowing beyond the boundaries that we reflectively and often defensively define where "I" stop and the world begins. The propulsive forces of this movement are to be found in the tastes, the textures, the touch, the colors, the smells, etc., which if embraced with a focused awareness allow for this floating beyond the ego boundaries in an exciting tide.

This means that insofar as one stays in possession of the ego boundaries, either using another person either as sexual object or submitting to them as abject worshiper, in order to bolster one's ego or abase one's ego to bolster the other person's ego, the erotic has been abandoned at that moment. There may have even been a spell which was cast initially in which one gave oneself up to the sensory currents to leave ego behind, but as soon as the experience becomes this means to overcome insecurity or feel power, the erotic spell has been left. It would be as if Eiseley in facing his insecurities had decided willfully to keep floating just to prove to himself he could overcome his fear of water by being braver or tougher. The erotic can be shattered. When one starts to use its intermingling spell to captivate or dominate or manipulate another (or even oneself) in some way, one has returned to the bounded self and left the magic of this dance with the earth's flows. The erotic is fragile, and requires concentration and fidelity to its spirit for its spell to last. Even less erotic are all the detached encounters of people or body parts or objects as sex objects, where there is no affective charge at all. This is a consuming of energy, a fix for missing vitality, that is the craving of the vampire.

Through each sensory current, Eiseley experiences the mingling of his presence, of his very being at that moment, with that of other beings: the *tingling cold in his fingertips* announced the mingling of alpine springs with this flow of which he was part, the *taste* of the water was the taste of the continent, the *absorbing heat* was the presence of the sun in him, etc. It is in the sensible pulp of the experience itself that we feel these other co-presences with us. This means that we must recognize that the body understands, that the senses have their own kind of understanding, and cognition is not just the domain of thought and reflection. There is a bodily knowing and a coming-to-understand-further that happens in the erotic, as well as in other sensory and bodily experiences. We have discounted them because of our dualistic prejudices that the body is dumb, a machine, as matter is dumb. We have, therefore, portrayed the plunge into the erotic as the plunge into the irrational, the unknowing, but this is not so. Intermingling with the other beings of the Earth, we come to understand them in very profound ways. After this day of his float in the Platte, Eiseley understood the river, its history, its place in the continent's ecosystem, his kinship with fish and sand, and many other things in a different way. It is a kind of understanding that flows through his veins, is felt in his viscera, infiltrates his later sensory experiences, spawns new imaginative figures, and adds depth to his emotional register.

Eiseley's experience also shows how we have misjudged the erotic in the opposite way; we have also underestimated reason and thinking in our dualistic oppositions between mind and body, feeling and thought. It is obvious that the knowing powers of the body, emotion, and the sensory have been belittled, but the mind—even though being continually lauded—has been seen too narrowly. We have portrayed thought as detached and bound by rules, and although it can be confined in this way, it can also be released to take other forms. In Eiseley's float down the river, the encounters with crayfish, alpine springs, and continental tides come through the senses, but they are equally made of the intertwining with sensitive thoughts about these things. Eiseley has thought and learned much intellectually about these other beings. Yet, rather than becoming absorbed in detached thought about them in the midst of his floating experience, his knowledge of insects, animals, topography, and geography has been allowed to mix in with his bodily senses, such that they become each other. There is a "letting go" of the mind (as well as the body, senses, and emotions) in this erotic experience, in which knowledge comes to dance easily and interpenetratingly with the sensory, emotional, and imaginative. It becomes a light, dancing, and caressing thinking. This only happens with a certain artistry of releasing thinking to these rhythms, like learning how to let a kite be taken up by wind currents. So, *the erotic is not the unthinking*, but rather the blending together of thoughtful sensitivities and knowledge about the beings announced and encountered sensorily. The reflective knowing has been released into the intermingling with our feelings and senses in such a way that that knowledge caresses us in that moment as a sensual and enveloping presence.

However, in the erotic spell not only does thought change from something detached and reflective to something that has a physical presence, as it becomes for the moment a smell or a feeling of temperature or a touch, etc., but also what is presented to the erotic partner are partners who evanesce in their singularity of identity. They lose the univocalness of identity in two different ways—both within themselves and with regard to other beings. The river he is floating in, the Platte, becomes also alpine springs and Gulf waters or present fishes become also commingled with their reptile forebears or other larger related fish. In the erotic spell with another person, for example, one can see in another person's face the faces of mothers and daughters or of grandfathers and sons, and of other women or men who resonate in the erotic current that moves through the dance of all beings on the planet. It is as though the other person or the other creatures or things become like reflections in a mirror caught in another mirror, which, if the mirror's glanced at from the side, recede into an endless march of differing aspects, layered indefinitely, but of one face too. Unlike the mirror, faces refract into totally other kinds of faces but belonging to the same series. The spell is even deeper though, for it crosses among species and categories of beings, so that fish and turtle, rock and cloud might start to interweave too, once the release from staid boundaries has occurred in the spell of eros. Yet, this happens in counterpoint to the particularity of the person with whom one is erotically involved.

The current that is that erotic charge also dissolves the person who encounters these dancing partners. Eiseley feels himself no longer one solid being after he had launched out into this tide. He extends not only beyond his boundaries, but moves through changing interminglining identities. He becomes the multiplicity of beings that have entered this intercoursing current—from frog, to turtle, to oozing jelly, to crayfish, to mountains, to all the waters of the world. Later, thinking back on this experience, Eiseley states, "I remember my green extensions, my catfish nuzzlings and minnow wrigglings, my gelatinous materializations out of the mother ooze" (*IJ*, 26). In much of what passes for the erotic in our society, the partners involved, or perhaps the consumer and the supplier, are far from losing themselves in their hold on their ego identity and far from discovering within themselves the ways in which there are currents of their own being which touch and are touched by myriad other beings—that they have no firmly bounded identity as shut off and separate from the world as revealed through eros. This is not erotic experience, although it may start out from sexual sensations that could have led into erotic experience if they had been part of a different kind of experience in a different context, namely that of this sensitive "letting go" with the world, where the world is channeled through one person or, as in our example, through one riverbed, at the moment. The so-called erotic that leaves us comfortably within our habitual bounded self and identity is an entertaining diversion or manipulation, but not the true eros of transforming identities and the playing out of different selves.

The often-asserted sense of the erotic represented as a "release" of energy—as if we were solid and rigid vessels of psychic energy that built up pressure that has to be "released"—is also easily seen to be alien to the sense of the erotic we're describing. A stiff vessel doesn't join in the dance with other beings of the planet, and is barricaded off from the flowing energies and rhythms that can bring us into this fluid interchange. The psychoanalytical notion that eros is the desire to join with others to become one, to get nearer to that primal state of undifferentiated unity with the world or the mother, is also at odds with true pulsing of the erotic. To become one is another version of the more common sense idea we've discussed of possessing the erotic partner, of somehow assimilating the other into ourselves, so our security can't be threatened. Yet, this too would destroy the erotic charge, rhythm, and meaning. It is because Eiseley also has a sense of himself *as* water, *as* minnow and catfish and ooze, *as well as* Eiseley, that the erotic can *link* him to all these dimensions and enrich him with this ongoing sense of *inter*change. If he were utterly swallowed up in the other identity, he'd be "gone" and then perhaps later "returned" to himself—"blotted out" and then "come down" to himself—as some seek in various fleeing, diversionary experiences, like drugs. However, eroticism is a sensitivity, a heightening of awareness, and the greater experiencing of the pungency of the sensory (with more packed into the sensory than normal). One "links" one with another (as the "inter" in "interchange" implies too), but what happens is neither one nor two—but rather the "earthbody logic" we discussed at the beginning of this book, instead of the diabolical "either/or" logic. We remain both distinctly ourselves and distinctly in one dance with others—different from the isolated self seeking to dissolve into oneness with the other.[8]

It is this fluidity of identity, of selves, of bodies becoming one rhythm (yet distinct) that is behind the emphasis of the "fluids" of the erotic. In the sexual experience of the erotic, fluids—the fluids of various secretions, the sweat of bodies in motion, the erotic power of water and fluids as flowing around and on partners, fluids splashed on or licked off or smeared around—often figure prominently in the experience of the erotic or in its explicitly heightening practices, because they are the material expression of this intermingling and becoming fluid as earthbodies and as selves. Also, they show that this intermingling takes places on sensory surfaces as well as deeper pathways of flowing (another prejudice the Platonizing tradition has brought against the supposed "superficiality" of "surface contact") The sensitive touch of skins or of warmth on an attuned skin can be deep and profound. It is fluidity as the sense of literal fluids and the ubiquitousness of water that brings Eiseley to a fluidity of identity that goes beyond the human. He remarks at the end of his experience: "Turtle and fish and the pinpoint chirpings of individual frogs are all watery projections, concentrations—as man himself is a concentration—of that indescribable and liquid brew which is compounded in various proportions of salt and sun and time." By contrast, the dry is the logical, as often noted. The erotic is fluid and tidal.

When Eiseley floats and describes how it feels, we readers can feel ourselves floating and can sense as if in that moment Eiseley is just "any human," has not only taken on multiple linkings of identity, but has gone beyond the boundary of personality. There is this paradox at the heart of the erotic (which reverberates into love as it draws on the power of the erotic): it is most personal and somehow most impersonal, yet impersonal in a deepening and liberating way, not in an offensively dismissive way. It is the pettiness of the ego, the sense that my individuality is so vitally important to the world, which is abandoned for the comforting and ener- gizing feeling that each of us belongs to this long river of lives and intermingling currents and each adds and nourishes the whole. The erotic makes this felt pun- gently, and viscerally: you excite me as woman, as man, as flower or fish, as beauty of back or breast or leg or petal, and there is an excitement of release from all the numerous labels, details, and quirks we pack into our everyday identities. Some- thing simpler and wider emerges, yet one gets to this place through launching off from the particularities that drew me to this person.

Before the long tradition of seeking to cut ourselves off from these flows of energy in our fear of death, as so well articulated by Plato and the classic Greeks, there is evidence the earlier Greeks thought of all existence as being *physis* (pro- nounced "phu-sis")—the "shining forth from within all things"—of a glow, a light. Similarly, Buddhist traditions, especially the Tibetan, speak of the "radiant light" that shines forth from all things until it is dimmed down by the separation of the person from the world by dualistic or egoistic thoughts. Let's think for a moment of this "shining" not just visually, as we might be tempted to do, but as a multi-sen- sory energy: as a light, a glow, a warmth, a felt charge surging, a pulsing, a hum, a singing, a vibratory ringing, a caressing, a tingling, and a swirling that moves within, through, and among all beings, animate and inanimate. This moving, sparkling, and resonating energy does not shine down upon them from some non-earthly source, but comes from the shared dance and interaction—a rhythm that is cre- ated by all beings stepping within themselves in time with all others.

Then to be erotic is to use the special ability of the body as material, as part of this flow, to "catch," "concentrate," "shape," and "spread" this shining forth. It is to make the other glow with this energy because one has opened oneself more con- centratedly, savoringly, and fully to this shining forth. The hand in the caress is able to both draw on this shining forth from within that person's gifts of caring, being perceptively resonant to the dance of the world, and from their excitement about the special beauties on all levels of being of the person they are touching. These shining, glowing vibratory energies are drawn along by the hand to open a path that allows an augmenting of those similar energies flowing from the other per- son. The hand in touching, in moving over the other person's body, in gliding over the skin, is able to bring forth and catch these energies, to direct and open the recip- rocal flow that moves between them and moves them to new places of being in rhythm and connection.

To really understand this power of the erotic caress requires we stop a moment to consider the power of touch and its relationship to vision, emotion, and the other senses and powers of apprehension and expression. Our culture's philosophy, psychology, and now biological sciences have long considered the senses and the other avenues of apprehending the world as separate "faculties"—as mechanisms of some sort doing their particular jobs of inputting information: e.g., the eyes take in visual data, the abstracting abilities of the mind draw logical categories, or the memory retrieves past, stored information. There are separable functions which work on the input from one objective world. We have already criticized the notion that each person performs these operations "internally" and instead proposed that the world, things, and other living beings "do" these things with us cooperatively—as when my hometown makes me remember something I never would have remembered without the cooperative power of that place or the hue of hawthorns awakens a feeling of certain sanctity and peacefulness I would not have felt without their presence.

Now, however, we must see also that each of these ways of "taking in" the world is also a way of "being" in a certain world. Each distinct sense is a different way of existing that dances with all the other ways of existing afforded by other sensual avenues of experiencing. There are worlds of vision and touch and smell, although they link in the same rhythmic enmeshment as our Matisse dancers to create a dance or the sense of one world. We "take in" visual inputs in seeing because we have "entered" a "world of vision" in which things and creatures exchange seeing energies. To see means also to be seen. This dual aspect comes from entering a world swirling with color, and shapes, and from moving over and among things in a seeing kind of way. For example, part of my body moves to the mountaintop as I look out over this porch to the peaks around me at this moment or is on the mountain's far side or even above its peaks or ranging through its forests, since part of my visual view from this vantage point is also having the sense of the visual views from those vantage points. Those other vantage points are not thought of deliberately and mentally—although I can do that too—but are just part (are "co-present") of how the currents of my body as visual circulate through the world around me. Of course, I am "here" on the porch with a multi-sensory richness, feeling the chair on my backside, the floor beneath my feet, the smell of the woodpile next to me, etc., but if I were to concentrate just on the visual dimension of my world, my body (in a "lighter," "freer," floating way) "is" in those other places too. If we followed the dictates of the diabolical logic my body would be "stuck" on this porch, since it would be either "here" or "there." However, I can feel my bodily connection, its flowing energetically through all these other spaces opened up for me at the moment by vision.

This visual sense gives me a very different set of experiences than hearing the wind whistling through the forest. In hearing, I am taken to the heart of a space that enters me aurally, but not to a definite projected location, as it is laid out in vision. Aurally, I enter a shared space where I have permeated its depths and details, as a second later happens when the sound of hammering travels across the valley, enabling me to hear the specific hard metal pounding the yielding yet resistant piece of wood. Hearing, I encounter even the "insides" of wood and metal in their substance as their clashing rings forth through the valley. Where I meet them is also somewhat directionally located—say, for example, further down the slope and somewhat to the right, but it is also somehow just floating through the entire valley. Once, to bring home this point, a class of mine agreed to conduct our conversation for two hours with our eyes closed. At the end of the evening, we had the strange sensation of having been transported to some indeterminate floating space within the circle of our chairs but upwards towards the ceiling, rather than our customary visual sense of being securely located in specific places around the room. We also had the strange sense that we were intermingled in this floating space, instead of being clearly at a distance from each other, as again we felt when we finally open our eyes and discovered each person at a certain distance in the more visual space of the room. It is in this way each world is a differing world.

The erotic is intimately grounded in the power of touch and in the world of touch, although our culture has focused much more on linking the erotic to the power of vision. To understand what could be unique to the power of the erotic calls for us to focus for a moment on what is unique about the "world of touch"— that strand of our ongoing experience that is somehow uniquely contributed to us by the unique aspects of tactility. To touch a person, creature, or thing is to enter into an immediacy that tends to intimacy. To look at something slimy is quite different than recoiling from its slimy touch, or to look with care at another person is different from taking trembling hands in one's own hands or entering an embrace with them. A boundary, a distance, has been crossed through the power of touch.

To touch something and be touched means to enter into the flow of what comprises that being at the moment. Our culture has been particularly harsh in its prejudice against the power of surfaces, such as when we declare disparagingly "that's just surface knowledge," as contrasted with intellectualist (and masculinist) sense of "penetrating to the depths" of something. Yet, the surface is the primary sensual offering of that thing's or creature's state of being, and especially of its current activity or expression. As such, the energy that is flowing through it, its current state of relation with its environment, and its sense of movement usually ripples along its surface. Splashed on its surface, on the thing's or person's face, its outward expression, is much of its life and meaning, but we have distrusted "surface appearances," fearing we'd be fooled by our body's immediate sense of the world, to such an extent we are often sensually uncomprehending of what is "right before our face." Yet, fear, love, anger. boredom, care, distrust, etc., are there in the person's facial expression, in the way they're holding their body, in their breathing, etc., to be experienced knowingly.

To touch something, some creature, or some person is often to wade right into this tide of meaning and energy that ripples along the surface of the other's body: we take in to ourselves some of that energy and some of that sense of the other's current being. We can have the distanced and detached visual and cognitive sense of the other that can wait for the ever-changing fluxes and flows of the emotional, imaginative, and sensual charges flowing from the world and through the person to subside and then "take stock" of the overall sense of things. However, sensitive and open touch can enter into this flow like touching an electric current and let it flow through both people. For example, when I embrace a grieving person, who had been "composed" at the moment before our embrace, suddenly that person and I start to cry as the access to the energy flow moving through their body opens, and is now returned back to them through me in an amplified resonance. The erotic can be a primary dimension of openness to these dimensions of energy flows of feeling by entering fully into the power of touch.

In other words, what is most distinctive about the "world of touch" and the power of the tactile is its *reciprocity*. In touching, one is touched by the other in a permeating way. The usual boundary between people blurs in touch, which is why we feel so vulnerable in being touched and why it is such a powerful experience, for both constructive and destructive purposes. We still have a sense of ourselves, but as permeable. To be touched by an adult in sexual abuse, for example, penetrates to the heart and psyche of the victim, because their boundary as a person has been forced open and violated by alien feelings and intentions, which they have resisted but feel guilty about and sullied because of the reciprocal nature of the touch. They have not been literally complicit with this abusive touch, anymore than I have literally soared above the mountaintop when I looked out at it with the sense of vision, yet with the sense of touch there is this feeling of reciprocity, here being turned to its damaging capabilities by this violation. In a positive experience, however, when partners are touching sensitively, caringly, and communicatively, this sense of reciprocity in touch can powerfully augment the sense of mutuality between two people. This gives eros its power to add a visceral sense of bonding to an already conceived and felt sense between two people. Not all touch is open to its current of reciprocity, nor do we always want it to be. For example, when we go to the doctor, we are not interested in augmenting mutuality with her or him, so we construct a context and safeguards that limit the natural tendency of touch to be reciprocal. However, notice this is testimony to the natural tendency and power of touch to embody a sense of reciprocity.

The erotic touch is more open to this power of touch because it is not just "handling" the other as a tool, nor as a striking of the other, or a "pushing" of the other, or any of the other non-contactful or insensitive ways of touching, but rather erotic tactility culminates in its fullest openness and expression in the special touch of the caress. The caress is unique because it joins the power of touch with the special earthbody sense of emotion. Again, because of our cultural tradition's denigration of the body and priority of staying separate as individuals and in control, we have also failed to understand the emotions and how they can enter into the power of touch in the caress. We are very dumb about how the emotions tell us about our world and how they work with perception and the senses.

In a later chapter, we will delve deeply into the emotions, but for the moment, a few preliminary aspects of the emotions in relation to earthbodies must be described in order to complete our discussion of eroticism. In line with the dualistic way of looking at the world we have been describing throughout, the emotions, too, have been condemned as "irrational," as "uncontrollable forces," and as a pull to a "dark,

animal nature" that threatens to overwhelm us, if we are not careful. Yet, if we look
at the world through the perspective of earthbodies, we see that we are only dances
ourselves, a swirling unfolding sense of who we are emerging through the ways we
join up with the other beings of the world, who are themselves dancing out abilities,
forces, and meanings in relation to all the linkages they've created with the rest of
the world. As a purely flow phenomenon, with an ever-changing dynamic quality,
our sense of who we are in relation to other people, things, and the world might
become too dizzying, if we didn't have a way to constantly feel where we are within
the dance that is itself part of the dance.

Yet, we do: emotionally! The emotions are called "e-motions," because they
are a constant motion or movement "away" (which is the root meaning of "e") from
our self-enclosure into the shared sense we have with the world. They are also the
reciprocal movement of the beings of the world "away" or "outside" (another root
meaning) of themselves into all others, including we humans, or outside of one
human into others. Within the dance, the sense of what is happening among earth
beings moves outside any of the participating individuals into the shared movement of the spiraling, graceful pattern. In our bodies, as open to the flow of sense,
through the senses, we also can sense, feel, register our *relationship* to these flows
coming through the other dancers (and the dance itself) viscerally as emotions. We
"understand" *how we stand in relation* to the world as these movements of energies
through our anger, our joy, our sadness, and our other "feelings."

Notice that the language of emotion is the language of touch and of felt
movement. When we see our friend lose a parent in death or fail at an endeavor or
lose their property to natural catastrophe, or see children starving or abused or suffering the ravages of war, or see how this person likes us or has made a new discovery that will help them, we say both that emotionally we are "moved" and
"touched," whether by sadness or joy. Emotions make us feel our relationship, the
way we regard them and the feelingful way we are connected to them, to the situations we witness. Situations that could be viewed or thought about dispassionately, from the safe haven of a psychic distance, are registered viscerally as situations of which we really are a part, as part of the flow of energies on this planet,
even if our minds dismiss them as "someone else's problem." The tear or the joy
belies the barrier we might try to rationally erect. Emotions never point us towards
"people out there" or "over there," or of events, creatures, and things in a distant,
quantifiable relationship to us, but instead we experience how they are "under our
skin": we *know* emotionally what their situation means to them and to us in our
bodies—as part of our kin in the dance, the largest family.

Since the understanding we get through our emotions is about wholes, the
whole situation, and is changeable, as the steps unfold, and is somewhat personal
and somewhat takes everyone into account, we discount this knowledge, since we've
defined knowledge as taking things apart, having certain, unchangeable answers,
and having separated off ourselves and the individuals involved. However, this
detached, calculating, and rational knowledge, although vital, powerful and indispensable, only occurs after our more immediate emotional knowing our place in

the world—how I feel about this person or that situation, etc., which reveals to me a lot about them and me and how we stand together.

Erotically, this emotional discovery and this emotional expression of what has been understood (and appreciated) can be allowed to flow into the power of touch in caressing another person (or even creature or thing). The moving touch, as it glides over the other's skin in a sexual caress or in a soothing caress between parent and child or between friends, or as increasing pressure is applied sensitively to bring singing bodies into harmony and sensitively fit into each other in embrace, can sketch out or spread rhythmically or splash energetically the sense of connection in the relatedness of emotion between people. The erotic touch in a caress can focus, communicate, and augment the resonance of the other's senses and body the moving emotions of care, excitement, love, gratitude, appreciation (of all sorts of beauties), discovery, and joyfulness (even in the midst of sorrow). This means, however, that such a touch uses the power of tactility to augment reciprocity becoming mutuality. This kind of touch even transforms the sight of the others body into an expression of the flow of emotion between these persons. This touch spreads a different vista over their appearance, like the Greek divinities' touch might make a mortal suddenly glow with beauty or vitality.

This kind of eroticism is the exact opposite of what our culture tends to promote as the erotic. In the sexually erotic, we are presented with breasts disconnected with women, men's buttocks or penises disconnected with men. Our culture has reached such a fever pitch of self-violating pseudo-eroticism that the body parts are often seen as most erotic when dismembered from the rest of the body. Body parts are erotic within the halo of who that person is, what they stand for, whom they are to us emotionally, how they are cherished, or how rich is our shared history with them. These factors of emotion, spirit, and thought are actually often seen in our contemporary culture as anti-erotic, whereas reducing someone to "meat" is seen as the purely erotic. Vision is given the lead in this presentation of eroticism—an exaggerated taking advantage of vision's ability to distance and to pick out details from the whole. Our culture's dominant eroticism seeks to soar around the erotic object as a floating eye or through the power of voyeurism. These tendencies are so strong they often seem to overpower our experience, such as when we find our erotic life seeming to borrow its sense from films, or at least feels like a Hollywood script.

Of course, the visually obsessive erotic fits with a cultural or diabolical logic that seeks to stay distant and control those beings who can't be felt in their kinship. Cut off from each other, we fear each other, at least on implicit levels. The eroticism of isolated parts also allows us to feel the erotic out of the context of our life situation with others and thereby disown responsibility for the erotic as part of our relationship to others and the world. The angry husband who has just beaten his wife can feel "turned on to her" a moment later, because he can just detach her body, her breasts, or her vagina from the shared history of depersonalizing and degrading that person. Similarly, an abusive parent who just brutalized their child can suddenly give them an excited hug of love by detaching the child's smile or adorable little form from the horror of what they just did to them. Excitement and brutality can easily follow one another as discrete detached bits of decontextualized input. There is a desperation to this sort of perversion which marks our culture's sense of the erotic and gives our media and entertainment a tawdry, alienated, and dehumanizing undercurrent.

The different perceptual senses each have special powers that are present to a lesser degree in the others, but are more fully centered in each one. Yet, using earthbody logic, they, too, are like those dancers, caught up in each other's rhythms and able to tap into the flow of each other's contribution to the dance. So, even though touch gives us immediate access to texture or smell to something's aroma, a good painter can make us see softness or hardness or see the smell of fresh-cut hay or the stink of a polluting incinerator. So, too, the vision of eroticism can borrow the power of touch to "see feelingly." Rather than using vision's focusing power to strip away the context of the other person and see them as dismembered body parts or as naked flesh, the erotic as sensitively responsive does the opposite: even the naked dancer can be seen caressingly to be moving in a gracefully weaving pattern or the loved person's body shines with their kindness or their integrity or their grace in helping others. Even fully naked, the person we love shines forth from their flesh in a transformed way gaining more brilliance and poignancy from the excitement of relatedness to them as a person.

If we allow all these emotions to flow through our bodies, and through the loving touch to be spread out in the shining forth from the other person's body, the erotic becomes an intensified connection to all these currents of our shared life with this person and even practically with the fuller sense of harmony with other people and the planet as crackling right through the heart of our embrace with another. Then the erotic is not at odds with love, friendship, decency, integrity, and a sense of harmony with the whole of life and the planet, as it often is in our culture's degraded eroticism, but becomes the way shared energy becomes more pungently flesh, in vision, in touch, in smell, and in launching out on the sensual currents, even of a Platte River estuary by an aging scientist. Then, however, boundaries are blurred. A sober scientist like Loren Eiseley can feel like he has crawfish eyes or I can become my five year old's silly puppy-like energy for a spell or, like in the myth of Innana (the oldest written story we have on the planet, and I believe the most erotic), we can become not only mixed up in the being of our husband, the farmer, the "honey-man," but in our hugs, kisses, and even in our genital sexuality, we might suddenly be the fields, the wheat, the grapes, the grain, the bees, the sun and the stars, as in the following passage:

> Before my brother coming in song,
> Who rose to me out of the poplar leaves,
> Who came to me in the midday heat,
> Before my lord Dumuzi,
> I poured out plants from my womb
> I placed plants before him,
> I poured out grain before him.

I poured out grain from my womb
. . . He laid me down on the fragrant honey-bed.
My sweet love, lying by my heart,
Tongue-playing, one by one,
My fair Dumuzi did so fifty times.[8]

In their lovemaking Innana and Dumuzi feel the flow of everything through their embrace, and for the moment become all things together, in a dancing, playful, and celebratory way. They call each other all the names and roles that can flow between man and woman—lover, friend, father, mother, brother, sister—and engage in prodigious sexual feats, but end with

He put his hand in her hand
He put his hand to her heart.
Sweet is the sleep of the hand-to-hand.
Sweeter still the sleep of the heart-to-heart. (IN, 43)

The verses mention the fish and birds chattering, the reeds growing high, the deer and goats in the forest multiplying, the lettuce growing in the garden, and so forth, right in the midst of their erotic scene together. What an undermining of the power of diabolical logic to keep us separate—from each other, from the "bestial" creatures around us, and even from the "dumb" inanimate things about us! Our culture has needed the security of feeling superior, the sense of control of being apart, and the ego protection from being part of the flux and flow of life, which means no one is all-important and everlasting. Yet, eros could bring us back to the flow of earthbodies as spectacularly healing and joining—if instead of seeing our melting of identity with that of grains and birds and soil as assaulting our "human dignity" as "higher" creatures than the slimy earth, we could feel ennobled as part of an earthly dance in which beings can be brought into a mutual shining forth of appreciation, of shared rhythm, and of interchanging excellences. Then this planet could truly excite us. Then, all perception, all sensing, and all caring emotion could be a potential kind of inter-coursing with the world and others, which would not compromise our commitments, loyalties, and values, but just make each of them in their special and unique form allow a flow from all the corners of the planet to become part of their felt sparkle.

Chapter Three
Discordant Contemporary Rhythms

Introduction: Detachment as a Curse upon the Land

A bone-chilling story is told by Leslie Marmon Silko as part of the fabric of stories, chants, myths, and poems that make up the novel *Ceremony*, about how there was once a contest of witches "in dark things," which here means acts of truly horrifying power. In the story, most witches create disgusting or surprising objects. They are all topped by one witch whose sex and people remains unknown. This one witch merely tells a story, which by being told will set an unfolding of events into motion. (The power of stories is something we will examine later in this chapter.) The witch tells of a culture, whose people "grow away from the earth/then they grow away from the sun/then they grow away from the plants and animals (*C*, 135)." This embodies the power of the diabolical logic we have discussed, whose vision is abstracted away from the dance of senses and feelings to use vision only in its stripping away and cutting ability, to see objects out of context and connection, as merely separate objects.

As Silko continues, "They see no life / When they look / they see only objects (*C*, 135)." In no longer feeling the interconnection as part of their sensing of things, and in removing themselves from the dance of vitality that runs among things, this people comes to make a distinction between themselves as animate and the inanimate world around them: "The world is a dead thing for them / the trees and rivers are not alive. The deer and the bear are objects / they see no life (*C*, 135)." Once separated from the pulsations of energy, of rhythm, and of kinship that run through all living things as announced within the swirl of the senses, one can't feel not only the dance running through rocks, soil, and water, but also through plants, animals, and, ultimately, even one's human dancing partners. All are objects, objects to be manipulated—as Silko says, "Objects to work for us / objects to act for us" (*C*, 137).

The poem-chant continues to tell how a people cut off from feeling kinship and vitality feel something else: "They fear / They fear the world. / They destroy what they fear. / They fear themselves" (*C*, 135). When the world is made of objects, which seem at a distance, which seem to be alien in some way, and need to be subdued since they are opposing forces, the natural response is fear—fear they will not be controlled, they will hurt, or they will deprive me of what is needed or wanted. The tale descends into the depths of these fearful ways of confronting a hostile world and reaches the inevitable outcome: "They will kill the things they fear / all the animals / the people will starve. / They will poison the water/. . . Killing killing killing killing" (C, 136). The tale relates how both inadvertently and deliberately, a culture that sees the world in detachment, as separate and separated, as not being alive in the same way its people are, becomes a power of death, a people of unparalleled violence, eventually turned against itself too.

Such a people would be a curse upon the land not only because they bring death to everything, but also because they are under a spell. They are not really aware of what they do. They can't see or feel fully with the kind of vision, with the kind of thinking that they employ while under this spell. They lead to a "Whirling / whirling / whirling / whirling" (C, 138), which is both a vortex that threatens to spin all down into destruction, but also is a motion of intoxication and speed that is dizzying and disorienting.

Silko's charge against European and American culture and its Plato—to—modern heritage we have been discussing emanates from the ecological sense of her Native American perspective. It squarely gives us, as members of this culture, the responsibility for what we've done, how our ways of experiencing the world and how our own sense of self lie at the heart of this destructiveness, but it also doesn't condemn us as a people or a culture. It sees we've have been in the grip of a spell: a way of seeing the world that spins mightily like a hurricane and doesn't allow alternatives within its force field. Yet, everything has a place and a role in Silko's world, including the European descended people. Silko calls for a vision where all the earth's peoples: white, red, yellow, brown, black are valuable kinfolk of all living beings. However, the witchery behind the European culture must be stopped.

I find this tale haunting because of the power of its connections, the challenge it gives us to take responsibility for the damaging side of the tradition behind the industrial and cultural context in which we live, and the sense that for all our modern knowledge, we are ignorant of the forces behind our actions. It also introduces in a bold way the themes this chapter will explore. How does this vision of the world as separate inevitably lead to violence? What kinds of violence? What is the nature of the spell we are under? Are we truly witches of some sort, even though we see ourselves as by and large "enlightened" and "rational"? Is our "sanity" really quite insane? What are the modern forms of witchery that cut us off from each other and the world, while seeming to do the opposite? How have some of our highest values had a destructive undercurrent we expended energy not to realize? How can we tame the forces our power has bequeathed us?

The modern American culture does not have the rich mythic background of stories passed down from generation to generation as Silko's Pueblo people does, but we also tell ourselves many stories in films that keep alive images which have appeared in older tales.

Ghouls: Our Love of Horror and Compulsion to Consume

Ghouls feed on life without being alive. They may have some sort of biological functioning, but that does not mean they are alive. The fact that this is so
striking in watching images of ghouls in our horror films should be a lesson to our
culture: despite our scientific intoxication that sometimes tries to reduce life to
mere mechanical operations—biological functions that we hope to endlessly
manipulate and manage—the ghoul displays to us that functions such as locomo-
tion, information gathering, eating, etc., do not yet make for human life, or even
life itself. In terms of this book's ideas, we can see right away that they are not earthbodies—open and flowing among all the other beings of the Earth. The fact that
they have a comparable biological functioning does not make them part of the life
of this planet—whether of the biosphere or the intermeshing of all beings in which
aspects of the other beings are inflected, communicated, and indirectly passed along
to other beings. The ghoul is driven in a way in which humans and even animals
can never be. It is relentless and impervious. Usually, it is impelled towards the
damaging of other life forms for its own subsistence, but usually even more so for
either no rational reason—just mechanically driven or in some sort of frenzy to
doggedly increase its own numbers, or in some instances, the ghoul seems to delight
in this destruction of others. This is rarely depicted, however, for ghouls don't
delight in anything for the most part. They simply exist. They simply function. In
their grinding along, they usually hurt the sensitive beings of the planet.

In the past few decades, one famous portrayal of ghouls has remained lodged
in our popular culture psyche as a striking series of images. George Romero's film,
The Night of the Living Dead, made in 1968. It is worthwhile to pay some attention to this film, because of some of the messages it contains about the possible
living death of our culture, as cut off from earthbodies. It is a very pessimistic vision,
which will start us in this chapter with the grimmest possibility, before we progress
to less fatalistic images of who we might have become or are becoming. I say
"images of us," because the ultimate horror of horror films is the not the carnage
we witness or the uncomfortable suspense about threatened doom, but the unnerv-
ing kinship vaguely felt with the monsters we watch. This is the subtler and slower
wallop of the horror show: the dawning realization later that in some way, that
thing may be me!

In this film, which opens with two characters visiting the grave of their
mother, the corpses come back to life, but not to pursue an afterlife. They have no
real sentience. Yes, they can track objects and their prey and manipulate their corpse
bodies around, but they give no indication of being able to communicate, of being
able to feel empathy for any other creatures, including the humans they devour,
nor could they seem to have any real response to their environment other than continuing the necessary motions to destroy and devour. They also seem to have no
real sense of their identity or even why they are doing what they are doing. Apparently, the only thing they can feel is a relentless hunger to devour human beings.
It is not even a matter of gaining numbers and therefore power, as many monsters

have desired, but rather a totally undiscriminating hunger to devour those who still are alive. The ghoul as traditionally depicted in stories has been portrayed as "a living soulless body which ate corpses but did not drink blood."[1] The blood of life, which has always symbolized the animating force of human life, a connection to the heart, the conveyor of passions, the source of vitality, and that fluid rich with spirits, is not what the ghoul seeks. Having no soul itself, being empty in the way only a machine can be empty of the animating spirit of humanity, it seeks continuously, as if there is no shut-off valve, to fill itself with the flesh of humans, the substance that marks human life, but this mere stuff will never be enough.

The existence of the ghoul in one or more ways usually defies the natural order. In this case, death has been defeated, as often wished for by humans, but in a monstrous way that echoes our misunderstanding of life and what our bodies are like. The ghoul echoes our emphasis on life as mere continued physical animation and as hunger, as obsession to just take things into oneself mindlessly, soullessly. There are three different warnings here in the ghoulish existence. First, when we become obsessed with mere continuation of life as a functioning biomechanical entity, we are becoming ghoulish. An image comes to me of a patient in a hospital in which I worked: he was elderly and had lost both legs to amputations, and had been very ill for a long time with diabetes, serious heart problems, and other complications. At this point, if his heart again arrested, he wished to die. However, when he did arrest, a cardiologist who was on call, who went around the hospital saying "Carl's my name and cardiology is my game," was determined not to lose a life. After repeated shocks, and injections, Carl opened up his chest and was physically massaging the heart of this poor being. Legless, chest cut open like a chicken's, blood splattered all over the room, this man and the code team had passed over into the realm of ghouls. What could be accomplished here? Only the horror of biomechanical functioning that has ceased to dance with the cosmos but stumbles ahead without sense or the chance of delight.

Also, we should pay attention to the image of the drivenness of the ghoul's pursuit of its prey, which makes the standard frightening fare of most of their portrayals: no matter how maimed, no matter how much destruction is turned against it, parts of it burnt or crushed or whatever, the ghoul pops up again and keeps coming. This should remind us that life is not about the one-track maniacal pursuit of anything. Yet, our culture often promotes and rewards those who become driven in such a way that other calls of the earth, the appeals of their families, and other aspects of life are shut out in the pursuit of money or fame or power. Perhaps we are more sensitive in our sphere of friends and family, where we do tend to realize that as any person starts to approach this extreme of not being able to really respond to anything else in their lives or to feel what anyone else feels, we start to feel concerned and uncomfortable in their presence—they are becoming monstrous. Ahab pursuing the whale may be a romantic picture of this horror, but far more gruesome, ghoulish, and prevalent are the many insentient, shuffling, and out-of-touch living dead driven towards success. Another famous literary sketch of a ghoulish human life is Ivan Ilyich's obsession with the right furniture, house, family, and position, which never allows him time to notice he is alive until he howls for days with this recognition on his deathbed.

The other aspect of the ghoul that seems like a warning to us is the nature of its hunger. It consumes and consumes, but not with any sense of satisfaction and not with any possible satiation. This obsessive consumption contrasts with that of earthbodies: if we take things into us as part of the interweaving of the dance, we come into concert with them and take in their rhythm or energy. We find our steps in accord or having slipped into the gracefulness of passing something delicate back and forth—like when two strings enter into harmonic accord, picking up each other's vibrations. The ghoul, however, is detached, cut off. It isn't alive in the sense of having the sentience of the flesh that is part of the round dance of energies, feelings, emotions, and dreams. So, its hunger is not about finding anything delectable or taking delight in that which it consumes. Both of these words—delectable and delight—have the same etymological roots, and derive their meaning from the drawing something out from something else as the source of pleasure and also as a source of illumination. The "drawing out" from something is the setting into motion the kind of energy transfer we have seen can happen in the depth of the senses and feeling passed among beings. This is the special glow we saw in the Yurok tale of Umai—the glow that at first Umai thought came from the Land-Beyond-the-World, but then realized it is within all things. We have also seen the ancient Greeks started with the idea that the reality to be perceived is "the shining power within all things" that could be received by humans in their kinds of sensing. Open to this glow, we are delighted and find the world delectable: it gives us luminous nourishment. With the dead body of the ghoul, we devour the substance of life, its flesh, without being able to catch the glow ourselves. If you walk about a shopping mall or go to an "all you can eat" restaurant or a "pick up" spot, notice how many people seem to be shuffling through the experience like the undead, moving their limbs, pursuing, and taking in things, food, experiences, and even the company of others, as the mechanical devouring of life. No matter how substantial, like the movie ghouls eating the living flesh itself, that which these people consume will not give them life or delight.

The Night of the Living Dead also makes very palpable the way in which ghoulish perception works versus the depth of the senses we explored in the last chapter. Earthbody senses do not operate like robotic sensors guiding us by cues through our environment or like the sensor screens on *Star Trek's* Enterprise that yield specific data: instead, they tell us what something is in all its connections to the rest of the world, how it feels, and what it means—even before we interpret it. So, for example, as I look out at the beautiful summer day, the sunshine and crispness in the air communicate a vitality echoed by the three new sunflowers which have opened up since yesterday outside the door, which echoes the love of my friend, and embodies hope; or, my dog's bouncing up to the door eyeing its leash immediately speaks of play and enjoying a romp and is connected to tennis and jumping up and down with childhood friends, and announces the lighthearted, viscerally charged dimension of opening up playfully to the world. The hustle and bustle of people outside my city door announces their concentrated intent to get to jobs, appointments, and activities, and they just don't pass me by as one mechanism might pass another with nothing passing between them, but rather I resonate to their energies. Similarly, the postures of the people slumped over, the blood on the sidewalk, the howling dog, and the flashing siren lights convey the shock and horror of the scene of this accident at the corner, as I walk by and I am rattled or saddened or psychically moved in some way. By contrast, the ghouls just march through scenes seeking their goal or their victim, not really understanding what is happening around them and certainly not being swept up into its tide of meaning and shared feeling.

One of the most grisly scenes of *The Night of the Living Dead* occurs after the little girl, Karen, has been transformed into a ghoul. Karen calmly eats her father, Mr. Cooper, in the basement of the isolated farmhouse where they had been trapped by the horde of ghouls gathered outside. She also mechanically stabs her mother, Helen, repeatedly as her mother approaches her, trying to reassure her by saying, "It's Mommy." When Karen, smeared with her parents' blood, looks up at those who are horrified by this scene, she does so with a blank expression, utterly uncomprehending her relation to the scene of which she is part, let alone feeling empathy or what others feel. The figure of the ghoul in general is a message to humanity: there lurks within us this ability to become a monster, and we become so not by any horrible disfiguring transformation, not by right of any particular hideous act, but by turning off our sensing of others and our sensing of being part of the dance with all other creatures we've symbolized by the image of Matisse's dancers. In this state of numbness and disconnection, where sensing has lost its earthbody ability to enter into all things as on a magic journey (as we discussed before), we feel empty and eat away at the flesh of life in a vain attempt to stop this terrible hunger. The culture of consumption seems to ever deepen. We need to take in more and more stuff—gadgets, things, decorations, toys, and delicacies—that gobbles up more and more of our life—time, energy, and passion.

This film intensifies the ghoulishness of the ghoul, however, by reducing its supernaturalness and the distinctiveness of its character. The ghouls of this film are not very spectacular—actually they're utterly unspectacular—drab, featureless, and having little ability. Their only way to succeed as ghouls comes from their numbers and relentlessness, otherwise they are so unaware, dumb, and stupidly stuck in the rut of devouring, they would not be able to achieve any feasting on the living. This too has meaning for us: it is in the sheer numbers and the relentlessness with which we allow ourselves to be driven mechanically to devour things and others that we can have such a cumulatively devastating effect. The ghouls are disconnected and leaderless in the film. They only end up coming together in concerted action because they all seek the same prey. So this, too, echoes how we destroy habitats just by so many of us following preprogrammed entertainments. We show up at the National Park in such numbers that we destroy what we come to see or we all seek the same spot in a rural area to escape the urban sprawl and in so doing we create a new urban sprawl. We often think it takes a leader and a plan to be so destructive, but in being tuned out and marching zombie-like to the same hungers insensitively, we can be murderous. One critic of the film says that what the living dead really lack is "personality."[2] I think what he is pointing to is that there is no sense in which the living dead's uniqueness is expressed: all are just consuming machines. This brings up the paradox that Philip Slater raised several decades ago, that as isolated functioning machines, we all end up doing the same thing and becoming uniform.[3] However, if we are really open to others in a flowing, interrelating community, then through the interaction of the many, the uniqueness of each person can shine forth. So, in the circle of the dancers, the one who keeps the best rhythm for the group, the one who has the most energy to infuse others, the one who can be most creative with new steps, etc., can shine forth in the fever pitch of the interaction. This interaction, in turn, solicits from each member aspects of who they are they might never have been aware of without the magic pull of the moment.

Several differences with vampire and other monster stories are significant to the import for earthbodies of *The Night of the Living Dead.* Unlike other tales in which finding a secret or a solution to some puzzle is significant to turning the tide, in this story, the knowledge of the scientists, the government, and the protagonists is to no avail and no one ever puzzles out the how or why of the ghoul's emergence (*LD*, 272). There is some speculation that it may be connected to radiation in some unspecified way, but insight never arrives. The posse which finally bludgeons, shoots, and burns this particular group of undead who have consumed our protagonists is led by Sheriff McClelland, who insists the "job" be done mechanically, dispassionately, and has no particular significance when he is asked to comment on their struggle during his interview. In other words, the posse, like the ghouls it is fighting, perhaps like much of our society, dully marches forward, not connecting to the swirl of sense, emotion, thought, and imagination, and destroying in an environment where nothing is meaningful and all ends on the rubbish heap. Not only that, but the posse kills Ben, the African-American who has survived the attack of the ghouls by holing up in the basement, shooting him with the mob of undead and throwing him on the heap to burn also. The posse, like the ghouls, has no power of true discrimination and sensitivity and doesn't realize Ben is a human in the midst of the ghouls. Given that Ben is the only Afro-American protagonist and the only one who shows real character in the struggle, we can't help but note that racism—or sexism or other forms of mass violence against groups—is possible with this zombie-like blind-numb marching forward in destruction which removes the perpetrators from the round dance of sensitivity and empathy which move through earthbodies among the planet's creatures. Like the emergence of the ghouls in the film, this is just "something in the air" of our current age. I think the film is right in portraying that no scientific or special knowledge will help us overcome the threat of ghoulishness: it is a way of living the body; of understanding the self, others, and nature; of believing in stories with a certain magical power of connection; of remaking time in timing; of feeling the erotic; and a host of other ways of changing our entire way of living, thinking, and valuing ourselves

within the earth community. This is a long, slow task of self-transformation—not
not open to a "quick fix."

One last aspect of the ghouls of *The Night of the Living Dead* should be
noticed. They seem to have no real pleasure in their consumption as we noted, but
also they have no sexual or erotic sense. Unlike many monsters who crave contact
or affection or at least sexual thrill of some sort, they attack the bodies of their victims as if attacking popcorn or dog food. Even this is too erotic a comparison to
make. We often find the warm steam rising from the popped corn, the bracing salty
smell, the crunching texture, and the rich buttery, slimy surface to be caressing to
our senses, and thus to have an erotic charge, as we take it into the mouth and
tongue, in the way in which we have seen the eroticism of the coursing of the senses.
However, among the living dead there are even naked ghouls and naked victims,
but they are just hunks of flesh, offering no more sensory delight than anything
else "perceived" by the ghouls. Their limbs touch things only to manipulate them.
They are not touched by things or others while touching them: they grasp things
in the way a key goes into a lock or a diskette into a disk drive, just to trigger further indifferent movements and functions, not to enter one being into another or
to initiate a crossing of boundaries of sensibility. Normally to touch is to be touched:
it sets up an inter-course of energies with the world. Our touch can become a
ghoulish mere grasping, manipulating, and impervious handling unless we return
to earthbodies as the reciprocal entering others in our senses. If we instead become
part of the day of the living dead and tune out the sensual richness of all the environment, then the danger implicit in this film reinforces our previous conclusion
that our culture could lose its erotic sensibility despite whatever proliferation of
sexual mechanics takes place.

The ghoul in film and story is a part of our culture's fascination with horror, and especially horror movies. Like the widespread proliferation of pornography and consumption of images and portrayals of a sexuality that fails to be erotic
in the ways we discussed in the last chapter, the fascination with horror seems, too,
a way of not being open to the very thing that these films, novels, and television
shows are about at a deeper level. Horror films are often seen to be portraying a
threat to normality represented by the Monster who is then vanquished, showing
how much we crave the normal, which without this appreciation of having escaped
its threatened breakdown can appear boring. Or, horror films are taken to be about
our imagined threats, the threats that appear to us in the dream dimension, now
suddenly made "actual" by the powerful illusion of the screen, and as a way to successfully reveal and master these "inner anxieties." Horror films are also often seen
to revolve around dimensions of life that we can't really fathom, where our access
to what they're about is somehow "blocked," like our understanding of what happens after death or how truly strange conjunctions of events do occur.[4] Although
these explanations of the appeal of horror may be true on some levels, to further
our understanding of earthbodies and how these voices always ring inside us, we
need to see how our being inextricably part of the planet's sensitivities may also
feed this habit. I would like to contend that the horror film or novel does reflect

our perception of the "actual" world—a "horror world" or a "hell world," as the Buddhists would call it—of the so-called "normal world," and focuses on our emotions, our perceptions, and our thoughts of the ongoing "day world." We are not "blocked" from seeing it, but rather we see it and feel it in our bones, in all levels of our earthbody sense, and then we desperately and vainly try to block it out from our awareness.

What is part of our everyday lives, what is our doing and not some supernatural being's doing, and what we see all too clearly that we must try energetically not to see, is the everyday fabric of violence in the world. This brings us to the last commonly noted aspect of the horror film genre: its pervasive "dehumanizing ultraviolence," and its usually benign interpretation that parallels the interpretations of the other three aspects of horror films. It is often taken that massive portrayal of extreme violence is some sort of "safety valve," a way of expelling our violent feelings that doesn't hurt anyone, as the film viewers can both identify with the monsters and their violence, but also enjoy how society usually annihilates the monsters through equally violent and gory means. Another interpretation would see this massive consumption and enjoyment of violence as either a way to express unconscious desires in a non-threatening way or to expose our deepest fears about modern life in a way that we can ultimate laugh at them and dismiss them as the lights come on at the end of the film and we go back to a more normal world.

What is common about all these ways of looking at horror films and horror in our society is that we don't have to be implicated or seen as responsible. Instead, let's consider that as earthbodies, we are caught up in the circulation of feelings, images, and sensations that pulse through all living and non-living beings. Then we see that we register in our bodies the pain of several children dying of malnutrition somewhere on the globe while you've been reading this page; of the several women having been raped in this country while you read this page; of the millions more children who live in chronically abusive situations; of many species of animals in their death throes as a species; of shore birds caught in oil slicks; and of the innumerable murders, annihilations, and violations that are occurring all the time as part of the unfolding of contemporary life on this planet. That is not to say that open earthbodies will become a channel for relentless, never-ending, and overwhelming pain. However, among the myriad joys to be registered, feeling an openness to the planetary circulation of sense is also to always feel a certain level of unavoidable pain and also to feel the impact of gratuitous violence causing yet more suffering.

If we would really focus on the starving child, the tortured political prisoner, the bleeding, raped woman, the swollen, uncomprehending infant kept in the closet, the animals crowded into cages and starved, etc., we would be overwhelmed by the horror that is part of daily life on this planet. It overwhelms Ivan Karamazov who keeps a collection of clippings of horrors, a collection which for him is fuel for his doubt that God or love exists. The conclusion that Ivan reaches that shakes him so in the *Brothers Karamazov* is that the perpetrator of all this horror is someone he confronts every hour of every day: the person in the mirror. We are all responsible for allowing this type of world to continue as long as we find our own lot at least bearable, and for most of us, often fairly enjoyable. These horrors, we rationalize, are just the inevitable price of these enjoyments.

It is probably true that most feel that we could all do more to try to prevent such ongoing violence, but there is a deeper level of emotional horror related to earthbodies that is closer to all of our experiences. The other side of horror is the *emotional cutting off* of others that precedes the kind of physically wounding of others: first, I must cut off the way I feel your pain and your life in me as earthbody and vice versa and make you a mere, distanced object. Although most of us don't perpetrate overt violence, this prior violence of objectification of others is something we all do, which often is not significant, but often is. There are so many moments each day for each of us when we could truly be open to the flow of feelings circulating with others, to feel "com-passion" (literally a "feeling with" others), but for a variety of cultural, social, and psychological reasons we harden ourselves against the permeability of interchange among earthbodies. Somewhere deep within us, we know how much more love, caring, nurturing, appreciating, affirming, tending, etc., of each other and of all the beings on the planet could occur, if we would choose this, but we do not. This horror within life, the myriad cruelties to each other and to animals and the earth, the turning away from more vitality, beauty, and grateful interaction into a darker and colder realm, is a level within our earthbody feeling that we flee. However, we know the avoidable horror of the planet is there and it fuels this enjoyment in projecting grotesquely horrible actions on alien or deranged beings. It acknowledges the horror world by making it something fantastic for which we have no responsibility or belief, and yet relieves the pressure of hiding from what we feel by at least experiencing the horror in another form, in an indirect form. The projected horror, however, is not our responsibility, so we enjoy absolving ourselves through this "fun."

Freud thought that our dreams were disguised ways of dealing with unconscious desires, but what is true is more radical than that. Much of our waking life has the shape of dream, takes on surprising shape and affect, because it is a way of projecting and dealing with feelings and thoughts we don't want to meet face to face. So, we project hatreds on a certain ethnic group or on a politician or are obsessed with some minor problem or remark someone made that suddenly feels as if it is a great evil because we dream while awake—we meet the fantastic shape of our suppressed emotions.

Film is particularly apt for this waking dream, because it is projected around us visually and sonically in a way that grabs our bodies as earthbodies and leads us into byways of fantasy, emotion, and memory, and a plurality of levels of experiencing that are uniquely gripping: we have the sense of virtually levitating from our seats and being "thrown" into the midst of the world projected before us. We flinch, we jump, and we cry, as if we were "up there" in that world on the screen.

However, it is not just projection of horror onto the events on the screen which allows us to deal with this level at which we are monstrous everyday, but also the transformation of the horror's shape. This shifting is another cultural tendency that deserves notice, what I would like to call the "supernaturalizing defense." We can take a dimension of experience, for example, the dimension of magic or horror, which is an ongoing and unsettling part of our everyday experience and acknowledge it in a disguised, supernatural form. By making them supernatural these aspects of life are *trivialized by being made spectacular*. Horror becomes something feared of lunatics or aliens, magic becomes part of an alien culture or fantasized sorcerers, and traveling in time and space becomes something done with transporters or through miracles, instead of seeing how all these aspects are part of our earthbody makeup, as we will do as this book proceeds. Now, instead of seeing the horror around us, for example, that five citizens in our city were murdered today, many beaten or raped, others going hungry, the curtness among co-workers, the lack of real care at the dinner table, the cumulatively crushing frustrations of not being heard or supported by those we love, etc., almost infinitely, we experience horror without being implicated ourselves or bearing any responsibility by watching the masked devil decapitate scores or the zombies devour humans on their way through the countryside.

A second defense is that of "literalization" which is part of the supernaturalizing tendency, but is also part of other ways we fail to understand earthbody reality. In a horror movie, the everyday violence between strangers, between family members, becomes substantialized as literalized violence, when much of it is more subtle, and also the perpetrator is literalized as an actual monster when it is "us" or actually just parts of us or rather dimensions of our behavior or emotional life. The real horror is often no one literal perpetrator, but rather a quality of our relationships and a sense of the atmosphere within which we live with others. As with supernaturalizing, we will return to this literalizing tendency when we look at how we actually continually "travel" in time, in space, and among various realms with our earthbodies, that we are transported in time and space and dimension all the time without any need for literalizing these voyages, which actually often undercuts their power and wonder.

Horror films are often recognized as the "pornography of violence," betraying the associative link we make unawares between the alienation of treating our sexuality through dismembering images and something else similar that's happening to the body in this genre (*AH*, 7–8). Like sexuality cut off from the context of the sensual openness making palpable the relatedness of partners, the sensibility of the ghoul is cut off from the context of openness to others and the world as the immediate conduit of intimacy, delight, and delectableness. For earthbodies, this spark within sensibility is what fuels our hunger for contact with others—a longing to open up and enter reciprocal sensitivities. However, by contrast, even before the ghoul devours the first kill, it is its insensate, bodily disconnection and endless hunger which is really ghoulish and horrifying. It is a way of encountering the world we can all fall into to some degree.

Vampires: Hunger for Experience and Fear of Intimacy

The ghoul who is undead, moving and eating despite being dead, is a different figure than the vampire, who, also being dead in some sense, is actually far more sensitive, preternaturally sensitive, than the living. Perhaps this helps explain why the vampire, although inspiring some of the dread associated with horror, also has a powerful positive appeal. When we introduced these two figures in the last chapter, we mentioned how the undead can echo our own existence as lapsing into "merely undead" and not fully alive, but also stated how the vampire has other dimensions that make it an ambivalent symbol. The vampire can see, hear, and smell things that mortals cannot. The vampire has greater physical strength, and perhaps even more sheer intelligence. Unlike the ghoul, the vampire is not the representation of our merely taking up space, stumbling through life, and devouring mindlessly the substance of life, but rather represents the swift, acute, and even voluptuous pursuit of the vitality of life—its blood. Anne Rice has reached a vast audience by portraying the seductive power of the vampire life and also expressing more fully its psychic flaws. Although our feelings towards the vampire and the vampire's feelings towards his victims have always been ambivalent, Rice's portrayals, as well as several recent film depictions and the popular TV shows, *Buffy the Vampire Slayer* and *Angel* have highlighted this tension. The vampire, too, can offer important lessons, not only as a mythic figure, but as representing a way of life into which we may also fall. The vampire is at the heart of how we can choose to live our body, our sexuality, and our emotional relationship to others, and we vaguely sense this as we read Rice's accounts or feel the seductive pull of the vision on the screen.

Traditionally, the vampire myth was often linked with those who had lacked spiritual strength and had committed suicide, been excommunicated, or been given over to evil.[5] It was seen as the torment of those who were pointedly antisocial, as we would now call these people. They were those who after death were condemned to feed on the living. The question the vampire might pose to us is whether many of us don't turn away from our bonds with others, and lose the faith that there is something more meaningful to life that makes it necessary to work with others in community—a loss of faith and commitment that kills something in us and leaves us with a vampiric hunger to then feed on the lifeblood of others. If as earthbodies, the faith we really need is in ourselves as part of the interplay of rhythms of the beings on this planet and we need the courage to let go and open ourselves to the depth of the sensual such that we experience the shared vitality, meaning, and compassion(s) moving through the materiality of the earth and our bodies, then to lose this faith is to excommunicate ourselves from this available shared sense. We might rage against this dying of the light in our relations with others and the environment, but this death will be our own removal of our bodies from the steps of the round dance. In this sense that is closest to us and non-literal, many commit suicide, many cut off communication or excommunicate themselves from communion with others, and commit evil in the primary sense of that word, before it takes on moralistic or religious overtones, as an act of negation, a saying "no," to what we are and can further be that is of intrinsic value.

Traditionally, the vampire was the opposite to the ghoul in other ways: instead of the symbol of the mindless conforming to the ultimate detriment to society, the vampire always evolved from those within society who both sought its sustenance but also flaunted its values and conventions. Bram Stoker's Dracula was based on the legend of the Transylvanian ruler, Vlad Tepes the Impaler. Tepes was both a mighty hero who defended Eastern Europe after the fall of Constantinople in 1462 to the Muslim Turks and a reputed mass murderer and villain. His name shows this dual nature: it means both "son the dragon," which is a reference to his being a leader in the sacred cult of the dragon (a group sworn to defend Christianity from the invaders), and "son of the devil" (*VF*, 43). The figure of the vampire seems to be the figure of ambivalence, not only in our reaction to it, but in its relation to society and in the heart of its makeup. The vampire scorns the merely mortal and yet longs for the lifeblood of mortals. It feels superior to us (and in some of its attributes is clearly superior), and yet in many ways is dependent and helpless.

Francis Ford Coppola, in the opening scene of his film *Bram Stoker's Dracula*, highlights the ambiguity of the myth that points to an ambiguity with which we all live and which can erupt into horrible ambivalence leading to destructiveness. In the opening scene, Dracula is plunged in the blood of violence that is necessary to uphold the sacred trust of the dragon. He must defend this cause and impale the Turkish invaders to stop them from destroying what Dracula believes is holy, the order of the church. Yet, the Turks trick his lovely bride into thinking he is dead rather than victorious in his quest, and she plunges to her death in suicide. She failed to have enough faith in her husband's vow that he would come back to her or in her church to bind her spiritual wounds, if he had truly met with forces greater than he. For his part, Dracula, drenched in the blood of battle and the blood of his beloved, cannot tolerate the law of his church, which will not bury his bride in consecrated ground because she committed suicide. Coppola has Dracula plunge his sword into the heart of the cross in order to make it bleed—so the blood he will henceforth take from his victims will always be the blood that now spills from the cross. The blood of his beloved church has nourished him until it turned against his love for his bride. From this moment on, he will crave more mightily than ever that blood, but henceforth in eternal opposition to that force of holiness that was its essence and that has enraged him. The vampire is always caught in craving what it despises, which is not only its nourishment but also its desire. It desires the blood of the spirit it loved, and still loves, in the midst of its anger and scorn. Were that attachment not still burning, there would be indifference instead of craving. Rather than the zombie-like bottomless hunger of the consuming ghoul, the vampire is the conflicted fever pitch of desire.

The vampire lives in a world that is an anti-world. The light of day which nourishes all beings on this planet by causing chemical reactions, growth in plants, offering a medium to see and comforting warmth, and standing as the symbol of energy, passion, and enlightenment, is deadly to the vampire, who must be shielded from it. Or at least in other variations of the myth, the vampire has no special powers in the light and is drained by it. Aside from the sun, the vampire manipulates natural forces to do its bidding. Even matter itself can be destroyed by its will. Not only is the vampire eternally undead, but it doesn't eat or defecate or take part in the organic functions that link all living beings on this planet in an immediate material circulation that matches the wider circulation of sense we've stressed. The blood that the vampire seeks from its victims is clearly much more than a physical or chemical substance: it is somehow the spirit of the victim incarnate—their vitality, their passions, their feelings for others and the world—that the vampire seeks to imbibe. In either way, physical or spiritual, the blood carries the nutriments which are the result of encountering the world, dealing with it, feeding on it, digesting its substance and turning that back into life-giving energies; or the vital feelings which inspirit us in our psychic lifeblood and which are also hard won from long interaction with others and the world, and from digesting these experiences. The vampire attempts to short-circuit these processes of life: it drinks in the life-giving results that those mortally vulnerable ones have had to work through painstakingly to achieve for themselves.

There is a kind of invulnerability that comes from this state: the vampire is physically stronger, has hypnotic powers of persuasion, is pitiless, is not able to be "killed" through most means, can almost "vanish into thin air" given its speed and defiance of gravity when necessary, and can turn others into vampires with the infectiousness of its state—when it chooses to give mortals of the Dark Blood. Its priority is to stay in control, and it is often portrayed hiding out in castles or refuges where it can be the master of its realm and exact a kind of tyranny among its minions. In Rice's amusing portrayals of the modern vampires, they are masters of controlling the modern world, amassing great fortunes in the stock market or other silly mortal societal ventures they can master with ease, given their powers. Of course, like most beings who seek to control others and themselves "from outside," because they are not caught up in the same constraints, such as gravity or normal vulnerabilities, the vampires themselves often are teetering on the edge of losing their own self-control, wound so tightly are they and held in check only by their own will. This is often their downfall, leading them to do foolish things.

Anne Rice's wonderful playing with the myth in *The Tale of the Body Thief* allows us to see clearly for a moment the vampire's strange inversion of the vulnerabilities and powers of earthbodies and so be able to see what the vampire symbolizes for us as an ambivalent path away from our earthbody fate. In this tale, Lestat, who has been part of the undead for two centuries, is given the opportunity to switch into a mortal body and leave the vampire existence behind, at least temporarily—something that normally wouldn't be possible, since once one drinks the Dark Blood one is eternally undead. Lestat is a strikingly handsome vampire, six feet tall with long blond hair and blue eyes. He is strikingly successful in his manipulation of worldly wealth, his aesthetic enjoyment of his home in New Orleans and spots around the world, and his connection with Louis, the vampire he made, and with David Talbott, the mortal who is a scholar for the Talemasca Society, the organization that studies vampires and similar phenomena. However, even Lestat, has felt the despair of "having a body" versus "being a body," as mortals are—as their gift and their curse. His despair over the driving blood-hunger has led him to attempt—unsuccessfully—to end his undead existence by exposing himself to the intense sun of the Gobi Desert. Despite the power, the eternal life, the thrill of drinking in the lives of others through their blood, as Lestat puts it, and the intensity of aesthetic experience with this fine tuned instrument of sensation his vampire body has become, Lestat jumps at the opportunity to become human again. In the switch, we can see the nature of the appeal of the vampire life in tension with both the uniqueness of being an earthbody and the deeper temptations to flee into vampiric existence when faced with the fearfulness of our inclusion in planetary sense.

When Lestat first makes the body switch, there are many comical moments, such as when he realizes, with horror, that he has to urinate, defecate, or to take substances into his mouth and force them down into his body in eating. He faces a host of realizations of how closely the world impinges through the body on the human sense of security. However, these messy entanglements with things start to threaten him in an even more startling way in his first erotic encounter with a woman:

> I kissed her throat again. I could smell sweat on her body too. I didn't like it. But why? These smells were nothing as sharp, any of them, as they were to me in my other body. But they connected with something in this body—that was the ugly part. I felt no protection against these smells; they seemed not artifacts, but something that could invade me and contaminate me. For instance, the sweat from her neck was now on my lips. I knew it was, I could taste it and I wanted to be away from her.[6]

No longer in a vampire body, Lestat is overwhelmed by the sensual experiences he is having, not because they are stronger, but rather because they are the means of being in connection with others, and he finds himself as this kind of body linked with others in smelling, seeing, hearing, tasting, and touching them. He feels "invaded" and "contaminated" by others through their taste or smell or touch: his impermeable vampiric boundary is gone, replaced by an earthbody which is an opening up to and linking with others in the way their being gets played out in and through all these sensual manifestations and expressions. Human sensing of another is not registering "artifacts" about separable entities in space. It is not collecting "data" about them, as we now attempt to simulate human perception in computer fabrications, but since we *are* our bodies, these perceptions are ways of "entering" others, moving into the whirl of a space that is the pulsation of energies of which we are all a part.

Lestat misses his "protection" of the vampire body. Descartes mistakenly described our human space and bodies thus: space is a void, an emptiness, which puts things, including other people, at a safe and objectively measurable distance, and makes my body a mere vessel, to pilot like a captain pilots a ship. This is what Lestat relied on as a vampire. The Western societies adopted this Cartesian space as gospel truth as we entered the post-Medieval, so-called enlightened world, in an attempt to keep others at the manipulable distance that the rise of industry, mass culture, and technology seemed to demand in the name of efficiency and order. This vampire metaphysics has worked with the diabolical logic we spoke of previously to maximize our sense of power and diminish our sense of vulnerability.

When Lestat first experiences with a woman this connectedness through immediate flow between human bodies, he loses all sense of the situation and feels impelled to be joined with her. He doesn't even realize he's forcing her to have "unprotected sex." He momentarily falls into senselessness, in which he is not even able to understand her words to wait while "he puts on protection." When he snaps out of it, he realizes his empathy for her, in seeing how open and vulnerable human contact is—not just biologically, but spiritually, given the nature of earthbodies. Her need for "protection" is only a physical one, whereas his need for protection is profoundly metaphysical. He sees that in some way as a vampire, he has always been able to choose to remain at a distance, and even sucking out the person's lifeblood, and their soul within it, he could control the amount he drained from them and maintain the barrier. Before this, people were like works of art, to be appreciated from an aesthetic distance and without the messiness of real involvement:

> And she, the poor being, she would have been beautiful to me simply because she was alive! I could not have been sullied by her had I fed on her for an hour. As it was, I felt filthy for having been with her, and filthy for being cruel to her. I understood her fear of disease! I too felt contaminated! But where lay the perspective of truth? (*BT*, 191)

The perspective of truth for earthbodies that this book is attempting to articulate, and which Lestat now seeks, is one of a different logic: through our deeper bodies and the feelings and depths within the senses they harbor, we are neither one nor two, both separate and yet joined in the fluidity of our interacting. Here, Lestat is experiencing the same lack of control and feeling of vulnerability as an individual in a human body that our culture at large has also fled.

Vampire metaphysic pervades not only our intellectual and cultural history, but comprises our psychological makeup in its profound ambivalence. Even as Lestat begins to experience in greater depth the kind of rich experiential possibility of being an earthbody, in which perception is a communion with the environment and others around us, and understands the potential beauty this allows in human relations (as well as the violence of which we will say more), he sees how this deeper possibility is terrifying. Being with his old friend David Talbott, now as another human being, he sees further how humans can embrace, either sexually or even just intimately and non-erotically, and have it mean something else than his previous ravishing of mortals had meant. As the moment continues, Lestat further sees that just being next to David in a humanly feelingful way through the flow of energies that pass along earthbodies opens up new possibilities:

> The idea paralyzed me. It sent a soft chill over the surface of my human skin. I felt *connected* to him, connected as I had been to the sad unfortunate young woman I'd raped, to the wandering tourists of the snow-covered capital city, my brothers

and sisters—connected as I'd been to my beloved Gretchen.Indeed so strong was this awareness—of being human with a human—that I feared it suddenly in all its beauty. And I saw that the fear was part of the beauty. (*BT*, 283)

Lestat has understood that our bodies are entranceways through which we become co-mingled with others, one's being is connected to theirs, not only in the physical act of intercourse, but in any sensory experience, even with those who remain physically and psychologically distant, such as those caught up in gazing at the blue of the sky together or at that work of art. It is this vulnerability of being opened through the human body that creates both the beauty of "co-munication," whose roots indicate a "being in common" and a shared being, and the fear of this openness.

The fear of vulnerability through mingled being is the opposite of the fear that Lestat had lived with for centuries as a vampire. As earthbodies, we can fear being absorbed into the common bond as part of the earth and its round dance of energy and feeling, whereas the vampiric fear is one of utter disconnection:

> She asked me to describe flying to her. "It's more like floating, simply rising at will—propelling yourself in this direction or that by decision. It's a defiance of gravity quite unlike the flight of natural creatures. It's frightening. It's the most frightening of all our powers; and I think it hurts us more than any other power; it fills us with despair. It is the final proof that we aren't human. We fear perhaps we will one night leave the earth and never touch it again." (*BT*, 232)

Using his body as a vessel, as a tool, and as a vehicle of power, the vampire isn't of the earth, and flying above it, it seems as if the vampire could just float away from any sense of connection. A bird flying on the air currents or even we in our airplanes are making an effort against the resistance of other elements, air, gravity, and wind flow, which we feel as part of our engagement with them, as we do with all the elements of the earth with which we are caught up. The vampire just moves through things and past them, whether the air or into another's thought without struggle, but also without enmeshment and engagement. The meaning that this engaged body imparts to us is that for a human being, even in an airplane, even walking on the moon or someday on other planets, we are always connected to the earth and part of its circulating sense. That is to say, we are always of this earth if we are open to the depths of what our senses give us, the emotional resonances, the imagination to dream of possibilities of further meaning, the pull of memories and their loyalties and commitments.

Now we can see fully the appeal of the vampire and also the true horror of the vampire. The life it captures in its image is the life of staying defended behind boundaries that can't be broached. It represents a kind of "undeath"—a kind of being alive that has also somehow died and can't partake fully of the events of this planet. It moves *by* people and things, but is never *of* them. Unlike the mindless, numbed consumption of the ghoulish life of buying more things or eating more food or consuming experiences with no real engagement, the vampiric urge seeks the lifeblood of others, their affections, their dreams, and their vitality. At least the vampire appreciates and desires the richness of experience that earthbodies make possible. However, the vampire has chosen an existence or been drawn into an existence distanced from life by abandoning its vulnerability in order to avoid its pain, but this has left it feeling empty. It needs the acuteness of life, but wants to keep the distance and control. As we might say, the vampire "wants its cake and to eat it, too." The vampire steals the richness of meaning that comes from engagement from the toil of others.

The fact that the vampire achieves a higher pitched sensibility—it hears better or sees colors more brightly or can read other's thoughts—but always hungers shows that the satisfaction of experiences, especially experiences that sensually plumb the depths of the earthbody's sensitivity, is not about a greater quantity of sensory "input," but rather a "taking to heart," a resonating with, or connecting with, what is experienced. However, the vampire in us fears to be so connected and openly vulnerable and pays the price of relinquishing greater satisfaction and empathetic sensitivity.

This is why Lestat decides that despite his desires "to walk in the sun for one day. To think and feel and breathe like a mortal (*BT*, 234)," he made the wrong decision. The feeling of being so vulnerable to others, so close to them, and open to the impact of their feelings on his own being is too frightening. In addition, as we will explore in depth later, the price of this sensitivity is being a body that is incomplete, that is resisted by nature, matter itself, and other beings, and is in many ways limited and fragile. Lestat, used to power and security, is horrified by this fragility, and it is his final reason for returning to the vampire life: "'I'd much rather be a vampire,' I said. 'I don't like being mortal. I don't like being weak, or sick, or fragile, or feeling pain. It's perfectly awful. I want my [vampire] body back as soon as I can get it. . . ." (*BT*, 234). To be part of the dance of life with the rest of the earth is to be part of a process that has a rhythm that can always be disrupted, whether the cells in our body suddenly start to multiply in discordant ways or we run afoul of others in a destructive tailspin or come into the path of a moving object, the rhythm of the unfolding of our life—biological and psychological—can always be disrupted because of the same open-endedness that allows it to be enriched.

The vampire is an important symbol for our current culture, because it represents an increasing threat to our psychic well-being. From MTV to Hollywood films to advertising, our culture promotes the idea that more input, whether more images bombarding us, more decibels of sound, more power in our cars, more frenzied adoration, more sales, more money, bigger penises and breasts, etc., means "heightened," more satisfying experience. This what the vampire seeks as compensation for losing the fragility and responsibility of sensitive reciprocal communion. The vehemence of an experience does not mean that it means more or involves more feeling or is more satisfying. Actually, it often indicates the opposite as the root meanings of "vehemence" recall. Literally, vehemence refers to being "without" ("ve" from the Latin) "mind" ("mens") or "mindless." This opposes the special quality of earthbodies and their "inclusive logic," as we've discussed, that joins emotion and sensual quality intermingled with meaning and mind. The vampiric "heightened" experience is more limited in being a blasting of certain channels without the intermingling of other senses, feelings, ideas, images, etc. It is a disconnected experience, of pure sound or of other pure sensations or of speed or of strength which actually disrupts the fragile rhythms within which different dimensions of earthbody sense enlace each other. Ultimately, what the vampire feels, or what we feel when blasted by these inputs our modern culture offers, is a feeling of power, which is not the same as a feeling of being moved or touched or graced with meaning or entering into communion.

It is certainly true that within the traditional masculine gender roles of many cultures, males have long been accustomed to learning to avoid the pain of vulnerability by taking charge and being defended from the world. I would sum up the masculinity's psychic defenses that males have learned like this: to be a "real man" or the masculine hero is to be able to soar to the heights beyond reach, to make the body into a tank-like structure than can "take hits" imperviously, to have a "missile sexuality" of going in for the "big splash" against females, and communicating through giving the "bottom line" or delivering the facts of the case in "the briefing."[7] However, this distancing from others and staying in manipulative control as dictated by the imperative to be "in charge" and "on top of things" leaves males, insofar as they fall into this pattern, feeling emotionally empty. Women are then desired as those beings that can somehow bring the male back in touch with emotional reality: women can be delegated the task of "emotional intermediaries" with the world. If the woman is supposed to handle these emotional matters for the couple, and the male can only be safely somewhat emotional with his female partner, this is a vampiric relationship. He will get his dose of emotion, of sensual aesthetic contact, and of connecting to others through the taking in his female partner's experience. This is why, no doubt, the majority of vampire characters have been men feeding off women.

However, it must be said that this is not exclusively a gender issue: females, too, acculturated by values of heroic achievement—staying in charge, being in control of emotion, and being "victorious" in life, seen as a series of challenges to be overcome, can follow the same patterns of psychic withdrawal from the sensitivities of being an earthbody. Certainly traditional heterosexual couples have no monopoly on vampirism: the male partner of a heterosexual couple or either partner of a homosexual couple can also be the one who is the designated "emotional intermediary" with the world while the other partner lurks at some non-reciprocal emotional, sensual, and imaginative distance from open exchange. Much of our current society's idea of success stresses these attitudes, encouraging even further the vampire life. A humorous, but disturbing film that focused on werewolves, *Wolf,* is a story of an executive in a publishing firm (played by Jack Nicholson) who is too sensitive and open to be successful in today's ruthless business climate and is failing, but once he starts to transform into an aggressive werewolf, he quickly climbs the corporate ladder (until the transformation goes too far). Our culture's advocacy of a certain monstrously detached and ruthless aggressiveness, although to be kept under control, makes a good climate in which vampires can thrive.

If we look at a few of the other symbols in the vampire lore, it is interest-ing to see how they might represent the flight from the more open and vulnerable affirmation of earthbodies. The mesmerizing and seductive power of vampires is striking. They offer even to their victims a kind of intensity and wildness experi-enced in ravishment not allowed in the drab, hum-drum day-to-day societal exis-tence. Francis Ford Coppola brings out this dimension of both Lucy's and Mina's seduction by Dracula. Both young women are engaged to attractive, but somehow rather boring men. Lucy has been raised in the stifling, upper-class world of pro-priety, and faces a life of being trivialized as the "beautiful keeper of the hearth" while her husband pals around with his well-to-do London friends. Mina faces the challenge of being faithful to her middle-class life of supporting her earnest, soon-to-be husband as company clerk and aspiring bread-winner. Dracula appears to Lucy in hallucinatory images and scenes of exotic eroticism amidst lush vegetation and shape-shifting animal forms of passion. Dracula first begins to seduce Mina by staging elaborate poetic scenes for romantic dinners and trysts, appearing to her in the shape of a cloaked, long-haired, and stylish eccentric, bohemian, and princely outsider to society. Ripping aside the confines of societal norms for the power of more raw sensation and vitality is seductive for people living in a numbing, sup-pressed, and driven culture.

Aesthetes: Obsession with Novelty and Control

The childlike intensity, the heightened sensation, the break with the hum-drum life of the ordinary, and the psychic defense of never being able to be caught emotionally and pained by the interaction which yields this emotional and sensual intensity is not only the mark of the vampire, but has been described less super-naturally as the "aesthetic life." The appeal and the power of the "aesthetic life" has always been to offer us the chance to "have our cake and eat it, too."

The threat of this particular seduction for society was foreseen and best described by Sören Kierkegaard, a Danish philosopher of the early nineteenth cen-tury who had incredible psychological insight into the individual and the dawning modern age of Western Europe. His picture of the aesthetic life portrayed in his *Either/Or* described the modern sensibility he foresaw as becoming increasing pow-erful: "If you marry you will regret it; if you do not marry, you will regret it; if you marry or do not marry, you will regret both. . . . Laugh at the world's follies, you will regret it; weep over them, you will also regret that; laugh at the world's follies or weep over them, you will regret both . . ."[8] Given the breakdown of a defined social structure and the sense of community, rather than being committed to the relationships with others that allowed working out of shared values and ideals, Kierkegaard saw that for most people any commitment to others would only mean the loss of individual freedom, if that freedom is considered to be the ability to choose whatever I want whenever I want it. Whatever committed choice was made would mean that I am involved with others and a certain situation, so I will regret that choice sooner or later, since I am no longer free insofar as I remain faithful to that situation. This purely negative sense of freedom, which has become widespread in its acceptance, means that I am only free if I never use that freedom to really make a choice to be committed to something or someone. This sentiment might best be summed up in a little parable the aesthete shares with the reader:

> The essence of pleasure does not lie in the thing enjoyed, but in the accompanying consciousness. If I had a humble spirit in my service, who when I asked for a glass of water, brought me the world's costliest wines blended in a chalice, I should dismiss him, in order to teach him that pleasure consists not in what I enjoy, but in having my own way. (*EO*, 30)

This captures many aspects of the aesthetic approach to life in one brilliant passage: first, that the key for the aesthete is to be in charge and to be in control of the situation; second, that the aesthete has no faith that the content of his experience is the key to fulfillment, but rather, it is what he or she can *extract* from the experience of the content while not being "caught up" in it; and third, that all experience, even a purely sensual one like tasting wine, becomes filtered through the mind or becomes an occasion for the mind to savor reality from a distance. This not only allows for a vampiric psychic relationship to others and things, so that we can maintain a safe distance "in our minds" from potential disturbing and involving entanglements, but as we will examine shortly, we are also continually structuring our contemporary world (especially through technology) around us to allow us to experience the world through images, like the television, film, or computer screen, that replicate this distanced, "mentalizing," or abstracting perspective. As the vampire extracts the lifeblood of its victims, taking in their experiential richness and vitality vicariously, so all of us who adopt an aesthetic stance can take in those around us from a carefully controlled psychic distance, keeping reflective control over ourselves, so we extract others' emotional life at no risk to ourselves.

Kierkegaard's aesthete gives a masterful lesson to his readers on how to manipulate their own psychological states in order to use others so they can have their cake and eat it, too. He calls this psychic defense the "rotation method." The crude form of the "rotation method" is to physically or literally never get caught in a situation, so one should always be ready to change jobs or move to a new house or change spouses or whatever. In this way one can enjoy them aesthetically, as if they were a work of art, until the inevitable complications, stresses, entanglements, and inherent challenges start to ruin the occasion of enjoyment, threaten one with having to do things that one didn't choose and be altered by the situation (including others), instead of by what one chooses. Instead of being "trapped," one is ready to switch, rather than lose this aesthetic freedom and control. Amazing that Kierkegaard wrote this in the nineteenth century! How he would laugh to see our divorce rates, restless changing of jobs, houses, families, locations, etc. He said the ultimate expression of this method would be for people to travel to other planets to switch from life on earth!

However, the aesthete warns that this literal switching is the "crude method" of the rotation method and is doomed to failure after a certain period of time, as we of this "postmodern" age are starting to discover: if one keeps changing partners or jobs or geographical locations, after a while they all seem the same. The problem is that one is placing one's hope in the inspirational power of novel objects, even though one has no real faith in the content of any object of experience to be redeeming in any real way—e.g., one beautiful or rich or faithful spouse is as good as another in some way—since this lack of faith was the original motivation for this strategy. One doesn't allow the relationship to the object of one's desire or affections or attentions the necessary time and process to build its nuanced meaning.

If the value of our experience is merely the sum of feelings that the other can occasion for us, whether the love or the excitement or the fun or the enrichment, and not something intrinsically enriching in them and the nature of the relationship itself, then the logical and aesthetic question is to wonder whether we really need to go through all the invariable complications of the entanglements of forming and sustaining a relationship. Why not have just enough emotional connection to them to be able to find ways that occasion the feelings we desire—whether they be feeling sexual, romantic, secure, excited, or whatever? If we realize that our satisfaction is the issue and have lost faith that anything or any person has such value that it's worth compromising our freedom and control, then why not just use things and other people to occasion those feelings without "getting stuck," if possible?

This means that avoiding "getting caught" will not involve literally always moving on, but cultivating the ability to always be psychically free from entrapment, or to be always "moving on" psychically, even though perhaps still in the same situation. We have this power to make ourselves vampires—to transform ourselves into beings who drink the lifeblood of others emotionally, but are impervious to being caught up in the ebb and flow between humans that calls for reciprocal emotional giving. The aesthete warns that one can always avoid psychic openness and commitment, as long as one never plunges fully into an experience. He tells us that "the carrying of concealed weapons is usually forbidden, but no weapon is so dangerous as the art of remembering," which is the key to his ability to psychically distance himself from others. What he means by this is indicated by this passage:

> From the beginning one should keep the enjoyment under control, never spreading every sail to the wind in any resolve; one ought to devote oneself to pleasure with a certain wariness, if one wishes to give the lie to the proverb which says that no one can have his cake and eat it too. (*EO*, 289)

Part of this control is a unique view of remembering; developing the strategy of looking back on an experience as it is happening for the sake of remembering it, or in his words, "remembering *the present*." Those who are open and vulnerable plunge into experience and *then* remember all its joys and all its pains: these people who are "caught up" in experience remember the past. The aesthete, in the midst of his experience, is regarding it as an image, as if it is a film or a video or at least as if it were something happening *to* him or her, instead of what he or she actually *is* at that moment.

If, as events are happening, we are looking back on them, then the interlocking rhythm of the dance is broken. There are only clips, in this case for Kierkegaard of the nineteenth century, only "mental pictures." One is there with the other, but one is really not there, not there as given over to our earthbodies to be swept up in this swirling emotional, erotic, intellectual, imaginative, and memorial tide that moves us. One is "standing outside" the experience as an observer and as a manipulator. As the aesthete boasts in an image which captures this aesthetic and vampiric life:

> Carking care is my castle. It is built like an eagle's nest upon the peak of the mountain lost in the clouds. No one can take it by storm. From this abode I dart down into reality to seize my prey: but I do not remain down there, I bear my quarry aloft to my stronghold. My booty is a picture I weave into tapestries of my palace. (*EO*, 41)

For the aesthete, the castle is his or her mind. He or she is not his or her earthbody—not fully given over to the flesh one touches or with whom one speaks—but is using the body as a vehicle of his or her bidding and it is to this empty vessel, this placeholder for the mind, that one is speaking.

For example, in *Either/Or*, the young aesthete has an older friend, Judge William, who loves him and is quite concerned about how his young friend is wasting his life. Judge William believes that they are engaged in a series of heart-to-heart discussions about the aesthete's problems, while the aesthete tells his readers:

> There was a man whose chatter certain circumstances made it necessary for me to listen to. At every opportunity he was ready with a little philosophical lecture, a very tiresome harangue. Almost in despair, I suddenly discovered that he perspired copiously when talking. I saw the pearls of sweat gather on his brow, unite to form a stream, glide down his nose, and hang at the extreme point of his nose in a drop shaped body. From the moment of making this discovery, all was changed. I even took pleasure in inciting him to begin his philosophical instruction, merely to observe the perspiration on his brow and at the end of his nose. (*EO*, 295)

The aesthete has transformed the experience by finding something interesting for him in the interaction, something that will give him pleasure instead of pain. It also means he is in control. When the judge thinks they are touching souls, sharing deep emotions, forging a friendship, the aesthete is just amusing himself, and is defended from any real hold on his feelings. It is not that the aesthete is really that amused by sweat balls, but rather the pursuit to always find what is fun, amusing, or interesting is a powerful psychic defense against the kind of compromising engagement where one is overwhelmed by the feelings and the closeness of the other that Lestat also found so horrifying. To always look for what amuses us can be our way to drink the Dark Blood and not really be present.

This is an extreme case, presented in a humorous but sad way, but the aesthetic defense is used continually in our culture. Consider how often a spouse tunes out what the other is saying by taking up the attitude, "oh, he (or she) is just like that—look how upset they get," as the spouse stands there shaking with anger or racked with tears, open and vulnerable to the loved one's response to their communication, but unable to reach him or her in a way that the feelings expressed have really been taken to heart and moved the other person into reciprocal vulnerability and expression. It is an aesthetic response because the person has been rendered an image—made into a memory in the midst of the present; he or she is dismissed as "oversensitive one who is so touching with her tears" or "the big fool who is unfair but powerful in his anger," etc. We also are aesthetic each time we do this as a group to our leaders or to other important societal figures, seeing them as a certain work of art, whether the "gentle-souled leader" or "the hard-boiled boss" or the "spoiled star" or whatever, if they are genuinely trying to speak to us: if they do, we are apt to take people's genuine emotional expressions as enactments of their roles or as aesthetic objects to be appreciated for how their suffering or sincere feelings look, taken as if it were only a show. Then there is no chance of a genuine expression being taken up as a beckoning for response and encounter. We then have endless amusement by making fun of these people and are relieved of the responsibility of truly responding to them.

We are so adept at this aesthetic trick we can even transform starving children or torture victims or the sick into just another one of those type displays—perhaps this time into more of a tragic soap opera—to occasion this or that response from us. We become like an audience at a play, instead of actually being in our earthbodies and feeling the various ways we can be caught up with them in the swirl of feeling, image, sensation, memory, etc. Of course, if we did this then they might really move us and transform our relationship to these people. If we can do this to human beings, babies, and even our loved ones, it is no surprise that we do the same to nature and inanimate objects: massive canyons, gurgling brooks, or the moon on the horizon have become a series of postcards and images, even when we are "out there" with them—interesting, amusing, or even frightening in an entertaining way.

However, the real problem is that we also treat ourselves as though we are aesthetic phenomena. In Kierkegaard's tale, the aesthete feels the despair of never really being connected to anyone as the price of having his sense of being in control intact. He never really grows or becomes transformed as others do from having to "work things through" with people and with the world. As he writes in his diary:

> Vainly, I strive against it. My foot slips. My life is still a poet's existence. What could be more unhappy? I am predestined; fate laughs at me when suddenly it shows me how everything I do to resist becomes a moment in such an existence. (*EO*, 35)

Inwardly, the aesthetic life means that one stands nowhere and is not really "there" with others, as Lestat also realized about himself. This way of avoiding the unhappiness of life—supposed derived from being forced to do what the situation and other people with whom you're involved need you to do for them—becomes instead what makes up the aesthete's life: once having fled this way he must stay in inward flight or feel like he is "trapped." Instead of the pain of deeply felt conflict or dealing with the moving circumstances others bring to one's life, the aesthete's pain or unhappiness is his own sense of disconnection or of "slipping" instead of standing within life. However, even his own pain makes for a story, an image, which he never encounters on a deeper level of openness. He writes his story, he amuses people with the tales of his suffering, he runs contests to measure and reward which despairing characters might despair the most, etc., but he never really connects with or takes to heart even his own sadness and unhappiness.

This sounds appallingly similar to our current fads: turn on the television at almost any daytime hour and you will find people who have come to the studio to entertain others with confessions of their sufferings and how they have brought pain and damage to their lives and the lives of those around them. It's a grand show, the newest spectacle,—or rather aestheticism gone amok. There are even shows with contestants to who compete in making their confessions and expressing their sorrows. The audience then votes on whose misery has made the most dramatically powerful scenario.

The trouble with taking oneself as an object is that one loses the only reality we have as part of the dance of earthbodies. We lose our inner movement that grounds us, and we lose that interrelatedness that is our lifeblood. Instead, we are left with the Hunger. The aesthete confesses that he feels intoxicated with possibilities ("there is nothing so intoxicating as possibility!" he says), since he is never really "in" any actual relationship, and that he feels as though he is spinning like a top. Both of these images are cogent to our society. We live in the midst of a constant atmosphere of intoxication. The newest dance, the newest tragedy, the newest scandal, the newest teddy bear, or whatever is "happening" is something we approach drunkenly and with a frenzy of excitement. Suddenly, we can't stop talking about this trial or even about this or that toy. We become frenzied, obsessed, and "high" about whatever has captured our attention, like our friends who stagger up to us at a bar. Our society is built on spinning and spinning like a top and getting people caught up in the motion, whether to take their money or their votes or capture their adulation or persuade them of some new policy. We conduct more and more of our lives like a drunk staggering from one occasion to the next. From the trivial, like the crazes of having to buy the newest, adorable stuffed animal, to the serious, like choosing our government or our values for ourselves and our children, how often do we really sit down and feel deeply, ponder long and hard, use our imaginations and memories to discover genuinely creative responses, enter into heartfelt and open dialogue, and become transformed by the situations of our lives which confront us? Instead, we laugh at ourselves or feel hopeless about ourselves and this frenetic and intoxicated way of doing things. We realize that there is something unhealthy and absurd for everyone to be so caught up in these images and life made into a series of sensational dramas, yet we blame it on the media or mass culture and take no responsibility or look no deeper for the way we're falling into these currents of society because of something about our way of being the kind of selves we are. We could only do this if we stopped the intoxication, the spinning, and the distancing, not only from the world and others, but also from ourselves.

Of course, in an aesthetic environment, no one rightly can take anyone else to heart—whether the politicians, educational leaders, or spiritual leaders, attempting to express themselves or the audience to genuinely respond. Both become staged performances. If we treat ourselves as aesthetic phenomena, then we do live by just donning masks for one another, to make a certain impression or to manipulate a certain occasion, just as the aesthete claimed he could become anyone for a time to make a certain impression and advised the government to use its funds "not to pay our debts, but for public entertainment. Let us celebrate the millennium in a riot of merriment" (*EO*, 283). Rather prescient advice, given that it is 1843 when Kierkegaard wrote this. Not only do more and more of our time and resources go to making all aspects of life "entertaining," but the creation of personae and fictions to elicit certain responses has become a trillion dollar industry of creating "spin"—using words, images, and entertainment effects to create whatever impression is desired, no matter what was the actual content of the experience.

Here, one danger for the vampire or the aesthete becomes apparent. For all his or her independence, as Lestat has scorn for his victims, for example, as the mortal vampires who disrespect their spouses or the other sex or have scorn for those foolish ones who are sincere or emotionally vulnerable, he and they are dependent on their victims to furnish the lifeblood or the real contact with others that they lack from their distanced position. If everyone took this stance towards others, everyone would be parasitic and there would be no real substance of life to be taken in by those who dart down and feed on others before retreating. Besides the dishonesty to those with whom the vampires and aesthetes relate (that they are not really in relationship with them but are rather using them as a mere occasion for their nourishment), there is also the self-deception about their freedom—they are not really in charge of their lives; despite the self-image, they are covertly utterly dependent. In a committed relationship, there is an acknowledged inter-dependence. In the vampiric relationship, there is a covert dependence the victim doesn't know about and that the vampire lies about in his or her inner heart. The only way the aesthete can carry out the manipulations of others and be nourished with the real substance of life that he or she or we are unwilling to obtain from being part of the round dance of life with all its entanglements, committed effort, and up and down emotional passages is to have a supply of victims. Instead of being free and self-sufficient they are just indirectly dependent: living a lie that they flee from by spinning ever faster and making their own suffering just a game on the spinning surface, but a vaguely felt cancer underneath.

This leads to a rash of absurdities. In Kierkegaard's aesthete's life it meant that he would start a book in the middle or go to the last act of a play, while being sure to avoid real friendship and being aware that "marriage brings one into fatal connection with custom and tradition" (*EO*, 293). What he meant by the first two suggestions is that it is easier to engage in activities or relationships that are arbitrary or accidental, whereas in the second cases, of friendship or marriage, entering into a situation that involves the powerful feelings of a group means "you have lost your freedom; you cannot send for your traveling boots whenever you wish" and that "traditions and customs are like the wind and the weather, altogether incalculable." If you truly take to heart a tradition or enter into a deeper relation with a group like a family or a community, then you are caught by reciprocal expectations, obligations, responses, and sensitivities. Furthermore, they are unpredictable like the rain, whether it is your spouse getting sick, your child needing comforting, or the community group needing someone to man the phones or help out with a disaster, etc. The result is that the aesthete takes what he wants from the book instead of struggling all the way through it, that he watches the sweat balls on his supposed friend's nose instead of emotionally being caught in the turmoil of the latter's anxiety for him, or moves on to a new woman when the last has reached some crisis. However, he is so intent on keeping this freedom he is not only a slave to his freedom, but he is a slave to the trivial, to the arbitrary, and to the distant. He does this in the name of freedom. He runs with intoxication from one interesting, but non-threatening event to another, or from one person to another who suddenly seems fascinating, but is still distant enough not to really ensnare him.

Again, it is staggering to stop and realize to what extent our current culture has fallen into this slavery of the supposed freedom of aestheticism gone amok. Husbands and wives, children and parents, people who live next door to each other or work together may exchange the barest bits of communication. Yet, these same people can't tear themselves away from watching the latest televised trial or from running home to spend hours at a video game or cruising the Internet compulsively or watching soap operas. Not only do they end up being slaves to trivialities consuming their time and energy, but also their deepest feelings are reserved for these distant happenings. One's own mother or father or co-worker dies and the person feels nothing, yet the death of Princess Diana or some celebrity they have never even known in the slightest causes them overwhelming grief and upset. This reaches such absurd heights that when a fictional character on a soap opera dies, the studio is flooded with condolences and flowers! This is not disconnected from the aspect of a culture where most people polled prefer to interact with an automated teller in order to avoid even the minimal human interaction with a human teller. When we are so busy avoiding real contact, the Hunger drives us to find distant, trivial, and arbitrary connections. In our intoxication, we are obsessed and addicted. People who couldn't watch the O. J. Simpson trial for a day would be depressed, whereas not having time for their families for weeks at a time would be no problem. This is the absurd price of aestheticism: we come to absolutely need the trivial, the distant, and the disconnected with a passion that we have withheld from our potentially involving commitments. The need for connection can't be eradicated, since as earthbodies, we are not solid substances, but are instead moving waves that exist only as part of larger rhythms. If we flee psychically from what is central to our lives in fear of the intimacy, like Lestat did, we only displace a fundamental need onto trivial and non-threatening forms.

Since the aesthete has no real involvement that can't be sheared off at will when it becomes too demanding, this person, or a society of people like this, are strangely blank or lack a content to their lives. They feel no "calling" from the world towards specific values, interests, or compelling passions. In such a world, the worst and ever-threatening enemy is boredom. Kierkegaard brilliantly defines boredom as "the nothingness which pervades reality; it causes a dizziness like that produced by looking down into a yawning chasm" (*EO*, 287). The bored person feels as if everything doesn't matter, has no weight, no bearing, and they are left dizzy and staggered, as if the world were vertiginous, as if it were only empty space into which one can fall. The aesthete also realizes that the person feeling boredom always wants the novel, the new, or the surprising to get beyond this empty feeling. The electric charge of the novel fuels the rotation method of finding something fascinating in that which is merely of passing fancy. In other words, they want to change the mood, but not the deeper disconnection that has caused the world to no longer call to them. Novelty will allow them to stay with the same superficial level of engagement, but "freshen it up."

Again, our culture seems far beyond the wildest aesthetic fantasies that Kierkegaard could imagine in its frenzy for novelty. Each day there must be new discoveries, new fashions, new breakthroughs, new economic expansion, new frontiers, new records in measurable activities, new images, new celebrities, new commodities, and even new values, new truths, and new faiths. When an individual lives in this quest for the ever-new, a strange phenomenon occurs. Kierkegaard points to this strangeness within the passage we've already looked at, which contains the aesthete's boast that he lives in his castle that no one can take by storm, from which he darts down into reality to seize his prey. He continues with this strange image: "Then I sit like an old man, gray-haired and thoughtful, and explain picture after picture in a voice as soft as a whisper; and at my side a child sits and listens, although he remembers everything before I tell it." The one who savors the series of images that the aesthete collects from life is a child. Remaining psychologically defended in his or her mind, this type person does seem to be like a child in some ways, or to be like Peter Pan in having the child's glee eternally. In the aesthete's experience, there is the rush of excitement, the glee, the momentary fascination of the child, which is also like the vampire's experience of being absorbed blissfully with his victim. There is something that seems naïve and unspoiled, like both the child who is sheltered from the grinding responsibilities and assaults of the world he or she is not yet equipped to handle in an ongoing, creative way, or the vampire, who also doesn't have to worry about sickness, hunger, or obligations, but lives for pleasure. This is the wonderful charm of children and part of the seductive charm and special energy of the vampires that draws their victims. In some ways both the aesthete and the vampire present not only the certain kind of vehement intensity we've discussed, but also a summons to remain a child forever.

However, the child's wonder and fascination are their introduction to the beauty and compelling nature of existence itself, of sensing itself, of moving itself, and all those human dimensions of apprehension and expression, that the adult will come to take for granted. The child first connects us to the world and the planet's dance.[9] It is important for the adult to have had this childhood period of being in love with the planet, with human existence, and with other humans, for if Merleau-Ponty is right, this is an "abiding acquisition,"[10] something we gain as a dimension of our being, which as adults we can "tune into." The power of this childhood dimension is resuscitated when we fall in love, for example, or feel the unity with others in friendship or comradeship, or feel that wondrous, buoyant energy flow through the landscape and through ourselves that is an "oceanic love," a feeling of our ego boundaries melting at that moment. When the adult's ego boundaries become well formed and usually too constricted, it may be essential to rediscover this childhood sense of openness in order to return to the earthbody sense we've discussed. Yet, notice, for the adult, both of these dimensions can infiltrate or reinforce, or to use the metaphor of this book, dance with, each other to give the richest experience possible: the adult sense of commitment, of having a rational grasp of the world, of having deepened emotional sensibilities to others, and of having developed its capacities can enhance this wondrous energy with a new meaning; and, the childhood sense of oneness and aliveness can infuse these various dimensions of understanding and expressive capacities which otherwise will become deadened and overly individualized. This mutual infusion does not occur with the aesthete.

The aesthetic life is built on separation and barriers, between the self and others and the world, and also within the self—at least by contrast with the kind of fluid and interpenetrating sense of self that earthbody sense comprises. The resulting fragmentation is embraced by Kierkegaard's aesthete as he is proud that his life has no unity, which in his assessment would be boring, entrapping, and a testimony to a lack of daring and imagination. Our contemporary postmodern culture seems to have reached the same assessment: celebrate the discontinuities, whether from identity politics, which see no chance or reason for larger community, or from aesthetic judgments that only harsh and grinding fragments of the elements of composition are acceptable in the new artwork, otherwise the work is judged merely "nostalgic" for a time when beauty or unity could be taken seriously. The reaction against earlier coercive senses of one truth and one norm are understandable, but this protest falls prey to diabolical logic in that opposing a coercive norm by a celebration of radical disunity maintains the same dichotomous framework and prolongs the flight from a more involving way to think of ourselves—one that has a "logic of inclusive differences" that allows for engagement. The postmodern form of flight, however, is one that masks the aestheticism it serves.

Rather than the integrative sense of "childlikeness" which can bring regained vitality and belonging to adult life, notice that in the aesthete's image, there is a child and no adult within the "castle no one can take by storm." There is a child who listens to one who feels like an old man tell his tales, but the child knows them all before they are said. The child confesses that "there I live as one dead." Despite the glee while darting down into reality and the intoxication of the rotation method, the child of this mind is a person old in the sense of knowing it all. With the vehement vitality, there is also connected a strange sense of being weary and jaded. The child doesn't bring childlikeness as being alive to the experiences because they have for him the quality of his having seen it all before. Why is it all the same for him? Perhaps, the answer lies in the fact that despite the glee of the experiences they never "hit home" or they are never taken to heart by the aesthete. By gliding through life this way, the "experiencer" or the self is never impacted and therefore never changes, is always the same. It is himself with which he is too familiar and bored.

What does it mean that the adult is missing from this scene? There is no one who, despite pain, despite infringement upon unlimited choice, and despite the need for repetition in an ongoing process, stands resolute with other people in a way that there is a true relation. There is no one who takes responsibility, sees commitments through, is emotionally responsive, and open to being impacted upon and changed by the exigencies of the other. The adult self is comprised by the sense that the rhythms of others as they are encountered are not limitations to my freedom as being able to choose whatever I want, whenever I want it, but are the grounds of being free to creatively respond within the bounds of the relationship or shared situation.

Culturally, all these telltale signs of aestheticism are rampant. There is a never-ending emphasis upon youthfulness, not in the deeper sense of childlike wonder at the world, which is often in postmodern assessments seen as naïve and silly, but instead of higher and higher energy levels, of an amusement park kind of gleefulness, of literally a youthful physical appearance, and a kind of quickly revolving attention span. Although children are quite able to sit quietly and wonder at the most simple objects or happenings, we promote the bombardment of stimuli and the lack of limits as the other aspects of the child that become contemporary culture's sense of "being youthful." A recent advertising campaign showed people jumping from a railroad bridge on a bungee cord or jumping off a mountain on a bike. The goal was to associate this sense of youth with a soft drink. These actions exemplify this need for experiences which rotate the world in new ways, give this vehement energy, and promote the idea that the thrill of life is in dissociative experiences, instead of in wonder at the details of the everyday, which is seen as humdrum or boring. Even the motto associated with both these "extreme sports" (as they are called), and also used in reference to other aspects of postmodern culture, could have come straight out of the Kierkegaard's aesthete's dairy: "been there, done that!" This attitude not only epitomizes the need for novelty, but also the same underlying jadedness and despair that life itself and the everyday aspects of it have no intrinsic worth except for the quest for the new angle on experience.

As a last comment on aestheticism, it might be helpful to turn to a story to give a concrete sense of this idea, but the story can only come from the culture that has centered on this way of life: the modern European-American culture. John Fowles' *Magus* is a novel about the struggle of Nicholas Urfe, an intelligent and good-looking fellow, to discover what to do with his life. In a foreword to a later edition of the book, John Fowles states that he thought of Nicholas as a "modern Everyman." Although published in 1965 with its story set in 1952, it clearly fits the current state of culture, especially American, even more closely. Nicholas is from a middle-class background, but as a bright fellow (although not brilliant), he graduates from Oxford and tries teaching in a "minor pubic school." However, a woman there, with whom he is involved, wants to marry him. Nicholas feels the need to escape not only her, but also the "boredom, the annual predictability, [which] hung over the staff like a cloud."[11]

As the novel opens, Nicholas is attracted to a stewardess, Alison. They immediately become lovers and quickly move in together. They live together for a few months and fall in love, but Nicholas has the feeling he always does—that he doesn't want to be trapped. Fate helps him in the form of an opportunity to teach English to Greek boys at a boarding school on a Greek island. As he leaves Alison behind, and walks away from their apartment, his thoughts are centered on his freedom:

> The thing that I felt most clearly, when the first corner was turned, was that I had escaped; and hardly less clearly, but much more odiously, that she loved me more than I loved her, and that consequently I had in some indefinable way won. So on top of the excitement of the voyage into the unknown, and taking wing again, I had an agreeable feeling of emotional triumph. A dry feeling, but I like things dry. (*TM*, 50)

Nicholas is pleased that he is free, not trapped by commitment, that he is in control of the situation, and has triumphed in that way. He recognizes already some quality of aridity about his life, but he makes it into a joke.

Nicholas feels relieved escaping from marriage and commitment with Alison, despite the fact that he had been happier with her than with any other person, had felt her loving affirmation of him, and had experienced moments like this one with Alison in the art museum: "I suddenly had a feeling that we were one body, one person, even there, that if she disappeared it would have been as if I had lost half of myself. A terrible deathlike feeling, which anyone less cerebral and self-absorbed than I was would have realized was simply love. I thought it was desire" (*TM*, 37). Nicholas always thinks in terms of the immediate, brute impact of feelings and sensations, and does not let himself be carried beyond his boundaries to see the world through the other's eyes, as we can as earthbodies within the spiral dance. In short-circuiting these deeper and further reaches of feeling, Nicholas simply fails to understand both the other person's feelings and his own. When he says he doesn't see or is confused, he is, but as a result of using feeling as an occasion, instead of embarking on an avenue of discovery.

It is not surprising that Nicholas has periods of depression once he slows down enough to realize how empty he is, as does the aesthete, as do many people in our society. Although he can't tolerate the emotional vulnerability he feels with her, he misses Alison. Finally, one day on the Greek island, he sits with a gun pointed at his head for quite a while contemplating suicide until he realizes "all the time I felt I was being watched, that I was not alone, that I was putting on an act for the benefit of someone, that this action could be done only if it was spontaneous, pure—and moral. But more and more it crept through my mind with the chill spring night that I was trying to commit not a moral action, but a fundamentally aesthetic one" (*TM*, 64). To commit suicide would take a despair Nicholas can't feel, since everything he does is like a show he's watching. Despair lingers at a depth Nicholas avoids. A moral action would be one that grew out of a deep commitment, a connection to something beyond himself, but Nicholas can't even connect to himself. Although empty, his life is too disconnected, too out of touch, to be truly tragic, which perhaps is much more sad, much more depressing—as might be much of our modern life. His suicide would be a show for others, just as so many of the violent acts of our contemporary culture are.

The *magus* or "magician" of the title is Maurice Conchis, a wealthy, brilliant, and non-conformist character who uses this Greek island as an experimental teaching ground each summer for the young men who take up the teaching post Nicholas assumed this year: they are his students, although that is unknown to them when they are recruited. Elaborate, secret dramatic productions of mythical, historical, supernatural, and above all mysterious happenings are produced by Conchis and his "cast" to create a situation for the student—this summer, Nicholas—so that once they have been drawn in by the charm and brilliance of being with Conchis they become increasingly unsure of what events on the island are "staged" and what are "real." Nicholas, who is by this time wishing he were reunited with Alison,— now that she has apparently returned to her previous boyfriend and fiancé,—soon is lured into fascination with one of Conchis's actresses, Julie.

Alison, meanwhile, is enlisted by Conchis to help Nicholas come to see himself and who he is. She suddenly comes to Greece and makes herself available to him. They take a wonderful trip climbing Parnassus, during which Nicholas is already devaluing Alison again and taking mental distance from her, because she is emotionally open to him. However, in spite of his aesthetic tendencies to flee, he really does—as much as he can—love her. On the mountain, hiking together through stirring landscapes, meeting others, hearing her speak of her life so openly, Nicholas realizes again how Alison "had always had this secret trick of slipping through all the obstacles I put between us" (p. 272). But even Nicholas knows it's not a trick, but rather that Alison is some sort of spiritual "sister" who can "evoke deep similarities" between them. There is a unique moment for Nicholas that occurs after this realization, when they reach a clearing in the dense forest, full of flowers and butterflies, which contains a little waterfall about ten feet high and a limpid pool of water. Alison takes off her clothes and runs into the pool and Nicholas joins her:

> The water was jade-green, melted snow, and it made my heart jolt with shock when
> I plunged beside her. And yet, it was so beautiful, the shadow of the trees, the sun
> light on the glade, the white roar of the little fall, the iciness, the solitude, the laugh
> ing, the nakedness; moments one knows only death will obliterate. (p. 273)

At this moment, Nicholas has let down his constant defenses, his unfailing retreat to his mind where he guards his feelings, and is swept up in a current of presence that moves through the water, flowers, butterflies, sunlight, bracing water, Alison's naked body and his own.

By letting himself go at this moment, Nicholas suddenly is able to both really experience Alison, his own feelings, and his relationship with her, and also realize that he is seeing through "to the naked real self of her—a vision of her as naked that way as she was in body" (p. 274). By allowing himself to go beyond his constricted boundaries, a choice for Nicholas as radical as Lestat's choice to be in a vulnerable human body, he discovers, "it rushed on me, it was quite simple, I loved her." As they lie there and Nicholas has this sudden insight into his feelings, they "make love, not sex." It is the opposite of his usual ability to have sex in a way that doesn't involve his earthbody and lacks any real presence with the other.

Almost immediately Nicholas has the thought that this is a kind of emotional honesty that is not usual for someone who has lived in habitual emotional dishonesty. Also, as quickly and with as much discomfort about being vulnerable as Lestat, Nicholas distances Alison, brings up his attraction for Julie, and confesses, "I don't know what love is" (p. 278). Alison, however, can see his ploys and his own aesthetic distance—not only from her but from himself—and confronts him: "Because nothing can hurt you, Nicko. Deep down, where it counts. You've built your life so that nothing can ever reach you. So whatever you do you can say, I couldn't help it. You can't lose. You can always have your next adventure" (p. 279). Given his manipulative stance, all his life passes by in his head, in a way that he is never "there." Human bodies can be made into vehicles for manipulative psyches seeking escape or they can be lived as earthbodies caught up in everything's and everyone's surrounding energy flow. This latter choice cements them into the fabric of the only reality there is—an unfolding of the beings that let themselves go and thereby become fully present and returned to themselves through others.

Many of the events in *The Magus* are staged by Conchis to demonstrate to Nicholas that "life is hazard" and can't be controlled other than by letting go and finding the magic in events coming together in unexpected ways. Nicholas is thrown into reenactments of the German occupation. He is fooled into thinking he is with Julie when actually he is with her twin sister, June. Both sisters act at not being part of the acting troupe or unsure about whether they want to be as they are fooling him. Finally, Nicholas is put on trial in a fantastic mythical setting by various magical beings in a wonderful performance by the entire troupe. Instead of letting go and becoming immersed in these productions and how they can reveal parts of himself, Nicholas is intent on outwitting Conchis in a competitive battle for control and superiority. Rather than taking up the opportunities to let go and be influenced by the miraculous events they stage for him, he becomes embattled in saving his sense of control and his own constructed sense of who he is outside of the influence of anyone else. For him, it is always a challenge to show how strong is his will.

When he once again starts to miss Alison, after forgetting her for a while in his excitement about Julie, Conchis arranges all the evidence to point to the fact that, in despair over their broken love, Alison has committed suicide. Conchis hopes this shock will penetrate Nicholas's defenses and make him think about his impact on others and how much they might mean to him. Yet, as shaken as he is by this news at first, soon he takes her suicide and begins "to edge it out of the moral towards the aesthetic.(*TM*, 400)" For Nicholas, nothing ultimately penetrates his castle that no one can take by storm. All is grist for how he can use it for his interest or as a reflection of his performance. At some point late in the events of the novel, Nicholas, too, can see his condition: "I had tried to turn my life into a fiction, to hold reality away" (p. 549). Yet moments like this are dismissed as themselves just another drama, a passing mood, and Nicholas persists in failing to make the connection with what Conchis has been showing him about giving up control, really embracing events, taking responsibility, seeing the interconnectedness of people and things, and how we can create magic in full presence to things.

Although Nicholas, like Kierkegaard's aesthete, has tried to set up his life so that he can have it all, the truth is that he can't have anything. When it is revealed that Alison is alive, Nicholas reacts with a period of fury that he had again been "made a fool," as he has reacted each time Conchis shakes up his previous sense of reality. He then searches long and hard to find Allison again. At the book's conclusion, it is not clear what will happen to Nicholas, but it is obvious that as soon as he is confronted with real openness and love, he must flee forever, chasing a poetic image that he can't bear in reality. Alison appears one more time, still steadfast in her love for him, but even after searching and searching for her, after Conchis and his troupe had disappeared after the events of the previous summer to allow Nicholas to think about what he had learned, he again rejects her. Actually, like much of our current society, it is the image he wants, more and more images, but not real connection.

Nicholas feels justified that his fictions are inevitable strategies we all must employ to maintain some psychic defense and control over our lives. He takes himself seriously and is self-righteous about his need for self-preservation being a right that condones distrusting others. Although he is never really "there" with people, he feels vindicated in demanding sincerity and stability from them. If they treat him with less than sincerity and commitment, he sees this as a moral affront and is outraged that they are so untrustworthy. His hypocritical demands come from his need that someone else provide the substance for his distanced, starved life. Whereas Conchis and his followers present the mirror image: letting go with the greatest feeling and vulnerability even during a drama, since all of life is merely a drama anyway, to be embraced with humor and danced with in a spirit of play. When hazard can be affirmed and played with for its revelatory and transforming possibilities, then magic can occur, where magic is that kindling of glowing connections among people and/or things that have no logical reason to become so connected. This means that Nicholas would have to take himself less seriously, something his mocking of himself and all those around him, does not undermine, but actually reinforces. Nicholas remains deadly serious in his need to be in control. His mockery is a hostile attempt to regain control. Letting be eludes him. Nicholas laughs one kind of laugh, which is very different from the laughter Conchis tried to allow him to experience.

Who Has the Last Laugh?

It is worth considering this paradox for a moment: we live in a cultural context in which there is produced ever more novelty in terms of new gadgets, objects of pleasure, and discoveries, and newer possibilities for experience for more people, whether traveling to a rain forest or going to the moon, and yet the new quickly becomes old. This trajectory is in stark contrast to most spiritual, philosophical, and psychological systems for human development that point the way to a level of experience in which the old forever becomes the new. As Kazantzakis phrased it in *Zorba the Greek*, "this is how great visionaries and poets see everything—as if for the first time. Each morning they see a new world before their eyes. . . ." The power of wonder that is truly childlike lies in being open to how the everyday is never just everyday, but is also infinitely rich and fascinating. It offers this side of things to us only through a dancing relationship of playful give and take.

This is not the frenetic energy we have taken as paradigmatic of the possible hyperactivity of children that we promote in a cultural childishness. Whether it is Jesus saying that unless you turn and become like children you will never enter the Kingdom of Heaven, or the Buddhist exhortation to return to the child's ability to be open in the way the child spontaneously lets go of one object and unhesitatingly picks up another as smoothly as snow falling off a branch or Jung and Erickson (psychologists), or William James, Gaston Bachelard or Merleau-Ponty (philosophers), to name a few figures of the many voices, there is a pervasive call for return to connection, quietness, wonder, openness, and playful transformation that could lead us to dive back into a remaining pool of childlikeness that is still within us. Unlike our culture that quickly tires of everything, this quality allows us to rediscover moment by moment an "ongoing originariness"—a never-ending quality of somehow still being at the "beginning," at that instant of never-ending creation and discovery that is the source of things in their meaningfulness and energizing vitality—within the most accustomed routines, objects, and relationships.

Notice that although this sense of experience is a childlike wonder, it is also a quality necessary to the adult to follow through on mature commitments. If I can't find something new and fresh, something I never quite experienced that way before, something surprising, in the midst of the old, then any long-term loving relationship will lose its power, meaning, and satisfying quality. It will become a worn-through routine. The same is true of our work or of projects we undertake outside of work like playing music, sports, gardening, building, etc.: we have to find something fresh, some of that same joy and surprise that we had on the first day of this profession or calling or job, or else we will sink into just going through the motions in a mechanical and not very satisfying way. Here the spiritual and psychological needs are in exact accord with the practical, for neither meaning nor quality performance will survive without this ability to find the newness of the old.

In our present cultural context, this need for the wondrous seems like a cruel joke. We long for the new, the novel, to bring us the wonder we had as children when the world was new, but now everything, including the most novel event or gadget, seems old. The oldness, the failure to inspire a jolt of delight and surprise, is not the fault of the object, however, but the result of our relationship to the world, ourselves, and others. Like the aesthete, who only has within his psyche a tired old man who feels no life and has the pervasive sense of having heard it all before, so do we in our culture have this inner decrepitude, that actually has nothing to do with age, but with an *attitude of seriousness*.

I'm sure that this assertion will strike most readers as surprising. It seems the one thing we must lack as a culture is seriousness. There is nothing that seems safe from ridicule, not our political or religious traditions, or even our political, religious, scientific leaders, or whatever institutions used to be held in such respect they were exempt from ridicule. However, ridicule and seriousness, in the sense intended here, are not opposites, but go together.

Seriousness comes about from a distanced relationship with things and people that leads to seeing them as somehow "standing in themselves," a kind of self-sufficiency, in a way that cuts off input from us. It also comes about from an experience of insecurity about one's own worth and identity, which also ultimately derives from the same distance one has in relationship to others and the world. In the first case, the serious person thinks that whatever has value has it as a result of just being what it is, instead of seeing that we are free in interpreting it that way. For example, someone who is "serious" about money feels that its ultimate value that rules people's activities is just a brute given, an undeniable fact.[12] This person doesn't see how others could acknowledge that money is important, but at times choose other values as more important, or decide that sometimes money isn't even very important in comparison to some other value at the moment. This person won't understand how it is possible for certain people or cultures to be happy despite a lack of material wealth. The imperious value of money is just "there," obvious to anyone who really pays attention to it. The only responsible attitude, the serious one, is to obey this imperative to gain money. It would be frivolous to make any other choice: there really is no other possible choice.

In the second case, the other aspect of seriousness is that in being cut off from others, one lacks the immediate sense of vitality and meaningfulness that comes from belonging with others, with nature, and with the richness of the material world in its sensual being. Feeling this inner emptiness from being cut off, one feels driven to do something, to achieve some value to give oneself identity and purpose by linking up with something through this project. So, to stick with the same example, my self-worth will be dependent on making a sizable income. If I can identify myself with the value I see residing in money by possessing it and having at my disposal its powers, then I feel and think that I can gain the security lost by not being part of the earthbody dance, by not belonging fully to one's world. This need for this identification presses heavily: if I have the money or whatever the value is I am trying to achieve, then I *am* something, otherwise I am thrown back on my sense of emptiness, of being cut off, and I really experience myself as *nothing*. We call this feeling of nothing "being a failure." I can't have humor about myself or my goals and values, for these matters must work out or I will cease to exist. To achieve this goal and realize this value is a life or death issue, and not to see this is again to be frivolous, to fail to have the proper attitude of being compelled by this imperative, which is seriousness. This is the source of heaviness: the pressure and the blindness to alternatives of serious- ness that can easily erupt into violence towards others or towards ourselves, at least in psychologically "beating" ourselves.

Both these aspects of seriousness resulting from the distance from others and oneself feed into each other in a vicious feedback loop and increase the feel- ing of emptiness and pressure at the heart of this attitude. Because Nicholas has this feeling of distance from himself—that he doesn't know who he really is or what about himself there is to treasure—he must try grimly to "come out on top," whether in love with Alison or in his friendship and interaction with Conchis. Both relationships become contests in his mind. Whatever they do or feel is being mon- itored on some level for how it reflects on Nicholas's attempt to construct a more secure self as measured by the implicit praise others bestow upon him through their love or by being impressed with him or being intimidated by him—or whatever feeling of theirs he can manipulate at that instant. This monitoring, manipulating of himself towards the desired effect on others, and this constant measuring of worth are what deepens his sense of being watched, of being "in a play," and of hardly ever being able to just be present with others or even himself in the world. So, his distance from himself makes him unable to become enlivened by others in their being truly with him, as Alison openly offers to him at moments, like the one at the green pool of the mountain.

His dismissal of his own worth both frustrates and defends him from being enriched by a spontaneous interaction with others that would give him a deeper, flow- ing sense of himself, and open the avenues for partaking in a visceral sense of worth in belonging to the flow of forces on the planet. His self-denigration short-circuits this flow and closes him off from what he desperately needs. However, he fears this connection and defends himself against it. He refuses a dancing enrichment with others, since it feels dangerous as not being under his sense of control. This is the plight of many in our current culture that feeds the fantasy of constant control of the world technologically as symbol for control of existence itself. Unknown to himself by never really fully being who he is, this distance from himself becomes an unbridge- able gap upon which he is dependent for safety, as much as Lestat craves his security of distance, at the same time it is draining him of a spontaneous sense of self-worth.

The flip side of this is that Nicholas really doesn't know others anymore than he knows himself. Others for him are unknowable. As a consequence, their love for him is also unknown. He never really feels their feeling for him. Feelings become something private and mysterious, and thus even more dangerous to someone who has started this vicious cycle with a vast insecurity. If one has given up the sense of control to spontaneously be taken up in a tide of shared emotion and interaction with others, the shared feeling becomes palpably felt by all within the circle, just as the dancers are swept up into the shared dancing rhythm. Feelings are quite accessible, my own and others, but not by looking for them within myself or by scrutinizing others from a safe distance. In the opening up to the feeling flows, I discover both my feelings and the feelings of others through each other. So, paradoxically, in giving up the attempt to control, I feel more in control as part of the shared interaction, which is palpable and can be contributed to, even if not dominated. That feels much less frightening than "working in the dark," which is what it feels like when the person is cut off and so really doesn't know what he or she feels nor the feelings of others. At each turn, the withdrawal from insecurity only deepens the problem and the dreadful feelings, even if kept at a distance.

This fear of what the other really feels and thinks about the self, and this insecurity about who the self really is, fuel the ridicule of others. Nietzsche has Zarathustra say, as he is walking away from the town in which he tried to help its citizens but was met with ridicule, so no one really heard what he had to say, "there is ice in their laughter." Laughter can be this coldness of heart and this frozen inability to be moved in concert by others. This seeming good cheer on the surface is actually a jeer. A very effective and a less vulnerable way to express hostility towards another is to make them the butt of this kind of humor, an unkind sarcasm or a making light of what they are. This kind of laughter is the humor that our contemporary culture seems to enjoy and spread across the media. There is no person nor any part of their existence that is considered sacrosanct and not apt to be put up to this ridicule. How is this the result of seriousness?

What function does it serve to make light of another, whether their sense of self, their beliefs, their behavior, or their situation? What is the pay off for others? If we take what has gravity, has weight, or is the substance of that other person's or group's life and make it "light," then we have diminished their stature. If in our distanced manipulation of others and ourselves, we are locked into a competitive race for self-worth, then belittling the other makes me take on more weight by comparison. The sense of insecurity behind taking oneself so seriously can be relieved by making fun of others, although it is a bit of a scary game—for they might retaliate by doing it back. Actually, much of our humorous energy seems to go into these sorts of battles of indirect hostility.

This is a much different kind of laughter and humor than the laughter of closeness. Humor, instead of being distant potshots, can actually be the way to establish a greater closeness and relatedness with the other person. Or another way to put it is to contrast the difference between laughing at someone or something versus laughing with them or it. We naturally get offended or hurt when we are laughed at or something in which we believe or hold in reverence is laughed at, whereas laughing *with* others is inclusive and forges bonds. Even when we laugh with others about a doctrine we all hold in high regard, we are expressing possible difficulties, but in a community-building way that doesn't undercut our reverence. We laugh at things or people—ridicule them,—when we hold them at a distance and refuse any real relationship with them, denying whatever common ground or rhythm there is between us. This is why so-called good-humored fun in making jokes that are really gender, racial, or ethnic slurs do not seem funny to those who are the butt of such jokes. Rather, they can feel the distancing put between them and the others who make the jokes, and the hostility that supposedly is not really there but is actually quite palpable. There is a felt difference when someone may even make a very similar joke, but do it with a sense of laughing with each other, as a declaration of not taking oneself or the other seriously, or of refusing to remain in a competitive or hostile relationship, where one party's security comes by denigrating the other party's worth. Instead, both can laugh with each other in recognizing their being in life's struggle together.

It is the struggle of human life that is frustrating, maddening, depressing, but also, if seen from another vantage point, is humorous. There is something very funny about doing ridiculous things. As Aristotle pointed out, this incongruity in our actions and their consequences, especially unintended ones, can be very comic. This is the appeal of slapstick humor, which reduces our simplest physical actions into a series of obvious miscues. There is a way to see that whatever we do is in some sense ridiculous, and especially those very actions that most infuriate us: when we do something wrong and make ourselves fail in our endeavors. However, to see this and, especially to feel this, both emotionally and viscerally, takes a shift in our normal attitudes, even our habitual way of holding the posture of our bodies.

The word *humor* comes from Latin and Middle English roots that designate moisture or liquidity—as when in archaic medical practice physicians referred to the various liquids of the body as various humors. To be in a humorous mood or to allow humor to take hold of one and to laugh means that one has to lose that rigid solidity of seriousness. In this solidity, we feel rigid in asserting our purposes and values, and about the necessity of achieving the goals they dictate. We even hold our bodies upright and stiff when caught up in this seriousness, and feel as if even our skin and perceptual organs are hardened to a kind of impermeability to appeals that would divert us from achieving our task. We can't be open to the full presence of others in their complexity; that would cause us to wander from the one-track purposefulness of seriousness.

In humor, we become liquid. Our boundaries that we have fought to maintain dissolve. The most distracting elements, those that seemed most tangential and trivial in light of the formerly serious plans and goals we asserted, can flow into us and take us over. Inclusive humor is not pointed like ridiculing humor. It is pointless, in the sense of not trying to achieve anything practical, in not being an aggressive thrust or word stab, and has no definite direction in which to take us, but rather makes us lose our way—but merrily so. Within the deepest humor, we see that somehow all life is pointless, that no goal, no one achievement, is the be all and end all. From the widest perspective, it is all silly: like through the child's perspective, all can be seen to be a game, an amusing and fun game, and not a cutthroat competition with others or with oneself. When we are wrapped in seriousness, we can think that we are indispensable or have achieved something incomparable that will give us glory, but in the widest perspective, no monument stands forever. One day our sun will explode and all that is in this solar system will no longer exist. From this perspective, there is a humor of melting down from the directedness towards achievement and the becoming released from this one-track mind of the serious person. Then everything is important—the smallest aspect of life that calls out to us in vitality—and nothing that offers to join up with us in our humor of dissolved boundaries is too trivial or distracting to entertain at the moment.

This aspect of the humor of childlikeness is brilliantly captured by the Zen Buddhist anecdote of the master about to die, who tells his students that he has one last poem to compose with them. He recites the poem, which goes: "I have been selling water / all my life while sitting / on the bank of a great river." For the serious person, this could be a statement of despair, but one who has dissolved their pretensions, they, too, might be able to embrace the lightheartedness towards existence embodied in the last line, which the master added after a brief pause: "ho-ho-ho!" He died while still laughing.

If we enter the liquidity of this sort of humor, we also lose our boundaries with the world, whether with the natural world, other people, or the larger community. The safety of the consuming ghoul or the feeding vampire or the amused aesthete may actually be a bad joke on them. With their lack of humor, their safety is an impermeability which traps them inside themselves: "From the perspective of the clown, who refuses to take any limitations and demarcations with absolute seriousness, the moat that protects the king's castle is also the moat that imprisons the king."[13] The person who can laugh at their goals, at their achievements, and thus at the identity that is associated with these deeds, is free from building themselves up and fearing what others think of them or even what they may come to doubt about themselves. As an absorbing and beautiful game, if this person of humor performs their deeds with concentration and care, their actions take on a gracefulness of lightheartedness that dissolves boundaries with others. In contrast, the grimly serious person marches through life with rigid boundaries, perhaps as I suggested of masculine heroes, as if he or she is inside a tank. The aesthete who is covertly serious despite the outward show of taking everything lightly, is a kind of phantom—that is, until ones searches in the distance and sees this poor soul within their gloomy and impregnable castle, which doubles as a prison.

The ghouls who walk the countryside eating the living, the vampires like Lestat who prowl the night to feed off others, or the aesthetes like Kierkegaard's seducer or Fowles' Nicholas are all sunk into a self-absorption that they consider to be a self-sufficiency and control over others. They are driven towards escalating power of various sorts like moths to a flame. We are no less frightened by their laughter than we are by a predator's growl, perhaps even more frightened. Their laughter can be said to be "sick" humor, as we sometime describe it, and seen in this light, we can see why it can make us uncomfortable or terrified. If we think of contemporary societal equivalents, the compulsive consumers, the emotional life-suckers, and the psychically remote manipulators and operators, and think of their humor, even though we often gleefully indulge in it, we also might find within us a level of discomfort about this ridiculing of others. Whether making fun of those with less material wealth, or of those who are more emotionally present and therefore seem naïve to some, or about those who are idealistic about beliefs, we know we are being defensive and making mileage for ourselves in a disguised hostile and destructive way.

Whether we take literally the fascination with Hollywood images of ghouls, vampires, and the supernatural of horror films, and the equal fascination with the James Bonds, the Supermodels, and the galaxy of fast-moving seducers, or whether we consider the way they symbolize our own behaviors of endless consumption, emotional vampirism, and distancing psychological inaccessibility, they present us with a pervasive desire to avoid our being mired down in the everyday. We seek the exotic or something more or something that escapes the everyday. We hunger, are disconnected and destructive to others in trying to find something to replace the vacuum within us, created by not being delightfully caught up in the everyday events, people, and difficulties they present to us.

Probably no tradition has remained as pointed in its criticism of this seriousness and insistent on reconnecting to the wonder of the everyday than Zen Buddhism and its lineage of masters, who often appear to be jokesters or clowns. They don't promise any great wealth, pleasure, spiritual afterlife, miracles, or anything else, only that we when we eat and walk when we walk. They use humor about the everyday, because humor not only opens boundaries, but also is contagious, and allows to one feel childlike as one laughs. Humor mixes things up that the "yes or no" diabolical logic tries to keep separate. If one even tries to introduce some other realm where the satisfaction and wonder lie other than right here and now in the everyday, the Zen masters are utterly dismissive.

Yu-men, speaking of the mythic representation of Siddhartha Buddha pointing to the heavens and the earth, said: "If I had seen him at the time, I would have cut him down with my staff, and given his flesh to the dogs to eat, so that peace could prevail over all the world" (*LB*, 93). This anecdote is related by Conrad Hyers in his book *The Laughing Buddha* as he is trying to show how the humor of Zen returns us to a deep connection with everything around us:

> Many such Zen stories reflect the same suspicion and humorous skepticism of the goggling delight in the fabulous that is the perennial soil for the strange human fascination for wizards and magicians, witches and demons. For in excess such fascination provides too great a diversion from the principal human tasks and dilemmas, if not a camouflage of the real issues at hand, as well as what then become, by contrast, the commonplaces of human experience. (*LB*, 93)

Whether in a religious sense or in a societally driven sense, if people think there is something beyond life to save them from the everyday drudgery of life, the Zen Buddhist response is a laughter that not only dissolves the supposed distance from reality of this refuge from life, but also makes all who enter the laughter feel that the everyday is wondrous in its mixed-up messiness. This is the childlike feeling that all is wonderful fun.

This is why the proper answer Siddhartha Buddha sought from his students about the question of the wondrousness of the lotus flower was simply to smile and laugh and fully take in the flower, which only one student was able to do. The others pondered it as sign or symbol that stood for something else, missing, as our contemporary culture constantly does, "the suchness and wondrousness of things in themselves":

> As one master exclaimed, "The beauty of a mountain is that it is so much like a mountain, and of water that it is so much like water." This is the acceptance and celebration of things as they are: beyond and before thought of useful and useless, subject and object, mine and not-mine, good and bad, holy and unholy, marvelous and ordinary. (*LB*, 93)

The joke is on us: as John Barth said, the key to the treasure is the treasure itself. Yet, in our contemporary culture, BMWs, evening gowns, houses on the right side of the town, Air Jordans and a countless number of commodities, objects, events, and even relationships with other people are status symbols. They are meant only to point beyond themselves to some greater value. How silly in our seriousness! We feel anxious, driven, and intermittently depressed by this competition with ourselves and others, leading us to be ghouls, vampires, and aesthetes in wanting to be safe and yet win—to have our cake and eat it, too.

Rather, we could laugh that we can't control others or the events of our lives, that others will have an impact on us and change the steps of our course in unpredictable and unasked for ways, that just when we think we're home free in our success or victory we're probably heading back to the need to start over again, and that rather than keeping all these realities at a distance, we could dissolve into them and let their comic face smile into our own. This humor would be a kind of freedom from our own restless imprisonment within our psychic defenses, allowing us to viscerally celebrate ambiguity, to become fluidly able to join the flow of transformations around us, and to celebrate being part of the everyday, of the earth as a mere earthbody.

Chapter Four

Cyberspace: Rootedness versus Being in Orbit

Introduction: A Different Kind of Materialism

The one place where we currently seem to have our feet on the ground might be in our technological mastery of the earth and increasing diverse areas of our daily life. There are new medical breakthroughs announced almost daily on the evening news programs: scientists can move single atoms, animals have been cloned, fifty-year-old women have given birth, the information and communication revolutions move at blinding speed, cars have the ability to tell drivers where exactly on the planet they are and how to get to their destination, and so on in what seems an endless line of new scientific and technological marvels. This seems to most of us the payoff of our taking charge of the earth in its most manipulable aspects, perhaps as the modern stewards of the earth turning the biblical injunction in a direction perhaps not foreseen, but appearing to be very effective in creating order, efficiency, and a vast potential of material well-being for people.

Even if we acknowledge that perhaps we have created just as many problems in succeeding in our technological initiatives—problems of overcrowding, continued violence against each other, destruction of natural habitats and perhaps the biosphere itself, the invention of forces which could be used to destroy life on the planet as we know it, etc.,—we certainly have advanced in many aspects of our technological ability to deal with forces that were limiting to human aspiration. Whether sending spaceships to Venus or the moon, taking photos of the surface of Venus or the energy emerging from black holes, traveling about the globe in remarkably short time spans, increasing the life spans of humans, exploring the microscopic world, mapping our genes, manipulating the subatomic world, the advances have been astounding. Whether in some ultimate sense we have made progress and of what sort, and what the balance is against the drawbacks, are not the questions I wish to pose right now. Instead of judging the effects of this state of affairs, I would like first just to see where we are and how we experience our world from this vantage point. I would like to do this in a way that critically analyzes—and by this I mean seeing *both* the opportuni- ties and the dangers—aspects of technology from a more basic stand than we normally do: at the level of who learning are we as human beings through insights emerging in our relationship with technology. I also want to see what aspects of the world's reality we can come to see that we might not ordinarily see without this prod of our own technological creations. The Socratic questions about who we are as human beings might have new answers in response to technology.

What would seem apparent to most people is that increasingly secularized, increasingly industrially developed, and increasingly technologically saturated mod- ern life is solidly on earth, in touch with material life, and focused on doing as much as it can to ameliorate the daily material struggles of people. Yet, I would like to suggest that perhaps we are the least *materially* in touch age in history. For the ways in which we seem to be hard-core materialists—from the emphasis put on mate- rial goods as key to happiness in life, to the extent to which our resources of time, energy, concern, and wealth are focused on working on the material conditions of life, and to the belief of many that there only exists as real a materially determinate world and nothing else—we may have an impoverished idea of what the material of the world is. Insofar as being in tune with the materiality of the planet is to be part of its rhythm and community, we might say that we have left the planet already.

In his videotape and book, *The Global Brain*, Peter Russell suggests that human beings have become like cancer cells in the larger body of the Earth. His version of the Gaia hypothesis is similar to the vision of this book in that he sees the earth being one body, but not as a simple "oneness," but rather as an open sys- tem of an indeterminate number of very different beings and entities that never- theless play off one another to come to work as one system. Once again, this is a logic like that embodied by Matisse's dancers. Our unity or disunity is not a given, but a matter of an unfolding process and the impact we have upon that process. Being called cancer cells brings home this idea that we can be in the midst of some- thing, even vitally connected to it, and yet somehow not be *of* it at all, as being at odds with its self-regulating and enriching unfolding.

Cancer cells are not within our bodies as part of our body, insofar as they are blind to the needs of the entire system of interacting community members that make up "the body." They take what they need and not what is best for the whole system. That is why they can be removed: they are not part of the body's self-augmenting fabric, its flow, or its melody—they are discordant notes or noise, are obstacles to the flow, or a rip in the mesh of cells and organs. There is nothing evil or even destructive per se about cancer cells. They are just living in a vast interweaving process into which they are not integrated. They don't experience the rhythms of the whole as what determines their own flow and unfolding. They go counter to the established ways these other beings are interlocked in their unfolding processes, and so end up disrupting this whole or this larger melody. This is the way we can not be of the planet or on the earth or not part of the dance of beings around us.

Technology can be used to fold us into the rhythm and weave of the earth, but it can very much be used to absent us while we are here, to allow us to skip off into other rhythms that do not resonate with those through which we have found much nourishment during our history up to this point. The earth is not some pure "Nature." The earth as an open process incorporates cultural histories and new technologies into its rhythms and sense. However, not all change is transformative and potentially resonant. Unlike the analogy with the body, it may be that we can find other rhythms that would sustain us in new directions that really do break with the old. However, we may be damaging the larger rhythms in self-defeating ways analogous to the way in which eventually the cancer cells kill off their own host community. What is more likely is that instead of a stark "either/or," we are both finding some truly new and helpful directions and also being self-defeating and unnecessarily hurtful to some extent. It will be hard to tell in the midst of this process. However, we can do two things already at this point. First, we can discern carefully what melodies or rhythms with which we are parting ways and distinguish what is to be gained and lost by these partings. We also have choices we can make as to what directions we do want to pursue and with what angle of separation and with what speed, if we want to follow these new trajectories. It may be that we can also find new ways of reconnecting with older relationships.

Cyberspace: A Material and Embodied Place in the World

Of all the technologies transforming life, probably none is as powerful as the computer and its information revolution. Although computers have transformed much of world, from weather reports to security systems, probably no application has as much straightforward impact currently on our daily lives as the Internet. The amazing thing is that it seems to be doing so in a way that uncannily echoes the dominant images and metaphors of this book, a book about the nature of the body which started with Native American stories and focused on the natural world more than the cultural world and certainly not on the technological. The two components of the word, "inter" and "net," are both expressions of the kind of linking and joining that we have discussed as a new vision of the body as rhythmic energy field. Also, they are terms at odds with the either/or diabolical logic, which we criticized at the beginning of this work in order to conceive this rhythmic linking. This seems at first quite ironic, since the basis of the computer is circuits and switches that are probably the paradigmatic use in our current world of "yes" or "no," "one" or "zero," binary logic.

If we look closer, however, it is not ironic. Rather, it is an another example of how we cannot assess what things are by merely looking at their components: they become something other when they build up complexity and take on functions and meanings within the vast web of communications and interactivities of the planet. That this evolving communications system, moving from its original purpose of being a military tool, came to be known by the name "Internet" belies a dawning appreciation by those who made this name popular of what these circuits could become when placed within a larger, more open social context. The prefix, "inter," indicates senses such as "between," "among," "in the midst of," "mutually," "reciprocally," "together," and "during." These words or phrases all echo the sense of linking together, timing, and getting between what had seemed to be oppositions and boundaries.

The other part of the word, referring to a "net," is equally interesting. A net is a peculiar object. In one meaning, "net" refers to an object that isn't solid in some sense, but instead is made of threads or lines or trajectories that keep folding over each other, interweaving themselves, or enlacing with others such that they form a loose fabric or a kind of "spanned reality" despite the spaces. We still can see the strands, but they have formed a woven or synchronized community that can hold things or ensnare other things within their meshes. A net is already a kind of "inter" being—it exists as the spaces between things being spanned, not really counting as empty spaces, as we have been trying to explain about the body which, as part of a dance among differing beings, incorporates the so-called empty spaces between them—or at least what would seem to be between them by an either/or logic of definitive or impermeable boundaries. So in some sense, the name "inter-net" is doubly declaring that its being is "between the between." This is apt for an entity that exists in the "between" of people and in the "between" of people and the things of the world.

I think it would be helpful for a moment to consider what we have seen in this book so far about the nature of bodies seen from an earthbody perspective. The body as earthbody is a kind of movement that accesses a larger moving, rhythmic flow of energy and meaning among all beings on the planet, it operates by a "logic of inclusive difference." Since the body is a living body, it has to be seen in its dynamic dimension, where it is caught up in its activities, or rather it *is* its activities. Whether it is thinking, speaking, writing, building, loving, struggling, remembering, the body does so only by allowing currents of meaning, energy, purpose, information to flow through it from the world around it. The "I" can't generate thought, love, gracefulness, or any expressive or apprehending force from within itself out of itself like God, who could create something from nothing, but rather the thought comes *to* me, the love wells up *from within* the shared situation with the other—perhaps from the sight of their face's expression, which itself shines with the reflection of many of their deeds in the world—and takes me over, or the memory *lodged in* the landscape pops up like a rabbit before me. In other words, we do things by opening ourselves up to a circulatory flow that moves through the world which returns to us through the perceiving body enriched by these acquisitions—gifts of others and the world. This is why in one of the quotations we discussed Paula Gunn Allen thanks "wind and sky, the trees and rocks, sticks and the stars" for usually being "in a teaching mood" and granting her the ideas and feelings she has experienced. *The body itself is a kind of "internet."* After meanings have passed among all things and creatures, they are delivered to us through being part of the link.

The body's time, we saw, is not some quantity of instants moving along in some other dimension which traps us within it, but rather is the timing among all beings, which gives time its unfolding motion. As such we are also responsible for time and staying within the sensitive synchronization with others that is most open and creative. This responsiveness makes for different kinds of timing and therefore different forms of time. Time doesn't "happen" without our being part of its process, and "all of time"—the past, present, and future is now, as being "timed out" among us and other beings. Whether it's the big bang, or the creation of the heavens, earth, humans, and all other beings in God's creation, or your reading this page, or the heat death of our solar system, the events that have happened, are happening, and will happen are doing so in a way that we meet up with them now. This means that there is always more beings from all parts of timing which might enter this dance. Equally, there are partners of all phases of timing who may become lost and drop out of timing. Time shifts. We are responsible to give other beings "the time of day" and let as many aspects of the world be welcomed into the larger movement into meetings that comprise the process or unfolding of time as timing. This allows time to become as rich as possible. So, for example, when we acknowledge the history of the African-American slaves in this country struggling for their freedom, people who had been kept invisible to many, or when we speculate on other ways to see past events that even science uncovers, such as the life of dinosaurs, or when we see other ways to understand language not just as grammar and syntax, but also as affective behavior, we allow "more time" to occur in a richer timing with more facets of the world.

There couldn't be this constant transforming of identity and unfolding of meaning within time's unfolding as synchronizing if all beings didn't have a distinctive shape or form and if they didn't have a way to both encounter the difference of other beings and yet also join up with them. This incredible trick of both keeping some of identity while changing somewhat can only happen through the wonder of materiality. This gradual working through or transforming differs from the yes or no, one or zero, instantaneous shifts in moving from one state to another. The melting, metamorphosizing, and unfolding quality of "being held" into a form or shape while also being somewhat relinquished in a gradual transformational process is the marvelous property of materiality. In an instant we can go from one purely conceptual idea to another, but most material states require a process of change. We too have this attribute because we as bodies are material beings. Matter holds onto shape, is shaped, and yet with a certain flow moves into new shapes. It allows for process, a retaining of the past yet a changing. Far from being a dumb barrier to spirit, matter is the mother, the matrix, the medium for the art of existence as never-ending process and transformation.

Perception, when it is understood as the source of the openness to the material matrix, we also saw, is not a gathering of "inputs," but the entranceway to innumerable elongated journeys. This is also part of the wonder of materiality and the body: they are joined in a thickness. There are layers and interweavings in which many can be held together and yet still be different too—like a twenty-layer cake of different kinds of cake, flavors, fillings, and icings that can still be discerned and that can be eaten together, with all ingredients adding something to the overall experience of the cake. Perception is the access to the way materiality holds together these multiple interwoven layers of meaning and the varied ways we have of teasing out these layers of meaning. By letting ourselves go into the mesh of perception we can become enmeshed in the other powers of mind/body, for it is the soil out of which they grow and transform, as we traced earlier. The most simple sensible quality can connect up to the most elongated and diverse paths of significance, if we choose to let go and linger with all the reverberations that are packed into each experience of the senses. Although Proust's narrator in *Remembrance of Things Past* or Willa Cather's archbishop may have been more artful in the passages we explored than most of us are much of the time, like them, we could journey with fragrances and colors, sounds or textures to far distant places in time and space, or to worlds imagined or felt or remembered or anticipated.

I can imagine some readers protesting that we have to distinguish the "reality" of the past versus the present or distinguish a journey to Rome made "in person" from one made within the pealing of a bell that transports one to Rome while lying in bed in New Mexico. There are certain problems we have to solve intellectually or practically for which this is the appropriate response: finding the right size of gap for the spark plugs in my car, for example, in the old days of more primitive ignition systems was one task and problem that always hit me with its need for precision of this sort of sheer physical presence or absence. However, for most kinds of understanding these other senses of presence are equally or even more important: whether the archbishop's sense that the reverberation of the bell has some quality that makes present to him the sense of the reverberation among people and living beings—which for him has something to do with God's benevolence in the creation—or whether the bell's tone makes real and present the history and tradition of the religion that has been located in Rome of which he is part, or whether like for Proust's narrator (and for most people in most cultures) there is something in the appearance of flower blossoms and their quality of color that is festive and uplifting, the dimensions of meaning are brought to us, made manifest to us, and held for further encounters within the qualities of the material world. As we have seen throughout this book, listening to the quality of our experience as earthbodies, instead of going with the prejudice of our culture that takes the case of spark plugs and diabolical logic to define reality as characterless masses in motion, there is a kind of flow of meaning and reality that has no firm, unchanging foundation beneath it, but that permeates matter in a rich but indeterminate way. At this point in the book, looking at cyberspace will help us understand how this makes cyberspace possible and how the characteristics of cyberspace may help us see beyond our traditional prejudices.

If this book has succeeded up to this point, the reader should have some sense of the body as a power of moving throughout the world it inhabits, because the body as woven into the world resonates with or reverberates with streams of significance that are located within the materiality of the world as conductive currents. Things don't block us, other people don't brutely bump up against us, and animals don't mechanically move about us. This is really a simpleminded view of reality that our philosophy has foisted upon us, especially in the Anglo-American tradition. The rock, for example, communicates some sense of tranquil solidity and centeredness, the other person's posture or their eyes move us into a felt sharing of their palpable suffering, or we feel the soaring through the sky by our body's resonance with the bird circling overhead—at least they do if we sensitively open up to all the meaning that's packed into our sensing of them. This is what the "logic of inclusive differences" symbolized at the opening of this book by Matisse's dancing women means in rethinking the body: leaving behind the idea of the body as merely a mass of biological stuff enclosed in a skin and instead seeing the body as the power within a moving, communicating, and transforming circulation through dimensions of the world. So, in some very real sense all these things, institutions, creatures, people, etc., are "part" of my body: not as some gigantic unity or ONE—which would be to stick with the same old logic—but as linkages and circulations. This movement is *asymmetrical*. I am "more" inhabiting my own flesh than yours, the dogs, the rocks, or whatever else. However, even this, too, is a continuum. It is a fuzzy phenomenon, since I also am somewhat unknown and opaque to myself on all levels and find myself at times "more internal" to myself and at other times utterly absorbed in the ocean waves, or the color of the flowers, or in the other person's feelings.

The space which connects people on the Internet isn't really a space in the Cartesian sense of the extended distance on a physical grid of locations. Yet, it has become a very real space. With this earthbody understanding of the body and matter, we can understand how there can be a "space" that is "real" within "cyberspace" (the term aptly coined by William Gibson in 1984). D. H. Lawrence, in his poem "Space," says that space is that liveliness that moves us about or that pulsation which moves from the world into our hearts:

> Space, of course, is alive
> that's why it moves about;
> and that's what makes it eternally unstuffy
> And somewhere it has a wild heart
> that sends pulses through me.[1]

Space is not a void between objects understood as mere stuff, but rather the openness anywhere that crackles with vitality, emotion, and meaning. This openness is not just between things, but is often within things, and not just within things in the simplistic sense of having physical volume to enter. Within the words of a book, for example, there is space: a much different space within Melville's *Moby Dick* than within Toni Morrison's *Beloved*. The first is a wild, swirling space above and below the ocean, swaying on deck and below deck, charged with tension among a multinational crew and a madman that ends bringing together man and animal, earth and sky, and yet threatening them with a vortex. This quality that can't be defined and I have only quickly alluded to is a unique space. The other book opens a space of oppression and cruelty, courage and kinship, insanity in the face of crushing violation and redemption in love and determination: another distinctive space.

There are kinds of space in different people's speech, in different city's habits and temperaments, within corporations and professions, such as legal spaces or medical ones. Dilbert, the enormously popular cartoon character, captures the "cubicle space" of middle-level workers in those corporate spaces, and that does not mean the literal distance between those partitioned walls. New York City's space is much different than the space of a small town in Kansas and that again is not about square footage, but a kind of electricity and commerce, a crowding of different enthnicities versus a rural space where clouds and natural landscape dominate even in the middle of town. We have various slang expressions that refer to "my space" or to an oppressive space in which people can find themselves. We think of these expressions as mere metaphors, but actually they point to a *primary reality* of our experiences, as earthbodies who dwell or inhabit places, not just take up some bare space. Having the bodies we've described throughout this book, those bodies move in joy, in pain, in sadness, in liveliness, etc., constantly through these spaces.

Currently, one of the most fascinating of these spaces is cyberspace. As the way I can bring these perceptual, emotional, imaginative, thoughtful, and remembering interwoven senses to bear in specific expressions, this is the power of my body in action. My body inhabits or moves into or takes up cyberspace in many ways. One of the main misconceptions about cyberspace is that it is a disembodied experience. If our bodies were merely lumps of matter, surely that kind of body couldn't "fit inside" cyberspace. *The bodies that we are, earthbodies*, that fly through the sky in our resonance with birds or live at the heart within rocks of stability and tranquillity, or by reading *Beloved* emerge into the world of slaves escaping from the South, *move right into cyberspace*.

Given the Western prejudice we explored earlier in this book that the "I" is not the body and will be trapped by the body—crucified by it—to be caught in a cycle of death and suffering with the mere brute and perishable matter, it is not surprising that one of the most exciting aspects for people about the whole idea of cyberspace is that it is a place where one can go to do things and meet others while leaving the body out of the picture. Stephen Talbott, in *The Future Does Not Compute*, discusses groups like "DigitaLiberty," who believe that cyberspace will be a place of infinitely extensible freedom and community based on individual liberty.[2] Talbott calls the beliefs of these people a "discarnate utopianism." It is part of the appeal of cyberspace that it is not an embodied realm. Howard Rheingold, one of cyberspace's greatest champions, starts his book, *The Virtual Community: Homesteading on the Electronic Frontier*, with a representative statement; "people in virtual communities do just about everything people do in real life, but we leave our bodies behind."[3] Certainly, in some important aspects of our embodiment are screened out by the on-line experience, and we will need to identify exactly what they are and what opportunities and dangers their absence portends for us, but first it is important to see that there can only be a "space" of cyberspace because it is a place we can inhabit with our bodies in this fluid, energetic, and circulatory sense of earthbody. Once we see this, it will help us explain a lot of what happens on-line to people.

In addition, seeing the bodily dimension of cyberspace will halt some claims in their tracks and, on the other hand, allow deeper understandings of the potential of on-line experience in a way that can then be integrated with our off-line experience or "in real life", IRL, as it is called in cyberspace. The phrase "in real life" points to a third advantage we may gain by looking carefully at how cyberspace has upset some widely accepted definitions used by our culture: by seeing the role of the body more clearly, we can have a richer definition of "reality" and "real life" that will help us understand our current overall experience—better, not just "on-line" but the rest of our lives, too. John Perry Barlow, co-founder of the Electronic Frontier Foundation, states: "Any time you've got a large number of people going somewhere where they can't take their bodies, you're engaged in spiritual activity. It's that simple. . . . It's not what we had in mind, but something is happening."[4] Well, Barlow is wrong. It is not that simple. In some ways cyberspace is a very embodied space and in some ways it's not. Spirituality, as this book is attempting to articulate, is also not a matter of leaving the body behind. This body (or matter) versus spirit dualism has been one of the most destructive pieces of the diabolical logic used in our tradition to defeat spirituality.

Sherry Turkle summarizes the comments of many people interviewed about their internet experience: in *Life on the Screen: Identity in the Age of the Internet*,: "Many people who engage in netsex say they are constantly surprised by how emotionally and physically powerful it can be. They insist that it demonstrates the truth of the adage that ninety percent of sex takes place in the mind."[5] Well, actually, as we have seen in chapter two, what this demonstrates is that erotic sex is about an experience of the body not as a mass of biological materials, but of the body as communicative gateway for a host of thoughts, feelings, imaginings, attitudes, memories, etc. The body as a material being inserted through perception into the rich significance of the material world opens a realm in which there is neither detached mind nor purely brute sense of matter as physical masses. Neither a mental substance nor a purely physical one could have erotic, moving, and communicative sex. However, earthbodies with multiple levels of sense and rhythmically gesturing ways of passing that sense on to others can find almost infinite ways of being erotically expressive, including Netsex. The Internet helps us see the body as a dynamic phenomenon caught up in the material life of the planet; it is about a medium of dreams and feelings, as much it is about agents of chemical and physical interactions.

We have already explored how erotic excitement is about an enlivening, playful, affirming, dispersing energy flow that moves into the visceral thickness of the body by intensifying its perceptual field. Textures, smells, rhythms, and all sensory qualities can become charged when swept up into erotic gestures. Matter becomes electric. The charge has always been there, but it is experienced more fully. The reverse works, too. Matter itself can electrify us into the erotic spell, if we give it concentrated attention. That is why eating foods with a certain openness to the richness of their sensory qualities can be erotic, or looking at a sculpture or a painting, or even just the color and texture of a fabric. Certainly, when another person opens our senses to the charge of our own bodies by stroking our skin, the body becomes enlivened and draws us into its richness, but it spills beyond the body itself. Objects or other experiences communicate the erotic, whether through the smell, texture and color of flowers, the speed, vibration, and gracefulness of a motor-cycle rider or the splendor of the crashing waves on the shore. In erotic experience, we become expanded and richer and more fluid and more multiple by becoming more intensely taken up with all around us that speaks to our body's perceptions. We find ourselves dispersing into the multiple dancing partners within us that can match up with these inviting flows as they rhythmically move through us.

Cyberspace is another conduit—a more constricted one—for these flows of energy. What is tough to understand about a lot of cybersex eroticism is that it happens through words typed on a screen. Despite our fascination with words, we don't appreciate that they too are part of the planet's dynamic materiality. Our bodies' energies can flow through words. Each word is in part a microcosmic "virtual world." Words that express eroticism or other feelings come from the depth of earthbodies with a thickness of entwined emotion, imagination, memory, sensation, etc., as part of their trajectory and energy. A book is a virtual world as much as on-line experiences are, and it is made of words assembled on a page. Each word is not merely itself in the sense of being physically comprised of brute matter. Neither are words just some shorthand for concepts encoded in them in various combinations. Words are conveyors, "magic carpets" we could say, that take us in varied directions. One word may have many directions and journeys packed into it, and many more when it is combined with others. Language does not point to itself, as many modern theories in the past few decades have asserted, but points outside language, to its gaps through which currents move from the rich surrounding world, especially when language is most expressive. Erotic language certainly points beyond language to the sheer thrill of certain aspects of the material world. Rich colors, textures, rhythms, shapes move through the language to transform our resonance with things.

The rules used to combine these words, the language's syntax and grammar, also do not wholly decide where these words will take us. It is the particular inflection or twist that each person gives to their words that equally gives the whole an overall sense of what is being stated or suggested or protested or proposed or appreciated, etc. This unique sense expressed by the person is carried in the way the words flow or have rhythm or a tone that has deviated from the unswerving standard usage—this hypothetical standard usage that a being with no loves or hates, excitements or special interests, psychological defenses or strengths would somehow employ in putting down word after word solely on the basis of a prescribed meaning or reference. Instead, our word usage, whether spoken or even typed on a page or a screen, twists and turns, dives and swoops, meanders and moves in rhythms that follow the contours of our loves and hates, fears and joys, prejudices and character qualities, background perspectives and motivating interests, etc. This tracking of rhythms and emotional movements encircles the person to whom our words are addressed.

Yet another way to convey this is to say that words can be bodily organs. They can be saturated with sensory qualities, rhythms, directions, fantasies, feelings, etc., if we do not dry them out. We can use words in such a way that we don't put these rhythms and flows and feelings into them, and then they are not expressive this way. But if we dare, of course we can light up the room, the other, or make love with our partners just through words. So, Netsex is not surprising, even the kind comprised by "mere" typed words. This does not show that sex or cyberspace is a "merely mental" thing. Rather, it shows words, images, pictures, can carry for us the dream energy of matter and bodies as dynamic patternings. Cyberspace is another avenue for this movement to circulate among us.

This is what is amazing about humans: their minds are of their bodies and caught up in its flow with the world around it. The "flesh" of earthbodies as we have been gradually describing it in its properties throughout this book is "thick." Its thickness is not a matter of layers of cells, but this circulating of meaning through the material of things. It is thick in that colors are lined with feelings that are lined with memories, which are lined with ranges of images and fantasies, which are lined with different thoughts, etc. The philosopher whose work is behind much of the thinking in this book, Merleau-Ponty, called this overlapping and layering of kinds of significance, "the flesh of the world." He said it was neither just matter or spirit, neither physical nor mental, but something in between and in motion, for which Western philosophy and culture had no name.[5] Since each sensual experience is thick with memories and with imagined scenes and with historical echoes and with ideas and with feelings and emotions, etc, if one points to one part of this on one layer and evokes it well, the other interplaying meanings resonate, too.

Merleau-Ponty's example is seeing a patch of red, which he says is also at that moment the vision of the tiles of rooftops (which in Paris were red), the sight of soil down south in France, the flags of gatekeepers and the Russian Revolution, the red garments of professors, bishops, advocate generals, and a certain historical group of gypsies that were in Paris, the eternal feminine from the conceptual realms, a realm of anger from the felt realm, or the fires of hell as imagined, etc. One could continue indefinitely. The meanings layered within each red percept which bounce around or dance with other reds of all sorts would be different somewhat for each person, given their cultural, historical, and personal context. However, it is this vibrating or dancing among all these interwoven senses when one apprehends something through the body that allows words in a sentence or colors on a canvas or a gestured pantomime to have such a thickness of meaning. When the other person types certain words on the screen, especially if they do so artfully in distinctive ways that call up shared contexts, resonates with them, then these meanings will also be reverberating within the words and Netsex is possible.

Of course, there is a very large difference in felt experience in actually making love with another person in the flesh and by using words over a telephone or on a screen through letters. When in the presence of the other's body, there is a richness of sensual experience that potentially overflows boundaries. Since, as we have explained throughout his book, emotions, thoughts, memories, fantasies, imaginings, feelings, intuitions, etc., are grounded within or woven into the perceptual sense that is given to us, the direct presence of the other flows into our sensual awareness and plays off all these other overlapping levels of being aware of the other, as if they are receiving constant fresh charges of energy and significance. Of course, as we have also been demonstrating throughout this book, "presence" being fully taken in, becoming a reality, is not a given or a freebie. It is not a matter of mere physical proximity. It requires an attention, an openness which is about letting go and being grateful, an allowing of the body to take up rhythms, a sensitivity that has to be learned and deepened through practice, and a willingness to be taken in directions that were not what one planned or hoped to control. If one has this willingness, matter has the density to hold the multiplicity of sensory openings and linkages through its qualities to take us on enriched multilayered experiences. The possibility to delve further into reaches of the psyche of the other within sensory openings, when confronted directly with the material presence of the other person or with their lining of emotion, feeling, thought, fantasy, etc., means that a screen interaction of any sort or Netsex will never be the same involving and transformative experience as the body-to-body experience. On the Net, what we are given is limited. Its parameters are set out in advance. We are dealing with the other's presentation, not with their open and inexhaustible presence.

Moreover, when face to face, or body to body, there is such a richness of possible perceptual experiences flowing towards one that not only is the person who opens himself or herself to the experience not in control of the flow of experiences that unfolds, but certainly the other person, in being perceived, is not in control over what aspects of him or her are being witnessed. Of course, we can try to influence or even manipulate the other person to focus on this or that part of us, but we express so much more than we are even aware of that this is an impossible project. Obviously, for many people this is the appeal of presenting themselves through words, whether in the past it be through postal letters or now much more accessibly and interactively, through words typed on a screen. Here, it does seem more manageable to dictate what the other person will experience. It is easier to hide and attempt to manipulate. However, even words, having all the intertwined significance we just discussed, will sometimes tell a person a lot more about us than we intended with their use. So the cyberspace experience is richer than our traditional view of reality would allow, but it is still "safer" or more manageable than direct presence. In other words, the Internet is much closer to the aesthete's dream of just presenting what he wants to present to others and control the extent of the interaction—a theme to which we will shortly return.

It is this "middle position" of dynamic earthbodies using words or other means of mediated expression that are neither "mere body" nor "purely mental," but rather the overlapping of the sensual with all other ways of apprehending and expressing, which makes Netsex powerful. Since the screen representations evoke all the entwined levels of meaning associated with certain words and situations portrayed verbally or pictorially, they immerse us into experiences that are fuller than those that would happen through a pure decoding of information by an abstract intellect. Although Turkle has many fine insights into on-line experience, she is wrong when she asserts, "The computer takes us beyond a world of dreams and beasts because it enables us to contemplate life that exists apart from bodies."(*LS*, 2). Rather, the computer is so powerful in all its simulations and "cyber-communal" experiences that Turkle documents throughout her book because it is a space in which beasts and dreams still lurk, a place in which the body still flows with its rich emotional, imaginative, intuitive, and sensual being in its "prolonged" or "extended" sense. The body is still there, just a shallower version, as if it had to "stretch out" its extent.

The Virtual Is the Heart of Reality

With the proliferation of computer graphics and Internet interaction with others, the power of "virtual experience" has been startling for many. Turkle focuses much of her book on the experiences of those who have spent a lot of time on-line in "MUDs"—multi-user domains. A MUD is where a group of people set up an ongoing environment with on-line identities, houses, and roles within the partic- ular cyber-society, which often has the form of some sort of game. For most par- ticipants, however, the game aspect is an excuse to spend time with others inter- acting in their newly constructed computer identities. Turkle studies many people who have used the Net much more extensively than most, but this may reveal what others seek in smaller doses. After following in much detail many of these case his- tories, Turkle states: "In sum, MUDs blur the boundaries between self and game, self and role, self and simulation. One player says, 'You are what you pretend to be . . .you are what you play'" (*LS*, 192). What many of the players in these games or communities find is that the line between "the real" and the "virtual" has become very blurred or even that the reality of their lives seems unreal compared to their experience on-line: "This is more real than my real life," said a man who was "play- ing" at being a woman pretending to be a man on-line (*LS*, 199). This sentiment is echoed by many of the people Turkle interviewed.

The fact that this virtual dimension is so easily accessible physically, (it can be layered in the Windows presentation of the computer terminal, in front of which many people spend their days in their occupational tasks), and is also psychologi- cally easier (by way of the technological structures which make it possible for the machine to do the work of opening up this virtual world instead of our relying on our imaginative powers), has brought virtuality to our attention in a new way. The dramatic sensory effects, displayed in myriad startling details—which are made pos- sible by the microprocessors' incredibly swift manipulation of data—or other visual or auditory effects, coupled with the feat that it spans distances so dramatically and conveniently has brought the virtual into a different kind of limelight. Internet vir- tual worlds also offer the benefit of being stored by the computer to be reaccessed— much like a book "stores" or "holds" a virtual world in its words, to which we can return at our convenience. Given our traditional prejudices, that what seems "purely physical" seems more real, and that the computer *seems* to have made the virtual into something physically palpable, now we can believe in it and become excited by it.

However, the virtual is what it's always been, even if we haven't noticed how virtual is reality. It is not "literally" there—not in the pixels in front of us or in the words on the page or in the motions on the theater stage. The identity of a person in an on-line MUD or in a chat-group or in the land of Myst, Kafka's gigantic cockroach who used to be Gregor or Shakespeare's Hamlet or Ophelia, are not "purely physically" anywhere, but neither for that matter are you, the reader, or me, the writer. The so-called virtual is just that extension of the material being of the world that comes to show itself through the earthbody sense that combines the perceptual, the sensual, the imaginary, the emotional, the intuitive, the fantasized, the conceptual, the reflective, etc., in one dancing, interplaying combination. In some sense, it is what has been the focus of this book, although not named as such. For "where" *literally* is the "dance" of Matisse's dancers? If it were in "real life," then "literally" there would only be bodies in motion of a certain velocity and direction. However, a "dance" is more than that: its virtual dimension is the key to its reality. This is Suzanne Langer's point in *Feeling and Form*, that all the arts are virtual. As for our continual references to a *painting* of a dance, which nevertheless presents us in a very palpable way with a dance, it is a virtual rendering of a virtual happening. It is vital to this book to experience something twice removed into virtuality.

When in his last play, *the Tempest*, Shakespeare declares in the last act that "we are such stuff as dreams are made on," he is indicating the virtuality of reality. Shakespeare is pointing to the fact that not only his characters, from Prospero to Romeo and Juliet, are a fabric of ideas, images, feelings, etc., but so is "William Shakespeare-ness" or "Caesar" or any person. We can never pin down exactly what they are. Whatever does comprise their identity is this strange compound. So, we could say that the real is virtual, or at least shot through and through with the virtual. Or, we could say that the virtual is not virtual, but rather is real, or at least is a vital part of everything meaningful that we understand as real. Computers are just making obvious what Shakespeare tried to show people, which was probably made all the more evident for him by spending his life involved with the power of theater. Hamlet or Ophelia can be a very real presence at times, and, at times, whatever we have thought we are actually can seem to be a mere dream. However, most of life is somewhere uneasily between where reality and virtuality are as opposite poles on a continuum of experiences. However, some experiences tend more towards one or the other pole and may fluctuate at different moments during the duration of the experience. Death certainly is the experience most crushingly tending towards the factual pole, undeniable and unchangeable, but even death is not absolute in that others can experience the ongoing presence of the deceased person, for example. Without experiencing ghosts, most of us experience the virtuality of the ongoing presence of the deceased, and they may impact heavily on "real life."

There is not any one characteristic or fact or set of them that constitutes the reality of what a person is. An interesting example of this was raised when John Brady, Ronald Reagan's press secretary, was shot in the head during the attempted assassination of Reagan. When he was finally able to return to the White House in a limited capacity, still hobbled by his injuries, *Newsweek* ran an intriguing article. He said that although, physically, Brady was back in the White House, in some sense Brady was not yet back. *Newsweek* noted that Brady had

had a certain way of handling questions, had a certain manner of dealing with people, a certain kind of humor, and it speculated that these indefinable, but very palpable, attributes had not yet returned to Brady and might never return. Without this certain quality, he might never be the same person the press had gotten to know before the shooting. This is what Merleau-Ponty called a person's "style" and he, too, thought it constituted their real identity.[7] Whether it is their gait, their manner of gesturing, or their use of language, there is a certain relationship to the world and to others that is expressed in a certain manner of entering into these other relationships that permeates all aspects of their existence. This manner of relating can be felt by the perceiving bodies of others. This quality of relating is more than the sum of any particular action or attitude that one expresses. Furthermore, it is not something under one's control or a product of will or intention—at least not directly. As with the dance, whose spirit comes over the dancers, or the "dance madness" that infected the town of Swift Creek in the Wintu tale we discussed, or an insightful thought or a graceful action or a feeling of joyousness, this quality "comes over" us, comes circulating "through" us in its streaming through the world. However, the way or the manner we have of channeling it or receiving it also shapes it, and is the distinctive mark of each person.

The *Newsweek* article concluded that there was nothing specifically quantifiable or just simply present in John Brady before that was now missing, but rather that this manner of relating to the world was a "certain way of happening." Such a phrase is a wonderful expression of how the missing identity is the manner in which the person is a dynamic process and is something outside of a willed set of deeds. This is exactly what the Taoists mean when they say the reality of the person, the reality of the world, and the reality of "the ten thousand things" (all the specific beings of the universe) is the Tao, which means the "way." The "way" of anything is what it is. Similarly, in his tribute to W. B. Yeats, "In Memory of W. B. Yeats," W. H. Auden writes that in Yeats's dying, what is gone from the world is "a way of happening, a mouth."[8] The mouth here means a way of speaking, a way of using language and forming images, part of Yeats's distinctive way of happening. These thoughts should make us realize that our identities are always "virtual," as a certain manner of being a process and of being shaped by the world. This is what life on the Internet can bring to our attention.

The same is true for objects, such as "the computer" or the "house" or entities like "The United States" or "New York City." There is not one exhaustive set of purely physically present characteristics that when added up fully comprise their identity. Also, we notice that this identity constantly shifts given historical, cultural, and personal contexts. New York City is not just a certain piece of land or a set of buildings and people, etc., but an "atmosphere," a way that things happen in conversations, in conducting business, in having friends, and in walking down the street, which is different from Paris, Rome, or Los Angeles. The same is true for "the United States." For some, it is the "land of opportunity," for others "the bastion of democracy," for others "the center of materialism and consumerism," or for yet others in the Middle East, "the land of immoral infidels" in opposition to the Holy, and all of these apprehensions are somewhat right and are not mere "subjective" phenomena. Actually, the United States' identity is a *current* made of all the facts about it, and of all these and other virtualities. Similarly, a house is not just a structure of rooms, floors, windows and a roof, but a whole way of being sheltered, brought together, made comfortable, etc. If our house or car is destroyed, it is not enough to physically replace it bit by bit perfectly, but somehow there is a devastating loss tied up with our identity, security, and sense of well-being caused by its being destroying, because its reality was intertwined in many virtual dimensions vital to that "way of happening" of our lives. We are not separate from our home, city, car, or country as one object, a subject, from a set of other objects. Instead, we are woven into the fabric of all these things in the virtual dimension of the real.

Probably one of the most blatant examples of this emotionally charged virtual dimension of our sense of self is the modern-day obsession with sport's teams. A whole city can be depressed because on a piece of Astroturf, a few men carried a leather sphere across a line on the ground or some other man hit a spherical object over a wooden barrier. In terms of "mere physical events," unlike a tornado which directly destroys many homes and kills many people, or the discovery of a toxic substance in a city's drinking water that threatens the health of millions, or the closing of a corporation that will put several thousand people out of work, nothing has happened with much practical import—except insofar as the virtual gets reabsorbed back into the actual and practical fabric of life and does have practical consequences. However, that is not the immediate source of upset and pain. The happenings on football fields or in basketball palaces are as "unreal" as the worlds of Super Mario Brothers or that of Myst, but they soon become as "real" as anything else, since the virtual feeds into the real and the real feeds into the virtual and they are a woven fabric—just as Shakespeare so aptly phrased it.

Given the sparsest material enactments, highly charged layers of feeling, emotion, sensuality, excitement, fantasy, imagination, memory, etc., can be woven into the fabric which is our actual world (of both the virtual and the real). We all knew this as children, when a piece of clay or a mound of dirt could become cities or magical lands, where heroes and heroines could live and die in the movement of dolls or games of wooden blocks. These virtual powers aren't fully extinguished as we get older and become responsible adults, nor do they disappear from the so-called sophisticated and enlightened cultural institutions that are sober, adult agents: they go underground and become disguised, but they are always there to be accessed.

Access to our virtual worlds often happens as a result of manipulation by others within our current culture, given that our traditional map of reality hides from us our awareness of this virtual dimension of our lives. Lacking in us are the familiarity with, the sensitivity to, and the practiced artistry of using these dimensions creatively. Yet others can appeal to them in us without our becoming aware of why we are responding the way we are. Whether it is casting a military action that has lost all ground in what is actually occurring in terms of mythical confrontations, or a consumer object in terms of a far off never, never land of enchantment, there are many ways we are manipulated by appeal to the virtual. Part of our gullibility to these manipulations is our impoverished view of the reality of the world as mere physical masses. Since we do not recognize and become masters at playing with the virtuality of our reality, we are made victims.

What the new attention brought by cyberspace and the Internet to the virtuality of the world can show us is how constricted our view of reality has been. Voices from the arts or philosophy that have tried to open us more to these dimensions of experience, whether providing virtual worlds through mythic explorations, novels, the stage, operas, etc. However, it is not only the arts or philosophy that have provided such regions to explore in the past. There have been many types of group fantasy games that kept open these virtual worlds for people—fantasy football or baseball leagues, Dungeons and Dragon games, or groups that performed rituals or ceremonies together, as well as much of the entertainment arena. If we were to become more aware of our need for the virtual and its power in shaping the meaning of the actual, then we could devote ourselves to cultivating virtual worlds to augment the meaning of our lives. Furthermore, if we were to really focus on the characteristics of the virtual, we could start to distinguish among various virtualities and ways of coming to experience them in order to understand much better how to use imagination, emotion, memory, intuition etc., in the virtual realm to make us more capable, vital, and enriched. We would see that the need we recognize for our children to hear bedtime stories or to entertain the coming of Santa Claus is a need for the virtual that adults have, too. This need can then be explored in light of the question that has always arisen about people's fascination with the virtual and that which now has arisen in response to people spending a lot of time on the Internet or playing in virtual simulation games: why, for some people, does it seem to add to their self-esteem, enjoyment of life, and meaningfulness, and why, for others can it be draining, or fall into the same self-destructive patterns as encountered in their "real life" existences, or become a mere escape from the difficulties that beset their lives with no relief or solution being gained?

The provisional answer to this question has to do with the inherent wisdom of our "common sense" response of limiting people's fascination with the virtual. When we imagine, when we fantasize, when we play at being something, when we exercise certain feelings we haven't had much experience with before, even in regard to simulated situations, there is a power that can be transforming. Given our traditional philosophical perspective and its logic that we have critiqued throughout this book, this should seem strange. If reality were just the brutely physical and tangible, then merely feeling, imagining, and playing shouldn't really affect reality, which is solid and substantial. Given our traditional way of seeing the world, we assume the only change that can occur is a subjective one: we have started to feel feelings which don't refer to anything and are internal bad habits or corruptions. We blame ourselves for being "weak" and caring more about the "make-believe" than the real. We feel like the changes are a matter of choice and can be simply reversed through "will power" and "proper discipline." Yet, perhaps, there is no captain above the ship (to use Descartes' metaphor for the indivisible core of self above the body, its emotions, sensations, and imaginings) outside of the experiences through which we pass, if we pass through them fully, that is to say, wholeheartedly.

In Hermann Hesse's *Steppenwolf*, the protagonist, Harry Haller, is stuck in a rut. He is at a loss for meaning in his life, despite his erudition and sensitivity. Later, he meets Pablo, who introduces him to the Magic Theater, a place which may be entered through drug-induced hallucinations, simulations with others playing along together in elaborate games or psychodramas, elaborate guided imaginings, or some other way of journeying to transformative spaces. The precise identity of the Magic Theater is never clear and is not important to Hesse. The experiences undergone there change who Harry is, as presumably the others who have set up the Magic Theater have become transformed before him. This is the idea behind Jungian "active imagining" or Gestalt therapy's imaginative enactments of dreams, feelings, and bodily states. Once one fully experiences these virtual happenings, the person becomes transformed and capable of feeling emotions, carrying out actions, and having sensations he or she could not have had previously. However, to state it this way, even though implying that the self is something changeable through imaginative and emotional passages, still focuses only on the virtuality of *personal identity* and not on how the *world itself* is virtual. That is a further step.

These transformational experiences, however, do suggest that the person has no unchangeable core or firm foundation, and can be altered by the power of the virtual, because in some sense they are "but the stuff that dreams are made of." This is also what Conchis is trying to teach our friend, Nicholas, in Fowles's *The Magus*: that each of the imagined psychodramas his cast is performing has the power to alter Nicholas from his rigid, detached psychological dead end, if he will allow himself to enter them in the proper "play spirit." This, however, is exactly what makes Nicholas panic: he realizes these "mere games" threaten the identity that he thought was firmly his, but he now can feel slipping away. His fight with Conchis is to prove the virtual is limited in power versus his underlying core of self and identity.

More frightening that the lack of substantial self is the simultaneous changes in the shape and reality of the world. It, too, has become something else that it was originally. The world is but the stuff of dreams, too. To return to an example that seems to be "firmly anchored in reality," let's return to the example of New York City, which as I write this book has undergone a renaissance from its plight and its identity of a decade ago. At one point, it was city of crime, of nasty people, of decay, of snobbery, of urban blight, it had a certain powerfully negative identity for many people in this country, which then also affected the sense of the city of those living within it. Of course, the very palpable atmosphere of a place actually alters what happens there—so with a negative identity, things went worse. Economic and social woes created an atmosphere that deepened these problems. (There are cycles of feedback within a reality that is also partly virtual—in which, as modern science has taught us, the observer and the observed are not separable.) As the negative identity was shed, however, the opposite cycle took hold. New York City now is a city of great interest for tourists, a shining global center of cultural activities, and of exciting happenings of all sorts, it contains interesting communities of diverse peoples, and there is an upbeat spirit among its citizens and visitors. As both a cause and a result of this felt change in the space, an upswing in its economic vitality allows New York City to attract and guide different events there. Then, these different events, such as media support, a decreased crime rate, or a renovation of dilapidated areas, feed back into the sense of the place, and so on, in cycles. Now, as I proof this book in the wake of the tragedy of September 11, 2001, New York City has altered again radically. Overnight, it has become a place of courage and resistance. It suffered a horrible, destructive physical blow, but it has shaped its new virtual identity as a city of resolve, and resiliency. Following similar cycles, Yugoslavia was once a place that celebrated cultural diversity, with its month long folk festival in Zagreb during the summer, and offered rising expectations for and improvements in the quality of life. Now it is a region of smaller countries torn apart by ethnic hatred, war, and the desire for "ethic cleansing" among its diverse ethnic groups, caught in a spiral of poverty, destruction, and grim oppression.

So, too, in the fictional examples we've been following, not only Harry Haller and Nicholas Urfe change, but when they allow themselves to be given over fully and creatively to the virtual experiences in which they've been included, the world in which they are located becomes a different place—one that has more light, more love, more trust, more celebration, and many more possibilities for friendship, self-discovery, and play. For Nicholas, the Greek isle is no longer a desolate and backward spot, but a charming and magical environment of peace and romance, and Harry can see modern Europe not only as a decadent and vicious culture bent on self-destruction, but also as one where comradeship, spiritual exploration, and love are still possible.

These changes are not just a matter of changed attitudes, or rather, if they are, it is a matter of seeing attitude or belief in a new way—as a powerful component of a reality that becomes richer than any diabolically split subject-versus-object dichotomy would have it. New events make new virtual constructions possible, since the virtual is grounded in real events, and real events come about because of the contexts that virtual experiences help to create, transform, and open up into new possibilities. New York City was probably attacked because it had achieved this atmosphere of vitality, expansion, and success. It had taken on a renewed virtual identity it's enemies sought to damage. To fully realize that there is no unbridgeable boundary between reality and virtuality, and that there is a feedback loop encompassing them both, entails embracing a view of reality, of the world, and selves, one that is not tied to an absolute foundation.

This lack of absolute foundation is what the Buddhists mean by *sunyata* or "emptiness," a term that has been terribly misunderstood by Western cultures. It does not mean there is no reality or that there is only a void and life is what we make of it, but rather as expressed in the famous Buddhist teaching poem by Master Seng-ts'an's (about 600 A.D.):

> The object is an object for the subject,
> The subject is a subject for the object;
> Know the relativity of the two
> Rest ultimately on one emptiness.
> In one emptiness the two are not distinguished.[9]

What the Buddhist master is trying to express is that there is no "reality," no "absolute," or no indubitable "firm foundation." Descartes said he needed this foundation to achieve "certainty," which would mean that the object would be the basis for the subject (or vice versa, but we usually feel the objective is the firm foundation), rather than the two existing only as for each other, as in relationship with each other. Hence, "emptiness" is the relativity that our culture has come to start to recognize during this century through science's revelation of the inseparability between the observer and the observed, and hopefully it is now starting to dawn in other cultural realizations.

Seng-ts'an sees only an ever-evolving interplay of the person and all the things in the world: "And each contains in itself all the ten thousand things." The web of interconnection means there is nothing "above" or "below" everything else, and each thing has an identity and yet is caught up in this identity of being itself only in relation to others. In other words, this opening to a world lacks an absolute foundation and yet is not merely whatever we make of it, as it has seemed to some of our postmodern commentators. Instead, there is the rich, indeterminate truth of an unfolding process which enfolds both subject and object. This can only be seen when we get beyond the diabolical logic we spoke of at the beginning of this work: "There is neither 'self' nor 'other': When direct identification is sought, We can only say 'not two.' In being 'not two,' all is the same" (*BS*, 174). There is not mere separation or opposition nor mere oneness, but a dance that joins differences. If subject and object don't exist apart from each other, reality and virtuality are interwoven in the kind of world both Shakespeare and Buddhist masters are describing. It is ironic that computers might help us to see what certain Buddhists of the Middle Way have been trying to articulate for millennia.

I mention Buddhism here not only to give another point of reference for the notion of reality that earthbodies can bring us to see, as well as of cyberspace and developments in science in this post-Heisenberg world, but because we need to understand why we resist seeing this deeply into the import of these experiences. We need to see why psychologically many of us can't take this liberating direction with experiences on-line—a fact that emerged and troubled Turkle in her interviews about cyberspace. One of Turkle's subjects, Stewart, had been very involved in a virtual MUD world; "he sums up his experience by telling me [Turkle] that it has been 'an addicting waste of time'" (*LS*, 196). Turkle concludes that "Stewart has used MUDs to 'act out' rather than 'work through'" his difficulties. Turkle, in seeing how different people use cyberspace, concludes, "MUDs provide rich spaces for both acting out and working through. There are genuine possibilities for change, and there is room for unproductive repetition" (*LS*, 196). The question to be asked at this point goes beyond the scope of Turkle's reflections, but fits our study perfectly. How is it that some people "work through" these difficulties given a virtual space to play out dramas and others "act out" their problems once again in cyberspace?

To admit that the virtual is at the heart of the real and the real is at the heart of the virtual means to let go of the security of knowing that there is an unchanging, definable, and graspable reality that we can come to master and rely upon. Our

Western and American cultures have founded themselves upon this belief and its optimism about technological progress, breakthroughs in knowledge, and social engineering: that we would gradually unlock the keys to this unchanging core of reality and come to master it. For the Middle Way Buddhists this has always been seen as a self-defeating trap: the need for some absolute foundation and the desire to master the world on the basis of grasping this foundation makes us unable to fully appreciate the world of the senses, the body, and the interdependent community of the planet which is always changing, flowing, and, like our central image in this book, dancing. As Seng-ts'an says in a verse right after the one quoted, "Clinging is never kept within bounds, / It is sure to go the wrong way; / Quit it, and things follow their own course." If one can give up the clinging need for an absolute, for the secure foundation, then both the self and the world can be affirmed in this ongoing transformation. If this letting go is realized, then, as the master states, there is "no more worry about your not being perfect" (*BS*, 175). There is no static goal above or beyond that would justify life, but rather an affirming entering most fully into its flowing transformation. This is not to say one gives up excellence, but it comes from a different motivation and has different virtues that the rest of this book will attempt to articulate.

The psychology of most of us within this culture relies on achieving, valuing, and relying upon an unchanging core of self in a world of definite parameters. To embrace the view this book is gradually articulating, and cyberspace has the power to suggest, is to see that reality is more changeable and more complex: that we are inextricably enmeshed in it and shape its unfolding. This not only is a terrifying sense of reality for many in its lack of constancy, but also one that gives us much greater responsibility. We not only have potentially dangerous impacts upon the world and others, we are actually responsible for the very shape of reality as it comes to unfold differently given our relationships with it. Or in other words, to return to the images of the beginning of this book, given the particular dance that emerges, we and our world are different with different possibilities. We do not create the world out of nothing in any way we please, but we do play out its rhythm together, and that is all the difference. This is a sense of existential responsibility that certain philosophers, artists, Buddhists, and others have espoused.

Cyborg Life: Protean Selves versus Fragmented Selves

The Buddhist comparison is also helpful in that for thousands of years the Buddhists have articulated how this clinging to a static and absolutist sense of reality correlates with a desire for a core of inner reality: the ego. It is not an accident that the "father of modern philosophy," as many have called Descartes, ended his quest for certainty and a firm foundation with finding the one certainty to be the ego, the "I." The Internet, however, has started many into questioning the sense of *an* ego or *an* I, as the personal foundation of security. At first, I think this can be confusing for many people, for we have been raised to have "integrity," which has often been interpreted to mean we should be "one defined unit" as its etymological roots suggest, as if being many or being changeable is a sign of psychological or moral weakness.

I have found in two decades of conversations with students of all ages that we use the word "ego," but have reflected little on what we mean by this; we just somehow assume it should be "strong." For Descartes, ego meant that there was an agency, some inner core that acted, that performed, above and beyond all his quirks of personal and cultural history, and for him the key action was thinking. For Descartes, this inner self, this core of reality, really was outside space and time in its own realm, which is why it later was scoffed at by some critics as "the ghost in the machine." If what this book has articulated, however, is correct, there is only a sense of self that emerges in concert with the actions and meaning of all other living and non-living beings as part of an ever-transformable, but still stable as materially based, process. In contrast to this enmeshed, earthy identity, where is this "outside" or "beyond" that is the location of the "pure," untouched and untouchable self? What could be an agent generating its thought out of itself, from some vantage point outside space and time, instead of thoughts coming to one with and through myriad other beings?

However, the more popular sense of ego is one that in some way is the opposite of Descartes' pure ego: the sum of the qualities, the events, the roles, the achievements, and the goals of a person in their everyday life. For most, this is the "I" sense, the ego, upon which their sense of self depends. This makes a person's history into an object, one they can display to themselves and others: owner of such and such, achiever of such and such, bearer of such and such qualities. It makes the future into the quest for a grail treasure: when I achieve such and such, when I am such and such, when others recognize me as such and such, then I will have made it. Of course, this, too, is a way of denying our existence as mere earthbodies that are caught up in changing relationships that can't be objectified without killing what they mean, and whose outcomes are not my sole doing, but the doing with and through others, not only of humans, but of all things. To return to our metaphor, as the dance moves through different stages, I am no longer what I was, and given whomever I am in relation with, there is a difference in who we are together and who I am at that moment. To really experience this transformative interdependency would undermine the security of an unchanging, self-creating ego. When we make our life events into some monument to our worth and security, somewhere within our feelings and awareness, we have this sinking or desperate feeling it doesn't really "fit" our ongoing messy existence.

The Internet has brought to people's attention not only the sense that the self is changeable, but also that it is multiple. Players of MUDs, participants in chat groups, and even those who use e-mail, have felt the freedom to "act out" other personae and then discover that these performances lead to a sense of new capacities and new dimensions—as if there were many potential selves and not just one, denying the central tenet of Descartes and much of our tradition that a unitary self is the firm foundation of human being. As Turkle puts it, "When each player can create many characters and participate in many games, the self is not only decentered but multiplied without limit" (*LS*, 185). For example, Turkle relates the case of Gordon, who as a college freshman began playing in MUDs through a series of characters.

One of the characters he says is like him, but "more apt to be flowery and romantic with a sort of tongue-in-cheek attitude toward the whole thing"; another is "quiet,
older, less involved in what other people are doing"; and a third is a female, who "is
more flirtatious, more experimental, more open sexually definitely" (*LS*, 190). Gordon is able to have a relationship to these characters he plays in the virtual worlds
as both him and not him, as somewhat real and somewhat not real, or rather, just
as we have been articulating, as a cycle of creativity and exploration between the real
and the virtual which is continuous: "For Gordon, playing on the MUDs has enabled
a process of creation and recreation . . . . Each of his multiple personae has its independence and integrity, but Gordon also relates them all to 'himself.'" Gordon has
been able to embrace the self as a "work in progress" and to forsake a certain security for the ability to use the virtual to enrich who he is.

The sense of the possible multiplicity of selves is also an old and diverse
wisdom, which the modern Cartesian and rationalist tradition has made us often
forget or ignore. Although the emphasis on the unitary self has often been a dominant cultural and social demand, enshrined and supported in many psychological
and ethical perspectives of developing a strong ego or sense of self, the voices calling for playing and learning from a multiplicity of selves also have a long tradition.
If Plato is the originator of the static perspective of a detached, rational, strong-
willed self able to transcend enmeshment with the multiplicity of the earthly, the
emotional, and the imaginative, then his star pupil and successor was the first to see
other possibilities for the self. Aristotle articulated an ever-evolving self responding
to its environment. Open to the changing demands of complex situations, the self
for Aristotle could always be shaped further, could learn from identifying with the
multiplicities of selves portrayed in the arts, (especially the theater, through a felt
identification with these characters), and was part of the natural world in which we
humans can be responsive to the developing whole. However, Aristotle, like many
of Western philosophers and theologians, still valued man's rationality as some sort
of pure reasoning ability that set humans apart from the rest of the natural world
and gave the self a self-sufficient integrity. Of course, even in the Athens of ancient
Greece, where Plato and Aristotle both had the first philosophical academies, there
were the Eleusinian mysteries, Dionysiac rites, and other chthonic traditions that
appealed to many in the populace. These involved the ecstatic surpassing of ego
boundaries and joining with the natural, with the multiplicity of voices surrounding the self as articulated in the many spirits of the forests, rivers, skies, seas, and
parts of the natural world and its cycles of transformation.

This tension, which at that time was perhaps historically based,[10] has remained
within Western philosophy, theology, literature, and other aspects of culture in the
standard of the rational self criticized by the more embodied, passionate, imaginative revelations of a multiplicity of selves in league with the many of nature and various virtual realms, such as fantasy or intuition. Within philosophy, probably Nietzsche's challenge towards the end of the last century to the preceding two millennia
of what he considers rationalistic, metaphysical, and moralistic philosophies brings
this issue to its most forceful confrontation. Nietzsche's work gives a philosophical

shape to what many disparate spiritual, artistic, and psychological practices had kept alive as an undercurrent, whether through alchemy, romanticism, or as borrowings from other cultures which openly embraced a world of many spirits calling to many selves within the person.

Nietzsche himself spoke many of his most powerful words on this topic through the "identity" of Zarathustra, who was more than a character for a book; as Nietzsche reported, Zarathustra was a presence dictating the words into his ear, and an identity that for Nietzsche clearly embodied what were some of his best qualities and thoughts, as well as his failings. Zarathustra was conceived as an echo of an earlier voice, that of Zoroaster, the prophetic messenger in the ancient Persian era who proclaimed the idea that the earth was the site of the struggle of "good versus evil." Zoroaster would live again as the messenger of these great issues in Zarathustra's mission, but now turned to the opposite cause: to reveal how such absolutist and binary standards of judgment destroyed the ongoing creative, involving flow of human life. Zarathustra's message was that the self was something to be overcome as "life itself confided this secret to me: 'Behold,' it said, 'I am *that which must always overcome itself*.'"[11] For Nietzsche, holding onto one identity, one set of values and truth, or an answer to life, was turning against the ever-changing flow of interacting beings in which "one atom affects the whole of being" and everything affects everything else in a "dynamic interplay of forces."[12] To be a self was to be a bridge beyond oneself to continual re-creation through interplay with others, to enter life as a never-ending-process with the childlike spirit which is "a new beginning, a game, a self-propelled wheel, a first movement, a sacred 'Yes.' For the game of creation, my brothers, a sacred 'Yes' is needed" (*TSZ*, 139). This affirmation of continual self-overcoming and re-creation is in distinction to the negative spirit "of revenge" which has fought time's flow and the passing of things in their dynamic quality. Nietzsche feels this "ill will" towards life, this "resentment" again time's flow, has made our Western history into a nihilistic one—one that is "sick of life itself."

Zarathustra states that the understanding of the dynamic and multiple nature of existence only comes when we stop retreating to the fortress of the mind, and detaching from our bodies, and affirm the material and embodied realm: "'Since I have come to know the body better,' Zarathustra said to one of his disciples, 'the spirit is to me only quasi-spirit; and all that is "permanent" is a mere parable'" (*TSZ*, 238). Nietzsche says that there has been a "reversal" of the "real and apparent worlds": what we take to be mere fiction, such as the arts, the theater, the dream world, in which there is a constant transformation of the self and world according to feeling and imagination and as expression of our creativity—the human will as artistic shaper—is the true world, the life-promoting world, whereas the world of absolutes, of unchanging eternal values, is the world of lies bred of the contempt and anger with life. The world of change and interchange is the world one experiences when one "remains faithful to the earth." This is Zarathustra's repeated appeal to his listeners: "to remain faithful to the earth" (*TSZ*, 188).

For Zarathustra and Nietzsche, this faith is not in something that one can envision conceptually, but is the belief in what one feels, in what one experiences, in the moment, in the present, as open to the natural world, and to the cultural world as emerging from the natural world, and to the perceptual, emotional, and imaginative realm as centered in the body. Zarathustra left society to be in the mountains for ten years gathering his wisdom, and his symbols of this wisdom, which now accompany him, are the eagle and the snake. The snake hangs on the soaring bird "not like prey but like a friend: for she kept herself wound around his neck" (*TSZ*, 137). Two symbolic opposites of the animal kingdom are flying together, because for Zarathustra, one must enter the realm of the senses, the natural world, and the human community at the point where opposites come together, and multiplicities can be entertained engagingly. The snake—who crawls upon the earth and had become identified with evil in the last millennia, after many thousands of years of being identified with the earth's regenerative cycles—is not at odds with the soaring spirit, which here we also learn from nature, but they come together still distinct.

The affirmation of the earth, the unending transformation, and the overcoming of self is achieved by reversing the thousands of years since Plato under the influence of "the despisers of the body." Rather than thinking ourselves detached from the earth by our minds or by an ineffable soul that makes us superior to the creatures and other beings of this planet, Zarathustra declares, "the awakened and the knowing say: body I am entirely, and nothing else; and the soul is only a word for something about the body." It is not the mechanical body that we have come to see in opposition to the mind to which Zarathustra refers, but the kind of body expressed throughout this book, which dances with layers of meaning of all dimensions, all of which grow out of the sensual richness of our rootedness within the rest of the planet. For Zarathustra, "The body is the great reason, a plurality with one sense, a war and peace, a herd and a shepherd" (*TSZ*, 146). The body thinks and understands, and the body is a multiplicity, which comes together in one sense, in is what we call our self, but which is nevertheless a plurality. There are many selves, yet they come to "treaty drafts of will"; they act together in response to the needs of a situation for the moment, but it is deceitful to our own experience to reduce ourselves to the one.

I have spent some time on Nietzsche for the moment, because he will help us understand why some people can use the internet experience of multiple selves creatively, to work out rigidities and add new potentials for meaning and behavior, while others just "act out" the same problems of self on the Internet. Why they are "stuck" is an important question. The other extreme is also another important pitfall to consider, which follows in the binary logic of our culture and is the experience of many who might be able to experience other ways to be on the Net or elsewhere in virtual realities, but then are left with a collection of fragments that have no relation to one another. The speed, the power of sensory virtual effects, and the multiplicity of experiences offered seems, like the increased compartmentalization of our employment opportunities, our social affiliations, and our mobile lifestyles, to be feeding a fragmentation of life. Despite saying the word "self" was a simplifying term for a multiplicity, Nietzsche also claimed that one should only have one thought, one virtue, versus those of us who were coming to live like the jester, who wore motley clothes, patches of this and that material sewn together. The patches remained just that: juxtapositions with no continuity or common thread. As we have seen, this is the defense of the aesthete who glories in this fragmentation. In it, he can never be held to the responsibility of any commitment, yet it is also an alienating condition that can be promoted by cultural conditions that make a coherent sense of oneself and the world difficult to achieve.

In our current world, it is not uncommon for someone to be loving and reverent towards others on the day they go to their house of worship and then take delight the next day when crushing someone else at work in a cruel or thoughtless way; then perhaps they return to being caring after work with their family, but then go off to some group of people who scapegoats another ethnic or racial group they don't understand or watch on the television about the newest famine or genocide and feel nothing. For Nietzsche, such a lack of "pulling together" existence was indicative of the "last man" who stumbles through life, "blinks," and "has one's little pleasure for the day and one's little pleasure for the night." Rather than trying to create himself or herself in any fashion, one drifts along, and "'no shepherd and one herd! Everybody wants the same, everybody is the same . . .'"(*TSZ*, 139). This tranquilized going along with the crowd means everyone just does, feels, or thinks what everyone knows they should do, feel, or think. This means that no one really has taken anything to heart, to discover its truth or meaning for themselves, but just follows along unthinkingly and unfeelingly, at least insofar as thinking and feeling can both be means of discovery and not just reactive powers. People feel and think about their lives, but only within the well-worn grooves of their society and culture.

The result is that our lives become like episodes on television, films, videos, or on the computer screen: well worn plots that mainly provide diversions; one lives looking for new forms of entertainment, "but one is careful lest the entertainment be too harrowing." The massacre of other people, natural disasters, political machinations, and even one's personal major life events become opportunities for entertainment and not very real, as half-felt, half-experienced diversions. This passive taking in of whatever feelings and thoughts are spread about as what one is to do, or whatever is demanded by the role we slip into at that moment to maintain our comfort, leads to an endless array of feelings, values, and ideas that move through us with no real connection to us or among those who hold them in common with us. Our lives are fragmented episodes without the deeper meaning that we could author by bringing our creative faculties to bear on these situations as chances to express heartfelt values unique to who we want to become. The world offers continual challenges, but only if we wake up and take them to heart. Engaged as challenges, they move us into transformation of self and world—an ongoing renewal and re-creation.

The key to this fragmented life for Nietzsche was the desire for comfort, for a kind of happiness as contentment, which reduces us to cows chewing our cud. Rather than trying to challenge ourselves with goals that form deeper and more encompassing meanings for us and others, "the time is coming when man will no longer shoot the arrow of his longing beyond man, and the string of his bow will have forgotten how to whir!" Nietzsche foresaw a time in which there would just be consumption of digestible diversions: "'We have invented happiness,' say the last men, and they blink. They have left the regions where it was hard to live, for one needs warmth. One still loves one's neighbor and rubs against him, for one still needs warmth"(*TSZ*, 139). This kind of happiness is a being contented to be comfortable and amused by things, but not to be challenged, to go deeply into oneself, to passionately connect with others or the world. For this kind of contentment, you need to superficially keep a kind of surface warmth going with others. In this kind of life, we are lost within an endless succession of roles, feelings, and experiences through which we drift with no real connection, and therefore no real sense of who we uniquely are. This makes life into a "hurdy-gurdy song," as Nietzsche called it. The key to what is wrong with these last men, for Nietzsche, and what makes them despicable, is that they can't despise themselves, as he put it. To despise oneself means to be able to continuously be critical of oneself and see the shortcomings of one's values and the person that we are at whatever point. Then, one will be called to re-create oneself. It takes experience of feeling how, despite our best efforts, whatever we have been needs constant re-creation to stay engaged with the ever-dynamic process of life, and its requirement of continual "timing" we have discussed to stay open to the meanings other beings offer up to us.

Another thinker who is helpful to keep in mind is Carl Jung, founder of the approach to depth psychology that stressed the shared depths of apprehension, rather than Descartes' "I think." For Jung, to go beyond the self-defeating dichotomy of clinging to the rigid self or dissolving into the senseless you must allow many selves to be experienced in what he called "listening to the little people." Jung, in criticizing the sense of the isolated, individualistic self, pointed to "archetypal" dimensions of the greater self. By this he meant there are apprehensions and expressions whose meaning resonates to the world in a collective manner. We all share certain apprehensions of the world, whether we feel, for example, that there are "wise old ones" or "villains" or "bearers of light" or "black holes of senselessness" that we see in people or situations, whatever our world is like. For one person, the senselessness might be in the painful death of an infant, for another in the inability of society to prevent starvation or murder, or for someone else in the suffering of their people or the extinction of species in nature. There are myriad events that can be seen and experienced within this one archetypal meaning, and the same is true for all archetypal apprehensions. In other words, Jung's point is that we have a shared pool of overriding meanings, even if our contexts and specific senses incorporating the archetype are different.

As different as cultural contexts are, and as different as historical epochs are, these common meanings repeatedly emerge—not as abstract concepts, but as feelings about the world, seeing it as a place of love, hate, desire, wisdom, greed, evil, curiosity, humor, etc., and always there are those who appear in these guises as their embodiment. However, it is not only outwardly we see the world this way, but also within us. The felt archetypes are "directly experienced in personified form" such that "in the course of this process the archetypes appear as active personalities in dreams and fantasies" and within "immediate experience."[13] For Jung, there is a multiplicity of voices and visions, selves, such as the Wise Old Man or the Poetic Muse or the Trickster, and so on—an indefinite number of psychic constellations for whom we should seek and to whom we should listen. For Jung, this was a mythic dimension to our lives that made up our shared psyches, the collective unconscious, that were vital forces he called "psychologems." These psychologems riddled our imagination, feelings, and thoughts in ways of which most of us are unaware. It is interesting that so many of the sites and the games on the Internet and in cyber-space have overtly mythical overtones and even allusions. Certainly, in Gordon's words to Turkle about his experience on the MUDs his personae, or as he called them, his "avatars"—the flowery, sensitive lover, the calmer, detached, and wiser old man, and the young, flirtatious, and boldly erotic female, an anima figure—are all similar to the archetypal identities Jung located within us.

One of Jung's followers, James Hillman, describes how, for the greatest full-ness of life, we need "to save the diversity and autonomy from the psyche from domination by any single power." Most of us, especially in contemporary Ameri-can society, would be aware of an external dictator who claimed to be the one capa-ble of acting, of thinking clearly, or of speaking for the country or the commu-nity—or even the family—but most of us seem oblivious to having created such a tyranny within our own psychic life in the guise of this ego or self or "I," until a crisis forces us to hear voices within us we normally drum out with the din of our everyday activities. However, other experiences, like those happening on the Inter-net or in our dreams, can also make us aware of other possibilities. As Hillman puts it, using the name "Number One" for this ego as boss or tyrant:

> The secondary personalities are apt to be fragmentary, intermittent, inconsistent, usu-
> ally without social sanction. The dream is the mirror where they show themselves,
> and their bodies may have surprising levels of reality. As Number One, we have one
> name, one vote, one social security number, even though our complete psychic real-
> ity is multiple and may be fragmented. We sense these other 'persons' and call them
> 'roles'—mother, mistress, daughter, witch, crone, nurse, wife, child, nymph, innkeeper,
> slave, queen, whore, dancer, sibyl, muse. But can there be roles without persons to
> play them? To call them roles and games is itself a game by which Number One may
> deny the autonomy of these persons and keep them all under his control.[14]

There are voices, which have their associated feelings, values, quirks, and even appearance if we would focus on them, that are within the depths of the kind of apprehended sense we have been describing throughout this book, with their lay-ers and facets and interconnections. They may be fluid and fleeting, but they return when appropriate. The varied voices could be savored and befriended, instead of ignored. To stop manipulating ourselves through the machinations of the ego, which dismisses these fleeting contacts as "nothing important," and let ourselves start to also become defined by "these little people" (as Hillman also calls them), Hillman states we have to develop the "imaginal realm" (as Jung too had suggested, and practiced with his patients in active fantasy and art works). This imaginal realm has to have its spaces by providing what he calls "inscapes" or constructed contexts in which these selves can be played out.

Myth used to provide a way of entering a different time and space in which emotion, fantasy, imagination, and memory could be freed up from their usual tie to everyday concerns and realities. As Jung pointed out, to a large degree we moderns have become alienated from our inherited myths and live with "our spiritual poverty, our symbol-lessness" which creates a "void" whose "vacuum gets filled with absurd political and social ideas." Jung would not be surprised at the past decades of increasing information glut, and media frenzy, and the entertainment explosion of bombarding images and superficial, gossipy stories which have been foisted upon us to fill this gap. Although cyberspace may well only add to this diversionary glut and add to our fragmented condition, it could also provide us—now postmoderns—some of the spaces in which to work creatively with the potential multiplicity of selves. This would be a way to address the need for ritual and ceremony that we have already discussed in the first chapters of this book. However, Turkle's question still remains: how can one person become open to these selves in a creative, expansive way, and how do others either get stuck or fragmented facing the same cyberworld? I have mentioned Nietzsche, Jung, and Hillman as three of those who followed each other's work in calling for a community of selves, within and without, because I think in their ideas we can answer these questions.

Internet experience has added impetus to the impact of other technologies in bioscience, medical technology, and other forms of information science to make many question the ways technology can multiply and alter the old sense of unitary self. The title of this section uses the term "cyborg" as an acknowledgment of the work of Donna Haraway, historian of science and social critic, who has written for the past few decades about humans as "cyborgs," that is to say, as "a cybernetic organism, a fusion of the organic and the technical forged in particular, historical, cultural practices."[15] She tells us the word "cyborg" was first used by Manfred Clynes and Nathan Cline in 1960 to describe a technologically enhanced human who could survive extraterrestrial space flight. One of the first cyborgs was a white lab rat implanted with an osmotic pump to inject chemicals continuously. Although perhaps first envisioned as a bringing together of the human or other organic beings with the mechanical in new sorts of combinations, it became apparent that new combinations didn't have to be literally "physically" implanted, but, for example, my sitting at the computer screen at this moment, watching my words appear on the screen, is itself some new sort of way for me to be, to write, and to think in combination with the computer's ways of processing information and displaying those products. Haraway, as a social critic, has shown how our human being is constantly being transformed by the systems into which we get plugged, and how we may not be aware of how they change who we are. She also sees hope in embracing the changing, multiple self, who is never finished and isn't complete in itself, but comes to know itself and the world through its splits and contradictions. Turkle's book ends in a chapter quoting Haraway and endorsing "cyborg dreams." She calls upon the views of Robert Jay Lifton (author of *The Protean Self*), Howard Rheingold, Daniel Dennett, Ian Hacking, and others to promote a "flexible self" no longer unitary, caught up in cyberspace multiplicities, but able to have these multiple selves open up to one another gracefully, rather than be atomized into significantly disconnected selves (*LS*, 261).

This is the right direction, but again the understanding of cyborg often gets skewed into an understanding of machine or technical systems that negate the body as the way of this becoming multiple and transforming. In the midst of articulating this vision of the flexible "cyborg dreaming" human, Turkle quotes artificial intelligence researcher, W. Daniel Hillis, as dreaming of the downloading of human selves into machines, so we could "live" for perhaps 10,000 years—once we overcame "the nostalgic love of human metabolism" (*LS*, 264). However, cyberspace is a mythic space because it is an embodied space. We feel it viscerally in its linking, emotionally moving, and sensually imagining rhythms which claim and compel us. Its roles and voices are (to quote Turkle's subject) "avatars" of us. This is the power of myth: we feel ourselves in these figures, and as Jung realized, we are broadened and deepened in this blurring of boundaries. Merely mentally entertained representations would be located in a series of spaces that would diaphanously float in self-sufficient isolation. We "plunge" into stories, roles, and rituals with our gestured body, with our guts, our senses, our heart, and with the body as a linking power which stays somewhat the same and somewhat altered—just the kind of "in between" logic, neither one nor many, that all these critics seek, but don't seem able to realize, especially given our traditional dissociation and misidentification of the body. Only the logic of inclusive ambiguity that is the body's and materiality's logic accomplishes this.

If we understand that humans are earthbodies, not as "joined" to a "body" as a machine or vessel, but rather that we are body through and through, we could see that we are "cyborgs" through and through, not just as a postmodern change in our condition. Our cyborg being has merely become more elaborate and emphatic. This point parallels the idea that humans have always lived in virtual reality. However, it is not just a matter of realizing a historical point that some supposedly new innovations are actually not so new. Something much more important and fundamental is at stake here that is a key to why I am writing this book. We have misconstrued the body in our dominant philosophical and cultural misconceptions for quite some time, which makes recent technological innovations and consequent cultural developments seem so startling. They have finally brought to the surface our misguided assumptions that have caused us past suffering. Now, they are also clearly too simple-minded, too reductionist, to allow us to confront the complexities of contemporary culture.

To be a body, to be a material being, means just the opposite of how our philosophies have often construed it. As earthbodies, we are not separated and isolated within "physical boundaries" (such as our skin), but rather we are open, able to be affected by other bodies, to "take them into" us through our senses and bodily apprehensions. Fleshly bodies are in a circuit with all the other material beings on the planet. The larger embodied circuit means that we are incomplete beings, beings in transition, and always in process, as indeed are all material beings, since "matter" is the process of energy exchange and transformations. To be materiel is not to be fixed, but is the way of partially holding onto a shape while being in the midst of becoming reshaped. Space is not the barrier, it is the means of connection for material beings, giving the room to move beyond themselves into other beings. They need that "roominess" of the material world, its spaces "between" things, not as separator (although it partially does that) but as area into which to move and to set up zones of commonness among them.

Heidegger's key insight early in the century was that a human being is a "being-in-the-world," and Merleau-Ponty's further insight was that this "being-in-the-world" was fundamentally an embodied being. Humans are "bodies-within-environments" or "bodies-emergent-from-contexts", not in the straightforward sense of needing an environment to causally interact with in order to function, but that our identity is determined only in a context. Throughout the sciences and social science there is this spreading recognition, but only ambivalently so, just as there has been in the larger culture. We know the importance of context, yet we still think we "really" are separable beings. However, we are not. This not only means that I am only what I am in a certain context. The hidden aspect of this condition is that the body is incomplete and "adds" onto itself diverse systems. A person in ancient Mongolia and one in the modern Manhattan, with subways, elevators and cell phones, experience space, time, emotions, other people, etc., in differing existences. When humans got on horseback, or used printing presses, or when they started to use machinery to produce quantities of goods, who they were was changed by these additions to their environments.

T. H. White expressed this insight about the incomplete and "additive" nature of human beings in a humorous parable in *The Once and Future King*. I believe it communicates most vividly this insight. At the end of Merlin's education of the young Arthur, who will become King Arthur, Arthur is instructed by a badger about how all creatures came to have their present nature. The badger explains that after "God had manufactured all the eggs out of which the fishes and the serpents and the birds and the mammals and even the duck-billed platypus would eventually emerge, he called all the embryos before Him, and saw that they were good." All the embryos looked similar at first, but they were given the choice to take the form of anything that would be useful to them, and so "some chose to use their arms as flying machines and their mouths as weapons, or crackers, or drillers, or spoons, while others selected to use their bodies as boats and their hands as oars." Last to ask for its nature was the human being, who said:

> "Please God," said the embryo, "I think you made me in shape which I now have for reasons best known to Yourselves, and that it would be rude to change. If I am to have my choice I will stay as I am. I will not alter any of the parts which You gave me, for other and doubtless inferior tools, and I will stay a defenseless embryo all my life doing my best to make myself a few feeble implements out of the wood,

iron, and other materials which You have seen fit to put before me. If I want a
boat, I will try to construct it out of trees, and if I want to fly, I will put together
a chariot to do it for me."[16]

As the parable ends, the Creator is delighted at this response and says that it will
make humans have dominion over the earth, but also that "you will remain a naked
tool all your life, though a user of tools" and be eternally undeveloped, and therefore have great potential. This is the source of all the great strengths of humans:
our openness to the world that comes from our incompleteness. The tool user
becomes remade by the tools it makes.

As human beings, we need to seek in the world for new abilities offered
to us by what we can use from the nature of the materials around us and find
meaning and insight in a hearkening to the lessons of the world. In one way,
this could lead us to an ecological consciousness of respecting and listening to
the world as it existed before us and still exists beyond our powers—a theme to
be explored in the next chapter. However, our incompleteness also means that
we have never been "purely" natural, that we have never been "pure beings" in
any sense of that word. We have always been *incorporators*. Our bodies take into
them whatever tools and gadgets the world can offer, and they and we become
transformed by the combination. Some of our gadgets are perfectly obvious in
this dimension: we know that the car's body, once we really know how to drive,
becomes an extension of our bodies as we drive and weave in and out of spaces,
just as the keyboard of my word processor becomes an extension of my body,
like the keyboard of a piano for a pianist. Our body as the open way station of
the worlds currents we've described is always conjoining with that around it. In
other words, we have always been cyborgs. Being a cyborg is what it means to
be a human.

The regard for nature and the appreciation of how the technological can
enhance our human being can actually go together, if we can find the way. The fact
that we are part of nature and that we are "unnatural" creatures who need tools,
machinery, and technology are not opposites, in the respect that they both come
from the same open and incomplete aspect of who we are. *It comes from a unity of
flow, not from a disparity*. The question is how we incorporate new tools and how
we can preserve the richness of the natural environment in ways that are most beneficial to the overall meaning of our lives. It is not an either/or question between
nature and technology, but rather a Taoist question of finding the centered way
between forces that move in opposition, yet are by nature mutually enhancing when
both are used creatively.

The prior question of how to find a way to embrace the multiplicity of selves
that somehow still come together, offering flexibility instead of fragmentation or
being stuck with a rigid self, and what is the way to get out of this nature versus
technology (or culture) dilemma turns out to be the same. Both of these moving
"between the opposites" require the open, embodied, belief-filled embrace of
incompleteness. Nietzsche continually posed the question of how to go beyond

oneself, and to enter the childlike play of transformation, where we let the world challenge us without resisting in terror or outrage. The challenge is to feel a joyfulness of being challenged, in the appreciation we have been given a nudge to move beyond our old selves. Zarathustra responds by urging "one must have chaos in oneself to give birth to a dancing star"(*TSZ*, 129). This is not the chaos of running here and there trying to "come out on top" nor the distracting consuming of pleasures we've discussed, but rather a willingness to let go of whatever idea of the Number One Self we've adopted. This chaos is about developing the humor of not taking oneself so seriously that to be proven wrong is a disaster, but rather is funny and a gift, and the sensitivity to listen for the echo of each voice within us that always has its opposite voicing itself somewhere else in our psyche. This chaos is more like a reverberation that shakes our inner core with harmonies, tones, and even melodies that are different from our dominant tone, and can only be felt in their vibration if we are willing to hold ourselves like tuning forks allowed to resonate. What starts to resonate can be represented as that multiplicity of selves people are starting to discover on the Internet. This sounds liberating, but how can this happen?

To be anything as a human is not the same as a chair is a chair or a rock is a rock. We *are* earthbodies, but we may not (really or fully) be earthbodies at any given moment. To be what one is for humans doesn't just come as a freebie or as a given condition. It takes an acknowledgment, an openness, and a gratitude to the experience of being whatever this is. To say humans are rational or emotional or imaginative or whatever is only true as a capability and potentiality. We can fail to be any of these things at any moment in our lives, even when that aspect is what we most need to be at that moment to give our lives sense or even perhaps to save our lives. We may most need to be imaginative or rational or daring at a particular moment, and yet may have walled ourselves off from that part of ourselves and from those selves which embody these abilities. To live as earthbodies and feel that sensitivity to reverberation takes a willingness to let go into the body, which is partly a decision, partly a cultivated disposition and skill, partly a matter of attention and concentration, but most of all requires a certain belief, a certain intention, and a certain emotional attunement.

The belief that is required is the belief in the reality and richness of what our bodies are telling us, that is to say, what we are immediately experiencing at the moment. Most of us have grown up thinking belief is what is required for aspiring to dimensions that we cannot directly or immediately experience, such as the belief in a transcendent reality or future redemption or in doctrines that defy logic, but offer answers to suffering. Nietzsche declared that such "metaphysical comforts" were actually a sickness with the life around us, a nausea, and a violence against what is offered to us by our bodies in the immediate senses, emotions, imaginations, etc. To believe in what is happening at the moment means to take seriously the present pain, the present thrill, the feelings we have about others and ourselves at each moment. Yes, I am angry at that adult for smacking that child for no good reason; yes, that beautiful sunset does suggest a joy and a peace that being caught up in this office gossip is pushing needlessly away; yes, something does feel violating and despairing about allowing the design of this device that will cause a certain number of fatal accidents but will cost the company less in lawsuits than in redesign costs; and so on, in the varied thousands of felt messages registered by our bodies daily, if we would believe in them. If we discount what the world can tell us through our linkages as earthbodies, we short-circuit the meaning our bodies announce to us from the larger context.

If we believe in immediate experience and the varied levels of the body's apprehension, we do not get the same payoff as belief in some abstract and inexperienceable doctrine that provides security in its clarity and absolutism. Rather, we get the opposite. We are plunged into depths that wash over us from the world and take us deeper into ourselves and into the details of others and the world. Since this belief lands us on grounds that don't have the same absolute foundation, that take us on long journeys where we are called upon to sensitively respond and become transformed, we shy away from this belief, discounting so much of our immediate experience as "nothing" or "just a feeling." Like Lestat, like the aesthete, and like the program of consumer life, we prefer distance and safety to engagement and complexity. A very powerful exercise that Fritz Perls used in Gestalt therapy with his clients was to have them declare how they felt at the moment and add, "this is my existence." For example, a client might say, "I feel sad and this is my existence," or "I feel paralyzed by this job and this is my existence." They might be asked to repeat this statement over and over, until the person's Number One Self let the other voices and bodily feelings, usually kept at bay, come over the person; suddenly they would begin to really feel, to have moving experiences about what did make up their lives, but had been only emptily acknowledged, like a statement about some specimen. Another very interesting experiment that Perls conducted was to have people eat slowly and really experience the tastes, the smells, the textures, and the entire sensual realm of what they were eating. By far, most of the people who did this responded by vomiting. They were so used to eating without experiencing, just stuffing whatever down there, that they were overwhelmed with really experiencing eating. Many found out how repulsive their food was. For Perls, this was a paradigm for all we swallow in life with no awareness, and so become manageable consumers, like the portrait we painted in the last chapter that perhaps we could call "the day of the living dead."

To believe in what one experiences as being real, as having meaning, and offering opportunities to learn also means to "de-literalize" our thinking. We often feel things that are vibrating between what diabolical or binary logic would call opposites. Accordingly, we force out of our awareness these ambiguities with the imperative of this logic that we must choose one or the other. Willa Cather's archbishop feels the grandeur of the Roman Catholic way, yet he also feels the wonder of the ways of being attuned to the world of the natives of the Southwest territories. He is unusual in that he can embrace both. He is even more unusual in that he is attuned enough to his body to find concrete objects and events that express this more inclusive openness to feeling. He builds the Santa Fe cathedral out of the local stone, whose colors capture the sunsets' landscaped brilliance of New Mexico, yet he has it shaped it into a facade that preserves the local sense of place and nature while still expressing the aspirations and values of his own European religion. He allows himself the fullness that goes beyond narrow boundaries of self-definition and thereby makes it possible for those around him to have a richer, many-sided experience that more rigid missionaries failed to achieve. Instead, the others were led into either/or standoffs with the local populations in which one group had to capitulate. For the archbishop, the symbols of his faith were not literal ones. They had a meaning that could be represented by many forms—a silver cross of European design or rituals he was used to, but equally the grandeur of the desert or the local customs of reverence for love and life. He believed in what he and others felt and were experiencing as genuine and valuable, a gift. The richness of sheer presence and its rich ambiguities of meaning were more important than the pale categories his more defensive compatriots clung to. He let the categories be redefined by the experience. What is most unusual about the archbishop is how he lets go into his sensual and emotional life, the life of the body, to allow the landscapes, the vegetation, the animals, the idiosyncratic characteristics of those he encounters, to touch him fully and find new avenues for creative expression.

It is this kind of belief that a thirty-year-old graduate student, Ava, in Turkle's study, brought to her experience in cyberspace. Ava had lost her right leg after an automobile accident, and during her recuperation began to use a MUD to create a one-legged character in cyberspace. This character's descriptions featured prominently her removable prosthetic limb, so that Ava and her friends in virtual reality had to deal with this aspect of her embodiment. When Ava took a virtual lover on the web, they dealt with the prosthesis in making love. Since Ava was able to believe in the reality of her experience on-line, to give it that reverence, credibility, and allow it that impact on her many-leveled embodied self, this experience had a great impact on her in allowing her to accept her prosthesis in "real life." She had the belief that her experience was real no matter what context. This allowed her to play with its possibilities in cyberspace. After this more circumscribed cyberspace experience, she allowed herself to trust more the reality of her new life outside of cyberspace, to identify with it, instead of fighting it as "not really my existence." If we can believe in the truth of our experience, then the virtual and the actual can both transform us in ways that enter an augmenting feedback cycle. For her, as she let go into the power of her experience on-line, she found the line between the virtual and the actual is blurred, is porous, for those who can allow Nietzsche's more childlike attitude of letting life play with us. By doing this, new sensual, emotional, and properly erotic possibilities opened for her that allowed her to go from making love in cyberspace to making love in her "real life." As she relates to Turkle: "I think the first made the second possible. I began to think of myself as whole again" (LS, 263). She believed in her experience as real and meaningful, despite being gained through cyberspace, and had the faith, the childlike, Nietzschean attitude, to let herself go into her emotional, sensual body, and embraced the ambiguities necessary for new selves to emerge.

Contrast this with Stewart, who spent forty hours or more per week in MUDs during college, but decided it had been an addictive waste of time, which ended with him "acting out" the same controlling, judgmental, and intrusively aggressive behavior towards his on-line friends and acquaintances. He would never let himself believe in the reality of his experience in cyberspace. Affected by heart problems and a "loner" throughout his life, in his life on cyberspace he constructed a fancy place to live, was the dashing character Achilles, and picked up his virtual date, Winterlight, in a limousine. Turkle describes at length how he carried on this courtship and was a focal point for this cybercommunity based in Germany. The courtship led to an elaborate engagement ritual and then a wedding ceremony. Besides taking pages and pages of text description on the Net, the wedding ceremony also involved twenty-five of the European players meeting in real space in Germany for food, champagne, and costumes. Staying isolated in his dorm room, for Stewart, Achilles was his "ideal self," but not a role that he himself could enter. In speaking with Turkle, he relates how he feels this self, this Achilles, is not him, and despite all his lengthy, detailed, and highly emotional experience with this group of people on the Net, he doesn't believe in it: it has nothing to do with him, Stewart. Why can't he believe? Well, Stewart states, "his main defense against depression is 'not to feel things.'" In other words, Stewart will not leave that fortress of his mind, as Kierkegaard's aesthete put it, and let go into his body and its feelings, its chaos. He states that in facing such visceral turmoil: "I'd rather put my problems on the back burner and go on with my life" (*LS*, 196–197).

For Stewart, the way to deal with emotions is to never talk about them and to throw himself into some all-involving project. He tries to stay distracted. For him, the Net is ultimately another distraction, a particularly powerful and seductive one. For him, cyberspace is like Rheingold's or Turkle's disembodied space, in that even the emotions he cultivates there he keeps at a distance to render it only a distracting occasion. People who are using the Net this way have found a postmodern equivalent to the aesthetic approach or to the parasitic feeding of the vampire. Stewart has taken advantage of the ambiguity of cyberspace's relationship to actuality to make it into an ambivalence, an "either/or." He keeps the virtual separate from the real, which helps him feel safe in distrusting and thereby disarming any potentially transforming experience on the Net. Ava, on the other hand, chose to trust, let go into her body, and believe in the so-called make-believe of the virtual as being both lighter and freer—a play space to try things out—but also vital and real to her life.

If it is true that many selves join creatively and yet keep their distinctive voices, and also that to combine the power of actual and virtual experience requires a certain belief, a certain intention, and a certain emotional attunement, then we must explore the requisite intention and emotional attunement. The required belief in the reality of our experience is not enough to give the Net transformative power. We must also have the intention that this experience will become the vehicle of self-transformation. By "having the intention" or "intending," I mean that we must have the desire, the focus, and the understanding of the nature of experience as containing this potential. The desire is part of the motive force that gives the process of transformation the momentum to begin unfolding. The focus is the concentration on those points of the unfolding experience that allow access to its meaning and power in terms of our relationship with the world and others. This means we have to bring to bear the significance, for each of us, of our history, our feelings, our particular ideas, and psychological needs. In these areas, there is enough "room to play" that leads us into our individual path. In common parlance, we could say we need to "make it our own," a popular echo of Heidegger's sense of authenticity. We must offer up the relevant connections to our experience for them to have their transforming power.

We are self-reflective creatures and some sense of where we are heading makes it more possible to head that way. Experiences don't just befall us, but must be met up with by us in order to take on their significance and potency through what we have called "timing" throughout this book. Even our bodies' movements through space happen because we are both "within" our body core and also, as earthbodies, we are "outside" our body core, looking at and even feeling ourselves kinetically from the vantage point of the sky, the buildings, the ground, the people passing by, etc. However, this is true on all levels of earthbodies: emotionally, memorially, intellectually, imaginatively, etc. We are "within/without" and absorbed in where we're going, if we're doing it well, but also outside ourselves guiding ourselves into the rhythms and openings of the situation. For example, in the fictional cases we've explored of Harry Haller in *Steppenwolf* or Tayo in *Ceremony*, both desired to become transformed and both had a good sense of the directions they needed to travel. Harry recognized that he was too serious, too guarded, too isolated, too alienated from the physical, and too closed to love and hope, he sought new horizons of humor, vulnerability, joy, sensuality, passion, and desire. Tayo knew that he and his friends had been poisoned by the killing and brutality of the war, the relentless discrimination of the Anglo society, the enforced poverty, and the disintegration of the community on the reservation. He sought a way to cure himself of his literal nausea with life, his feeling of dislocation, and his feelings of violence turned against himself. Tayo knew he needed to find ways to become nourished by the land's beauty and bounty, to meet others who would affirm his sensitivity, bravery, and intelligence, and to find a place for himself in the community doing something meaningful and constructive. It took effort over time for Tayo to cultivate these desires.

Harry at first could not focus on what was important in the experiences he discovered. However, through his belief and his sense of direction, Harry paid careful attention, almost comical at times, in studying the lives of his new friends. He came to recognize in Hermine's and Pablo's lighthearted, imaginative, sensual, and exploratory attitudes and characters that there was something here for him to change in his focus in order to follow their lead and release him from his rut. He could have been sidetracked by his prejudices that Pablo was seemingly uneducated or took drugs or was too frivolous, or by paying attention to Pablo's or Hermine's failings, but he chose to focus on the most imaginative and liberating aspects of his time with them. This was essential to his embracing all the fantasies, games, and psychodramas of the

Magic Theater. For his part, Tayo could have been put off by the idiosyncratic Betonie's ramshackle dwelling, his abrupt manner, or his unorthodox views, but instead he focused on how Betonie's stories and rituals could resonate with his own sense of the landscape, his people's history, and the events of his life, to find a way to enter his transformation. No matter how unlikely Betonie's medicine man proclamations were, such as those about the importance of his finding his uncle's cattle or his need to pay attention to the star's position in the sky, Tayo kept open to whatever possibilities this journey he set out on could provide.

Both Harry and Tayo were given explanations about the power of making connections, entertaining images, listening to stories, playing new roles, that could become magical in connecting them to forces beyond a simple cause-and-effect relation; even though their understanding was sketchy, they chose to follow it in the faith they could decipher a path to discovering more selves and more meaning in their lives. They chose not only to trust their experience, the power of imagination, of emotion engaged in involving play, but to stay focused on their intention to pursue a new direction. The result was different powers of the world now addressed them and addressed new parts or selves within them.

Without this kind of care, effort, and orientation, cyberspace will not offer us transformations of our lives, the discoveries of new selves, and new ways to be, but will only be another distraction and another place in which we keep repeating the same deficiencies.

Deep-rooted Emotion versus Cyberspace Sentimentality

At the start of this book we considered Philip K. Dick's novel, *Do Androids Dream of Electric Sheep?* (perhaps better known in its film version, *Bladerunner*), as a possible vision of how we can become starved for connection in a world without animals. The world presented suffered ecological devastation, and was dominated by corporate planning and material consumption, in which traditional communal structures had been ruptured. The threat this represents is that we could feel empty of the meaning that flows into us from encounters with other living, non-living, and human beings, as indeed androids might "feel" if they were constructed as self-contained, but sentient units. Another dimension of Dick's vision—and it is a state of affairs that many would argue we are approaching or have already achieved in ways—is that emotional life, even if it survives, will become "flattened out." Decker's test to discriminate whether he is confronting a human or an android is to use instruments to register the bodily changes that accompany certain emotions. The confrontation in which an android challenges Decker as to whether *he* feels emotions deeply enough to pass the test hovers without answer as a challenge to the book's readers or the film's viewers whether we as a society still feel very much emotionally. The question is at the heart of evaluating what's going on in cyberspace. It's hard to answer, because our culture is handicapped in judging emotional experience. We have such a warped view of the emotions, we can often be satisfied with an emotional life of "kicks" or thrills that fail to draw upon the emotion's potential to be revealing and expressive. Given this handicap, these potential dimensions of the emotions should be explored first.

William James tried to locate the emotions in the body in his essay "What Is Emotion?" He saw emotions as registering the feelings of the body as it underwent certain physiological changes in response to situations perceived. This type of explanation has continued to this day in many variations as one way to explain emotions. As Alan Lightman expressed so aptly in *Einstein's Dreams*: "They know that the body is not a thing of wild magic, but a collection of chemicals, tissues, and nerve impulses. Thoughts are no more than electrical surges in the brain. Sexual arousal is no more than a flow of chemicals to certain nerve endings. Sadness no more than a bit of acid transfixed in the cerebellum."[17] However, as had been often pointed out, differing emotions, such as fear and anger, engender similar physiological responses, yet mean very different things to the person experiencing them, or in other words, the same physiological processes are present in very different emotional states. Emotions are more than registering chemical or metabolic processes, even if it is certainly true that emotions are *accompanied* by them. What is wrong in such an approach is, as Lightman says in the next sentence, the ultimate conclusion of this attitude: to live as if "In short, the body is a machine . . .". These people become "those who think their bodies don't exist. They live by mechanical time." Their bodies don't exist for them anymore as earthbodies, as "a thing of wild magic." The body as mechanism is not the human body, not the earthbody, but just a necessary (but not sufficient) ingredient.

However, what is right about such explanations, even if they have walled out the earthbody and replaced it with the idea of a machine, is, compared to other approaches, at least they pay attention to the fact that emotions, whether called affect, passion, feelings or emotion, are grounded in the body. We feel love in our stomachs, pulse and metabolism, or fear in our shaky knees and breathlessness, etc. We live the power of emotions viscerally. However, as this book has articulated, all our apprehensions grow from the sensual soil of embodied perceptions and therefore do certainly have a physiological component, but are also bodily, as being part of the earthbody sense of being connected with the whole environment that flows through me in its energies and meanings. As we have described, mind, body, emotion, and other levels of awareness are one intertwining phenomenon, so of course they are experienced in the body and its material elements, but this is not merely registering physiological changes in functioning as the mechanism of biological processes.

What is unique about matter and the human body as open to and linked within the round of perception is that everything is "held together," has a kind of thickness or layering, that allows for the gradual unfolding and intermeshing of these levels. This wouldn't be true for more diaphanous experiences, which would be transparent or "all there" at once and of one meaning. As contained within the materiality of the body and its environment, feelings linger, resound, endure, and have a depth that can be explored: they are mixed, partly hidden among other meanings, and needing to be drawn out. The heaviness in my eyes and their sting as I feel like crying or have cried is part of the way the mood of sadness or grief lingers and has further depths to explore and can unfold in numerous ways, whether unfolding further into nostalgia, or changing into gratefulness for what was, or even moving into depths of sharper pain. The meaning of the experience is partly visceral. Sadness may be partly comprised of more cognitive realizations of discouragement, feelings of loss, or a sense of bleakness about the future, but it is also a heaviness in the limbs, a burning or pinching around the eyes and face, the feeling of slowness in the body, the lack of energy, etc. Emotional meaning is both "physical" and "mental," or in other words, is material or embodied in a deeper sense which encompasses both, and allows emotion to be jam-packed or multi-layered. There are always more connections with parts of the world embedded within them.

This multilayered, embodied aspect of emotion is key to the power of poetry, for example, whose importance to earthbodies we will discuss in the final chapter. Poetry's ability to use sensual images to disrupt customary language use explores the feelings, the fantasies, the memories, etc., that we all share to some degree as embodied beings. It brings us to these experiences more than other ways of using language by making us encounter the bodily feelings, the sensual dimensions, the particular resonances in the material environment that are part and parcel of these meanings in our lives, whether the brilliant magenta of a flower that might be part of a joyous feeling or the lightness and spring of step that is also part of joy. How it does this we'll discuss in the next chapter, but the fact that poetry meanders and points beyond the mere conveyance of mental representations of standard usage, to get us to slow down and feel these sensual, emotional, and imaginative branch-ings of these meanings, is an instance when we can become aware of the emotional layering we might not often notice. The poetic lines are ambiguous, pointing to the many levels of meaning within our intertwined sensual, imaginative, emotional, and rational experience. Poetry points us outside the normal round of language as cognitive representation or as a collection of word tools, towards the material and embodied thickness of the experience which is the wider source of this clearer and more abstracted meaning that we are usually content to convey.

Although it is true that as human, we have earthbodies that can bring together matter and spirit into one depth, it is also true, as we have articulated throughout this book, that we are free to turn away from these resonances. Some-times, it is necessary that we tune out these complex and absorbing layered emo-tions in order to get a practical job done or to concentrate on something else. We can also continually flee certain dimensions of our existence. When I say hello to my neighbors walking down the street or to my co-workers walking into work in the morning, I may well need not to have involving and informative emotional apprehensions and communications with them. At these moments, I may need to entertain very generalized feelings towards others, such as my genuine friendliness in greeting my neighbor, but not tune into the sensitively apprehending possibili-ties of my emotions to see nuances of his discouragement over his illness or his concern about his daughter's job or even his mix of various feelings about why we haven't done more together lately when we still really like each other. I do not want at that moment to express in a powerful and sensitive way all the complexities of my feelings about him and the rest of my life.

The same is true of all our faculties. We don't always want to use our reason to get to the bottom of everything or our imagination to entertain all possibilities, but rather all must be at least partially tuned out at many occasions. However, the problem is when one comes to rely on not feeling deeply and sensitively or upon feeling just these generalized or stock emotions towards the world, just as it becomes problematic to be continually unthinking or be only able to think in oversimplified formulas about life. The distinctive power of emotion is that it can open us into the specificity of the other person and their situation, that we can feel things about them that are unique to them, and then explore with them what this means for them or us or for us together. The emotions bring us deeper into our particular situation with another person or with our environment, if we let them carry us there.

Our culture really needs another kind of comparison than the one we usually make between strongly felt emotions and weaker feelings—ones that have less amplitude as a wave that rocks us. We should also discern between emotions that are many layered, thick, and complex in their possible apprehension and expression and those that are straightforward, univocal, and generalized in their focus, like our friendliness in the morning which is meant for one and all with whom we are on good terms. It is also possible to feel such simplified emotions very strongly, such as we might when feeling the happiness of cheering an athletic team on to victory, the excitement of buying a new car, the frustration of losing at a video game, or the sadness when a daytime soap opera character loses their relationship. The feelings engendered here are not part of the emotional complexity one feels when things are not going well with a spouse or a child or, conversely, when one has perhaps opened up a new level of communication with this spouse or child later, but rather are very non-specific emotions that we can use to unite ourselves with the crowd with whom we have no particular relationship and no desire to really know, other than joining with them as Yankees' fans or Corvette owners or devotees of *Days of Our Lives*. If we wish to understand what are the emotional benefits and dangers of cyberspace community, we will have to pause for a moment and look at the nature of emotion and figure out how strength versus weakness and generality versus specificity have repercussions on our emotional well-being.[18]

When we see that the earth is made up of objects, creatures, and other humans who are locked in a dance together, a rhythm of interchange of meaning, such that each keeps becoming what it is at that moment from the nature of timings or interconnectings it is making with others, then we can see that space is not the void between things, but rather is the medium of pulsations. In D. H. Lawrence's poem entitled "Space" cited earlier, the last line reminds us that

> Space's "wild heart"
> is the power that sends pulses through me."[19]

Space is the way the world pulses through me such that I can feel the meaning of these interconnections in my body as resonating or within the sensual depths of things or beings perceived. The most inert object, such as a rock, is in my field of pulsation as a presence communicating solidity or tranquillity or immovability or stubbornness, let alone those dynamic beings that most concern me, like my child or spouse, who may continually interweave very changeable melodies with that of my own being from moment to moment.

This kind of understanding—emotional understanding—is what Merleau-Ponty called "lateral" knowing. By this he meant it is not deliberate, not something that comes from a frontal confrontation with something or someone or some being, but rather is indirect, insinuates its sense into us within our perceptions, and is a continual kind of whispering to us from the world which we mostly do not explicitly heed, but still register in our bodies and in the depths of what we see, feel, hear, touch, and smell. Within our bodies, we have this sense of what other things mean, what their *qualities* are about, and not just whether they exist or not or other quantitative concerns. For example, we know when we walk into a room, we immediately sense whether we are in a hostile environment or a welcoming one, or whether the group we have joined is happy, depressed, or scared. Perhaps even the most emotionally sensitive may not know immediately with certainty, but even the least sensitive will have some feeling that permeates us as we enter and then remain in that space.

However, it is not just the qualities of other things, creatures, or people that resonate within us in this implicit understanding, but rather their conjunction with our own life at that moment. If the world is a circulation of energies and meanings from the environment that moves through its participants and back into us and then out again, what gets felt within our sensing bodies is how it stands with us in regard to these energies and meanings. The emotions register the relationship between us and whatever we have the feeling about, or how things have touched us in our sensitive body/mind. The emotion conveys the texture, the tone, the rhythm, the direction, the fittingness, the flow, etc., of the unfolding relatedness with that being.

The etymology of the word "emotion" and some of its associated terms is interesting in regard to gaining a sense of our dynamic relationships to a world seen as a dynamic unfolding of energies and meanings. E-motions are themselves a kind of motion, hence we say we are "moved" when we experience deep emotion, but as the root "e" in the Latin *e-movere* suggests, it is movement "outward" or "out from" that person into the world. However, sensitive emotion is not merely "ex-pressing" as a "pressing outward" of what is registered onto the world, for then it is only "e-moting," which is to make a show or display of some affect for the benefit of others. Sensitive emotion also has the sense of "passions," which literally mean "under-goings" or "sufferings" or "submissions" to the movements of the world acting upon us. Passions in this sense would be passive.

However, to be merely passive is not to be emotionally sensitive either, and actually can come to verge on emotional indifference. Rather, emotion captures clearly the sense this book has struggled to achieve of an activity that is a passivity, but a moving out to the world which allows it to move into the person, or in other words, a joining up, a dancing, or a moving together that is both active and passive, or may best be called something else outside these unhelpful "either/or" terms. To "feel" comes from the Icelandic root *falma* which means to "grope." This is another apt expression of moving forward and outward, but only to encounter something sought for, or that one is open to, in order to take it into oneself and know more about the world into which to further move.

This aspect of emotions we might call "reversibility," to again use one of Merleau-Ponty's terms. He used it to describe the way in which, within all sensitive embodied experience, we are seen in seeing or touched in touching, and so on, or in other words, active and passive in such a way that we learn about aspects of ourselves in learning about the world. Also, we find the world within us, expressing itself, when we introspect. Our boundaries are a permeable give and take, and the sense of others and ourselves and the rest of the world is promiscuous, insinuating itself within other beings. However, of all embodied experience, I would contend sensitive and expressive emotion most draws upon this give and take of reversibility. It is the way emotions explicitly work and it takes special defensive maneuvers to not have the other person's emotions impact on us as we express our emotions with them. Similarly, to apprehend the other's emotions feelingly usually also expresses our own emotions.

Feuerbach said that "Feeling changes the active in man to the passive, and the passive to the active. To feeling, that which thinks is the thing thought, and the thing thought is that which thinks. Feeling is the dream of Nature."[20] In feeling, the boundaries of the defended self and normal opposition with the world, when it is seen as adversary acting upon us before we act upon it, are superseded in this flow of interchange. If we take up the dance of emotions as registered in our bodies, however, what we find is each sense of relationship is nested within contexts of other relationships, and so on within ever larger contexts. This is why Feuerbach ends his statement by saying this kind of taking up of relationship by sensitively feeling ultimately takes us to nature as the widest context. Not only do feelings ultimately take us to nature, Feuerbach asserts, but also into contact with its deepest meanings, such as we, too, express in dreams. Thus nature dreams through us in our perceiving its sense. The permeability of boundaries in emotion, its reversibility, takes us "deep and wide" in the world.

Another aspect of sensitive emotion to note is that if what is emotionally understood is the way in which we are related to the world and parts of it, this is rationally ungraspable and unique to each person and each situation. When we explained the nature of virtuality and its power, since the self has no foundation, but is rather a "way of happening," we pointed to how palpable a person's "way" in all their activities might be, but that it cannot be captured by any static or general description. This is certainly most in evidence in trying to understand or grasp a person's manner of relating to others in their way of being emotional. It is not comprised of any single fact or deed, but is a style, a rhythm, an orientation, almost like a flavor or an aroma or a melody, impossible to grasp from above or straight on with rational categories. This does not mean it is subjective or irrational, but just

that its understanding takes a joining in synchronization or a resonating or a dancing in an emotionally sensitive flow with another. As somehow including a myriad of specific aspects that comprise a person's way of relating, it is really quite complex in all its strands. Sensitive emotional understanding is often immediate, but
very complex. This is why it can always be plumbed for greater depths indefinitely,
as pointed out in a humorous way by the many Woody Allen film characters who
spend decades in psychoanalysis.

In letting this power of e-motion move us outside our habitual sense of self
to be sensitive to the other, there has to be a *groping* or *openness*, a *flexibility* or *mirroring*, otherwise we will impose our own rhythms onto the other's way, rather than
vibrating to theirs. If one is truly sensitive, then one will really cast oneself far outside one's usual patterns of movement, and be impacted upon by the others. This
gives the emotions their transformational power, which might alter our own customary kind of psychic movement for a time or for a longer duration. In this moving into the dance with another in their relatedness to the world as understanding
them emotionally, there is a real encounter, far from the safety of the sheltering
ego, even if its duration is brief. This power of emotion is what was so horrifying
to Lestat. Emotions have a movement that he was not the source of and therefore
not in control of, these encounters penetrated him, and emotions' transformation
threatened his own stable identity, since even a brief resonance can reverberate for
a long time.

We have been describing the deeper e-motions, the visceral, moving, and
non-rational specific opening and enmeshing with another being, which is the
distinctive gift of emotional life. However, there are other ways to be emotional.
The way of emotion we have been describing might best be called *exploratory* and
personally expressive. They are also *interpersonally intermeshing* and *transformational*.
I have stressed this kind of emotion, because it is perhaps what is most uniquely
revelatory. It is the way we can find out what is most unique about our relationship to the world and others, and follow out these complexities and depths to
fathom new qualities in us and others. This kind of emotion is powerful in the
sense of its potential to discover aspects of our lives that can only be found through
these emotions, but they do not necessarily have to be the most overwhelming in
terms of quantity of affect or vehemence of emotion. Writing in one's diary or visiting a strange child in a hospital or listening to a friend share their fears may be
an emotional experience which moves more slowly and quietly than cheering for
your team to win the championship or getting so furious at the person who damaged your car, but may be more powerful in revealing the depths and complexities of who you are or how you are related to others.

Given our culture's bias towards the quantitative, that more is somehow better, vehement emotions have been the ones cast as "powerful emotions." The "power"
in this case might not fit the distinctive power of emotions to be revealing and
expressive. The word "vehement" is interesting in that its roots suggest "without
mind" or "sense"—as if reason and emotion were opposites and could only be most
powerful when the other had been negated. This notion would have emotions only

really powerful as they become overwhelmingly present with no reason or sense involved to counter their irrational onslaught. However, in the earthbody layering of different kinds of apprehension, reason and emotion can be intertwined with imagination, memory, and other ways of apprehending the world and still be very moving, even if quieter and more sensitive. Then, emotions might be "powerful" in their distinctive sense of relationally revealing, and transforming, and forging connection and community.

Proust articulates this contrast between vehement and more revealing, transforming emotion well. In the passage we examined earlier, in the "Combray" section of *Remembrance of Things Past*, a momentary sense of the wondrous, the depths of the sensual, and of gratitude to natural beauty are felt by Swann in a subtle frisson while experiencing the flowers. This becomes a moment which returns throughout the narrator's life in inspiring a feeling of connection with the world and offering him a sense of vitality. By contrast, the hundreds of incidents of Swann's being torn apart and carried to extremes of vehemence by jealousy, hurt, sadness, and despair in relation to Odette, in *Swann's Way*, are like thunderstorms passing by which really reveal nothing to Swann except perhaps his foolishness. These vehement emotions are not really sensitive to what matters in Swann's world and are more a product of a fantasy of love detached from reality. These emotions are more of a series of charades on both Odette's and Swann's part. These emotional storms have no power to allow Swann creative transformation, but are empty storms, truly irrational in not making much sense, which is what Swann sees once when they've passed.

Actually, our cultural standards may be exactly wrongheaded. Although vehemence of emotion may sometimes betoken a really sensitive revelation, expression, or transformation of our lives, more often it is an exercise in arousing an affect that is pretty shallow and disconnected from people's more complicated and meaningful situations. For example, the despair we feel when our team loses the big game or getting angry over someone cutting in front of us in traffic are common occurrences. We may "have a fit" at those moments, and loosely say we are "powerfully moved," but we know we have avoided our deeper emotional life in claiming this. The most uniquely powerful movement of emotion is to change who we are and how we experience the world, as the main protagonist in Margaret Atwood's *Surfacing* expresses, after her harrowing emotional transformation at the climax of the book, "it would be like stepping through a usual door and finding yourself in a different galaxy, purple trees and red moons and a green sun."[21] The greatest power of emotion can be its revealing and transformative power that suddenly allows the world, others, or ourselves to be apprehended in an utterly new way.

Addictive Sentimentality

Approaching the question of the status of emotion shared on the Internet, we can now compare it to the multilayered, complex, "reversible," unique, and spontaneous resonance of sensitively revealing and expressive emotion. An instructive example is provided by the usually sober *New York Times*, who on April 23, 1995, joined the bandwagon in declaring that the Internet was affording break-throughs in emotional expression, widened circles of intimacy, and new possi-bilities of genuine community. The article was about Tom Mandel's experience on-line in the five months before his death from lung cancer. Mr. Mandel's death and his interactions while dying have become part of the lore of the Internet. The article, in a large and bold headline declared, "A Death On-line Shows a Cyberspace with Heart and Soul." Mandel had fought the cancer with a "cyber-family of interlocutors from the far reaches of the internet," as the *Times* put it. From his Web site, he shared the various stages of his discovery of the disease, his treatment, and eventual demise, with a constant barrage of communication with people through the Net he did not otherwise know. One person cited in the article as overcome with grief, sympathy, and anger when Tom's diagnosis was confirmed, had pounded out on her keyboard the message, to Tom from "DONNAH1066," "Oh, Tom . . .Damn, damn, damn, damn . . .I am sorry." These certainly sound like vehement emotions, but are they indicative of inti-macy, of enhanced opportunity to express deep emotion, and the creation of community as the *Times* proposes in this article? What does this say about the community Turkle's many subjects, and an increasing number of people glob-ally, seek on the Net?

Even though we have described how the internet is an embodied space, and this is what makes the emotionally moving and imaginatively elaborated experi-ences on the Net possible, there is a *screening off* of the body-to-body presence that diminishes many of the fleshly communicative possibilities. Part of the sensual "thinness" of projected photographic images, animated scenes, or even projected video clips is a screening of the material medium needed to carry the emotional depths we've been describing, which require the full sensorially present body of the other person sharing the situation. Of course, this is many times more the case if only language on a screen is the medium of contact, even though language, too, as we described, can elongate some of the body's presence. The chances to go deeper into layers of emotional interchange, to follow out branching complexities, to feel the other person feeling themselves through you, as you to feel yourself within the other person's feelings (in reversible boundaries), and staying open for any possi-bility from the other, are filtered from the screen interaction. These possibilities occur in the energy and meaning circulating through the sensual perception of material presence. Notice, however, that they are not totally absent either. This is not an either/or situation. We have shown how the echoes and elongations of these material energies are never fully lost. However, even more fragile and requiring immediate presence are the ways of non-rationally grasping the uniqueness of the other person's style or way of being and the kind of spontaneous resonance that occurs in apprehending the gestures, the facial expressions, the second to second variation in bearing, mood, and attitude that we read in the body of the other per-son, and in facing the myriad of unexpected shared challenges of being caught in the material situation together.

I will give a personal example from my family's interaction with one of our relatives, who also died slowly of cancer during an eight-month period as a comparison to peoples' experience with Tom Mandel on-line. Admittedly, this was an unusual case, and it involved what I think most of us would like to have happen in a period of dying. However, this is also the question at issue: are there other desirable emotional possibilities that we can't achieve on-line? There is too much to tell here, but briefly, as I sat with this relative, I often became aware of resonating to feelings emanating from her, which were unexpected to both of us. She was a woman who had lived most of her life as a rather unapproachable, critical person, who mostly seemed concerned with being in control of situations in order to get what she wanted. She had never been very comfortable expressing feelings, was a very nervous person, and seemed to express constant criticism and dissatisfaction with the situations and people around her. At first, I think I approached spending time with her during her illness as a regrettable familial duty.

However, it didn't take too many visits to realize that a transformation was taking place: a coming to terms with whatever had rankled her about her life and caused her to lash out at others and keep them at a distance. The look in her eyes changed. She was able to look at me with a steadiness, a warmth, and an openness that had never been part of her facial expression. Suddenly, there was a lot of laughter about all the daily frustrations that she had found so vexing throughout her life. Now, inconveniences that should have been really trying as the devouring cancer made her weaker and weaker were met with equanimity. It was also true that besides giving these emotional cues, she was able to articulate verbally some measure of how she had become awakened by her illness to what was important in life and her sense of appreciation for all of the mundane activities of living. She now could articulate her loving feelings about people. A lot of her coming to this point was achieved through her emotional interactions with people of the kind that could not have happened through a computer screen.

One day in particular stands out in my mind, at the beginning of those months when she was still physically robust enough to go for an extended walk. We walked along the beach and also sat looking out at the water together for quite some time. My love of the water I know was communicated in my expressions and postures, and I felt her resonating to them and also taking delight in the scene around us. Also, at one point, when we were discussing our lives together, for she had been a caregiver to me in childhood, she took my hand and expressed through this gesture a directness of affection I had never experienced from her before. Also, there was a new gentleness and openness. The presence of the waves around us, the peacefulness of the scene with the gulls and the sand, as well as our gesture of sharing, I also know had something to do with the meandering path of the conversation during our walk. She shared emotional aspects of her life history—like being a young woman going off to work in a strange city during World War II— that she had never shared with me before. Not all of the emotional communications were so idyllic as those that day, as the months brought for all of us moments of dealing with her falling or vomiting or being unable to eat, etc. However, even sharing in these events, with all their material inconvenience and sometimes visceral distaste, also forged bonds and understandings about the other person's situation. What they are actually going through becomes real and challenges the people involved to find new resources in themselves (and also together within their relationships) of compassion, courage, humility, considerateness, honesty, stamina, patience, humor, and a host of other qualities.

For the people sharing Tom Mandel's illness on the Net, and for other screened Internet communal experiences, there are some of these emotionally challenging aspects present. It takes courage to write to the other in the face of pain, embarrassment, and the threat of death. These people did show significant empathy, compassion, perhaps affection, differing degrees of openness, concern, loyalty, diligence, etc. However, as an example of probably one of the deepest ties that can be formed through screen contact, this cyber-community hailed by the *Times* was forged by *sentiment* and not by what we called "exploratory and personally expressive, interpersonally intermeshing, and transformational emotion." *The emotional content of sentiment is the registration of the felt quality of relation through generalized representations.* We understand in general, through the experiences we've encountered and can abstract from and represent in an image or idea or notion, what this situation feels like. We apply it to this specific case. All of us know what it's like to get a threatening diagnosis, whether from our own experience or from other people we know or from reading about cases or watching them on television or even from fictional cases in novels or films, etc., and from this knowledge can represent to ourselves what that person feels emotionally and react to that. So, even though our response is geared towards the specific individual in their unique situation, it is a response engendered by what we have understood to be the "meaning this would have for anyone in this kind of situation."

Besides this generality of content, there is a quality of sentiment which is called a "mental feeling" in the dictionary.[22] This common usage recognizes that this emotion has been filtered through the mind, instead of welling up from the senses and the body. Instead of an immediate response, it is a mentally or cognitively engendered experience that we bring to a situation which seems to fit its contours. This is not to say that the sentiment, once brought to bear upon a situation, doesn't frame it in a meaningful way, but it does point to a different level of spontaneity and discovery than the more groping and spontaneous emotion we have been discussing. Sentiment is powerful in that it gives us a very public way of sharing certain feelings and emotional understandings. Especially in a culture in which there is increasing emotional isolation and lack of ready community, sentiment can be as refreshing and nourishing as a spring in the midst of a desert. As we said before, in many situations we do not want depth of involvement or revelation, and sentiment is often the key to creating an amicable and cooperative atmosphere among people. Emotionally, it gives us a "generally applicable" apprehension, which is usually sufficient.

However, it is important to avoid false expectations of sentiment. It is even more important to be aware of sentiment's abuses. If we return to a few of Turkle's cases, she relates how Peter, a twenty-eight-year-old lecturer in comparative literature "thought he was in love with a MUDding partner who played Beatrice to his Dante (their characters' names)." They had felt there was a deep intellectual, emotional, and erotic sharing in their screen interactions, since they had typed out detailed descriptions of their thoughts and feelings. However, when Peter flew from North Carolina to Oregon to meet the real person behind Beatrice, he returned home crushed: "'[On the MUD] I saw her as I wanted to see her. Real life gave me too much information'" (*LS*, 207). The body-to-body presence of the other gives one far more than the representations, the generalizations, or these feeling-laden but mental notions about the other on the Net. The affection of sentiment is real, but it can't be substituted for the love between two people arising from shared immediate experience, since it is a different kind of emotion which takes its particular quality from the context in which it arises.

Sentiment, besides having a distinct, but limited, value of its own, can certainly become a step towards developing deeper emotions, but only if it is surpassed to take the plunge in encountering others without a safety net. The experience of Stewart, who found his on-line emotional involvement addictive and not leading to transformation, began after he realized that the woman who introduced him to the MUDs on-line sought her emotional solace from the net. She "turned her back on him to talk to the people in the machine." Stewart's reaction had been "I mean when you have that type of emotional problem and that kind of pain, it's not an intelligent move to log on to a game and talk to people because they are safe and won't hurt you. Because that's not a way out of it" (*LS*, 197). Yet, Stewart himself, when he began his life of more than forty hours per week logged on, felt addicted to the sentiments he was sharing on the Net, but wasn't willing to attempt with others outside cyberspace. Even his more than twenty pages of text shared on-line of the engagement and marriage ceremonies as Achilles joining with Winterlight is only an opportunity for sentiment. All the participants feel what one would feel in such a romantic and mythical space of love's enchantment, but not the messy reality of an interaction between two people with all the quirks of their histories, personalities, and specific situations that moves beyond sentiment.

Since sentiment only requires one to play a general role and not to really encounter the other, there is not that immediate tug of reversibility drawing the other person into unknown feelings and responses. This makes it feel safe, since it is a predictable acting out of general, agreed upon roles. People can maintain a feeling of control in the sense of knowing the self that is being exposed, even if the feelings are vehement and become overwhelming and "out of control" in that sense: they still fit established patterns for that person or for the group with which they identify. For example, a husband who "loses control" of his anger and becomes physically abusive to his wife and children for some trivial act that irked him, and then perhaps is contrite afterwards, is acting out of a sentiment that has had validation as being part of his identity or as part of the male behavior patterns with which he identifies. He would probably feel more "out of control," in the sense of being pulled into unknown waters, if he were to be quiet and discuss his pain and frustrations with his family, and resonate to their mutual hurt. Perhaps, then he would do something unheard of and dreaded, such as crying with them as part of the communicative process of working things out. We think sentiment is pretty. It has a very ugly face, too.

The vehemence of feelings does not succeed in substituting for the intimacy of real emotional encounter and the being challenged to respond and become transformed by the parameters of a uniquely shared situation. Accordingly, there is an emptiness that can't be filled. This leads to a compulsive, addictive longing for more sentiment. As Stewart put it, "the more I do it, the more I feel the need to do it" (*LS*, 198). In a way, this is even a step backwards from being a ghoul, vampire, or aesthete, since all those strategies attempt to manipulate the other into a vulnerability that can then be appropriated dishonestly in such a way that the appropriator was not made equally vulnerable. At least real vitality and depth of feeling in their unique expression is the goal sought, even if dishonestly taken from the other. Here, both people (or the many people involved) agree only to seek sentiment and not go beyond this limit, so no one is vulnerable and no one really encounters another in their unique identity and emotional complexity. With this fear-riddled need to be safe, the cyberspace community and its shared emotion can become a diversionary mutual hypnosis and a filling of a hunger with an emotional nourishment without any substance. The resulting emptiness renders the hunger insatiable. An unacknowledged dissatisfaction and addiction easily follow.

We do culturally acknowledge that sentiment can become degraded from its more legitimate form of making wide but not very complex or involving emotional experiences able to be shared by many. When it becomes more of an empty, diversionary emotional exercise, we call the associated events or objects "kitsch." Kitsch is bad art or entertainment or events, in the sense that they are constructed merely to meet people's most simplified expectations, to give them an emotional experience whose main pleasure is its comfortable feeling, because it involves no real active response on their part. It is utterly digestible or without any challenge to them. Most people will feel little puppies are cute or children hugging their parents is heart-warming, so we can construct paintings or films or television shows or events that limit themselves to portraying in an emphasized way these "stock situations" with their "stock feelings." If we become a society addicted to a diet of kitsch, then the produced emotions will fail to release us beyond our old boundaries of self, fail to make us encounter aspects of the world about which we are ignorant, and fail to bring us into engaged relation with others. Insofar as the Internet is a screened experience dealing in sentiment, it could easily degenerate into a "kitschfest," which could become the focus of empty emotional lives.

Emotional Fiends Can Become Adolescent Killers

This brings us to the most destructive possibility of relying upon sentiment to the exclusion of a more open, reciprocal, and challenging emotional relation with others. In keeping with the other images of this book, I will call this possibility "emotional fiendishness." As we often use the word nowadays, a fiend is addicted to something, but it is recognized that it is something that is often self-destructive or destructive to others, such as the older "opium fiend" or the more current "dope fiend". Sometimes, when we call someone a fiend in an informal way, we mean they are addicted or possessed by something harmless in itself, but it can become dangerous to the fiend and others when that person will only pursue this object to the exclusion of other necessary or creative parts of life. So, a coffee fiend might skip the food he or she needs or a speed fiend might endanger passengers. Of course, fiends traditionally were evil spirits, especially those that seemed to thrive on destruction and being cruel, taking pleasure from inflicting pain upon others. So, in Mary Shelley's *Frankenstein*, the creation is referred to as "the creature" at first, then "the monster", but finally is continually addressed by Frankenstein as "a fiend." The fiend inflicts cruelty on Frankenstein (as well as on his victim) by hurting innocent people whom Frankenstein loves; Frankenstein becomes torn apart by pain at indirectly causing their deaths by creating the monster. This use of the term fiend resonates to its etymological roots in the Icelandic, which designated "foes" or "hating." The greatest sense of fiendishness is to be addicted by or obsessed with pursuing acts of hostility, of destructiveness, and of being foe to one and all.

It is in indulging these aggressive emotions as sentiments that the Internet and other aspects of cyberspace have been most upsetting to many. The myriad games that call upon the players to kill unrelentingly, to even tear their foes apart limb by limb, to move through hostile worlds in an orgy of violence, destruction, and conquest, engender an appetite for sentiments of the worst kind. They are sentiments in the same sense we have been discussing, as generalized and shallow emotional contents meant to appeal to anyone in a easily identifiable way. They don't require any vulnerability, any groping openness and transformation as in sensitive emotional interaction. They actually act as emotional shields. If one can settle into a constant diet of indulging these violent sentiments and then project them onto other situations outside the video game setting, the call to be emotional in a slower, open, and reciprocal way is crowded out and its summons is drowned out by the vehemence of these sentiments. Since sentiment requires us to bring an "emotional concept" to the situation, if one is relying upon it addictively to maintain a defensive posture, such persons could now screen out the actual presence of others. It is perhaps not surprising that Turkle's Stewart, after indulging compulsively in MUDs, not only could not connect with the affectionate, friendly, open, and vulnerable sentiments he had shared on the Net as Achilles. Lacking the intention, belief, and openness necessary to bring these positive internet feelings into deeper emotion, he clung to them as sentiments, which demanded nothing of him. After this period, he ended up moving into a subsequent period of being invasive, intrusive, and hostile on the Net (*LS*, 199–200).

If our descriptions have been accurate, the possibilities for sensitive, transformational emotion become greater as people have discovered more selves within them, as they have come to understand their emotional strengths, and as they have a better sense of the directions in which they need to open themselves to make up for deficiencies. Given the experience, skill, and history necessary to do this, adolescents must rely upon sentiments more than adults. When we are beginners—and emotional artistry is a learned achievement—we start with a more generalized approach according to a more conceptualized notion of the process and gradually learn the immediacy of response, the intricacies of situation, and the ways to direct ourselves. Since, in the emotional realm, this means we have to start with more sentiment and less highly tuned emotions, adolescents will be particularly vulnerable to the Net, as well as to other modern forms of portraying and inculcating sentiment. Given this vulnerability, society has an obligation to recognize the danger of how this starting point can lead to an addictive substitution for more challenging emotional development.

A horrible example has been provided by the rash of adolescent shooting sprees at schools in rural settings. With this adolescent vulnerability to the abuse of sentiment on the Net (and other media) in mind, it is startling to ponder the lives of the seven boys who went on murderous rampages during the years 1997 to 1998. All are reported to be/have been socially withdrawn and but very taken with images that appeal to violent sentiments through television, films, music, and the Net. The Internet has the potential to add to an obsession with sentiments of violence that are not engendered by a response to murderous environmental conditions, but are the result of a fantasy world gone awry—in that it has become a substitution for emotional interactions which really are responsive to the complexities of other people and situations. There are many other factors which need to be examined in regard to the plight of these boys, but in terms of this chapter, we should conclude with looking for a moment at why violent sentiment has such an appeal and danger for adolescents (especially for *boys* who are socialized to be much more uncomfortable with emotional sensitivity and expression than girls),[23] as well as for the rest of our society, and why the split between the virtual and the actual in our culture's philosophical heritage actually makes us apt to act out our fantasy worlds in destructive ways.

A life confined to sentiment would be an impoverished one without the complexity of emotional sensitivity. It lacks a real give and take with others in response to their unique attributes. However, a life of obsession with violent sentiments is more than impoverished, it is dangerous to all. If retreat to sentiment is a retreat from having to resonate to the other and to the energies of the landscape and larger world in a way that takes unplanned and unforeseen directions, it can seem to provide a sense of control, distance, imposition of will, and power. The power comes from the sense that this person is the agent, doing onto the world what is wished and being invulnerable to other people's desires and wants, at least emotionally. As Sartre pointed out fifty years before these attacks in *Being and Nothingness*, in the face of a sense of emptiness, distanced from the world in alienation, and on some level frustrated by this sense of disconnection, the need to gain control of this situation leads people to find destruction far preferable to maintaining relation, or even to attempting to control others through possession, and also to find hate preferable to love. Actually, in the logic Sartre articulates, the perfect solution to love's fragility and complexity is murder. I know there are, as I said before, other factors involved, but our culture is incredibly resistant to looking at how our way of conceiving of reality, our philosophy as it shows itself in our spirituality, in our psychology, and in our ethical standards, also has a great impact on how we lead our lives and treat others and the earth. Philosophy has been consigned to the academic ivory tower, yet it uncovers vital forces in our actions. So, I propose using Sartre for a moment to look at the philosophical reasons inherent in our culture for violence and murder, and for our addiction with violent sentiment as displayed in our saturation with violence in our television, movies, literature, video games, and on-line.

The central thesis of Sartre's *Being and Nothingness* is that an approach to the world that operates by what we have called "the diabolical logic"—which sees human beings as standing over and against the world and other human beings—is destined to always feel at its deepest levels of consciousness that it is incomplete and threatened with a sense of emptiness, non-being, or "failing to be anything." This book should make us see that the irony of this relationship to the world is that it creates the sense of being cut off from an inherent belonging to the rest of the planet as a sensing body interconnected within a weave of energies and meaning. Yet this is the power of the mind, to say "no," as well as to say "yes," to deny or to affirm. Yet, it is more than a thought. It creates an experience of feeling separated, and as it deepens, even an experience of being alienated. This is why in *The Brothers Karamazov* Dostoyevsky makes the devil appear to Ivan, one of the brothers, and confess that he, the devil, is nothing else than this power to negate, to say "no" to what we are. One starts by saying "no" and can become alienated, as Ivan suffers throughout the novel.

If we have cut ourselves off from being part of the dance of interconnectedness on this planet that is rightfully part of who we are as embodied beings, as earthbodies, and which still always survives on some level that we tune out, disbelieve, and stay distracted from, then this is a loss no other substitute can heal. Only a change in our way of seeing the world and embracing a different relationship with it could do that. So, Sartre shows that all our frenzied pursuit of success, status, power, achievement, possession, and love is an attempt to have these other things symbolize for us the value of this part of us that we are missing, this non-being our way of seeing reality has created. This attempt can't succeed and so these pursuits are part of a "vain passion" that haunts our lives lived within this perspective. However, what is relevant to this chapter is that Sartre shows how this poisons our "concrete relations with others"—our friendships, our sense of community, and even, or perhaps especially, our loves.

The reason we never can dispel fully feeling insecure when we see the world as me versus them or it, is that no matter how many successes, how much money, or how many friends we have, they still are at a distance from me given this boundary. Also, as the key to filling my emptiness, these conquests can always fail by being taken from my control. No matter how much someone may put their mark on their house or on a corporation or their spouse, someone else or something else may destroy it or take it away. However, even if we are fortunate to maintain strict control over our possessions, or successes, or even people we feel we possess, in this isolated individualism we are left to always wonder how others see us and what they think of us. Even if my house or corporation or fortune is not destroyed or taken away, it can be devalued by others in such a way that it no longer adds to me and fills up my hole. Instead, it can be transformed into another negative. The other person can always think what a joke to think that this sports car, this fortune, or this spouse is the ultimate prize, and reintroduce the insecurity that these relations or possessions were meant to dispel.

Given this stance of the "I" versus the world, Sartre says the basic meaning of human relations and even love is hostility. We don't want to be devalued by others, so we manipulate them in blatantly hostile ways or sometimes in covert ways. If we have this separation and insecurity regarding the world, then, for Sartre, love is the attempt to get the other person to freely choose us as ultimately valuable, as the "be all and end all" in some way. However, as is apparent with a moment's reflection or by looking at the daily fare of television shows or movies, this is an inherently unstable situation. It only works to overcome our insecurity if the other person *freely chooses* to affirm me as this be all and end all. If they are utterly enslaved because they have been forced into this choice or have no judgment and are addicted to their love, their love won't help overcome the insecurity, for there is no discernment on their part the loved person can credit to themselves. However, if on the other hand, they are still free to choose in some other way, then the insecurity also still remains: they might choose someone else tomorrow, hence the endless demands of proof of love and its permanence. We want them to choose us, but the choice is to be so overwhelmingly clear it will never be questioned. If this were not an impossible enough demand, there is the problem that each partner of the couple is trying to get the other to do the same thing that has been aimed at them. At best, this is a precarious seesaw.

However, think of the advantages, if we are insecure, of making the hostility between people trying to win over others become overt. To keep others enthralled with us as lovable is difficult and always open to question. Have I done enough? Am I really wonderful enough? It seems a lot easier to be the object of scorn and to scorn others back in return. If one can take pleasure in being hated, then it is a rather more secure position, one's identity seems less in question, since it is much easier to gain enmity than friendship or admiration. The price for being a hateful person is to have the strength needed to scorn the approbation that comes with this identity. However, if the person in question has already given up on forming sensitive human relations with others and has retreated to living life behind the screen of sentimentality, then being the target of hate will not have the same impact as it would for sensitive people. Furthermore, it has the distinct advantage of usually involving sentiments that are quite vehement, so in retreating to sentiment, the person forsakes the quality of emotional life for the quantity of affect. Living amidst hate, hostility, and violence with others will give the person a powerful affective charge and the security of knowing where they stand.

In an analogous fashion, if we approach the world by trying to gain our status through possessing things, we are always struggling to get more things and to keep others admiring these possessions. It is hard to maintain control over possessions and thereby keep insecurity at bay. However, if we destroy something, we forever control its destiny. If I own something, I may lose it, or it might be destroyed, or it might be stolen, or taken from me in some way, but if I destroy something, it will always be the thing *that I destroyed*. As Sartre cogently put it, "This is precisely why the recognition that it is impossible to *possess* an object involves. . . .a violent urge to *destroy* it. To destroy means to reabsorb into myself . . . . In annihilating it I am changing it into *myself*. . . .*I am* this barn since I am destroying its being" (*BN* 756). Its being has become added to mine in a way that can't be touched since I am forever linked with it as its destroyer, whereas adding its being to mine through possession can always be altered. This logic can be taken to its ultimate and grisly conclusion with people. If we look upon people and our relationships as possessions, we are always apt to lose them. However, if we destroy them, we are always with them in this destruction as the one who did it to them. The final emotional destination this leads to is murder.

For adolescents who are not yet secure with sensitive emotion, given the self-understanding it requires, and who rely on sentiment, it is easy to see that feeding them a diet of destructive and hateful sentiments might lead them to deal with their insecurities, also much heightened in adolescence, in habitually hostile, increasingly violent, and eventually in some desperate cases, even murderous ways. Even though it is more a danger for adolescents, it is also a danger for a population at large that feels increasingly cut off from others, insecure about their value and emotional ties to others, and who come to rely, through the Net and other media, on a sentimental connection with others. Even when most of us may not be led to extreme sentiments of hostility and hate, we can be led to living with a diet of more and more hostile sentiments, where we treat fellow drivers on the highway as if they are cars in a crash derby on a cd-rom game or as obstacles, we can blow away in cyberspace "harmlessly." We can go through life as if we were making our way through the worlds of video games just trying to avoid the obstacles and never be open to really experiencing the world or others in an open, groping, and undefended way.

Integrating the Virtual and the Real

The split between the virtual and the real is the latest tragedy of the dualistic kind of philosophy we've been trying to get beyond throughout this book. If cyberspace is taken as mere cyberspace in distinction to a reality that is reality, then we lose track of the far more changeable and complex place in which we live, which is a mixture of both. We also do not see ourselves as unfolding processes that can branch off in many ways given with whom or with what we truly connect. We take reality literally and we take cyberspace literally. If we would see that reality is made up of virtuality, we would see how we could play with virtual experiences in such a way as to try to connect them back to our everyday relationships. Another of Turkle's subjects, Case, a male industrial designer, successfully integrated the two when playing several female roles in MUDs in cyberspace. For Case, virtual reality was not separate from reality, nor was it purely virtual: "For virtual reality to be interesting it has to emulate the real. But you have to be able to do something in the virtual that you couldn't in the real" (*LS*, 219). Cyberspace can been seen as a more imaginary realm that has more space to play and to try out new things, but only does so in a transforming way if its overlap with the "real world" is kept alive for that person.

This insight has to go further to acknowledge that the so-called real world is made up of roles, fantasies, and ever-changeable stories. When the two realms are kept open to each other, then we can use cyberspace or film or other virtual realities, as Case did when he reports "I am able to do things—in the real, that is—that I couldn't have because I have played Katherine Hepburn characters." This means that we as individuals and as a society need to start connecting these realms, to be more imaginative, to see the virtual in the real and the real in the virtual. As Case learned through his experience in cyberspace, "MUDs give me balance" (*LS*, 220). There needs to be a balance established between the real and the virtual within and without cyberspace, in our day-to-day lives, and in our learning to experience nature and culture.

If virtuality is not seen as part of "the real world," we risk acting irresponsibly, feeding ourselves a constant diet of violent and hostile sentiments, which bleed over into our real life. Since we are only a process, ever apt to alter our rhythms, our emotional tenor, and our ways of relating, what we do in cyberspace or in movie theaters changes who we are. Furthermore, for those more insecure individuals who indulge in these sentiments in flight from so-called reality, they, in the end, might substitute one for the other, trying to blot out the more threatening real world and substitute for it a video game world. They may well mow down their classmates or fellow workers, or at least treat them as video characters and not as sensitive people. Since they've literalized them as separate realms, they can switch one for the other in a desperate choice of either/or. If virtuality and reality were part of each other for them, they couldn't hide or substitute or screen out sensitive life.

On the other hand, if reality is seen as purely and substantially real, like a rock is a rock, and not seen as part virtual, then we act humorlessly and unimaginatively. We lack ceremonial awareness of our place in the many dramas of existence and of ourselves an erotic adventurers with the openness to trying new selves in new dances. We don't see our dynamic ability to change and transform in relation to others and voyage to new universes through the imaginative depths of our senses. Without seeing this dimension of layers of meaning, of ambiguity, and of indeterminacy, both the real world and cyberspace become narrow corridors that don't challenge us beyond our established place in each. In this way, both can fall into mere sentiment to the exclusion of sensitive emotion. Then the real fades into an empty show of routine gestures and practicality, while cyberspace becomes a compulsive addiction to a "time out" from reality that substitutes for real change and robs cyberspace of its transformative power. Two recent films demonstrate the problem of keeping fact separate from fiction and therefore lifeless, or indulging in a separate fictional or virtual realm to the exclusion of its relationship to reality that also makes it sterile and potentially dangerous.

During the year of 1998, the film *Titanic* set all sorts of box office records. It is an interesting retelling of this tragic story, not only because of James Cameron's insistence on the series of brilliant special effects that gives the audience all the bodily feelings of being trapped on the *Titanic*, but even more so for the wonderful "frame story" which uses the story of the *Titanic* to tell a powerful tale about our culture. In the movie, the crew of a salvage ship has been working obsessively for three years, mapping every inch of the wreck in order to find its treasures, especially the diamond, the Heart of the Ocean. When they finally locate the safe they believed the diamond to be in and find it's not there, they are crestfallen. However, during a televised interview with the captain, the surviving passenger, Rose—the subject of the love story of this telling of the *Titanic* story—sees her picture, drawn on the night of the sinking. They have found it in the safe, and she contacts the captain as the one who wore the diamond as portrayed in the drawing. They fly her out to the site at sea, and most of the movie occurs as Rose retells her story, and the story of the sinking, to the spellbound crew of the salvage operation. The crew has every technological marvel at their disposal, and with their submersibles and banks of instruments seem like they're in outer space.

When Rose arrives, the crew chief takes her through a computer-generated series of simulations of the collision with the iceberg and a detailed, fact-laden, and statistically exact rendering of every aspect of the accident. Rose responds by saying, "thank you for that forensic presentation, but it's not quite the way it happened if you were there." They are so lost in this objective reality, they are truly ignorant about the sinking of the *Titanic*. As they listen through the night to Rose's account of the stories of the people on the ship, to the network or relationships among the people, and to the feelings, the desires, the fantasies, and the sensual experiences of the people on board during the sinking, they are absorbed in an involving dimension of reality from which they had been effectively screened by their quantified version of the "real sinking." When Rose finally finishes her story, they sit there stunned. Finally, the captain speaks with Rose, and, husky with tears and visibly shaken confesses, "I have been obsessed for three years with every detail of the *Titanic*, and I never got it." They thought that reality was objective, a set of true facts, as our culture has tended to assume for millennia.

The captain never got it, because he didn't feel the emotions, the sensations, the fantasies, the relationships, etc., that give the reality of an event its meaning. Something means something only within contexts, within horizons of hopes and fears and values, and as it has impact on the many beings involved and within the social, historical, and natural context. The abstracted facts and rational calculations left the captain with what I called, in my book, *Emotion and Embodiment* "emotional blind/numbness." It wasn't real for him or meaningful, nor did he form a relationship with what he was supposedly understanding that could transform him in any way. He was out of touch with the *Titanic*, its story and significance, during the whole time he crawled through every inch of her and obsessively thought about her. With his literalness about the facts and his "objectivity" that separated him from the passengers and the pathos of the wreck, the "me versus them" of the diabolical logic kept him safely hidden behind his firm boundaries and rendered him incapable of seeing the depths of meaning that an open and feelingful taking up of earthbodies allows.

In a strange juxtaposition, *The Truman Show* was released right after the initial frenzy with *Titanic* died down, and its theme is the mirror image of *Titanic*'s. In *The Truman Show*, Peter Weir presents us with a world in which there are no facts per se, but only fabrications of a "fictional world." Truman Burbank's entire life has been spent on an elaborate soundstage in which everyone is playing a role, and being constantly directed by "the Creator"—the television director, Christof, and his assistants, who are continuously observing and manipulating "the drama." This round-the-clock "candid camera" show is a smash hit, with a generation of people having watched Truman's life since he was born onto the soundstage, nearly thirty years ago. The catch is that only Truman doesn't know that it's a show. He's been kept in the dark. Whether it's the sun or the moon or the depressions of his lifelong friend, all is a manipulated prop or plot device. Every article of clothing or food or furniture is for sale to viewers through the Truman catalogue. However, given our lives in this culture, Truman has been happy. He greets the day with packaged sentiments for his neighbors, fellow workers, or whomever he encounters on the street, as most of us do. They respond with their portrayed sentiments according to direction and script. He is equally playing a role to theirs, as do most of us, so all proceeds well.

The interesting aspect of this charade is not that Truman begins to suspect that something is fake, but that he was comfortable with this life for three decades and that his audience was fascinated. Truman, has been locked into the sentimental, emphasized by his daily greeting to his neighbors: not only "good morning," but "good afternoon and good evening, in case I don't see you." This carries to its conclusion the logic of sentiment that requires no real presence or interaction, and so absurdly could just be given out in blanket quantities to cover all occasions or events. Given his decades of contentment in this safe environment, not ever even noticing that his wife has no real passion for him during their marriage nor that his mother doesn't really love him, Truman has been living a distant, disembodied life in sentimental hypnosis. In terms of this chapter, he lives within the supplied fantasy world in a literal way, substituting sentiment for any real contact, so he hasn't even missed "reality." The Internet, and other modern media including film, television, etc., offer us substitutes in which sentiment is the rule.

As for Truman's audience, they have been absorbed in his life for decades, avidly consuming this sentimentality as if it were the real emotional contact possible in their lives. We see a number of viewers, who seem to care more about Truman's "life" than their own, as a way of literalizing the sentiments and substituting them for vulnerable, involving emotions. Such a substitution of sentiment for other emotions was never more apparent than with the fascination with the life and death of Princess Diana, the most photographed person in history. The sentiments presented are not used as ways of getting back outside the show to open up aspects of themselves that viewers could "try out" empathetically with Truman, but are just consumed whole, as sufficient fare. When Truman begins to suspect that his life is a fake, and he rejects Christof's confrontation and challenge that "we accept the reality of the world with which we are presented," the audience seems to cheer for his rebellion and attempt to escape this imprisoning virtual reality. However, this phenomenon seems to be more centered on the good drama it provides, a heightened "special effect" that is more "lifelike" than the audience's desire to really connect with life and their lives and put aside the canned, consumable sentimental fare. It may be more exciting if we can go on-line and be sentimental about someone's illness or financial problems or romance than playing a purely fictional game, but these facts have been absorbed into a sentimental, virtual context where they can't challenge us with the complexities of our face-to-face lives. Truman may want to leave a world in which all is done for public consumption and distanced amusement, but probably not his audience. The film's last image is of the two viewers who have been obsessively watching "The Truman Show" during the time of the movie, immediately turning for the television guide to find another show to replace "The Truman Show," when it's obvious it has come to an end.

If virtual reality becomes literalized and is a world unto itself, it, like our other mediated realities, can become an escape, or even more dangerously, a place to exercise and habituate destructive sentiments. It could also be used as a meeting place in which to hold ceremonies, to use our imaginations, and to construct contexts for exploring unknown parts of ourselves, if it were identified and valued as a place within the real world. Then, we would have to find ways to insure the Internet overlapped with the real world. Its content would have to come into contact responsively with the larger context of culture and nature. The so-called real world can't be literalized either, for the "objective world" of "diabolical logic" is no place where humans, as involved with the larger flow of life energies on this planet, can thrive. The timing, the ceremonial awareness, the depths of the sensual, the enlivening erotic, and the multiplicity of dimensions of reality and the multiplicity of possible selves can only open up for us when we make "magic theaters" for ourselves to allow our emotions, imaginations, intuitions, senses, and ideas freedom to roam.

Chapter Five

Planetary Meaningfulness

Introduction: The World Is Our "Out of Body" Body

As he was dying, Descartes proclaimed his joy at being released from the prison house of his body, a sentiment that has been echoed by many in the Western cultural tradition and globally. The body is imprisoning in the sense that our bodies are commitments. Our bodies commit us to an indissoluble relationship with all other living and non-living beings on this planet. To be a body is to be part of everything else and to be caught up in this circulation of energy and meaning with other beings on this planet, as we have described. Much of New Age thinking is not very new in its repetition of this desire to transcend the body towards the "white light" or other realms of pure spirit that are not "confined" to any organic or material form. They are about becoming released from the complexities of the earth, which for them are "snares." However, from what are we to be released? It is usually stated that we are to be released from this "vale of tears," from suffering of various sorts. However, what we are really to be released from is not suffering, for in the end suffering is bearable and can even, if used well, "suffer us into wisdom," as Sophocles put it. The release is from responsibility. Commitment is about being responsible, in both the traditional sense of being morally accountable, and in the modern sense of "being able to respond to" someone or something.

Whether it is white light, some supernatural force, aliens, or some caricature of the world's great religions with God represented as an all-powerful man with a white beard or gods and goddesses as groups of beautiful men and women scantily attired, the scenario of leaving the body is always to join up with some force or being that has authority and provides sheltering security and peace. For Freud, this desire was the "death instinct." To give up the trials of human life for the inert peace of utter unity was to desire to exist no more as a human. There have been innumerable myths and stories about wishing to soar above the body, to fly free in space, or to journey to some realm of pure spirit. These journeys are all escapes. One is taken care of, sheltered, and no longer vulnerable. It's a "free ride." Whatever is to be done next comes from the light itself or whatever realm one has joined: the constraint of earth is gone. Everything on earth is constrained: each footstep fights gravity, as does the beating of the heart, the circulating of the blood; eating food is a struggle with others for resources and with the earth itself and its soils and animals, and leads to wastes which must be disposed of; moving means avoiding the paths of others, fighting weariness; communicating means one has to learn a language; and all is limited by time. Another way to say this, however, is that everything on earth is a matter of working with other things, of having to respond to the forces and presences of others of all sorts, and to not have willful control to just do whatever one wishes. We have to work with the plants, the gravity of hillsides, the need for our hearts to have fluids and a way to circulate those fluids, to accommodate those other creatures in our common space, etc. This interwoven condition means we are responsible for our part of making it work for all. It takes cooperation. It takes commitment to keep working with all other beings.

Commitments take work, and work of a special kind. They require finding ever anew the energy and sensitivity required to be responsive and the openness to become touched by those to whom we are relating. Besides the fear of death and fear of not having ultimate control we have discussed in terms of taking up the body sensitively, there is a greediness of many about "holding on" to their energy and safeguarding themselves from change through interaction with others, as if these were finite resources that would be used up. This stems from understanding ourselves as substance, quantities of stuff that can be counted up, rather than as a dynamic process that creates more energy through its interactions and feeding back into itself.

These concerns seem to be behind our almost willful misunderstanding of what our bodies are. We can on rare occasions hover over ourselves from the vantage point of the ceiling, we can for a moment have the uncanny feeling of being thrown back into our past of twenty years ago, or we can fly to the moon in our dreams. However, even when awake, we can't fully avoid even being partially walking on the moon, even if we wanted to do so, especially now that humans have walked on the moon and their images and echoes are part of our history, and part of our makeup as bodies of meaning whose knowledge of history intertwines with our bodies' sensing, imagining, remembering, moving, feeling, expressing, etc. In the moments that make up a lot of our day, amazingly almost at will, we can travel through time to relive experiences or even to times far distant, like that of the Ancient Greeks at Athens, and see for a moment Socrates in the market discussing philosophy with the young men after their athletic training. Or we move through space to a spot visited many times before on the other side of the world or to other spots only visited through pictures, accounts, or films. We can move into realms of other galaxies aboard the Starship Enterprise or to a Denmark of an anguished Hamlet over the grave of poor Yorick. Our bodies are not barriers, but are rather our way around times and spaces and differing dimensions. Without the body and its sensual presencing, without the body and its being moved into emotion by feeling viscerally our relations with other beings, without the wonderful imagistic power of imagining, we would arrive nowhere, at a point with nothing given to us

as experienceable. Fortunately, our bodies move throughout the world and its layered dimensions to many possible places.

Our cultural response is to claim this is not really "going" anywhere in time
or space or dimension. If we "move" this way, it is just "mental," just "our doing,"
rather than "being there." What does just "being there" mean in this case? Somehow to be in "another time," for example, would be to take a "free ride," where we
could be totally passive and just have it all utterly given to us. It only counts as real
if we were infants being cradled by some power that would have taken care of all
the creativity, all the effort, for us. The fact that the body is dispersed throughout
the world, wherever we wish to focus ourselves, is incredibly powerful. However,
it is not all-powerful like a god. The fact that, when we look at a tree or a skyscraper, our body enters a flow of energy such that we see a view encompassing (as
part of what I see at the moment without even especially focusing on it) what the
treetop or top floor of the skyscraper "sees" from that vantage point is an amazing
ability of the body's sensorium. Even sitting at my desk, I can at this moment
assume the vantage of a bird flying above my house to see "down" on it. Actually,
this view, although just a submerged part of my background perception, was part
of my sense of sitting here at the keyboard, anyway. My body as this circulation of
sense in perception moves through the treetop or the skyscraper or is in some sense
everywhere in the world that I have or will reach through my intertwined powers
of apprehension. My body is like a weed that grows its extended presence everywhere I have gone through my faculties. Yes, it is more forcefully somewhere if I
have been literally present in the spot, because of the greater richness of the input
we have described in the last chapter of straightforward perceptual contact. My
body can't go "out of itself" because this is what it is already: a journey through all
these times, places, and differing spaces that are now part of me as this always further unfolding flow.

Animals and Humans as Part of the Same Dream

One place where my body always is located is everywhere in the world that
animals move sensing, running, crawling, swinging, soaring, playing, hunting, rest-
ing, dreaming, communicating, caring, encountering, fighting, and gathering. If
the human body were not extended through all its animal fellow-beings, as a circulation of sense and vitality, we would be missing a lot of what we appreciate from
the world, understand about the world, and can sense in the world. We have alluded
to this phenomenon in brief flashes throughout this book, but it is time to focus
on how this is the case and what ramifications follow from it.

We edged up to one of the key points to be explored in the last chapter, when
we turned to T. H. White's tale of the badger in *The Once and Future King*. This tale
concluded with the admonition that humans have the most "incomplete aspect" to
their bodies of any animal, and, therefore, are always in need of tools or constructed
additions that become incorporated into their bodies as ways of sensing and dealing with the world. This is how we explained we are cyborgs: incorporators of tools,

mechanisms, and institutions which become part of our bodies. Our human body is like an "open circuit" into which many "extenders" of its capabilities can be plugged to widen our powers,—like binoculars or glasses which extend our vision by extending our eyes' capacity or the bodies of our cars which become part of our bodies with an extended scope of speed and agility with which we can move over the earth's surface. However, another aspect of our bodies' "open-endedness," which would be a less judgmental way to express this "incompleteness," is that the natural world, and especially its most active and interactive parts, the animals, are also incorporated into our bodies. "Through" the powers of animals our bodies have further ways of sensing the world, fitting into the world, learning about the world, and acting in the world. It is the same dimension of the body that allows us to be cultural beings and therefore to be cyborgs that also means we are part of the circulation with nature and animals. Our body as a unfolding process runs through them. How we add to our bodies routes or paths of circulation through the world changes who we are and what we are capable of experiencing.

Yet another way to point to the link of our being with animals would be focus on the "earthbody logic" we've been articulating throughout the book, where humans *are* and *are not* something at the same time. This means we are one with things, but not utterly so: we are suspended between separateness and oneness. Animals may be more seamlessly tied into their surroundings than we are, whereas we wander more loosely tied, able to switch environments or objects within environments or other creatures with whom we enter into relation more easily than other animals. This allows us to transform ourselves more easily through entering these differing relationships. An outcome of this is the wider scope of all of which we are caught up with, as more mobile and far ranging. Animals, however, may not be as locked into their surroundings or into their habitual actions as we have thought they were.

We could have skipped right to commenting on the nature of our belongingness with animals and what values to which this leads, but in this book, we are trying to give the underlying philosophical reasons for values grounded in our bodies. It is powerful to see how the nature of human and animal earthbodies are different than the tradition supposed, and how this gives deeper reasons for some of the values people are coming to hold today in regard to a changed relationship with animals as kin, helpers, friends, teachers, equal members of a community, and interlocutors in artistic, philosophical, and spiritual matters. Whether it is through animals being brought into senior citizen homes and discovering that their relationships are more healing than medications in many instances, or whether through juvenile delinquents being asked to train seeing-eye dogs and finding them more "rehabilitated" through this interaction than many traditional correctional approaches have achieved, or whether through Koko, the linguistically sophisticated gorilla, when responding to questions from around the globe on the Internet for a few hours gives more interesting responses than many of the humans interviewed in the media—to cite just three of the many stories in the news during the recent past—humans are beginning to see that animals are partners in ways that our reductionistic philosophical approach to them hadn't allowed. It is important to start to see them and us through a different philosophical lens.

The same tradition we have been criticizing throughout this book that separated human beings into a spiritual part, whether of mind or soul, and a bodily part, that was merely a vessel and a mechanism for man's spirit to use temporarily, also arrived at the conclusion that animals were mere machines. At the rise of the scientific revolution, Descartes not only projected an unending progress of finding mathematical and purely rational reasons to understand and engineer the world, to isolate the mind from the influences of the body and its emotions, imaginings, memories, etc., but he also made it possible to use animals as raw materials, since they were regarded as mere mechanisms. All of what we perceive was made of senseless matter, and the only intelligence and spiritual ability resided in a realm of pure mental substance that we among creatures monopolized. Descartes also thought and asserted that God was the sum of all this pure mental substance. The Church, however, perceptively decided, despite Descartes' words, that Christianity was about the incarnation, and this was a rather sterile universe Descartes described, stripped of both divinity and humanity, despite Descartes thinking himself a good Catholic, and they banned his works. However, Descartes got his dream of being the foundation for modern Western knowledge, science, and technology. Animals came to be seen as automata we could subject to any use that benefited humans.

Descartes' reasons for dismissing animals were that sensual experience, feelings, imaginings, intuition, and any other kind of seeming apprehension other than purely rational judgment told us nothing real about the world and meant nothing in itself. These experiences only took on meaning after our rational faculty constructed their sense, and in themselves merely "subjective." For Descartes, the most foolproof kind of rational judgment was mathematical, so the more everything could be put in quantitative terms, the more we could see its meaning clearly and arrive at truth. Unfortunately, Descartes' ideas represented powerful forces in society and became the "common sense" for most of European-influenced cultures for centuries. He solidified what Plato began: the conviction that the real is the rational and the numerical. This is how we have measured the intelligence of animals and even our own intelligence. Then, of course, we get the result that we, and now perhaps in some ways, computers, are the smartest entities on Earth. Animals as sensual creatures, able to seemingly intuit delicate nuances about their environment, to display great sensory acuity and physical dexterity, or to react with emotion to other creatures, were not for Descartes able to register anything about the world or express anything. They were merely the outcome of matter in motion, driven by determined laws of physics. Descartes' wish for humanity was to overmaster any "animal spirits" which raced through our blood as contamination of this driven, physical world, which acted on our mechanical bodies as it did on animals, and to take rational control over all such impulses.

Merleau-Ponty, who has been cited throughout this book as the philosopher who endeavored to make us see that our perceptual bodies are our way into the world that also make us part of a "flesh of the world," spent the last years of his life lecturing about nature, modern biology, and animals. Unfortunately, his work was cut off abruptly by his sudden death at a fairly young age, but transcripts of those three years of lectures have been published in France in the past few years, more than three decades after they were given.[1] There, Merleau-Ponty utterly reverses the way we have come to see animals, their physiology, biology, and relationship to the environment, and what this means for our connection with them. Rather than animals being built up from the "lowest" organisms to the "highest" by having more and more simple mechanical processes added to their makeup, to give them a clearer and closer to rational grasp of the world, Merleau-Ponty shows how animals are basically *creatures of dream.*

Dreaming has a curious standing in the European-influenced philosophical and spiritual traditions. On one hand, there is a continuance of the widespread belief in many cultures and historical periods that great truths sometimes arrive in dreams or that dreams can predict the future—occurrences mentioned even in the Bible. Yet, for the most part, dreams are dismissed as "idle fancy," as the mind "on a holiday" from the serious business of making sense of the waking world and helping us negotiate our way. There are traditions, like those of many of the Native American nations' whose stories (are given early in) this book, in which dreaming is a site of great revelation, or like those of the aboriginal peoples of Australia, where "dreaming" or "dreamtime" not only is revelatory in sleep states, but also infiltrates and underlies the fabric of the waking world. Yet despite these, our "common sense," the classic Western tradition—dictated by a quantitative approach to a reality of fixed forms,—sees dreaming as an irrational or even a nonsense realm. Even Freud's attempt to take dreams more seriously still made them the product of our "inner psychic selves," and even he thought dreams had a rational translation that could make sense of them out of their original irrational form. So, even Freud saw them as "subjective" phenomena that were also leading us away from a more logical message trapped within their imaginative shapes.

To contrast this view for a moment with one of many possible alternatives found in other cultures, let's return to Paula Gunn Allen's description of the role of the Dreamer within varied Native American nations. In the Kashia Pomo, for example, Allen relates, "The Dreamer is the person responsible for the continued existence of the people as a psychic (that is, tribal) entity. It is through her dreams that the people have being; it is through her dreams that they find ways to function in whatever reality they find themselves" (SH 204). Dreams, in this view, are what help people find their way in waking life, the source of talents and abilities, and what holds them together in a sense of belonging with each other. The sense that dreaming is at the heart of existence is so strong that this dreamer is seen as "the mother of the people not because she gives physical birth. . . but because she gives them life through her power of dreaming—that is, she en-livens them." Maintaining physical existence is not what "life" is about, that is what we have seen in this book—ghouls, vampires, and aesthetes physiologically function, even in superior ways, but know they are missing the key ingredient: vitality, a sense of their own aliveness, and being involved with the life of the planet. This is what dreaming is about, as explained in regard to the Pomo culture: "The Dreamer, then, is the center, the hub of the wheel. It is by virtue of her gift, her ability, that the people live and are a people, connected to one another in ways more than mere language, culture, or proximity can assure" (*SH*, 204–5). What draws us together is dreaming, not just being in the same physical location or a shared history.

Allen also explains that this being drawn together is not only true of people, but the material and the spiritual, objects, and the different forms that objects take in their transformations, the communication with animals, plants, and things, and spiritual realities are all brought together by the power embodied in dreaming. For the Keres people, it is the corn that holds this connective power that is the divinity of the earth, and it comes to people through the heart of Earth Woman, Iyatiku: "It is likely that the power embodied in the Irriaku (Corn Mother) is the power of dream" (*SH*, 22–23). This sense of dream brings us back to the beginning of this book, when we spoke of timing as another way to see time, rather than the linear progression of moments outside of us. If we *are* time in the ways that we contribute to the flow of the way things, people, and creature interweave their existences as processes and come together, then this time can be packed with all sorts of experiences, including dreaming. It is a matter of achieving a "fuller" time or timing with the world and, as Allen comments, dreaming is vital to the mix of different "times" that are brought together in ritual or ceremonial time (*SH*, 94). Perhaps, the only Western thinker who appreciated this power of dreaming was Jung (and his followers, especially James Hillman), who bemoaned the modern European detachment from the realm of dreaming. He considered it a spiritual poverty that deprived us of the ability to understand the deeper messages of the world, including those of the animals and the meaning deeper in materiality. Jung felt the meanings experienced through dreams connected all peoples and also humanity with the larger planet in archetypal apprehensions. He said modern man was "solitary," celebrating a sense of progress that "removes him further from his original *participation mystique* with the herd, from submersion in a common unconsciousness."[2]

For this to make sense, however, for readers influenced by the Western cultural and intellectual tradition, we have to see dreaming as not something "done" by people "in their heads," but rather as another dimension of reality given to us in the layering of our sensual contact with the world, within the layers of perception to which we ordinarily don't pay attention or even block out of awareness. If on the subway platform at night there are visions of hell or of underground burrows of gigantic lizards or the sense of walking through the unconsciousness of the city, or if in the forest at night there is the sense of wizards and mischievous little people or of spirits of trees and waters that seek to entangle us or seep into our bones, our Cartesian way of looking at things says these are "products" of the mind "projected onto" the world. However, there is obviously some quality about these objects, shaped by culture or of purely natural origin, or probably some of both, that flows around and through them in different possible meanings. They are the places, the sites, or the objects that "gather together," that embody in a material way, or that focus into themselves, these various meanings which would not be apprehended without these material places or things. Without rocks, it is harder to know what solidity means in all its nuances. We need to see we are in a dialogue with the inanimate and animate world that whispers in our ears or that suggests not one paltry meaning, like those limited choices we are comfortable calling "the real" because they are simple, easy to handle, and not very involving, but a rich multiplicity. If we can see that the world has meaning as a process interweaving people, culture, nature, material things, and living creatures, we can see there are dimensions of reality or layers of meaning, for which all these entities are responsible together, and dreaming is one of them. It is one of the important ways ranges of meanings get passed along.

To return to Merleau-Ponty's conclusions in examining the work of biology, physiology, embryology, and zoology, they wonderfully agree with these Native American formulations. Merleau-Ponty interpreted these studies to show that organisms that had been seen as mechanical were actually enveloped in a sense of their world parallel to what humans experience as dream. He articulated how animals have a sense of "world" that surrounds them, what biology calls an *Umwelt*, or, literally, an "around world" or "surrounding world." This *Umwelt* is not elaborated in a rational way, but is nevertheless at enough distance from the animal that they are able to be both caught up in it and respond to it. Some "lower" organisms that lack this ability, like an ameba, are also caught up in its surroundings—not like a machine, but rather by being so fluid they move through transformations immediately synchronized with changes in their surroundings. Being so fluid, there is no sense at all of difference, of being something else or of confronting anything like a world. Some other "lower" organisms, like sea anemones, are not integrated enough, but instead respond in separate, set patterns in their motor or digestive functions, so that there is not a sense of the whole environment or the whole organism, but just a bunch of functions grinding along side by side. A machine, by the way—even a simple machine—can react to the environment. Consider a thermostat that turns a furnace off and on given the air temperature, but it does so only in ways that are determined ahead of time by its designers and makers. However, the "higher" organisms are both flowing along with the changes in their world, and at a distance from the world such that surroundings can have different meanings and allow for choices of behavior. The animal has a sense of its world and of others within it, but obviously not a fully clear and purely rational one. Rather, as Merleau-Ponty demonstrates, they live in a world like the dream world, in which the different parts flow along with connected meanings, but ones which refer to each other in felt ways, in senses not fully fathomable, and in sparking more images and feelings, but not as distinct, static categories.

When carefully considered, even instincts, which are often used as an example of why animals are machines, are also like the phenomena of dreams. We have often said that instinctive actions are triggered like automatically so that animals achieve certain definite goals to make the machine of nature run smoothly. However, when an animal is doing something instinctive, it is the time they are least aware of goals, which is a consciousness that they can have at other times. They are not even aware of objects around them, which is strange for animals, who usually have such an acute discernment of the sensory aspects and nuances of their environment. As Merleau-Ponty puts it, at this moment when instinct comes into play, something in the world utterly fascinates them, obsesses them, and is like a human fetish,—an irrational craving for something that means something vague and mysterious that makes no sense to the person experiencing it, but who feels compelled to pursue it. So, to take a few of the examples Merleau-Ponty cites, the butterfly of a certain species is so drawn to the secretions of the female it will copulate with a glass rod smeared with it, or the male of a certain species of bird is so taken with the red patch normally found on the female of the species that if we paint a red patch on males, or even other species, the male will try to mate with them. It is as though they are "out of their mind" or more precisely, they are in a dream state, like we are when we are caught in obsessions, and we act as if under a spell. However, the point is that even when not in the thrall of instincts, which are usually given as proof animals are mere automata, animals live in a world of meaning, but one where feelings, associations, intuitions, and the sense of things is moving and not fully fathomable—this sense of an enveloping whole like we feel when we are in dream.

Human beings like to think of themselves as the "rational animal." This might be true, if by this we mean this is how we are different from other animals, but it is not true if by this we mean that this is our essence, our true being. We are animals, who happen to be able on the basis of being an animal to also be rational. Dreaming is a way to see both this aspect of how we are animals and also how animals are us. Twenty years before he gave his lectures on nature, Merleau-Ponty, in examining human perception in great detail in his book *Phenomenology of Perception*, stated that, "The phantasms of dreams reveal still more effectively that general spatiality within which clear space and observable objects are embedded" (*PP*, 284). This was a puzzling statement to his contemporaries, but Merleau-Ponty meant that we lived in a world whose farthest horizons were like those in a dream. Directions in a dream ,whether moving up or down or looking into the distance or spinning around, all have a certain feeling, whether fear or excitement or dread, etc., that goes with them, as does each color, or the details of the appearance of each object. For example, in a dream, that hats are squashed or that this man's walk is so stiff or that the building is so unsteady inspires many feelings, emotions, fantasies, and possible meanings. We feel them in our bodies somewhere. Also, within each feeling, whether engendered by the mountain blocking our path or the elevator that is plunging downwards or the sea crashing in front of us on a beach, are flows of memories and associations that move from these objects and emerge from within the feeling to give rise to many more feelings.

When we sometimes do say we are animals, we usually mean we have muscles that run like a deer's or have appetites to devour some morsel of food like a lion or feel intensely sexual urges or inexplicable viscerally stirring fears or aggressions, etc. We mean that our body and the feelings that obviously stem from it are

like those we attribute to animals. Usually behind this comment is the prejudice of
the mistaken Cartesian view that at this moment our rational minds are turned off,
and the underlying animal level of our bodies has gained the upper hand. However, if we discount this view that chops apart mind from body, what does it mean
to say we are animals as sharing a dimension of our bodies? These comparisons are
distorted by this prejudice about both the so-called mechanical nature of animals
and the so-called mind versus body split in humans, but they do point to the deeper
shared reality of earthbodies, which both animals and humans have together. To
see these comments in this light means that we live in a perceptual realm that is
one of feelings, intuitions, fantasies, and emotions that move in rhythms from the
environment in and through us in such a way that we are always swept along in a
current that we can never quite fathom. It also means that always, when focused
upon, it can yield layer after layer of possible meaning and interconnection with
others. This means we are both—animals and humans—creatures of dreaming.

Dreaming here is the dimension that makes us feel at home in a world, *connected* and *directed* by felt pushes and pulls, that we then can elaborate and extend
upon within clearer spaces by more rational and orderly means. This widest horizon in which we are placed and have to carve out our areas to settle, like our homes
from the wild landscape, is always with us. This is the deepest meaning of Shakespeare's wisdom in *The Tempest*, when he states that "our lives are but the stuff that
dreams are made of," which does refer to their brevity, their lack of stable foundation, but also might point to this wider horizon, one which Prospero, as magician,
should be able to intuit. The sense of enchantment on the island during *The Tempest* is certainly one in which animals, plants, rocks, seas, and people are all in some
sort of fluid exchange and share some common unfathomable vitality and striving.
In many of Shakespeare's plays there is a sense of entering a realm of dream, in
which characters and the fates of worlds are under spells of enchantment, attraction, repulsion, and action they can never fully fathom, as is the fate of the dreamer.

Our sense of belonging, just as the animals' sense of belonging, our sense of
attraction and repulsion, expansion in delight and contraction in despair, and other
overall senses of our world and parts of it, is not at first rational—not in the sense
of being the result of a reasoned judgment—although, we later often find rational
ways to make sense of these vectors of movement and rhythms of life. Our sense
of the mystery of the things that mean the most to us, our highest values, our religious beliefs, our loves, loyalties, and friendships, the pull of family, etc., means
they exceed any rational source. These characteristics are those of the sense of the
oneiric, the dream dimension of waking life, which is between the idle fantasy of
the daydream and the trapped fantasy of the night dream.

It is not only our sense of belonging, of feeling connected, and of being oriented, but even the purposes that motivate our daily actions that are the stuff of
dreams. We often say that we know we can't live without our dreams, but we tend
in our obsession with practicality to explain this notion of "dreams" in terms of
achieving certain definite projects or goals. Yet this stops short of really seeing our
deeper selves: these goals in their ultimate aims are dreams in the same sense as

our dreams when we sleep. We know that we haven't come to them by rational decision, but rather they take shape in a context of feeling, intuition, imagination, and other symbolic associations with our past, our cultural influences, and with our fantasies about parts of the world and others within it. One person seeks his "dream" of money—how much he or she doesn't really know,—another person wants to be seen as attractive, another wants political power, another wants to be an artist, or someone else wants to break the law or be a wanderer with no ties. Each of these goals means many different things to the person, as does those whom he or she thinks possess these qualities or have achieved these things. The person can then give rational explanations to justify to others their dreams, but others will never really understand the life and death nature for them of being a published writer, a star athlete, or the person who decides who is fired; another may never see the thrill in rolling an F-17 jet in the skies at Mach 1,—just as no one else can really understand another person's dreams during the night.

In order to relate this dream to another, we make it more rational and can't express all the layers, fringes, and outcroppings of meaning that we can never see clearly, but which pull us in different ways. We, like all animals, emerge from a mysterious sense of what matters, where we are, and who we are that is the life of the dreamer. Gaston Bachelard, who spent his life exploring the contours of how our waking life was another sort of dream than the night dream (he called it the level of "reverie") expressed the human situation this way: "I dream the world, therefore, the world exists as I dream it."[3] Bachelard goes on to say that such reverie or associative apprehension of depth and nuance that is dreamlike is engendered by all objects around us, by sorts of spaces, and by encounters. A kind of dialogue with the world, a non-verbal one, is opened: "A communication of being develops in both directions between the dreamer and his world" (*PR*, 163). This give and take is not about information, but is one of being, about who we are and what shape the world takes for us. This communication in feeling, image, and rhythm is presented to us by the world in this dreamlike state and we, like other creatures and things, contribute to it.

This is at least partially what many cultures mean in their tales about how we used to talk with animals and how we share the realm of dreaming. In a White River Sioux tale, it is explained, (as it is in many Native American tales), "in the old, old days . . . we were closer to the animals than we are now. Many people could talk to a bird, gossip with a butterfly."[4] This can be taken in a literal way, which certainly was true—there was more direct and immediate interspecies communication—but it also means there occurred communications of all sorts on the many different levels of reality Native Americans entertained. However, even in our alienated state, animals speak to us at this deepest level of our dreams. Some person may see themselves flitting about with the delicate beauty of a butterfly, like Blanche in Tennessee Williams' play, *A Streetcar Named Desire*, or our hypothetical F-17 pilot has been addressed, no doubt, by the streaking falcon, the soaring eagle, or even the gliding gull, which has slipped into his heart and imagination in dreams of flight and makes him hold his body a certain way, ready to spring off the earth.

Now we tend to screen out animals' presence, except perhaps our pets, although, as we examined with Philip K. Dick's book, perhaps we long for increased contact with them. In the next sentence of the Sioux tale, it says that in those old days, "Animals could change into people and people into animals." The stories of all Native American tribes are full of animals who teach the humans lessons about the earth, and about how humans and animals are woven together in inhabiting the earth.

Animals and Vitality, Morality, Spirituality, and Play

We can be taken in by an animal's spirit in an encounter in unusual circumstances, but for many of us it's a fleeting and rare moment. In the beginning of his book *Wild Hunger*, Bruce Wilshire relates being at his desk writing when suddenly he sees a large bird outside in his yard:

> A hawk or large falcon—mottled brown and white, standing erect and alert—an inert pigeon lying, purple breast up, between its great clawed feet! The raptor scanned the scene with its golden eyes, then with rapid movements of the beak plucked feathers from the pigeon's breast. Its watching ceased momentarily. A patch of skin exposed, it tore off small strips of flesh. Instantly, the scanning resumed as the bird swallowed meat.[5]

Wilshire is fascinated, then becomes suddenly alert and excited. He realizes that on some level he has been in a trance, even though he thought he had been awake and highly functioning. He realizes he has been in this trance state for a long time. The raptor has broken through the clutter of an existence in which "I live in a one-family house with locks and tight-seal storm windows, and travel strapped in a car. My feet encased during waking hours in leather and rubber, are rarely bare and seldom touch the earth." He realizes that, usually, like most of his friends, he is a somnambulist. However, here the raptor has communicated its alertness, its vigor, and its presence to its own environment. The communication is not one that Wilshire could ever put into words and is almost like a waking vision, a dreamlike power but one present face to face, that changes the body, its energy, and its feelings.

For Arthur's first lesson in *The Once and Future King*, Merlin turns him into a perch, and Arthur discovers "flying in the water . . . with his own body . . . it was like the dream people have" (*FK*, 48). Yet, animals are not only about the extensions of our bodies to feel what its like to soar in the sky or burrow beneath the earth or to swim through the green-blue world of the water. Animals also show us the power of sheer presence. If we are open enough to them, they not only show us, but they communicate in a bodily connection that makes this *vitality of presence* infiltrate our whole being. It is the opposite of the lore of the ghouls, vampires, and aesthetes that we have discussed, who fear being fully present because they want to be shielded from different aspects of the hurtfulness of genuine contact with the world. Animals are both *spontaneous* in expressing their reactions to the environment and *acute* in their sensory appreciation of the world. These dimensions are expressive of vitality. Human beings are uniquely handicapped in being prone to negate their own sense of vitality and to complain that the many means of cultivating their vitality is too much of a burden or too much responsibility. Animals can teach us the power of being attuned to the environment, to fully luxuriate in the exercise of physical powers, and to delight in the simple sensorial presence of sunlight or warmth or coolness or liquidity or swimming or running or jumping or cuddling, and so on in innumerable bodily satisfactions.

When Descartes includes justifications to violate our own felt sense of kinship with animals by the rational representation of them as mere machines, he is also justifying another way to not only be cruel to myriad other living beings on the planet, but also to strike out cruelly at our own embodied being. He had already advocated suppression of the emotions, the sensual, and all that was not under rational control, but the denigration of animals and their treatment as unfeeling mechanisms also damages our own sense of embodiment, our link with the rest of the planet. If they are our teachers in vitality, in sensory acuity and appreciation, and attunement with the body and environment, then to silence them is to silence a voice within us. At some level—similarly to how we discussed at the beginning of the book that self-infliction of injury is inherent to the "diabolical logic"—to cut animals off from our own sense of being is to cut off part of ourselves, to indulge in self-laceration. We know this, in some more sensitive but suppressed part of ourselves.

The unnecessary extinction of countless species, the deplorable conditions in which so many animals are kept, and the sense that we are "superior" to them and they are morally insignificant also creates many utilitarian problems for humans. In this book, however, it is the damage to being humans as earthbodies that is the focus. *When we assert that animals have no souls, it is the destruction of our human soul that is the issue.* On an ethical level, what does it say about humans if we treat as "below us" those beings who seem to have an unconditional trust in their relationships with each other and when they enter into relation with us? The ethicist Thomas Hill asserts that it means that we are not cultivating those ways of being with others and with the world that are virtuous. Being sensitive, being generous, being concernful, being loving, being trustworthy, and being honest are some of the key ways to exist as a virtuous person. Therefore, it is a lack of virtue to treat as objects those beings who never in unprovoked ways go on campaigns of slaughter or torture of other beings, as we often have, but instead demonstrate gracefulness in contributing to the health of the planet, its beauty, and its sense of vitality. If morality seems to be at a crisis (our age has been called the age of "moral minimalism"), a first source is how we fail to enter into reciprocal and fully communal relationship with animals as equals. It is not surprising, if we realize we are joined with animals, to find that those who are cruel to animals are often those who commit violent crimes against human beings. From voices like Gary Snyder's in *Turtle Island* to Starhawk's in *Fifth Sacred Thing*, there has been a call for representation for all animal voices in all decision-making processes that effect the earth, something that was taken for granted by Native Americans and other indigenous peoples. However, even before we reach the level of public policies, there needs to be a change in feeling our flesh as inseparable from the flesh of animals.

It is heartening that a minister, Gary Kowalski, has written a book entitled *The Souls of Animals.* The only coherent argument that has ever been put forth that animals would have no soul is their failure to engage in rational calculation and abstract reasoning on the level that humans do. If this were the essence of the spirit, the soulful, it would seem that animals were lacking this dimension. However, as Kowalski cogently points out, spiritual capacity "means many things: the development of a moral sense, the appreciation of beauty, the capacity for creativity, and the awareness of one's self within a larger universe as well as a sense of mystery about it all." Kowalski concludes that "spirituality is quite natural, rooted firmly in the biological order" and that animals are as soulful as humans.[6] For Kowalski, to see animals in their loyalties, acts of altruism, courage, spontaneity, empathy, playfulness, and sorrow is to see all the manifestations that could be given of a soul: "to me, animals have all the traits indicative of soul" (*SA*, 5). Kowalski goes on to cite many examples where animals give direct evidence of having these specific traits in ways very comparable to humans. It may be helpful for us, insofar as we have a hard time leaving our categories of human behavior, to very briefly mention some of these, but the point is that animals also have their own ways peculiar to their own existences for expressing these qualities. Other cultures have gone to great lengths to cultivate ceremonies, trance states, meditations, and active dreaming or imagining to fathom an animal's own way of expressing these qualities.

In speaking of the moral sense of animals, Kowalski cites many incidents of animals putting themselves at risk to save wounded or sick companions: dolphins will surround a sick dolphin to prevent it from beaching; African wild dogs will attack cheetahs to save a pup; monkeys will attack an eagle en masse to prevent it from carrying off a member of the troop; pelicans and crows feed and care for blind comrades; and so on (*SA*, 54–55). Even the strictly scientific Darwin had no doubt that animals had concern for each other, performed sacrificial acts of behalf on others, and even that the dogs he observed felt both shame and magnanimity (*SA*, 55). However, given the traditional Western prejudices about the nature of morality, he refused to call animals moral because they could not reason abstractly in order to articulate a universal moral code and to make judgments according to it. However, it may be this is another prejudice that fails to consider, as many other cultures have, whether morality may not be better considered the ability to feel sensitively other-directed emotions that prompt an immediate action on the other's behalf. This is what the Buddhists call "spontaneous right action." Maybe being ethical is more about being attuned to the earthbodies that open up to one another in a flow of feeling. In this way of thinking, the need for ethical rules is an initial step of trying to teach someone who isn't yet sensitive enough to feel all the rhythms within a situation that would call for a creative response to the well-being of those involved. We will explore this question in the next section on earthbody ethics, to which this book leads us; for the moment we conclude that animals certainly have demonstrated a spontaneous responsiveness to each other that might well be called a moral sensibility—and one that might often put more egocentric humans to shame.

Some consider it vital to either a moral sense or to a spiritual sense to have some sense of death and to be able to register its painful impact. The serial killers among us, for example, don't seem somehow to really register in a sympathetic way the tragedy of another's life being put to an end or even just ending in its natural cycle. Not feeling the other's pain nor being shaken by grief, their actions become a part of a plan to meet their own insufficiencies without the victim entering their true cognizance. Kowalski cites numerous incidents of prolonged grief in animals. One case, observed by Cynthia Moss (director of the Amboseli Elephant Research Project in Kenya, who observed elephant life for more than a dozen years), is so gripping and makes such a forceful statement about animal's recognition of death that I repeat it here as related by Kowalski:

> In 1977, one of the family groups who Moss studied was attacked by hunters. An animal that Moss had named Tina, a young female about 15 years old, was shot in the chest, the bullet penetrating her right lung. With the larger herd in pan-icky flight, Tina's immediate family slowed to help her, crowding about her as blood poured from her mouth. As the groaning elephant began to slump to the ground, her mother, Teresia, and Trista, another older female, positioned them-selves on each side, leaning inward to support her weight and hold her upright, but their efforts were to no avail. With a great shudder Tina collapsed and died.
>
> Teresia and Trista tried frantically to resuscitate the dead animal, kicking and tusking her and attempting to raise her body from the earth. Tallulah, another member of the family, even tried stuffing a trunkful of grass into Tina's mouth. Tina's mother, with great difficulty, lifted the limp body with her mighty tusks. Then, with a sharp crack, Teresia's tusk broke under the strain, leaving a jagged stub of ivory and bloody tissue. The elephants refused to leave the dead body, how-ever. They began to dig in the rocky dirt and, with their trunks, sprinkled soil over Tina's lifeless form. Some went into the brush and broke branches, which they brought back and placed on the carcass. By nightfall the body was nearly covered with branches and earth. Throughout the night members of the family stood in vigil over their fallen friend. Only as dawn began to break did they leave, head-ing back to the safety of the Amboseli reserve. Teresia, Tina's mother, was last to go. (*SA*, 14–15)

There are also reports of elephants staying for days with a dead baby, as Jane Goodall has also reported with the chimpanzees she has observed. Lorenz observed signs of grief in jackdaws who lost a mate and remained for some period of time demon-strating "listlessness, loss of appetite, drooping head, and downcast eyes" (*SA*, 68).

Although not necessary, we even have well-formulated discourse about this spiritual and emotional sense of death in an animal from Koko, the female low-land gorilla who has been observed for decades in an ape language study and com-municates in American Sign Language (with a vocabulary of over five hundred words). After she asked for a cat as a pet for her birthday, she took good care of the cat, which she named "All Ball." They played together and obviously liked each other. When the cat escaped one night from the Gorilla Foundation and was accidentally killed by a car, Koko cried with high-pitched sobs. For a week, whenever the cat was mentioned, Koko would cry and sign "Sad/frown" or "Sleep/cat." Seeing her grief, a staff member asked Koko about death. "Where do gorillas go when they die?," she asked, and KoKo responded, "Comfortable/hole/bye (the sign for kissing a person good-bye)." Then she was asked, "when do gorillas die?," and she responded "Trouble/old." In one further give and take, Koko stated that after death, there is "sleep" (*SA*, 11–12). Because of Koko's language skills, we now know, even in our human way of gathering direct testimony that an animal recognizes death, feels grief, and even has a speculative sense of the after-death experience.

Similarly, due to the curiosity of humans about animals or because of scientific studies, we have the testimony of experts that animals have displayed artistic sensibilities, love and loyalty, capacities for reciprocal relationship, and the creative sense of play, as well as these feelings of empathy, grief, altruism, courage, and the other indices of a spiritual nature. There is Siri—an 8,400-pound Asian elephant at Syracuse's Burnet Park Zoo—who impressed Jerome Witkin, a noted art critic, with the skill and beauty of her charcoal drawings. Witkin felt they were a lot like the work of Willem de Kooning, in their kind of "energy" and "joy in responding." When Witkin had them brought to de Kooning and his wife, also a noted artist, both were impressed with the work, as was their circle of artist friends. Desmond Morris also found non-human primates both adept and enthused about drawing and painting. The chimp Congo, produced more than four hundred drawings (*SA*, 41–48).

As far as affection and loyalty, the jackdaw, referred to earlier, courts for a year and remains faithfully with one mate during life, seemingly, showing great mutual attention, assistance, and affection throughout their lives. Probably the philosopher-theologian best known for thinking deeply and articulating ably the depths of friendship, love, and reciprocal relationship was Martin Buber, who first found the capacity for the "I-Thou" relationship, a recognition of the wonder and worth of the other in open celebration and honesty, through his encounters with animals. Although most of his writings were about forging this kind of relationship among humans, he always felt this ongoing possibility with animals and valued heavily these relationships. As Buber stated, "the eyes of an animal have the capacity of a great language (*SA*, 106)." The communication might be fleeting, but for Buber, it was not cluttered with the obsessions by which humans are so often. Humans can be so preoccupied by how to achieve their tasks and goals that they frequently see other beings only as objects or instruments (Buber's "I-it" relationship). Communication and understanding do not have to be verbal, and the eye-to-eye contact often says more than words could.

It is interesting that perhaps the hallmark of freedom, of enjoying the process of life beyond the mere struggle to survive, and of an open-heartedness that may be at the root of all these more spiritually oriented dispositions—whether of aesthetic appreciation, engaging others in community, or joy for sheer existence—although shared by humans and animals, is probably more in evidence more consistently in the animal world, and in ways perfectly analogous to the human forms, and that is play. Huizinga's famous book, *Homo Ludens*, argued that all of our spiritual accomplishments, including religion itself, were rooted in the human capacity for the "play spirit." Yet the book opens with this sentence: "Play is older than culture, for culture, however inadequately defined, always presupposes human society, and animals have not waited for humans to teach them their playing. We can safely assert, even, that human civilization has added no essential feature to the general idea of play. Animals play just like men" (*HL*, 1). The conclusion that follows, since humans are the "playful animal," is that humans are just that, *animals*, since animals continually play. However, it also meant for Huizinga that animals could not be seen as machines, but as more aware and self-directing beings. Animals all round us are caught up in play, whether it be birds swooping, squirrels chasing and running after each other from tree to tree, lions rolling around in mock battle, chimps swinging on trees after one another and ending up in wrestling or tickling matches, cranes doing elaborate dances together, or our own pet dogs approaching us in that inimitable crouched-down posture with both paws spread out initiating and inviting play. They are caught up as we ourselves were as children, and hopefully are even as "serious adults."

In looking at animals, both Huizinga and Kowalski declare that, of all the undeniable aspects of existence, play may be the most undeniable, and it is something that clearly flows through the "sacred hoop" (to use that Native American term for the circle of life among animals, humans, and the inorganic world) of the world into human beings, as much as flowing out from them. Kowalski puts it wonderfully: "Frolicking is everywhere, glad and irrepressible, confounding our desire for an orderly world" (SA 80). Play is a dimension of reality, in which it's not pragmatic results that matter, but a sheer exuberance of vitality and a celebration of the inherent value and gracefulness of physical existence. It is about taking delight in what we can do, what we can experience, and what is about us. Its feeling of "unreality" is about taking time out from our defined roles and tasks, and just letting ourselves go. Play is the vehicle for this feeling of effervescence, of lighter spirits and satisfaction in just the sheer doing of what we're doing, which seems to be a gift of the animal world and the more animal dimension of our own being.

Despite finding examples of animals who paint like human artists, or perform altruistic acts of the same sort as humans, or who can master human language like Koko, it is rather on this level, of the dimensionality of the world itself, that humans and animals are fundamentally interwoven. It is important to articulate this deeper connection among us, so that it does not depend on whether we discover more talented animals or idiosyncratic humans (like Hesse's character in *Steppenwolf*, who feels more wolf than human), in order for us to fuller appreciate how we are animals and they are us. *It is not a matter of finding ways animals can act just like us or ways that humans act like animals, but rather to see how both are called upon by the same kinds of meaning or how both are implicated in certain levels of reality or energies which both express in some parallel ways, but also in some unique and different ways.* In explaining the highest spiritual achievement of the Lakota,

Lame Deer says of those who "see with the eye of the heart:" "He talks with plants, and they answer him. He listens to the voices of the *wama kashkan*—all those who move upon the Earth—the animals. Something from every living being flows into him, and something flows from him."[7] This experience is possible for us all, if we open ourselves to the kind of ceremonial way of living our earthbodies that we described at the beginning of this book. If we are quiet, slow, and concentrated, and let go into the layers within our sensual encounter with the world with the open-ended intention or invitation to hear these voices, there are resonances and pathways to follow with our emotions, with our imaginations, and with memories that will open up for us to enter. On these paths are many feelings, images, sensations, attunements, and relations passed along by animals.

Many Native American tales start with the opposite assumption than the one the Western world has assumed (and which Huizinga criticized immediately in his book in order to open his readers to the full scope of play): that humans had to learn from the animals and from the inorganic world those lessons most vital to a robust and righteous spirituality. In many of the Trickster tales, the Trickster figure the source for human's learning how to get along, to form communities, to have the curiosity necessary in order to learn about the world; in that sense, the Trickster is the creator of the world,—not of its material being, but of its interconnectedness. Interconnection involves a lot of friction and conflict, as well as harmony and cooperation, and the Trickster figures demonstrate how these painful and potentially destructive dimensions of existence and community can be suffered with humor and a sense of play. At the heart of much play is the *agon*, or contest, taking the competitiveness that can exist between humans or within other species or among species and transforming the struggle into something in which one can laugh at oneself and the other, and the point of which is to appreciate the process involved and the excellence of performance that it brings out in the contestants. The Trickster is so open to the play spirit that he often is tricked by his own tricks or is willing to enter an arena in which he might end up seeming as silly and being the fool as much as his opponent.

The point here is that the Trickster is usually represented in the form of an animal, a coyote, raven, crow, hare, rabbit, spider, fox, duck, bear, or other animals or insects that often shapeshift from one form of animal into another or into a human and then back into an animal, etc. This playful spirit, this sense of frolic, which is at the heart of being able to maintain relationships of any sort, is an animal energy which infuses the world. It is one we are very much a part of, but not as its source and not in any way as above other creatures. The very idea of humor, which means to become fluid (its roots mean "to be wet"), to overcome the dryness of life and to allow our normal boundaries to be dissolved, suggests the return of both animals and humans to a level of vitality and sheer delight in their existence and their bodies as a release from their normal shape.

The particular humor of the Trickster would seem to intensify this loss of boundary, since it works by ensnaring the creatures or people with whom he is playing by their desires, goals, or quirks of behavior, and they do the same back to him. He constantly uses their habits, their ways of getting stuck in a certain rigid way of being, a certain fixed shape of character, and explodes them. Those tricked are really tricked by their own rigidity, until they learn to "loosen up." The players not only lose their usual, more serious boundaries, but they become all mixed up with one another, sometimes even exchanging body parts. Most of the desires used to trick others are bodily, about food or sexuality or aesthetic pleasure. There is the Cherokee tale of the rabbit fooling the otter out of his rich, brown coat. He tricks him into diving into the water (where he remains as his new home) by making him believe fire is coming from the sky —but first the otter has hung up his coat to protect it from damage.[8] There is a Winnebago Trickster who is human in form and a male at the beginning of the story cycle, but who in one tale takes an elk's liver to fashion a vulva and its kidneys to fashion breasts, and then mates as a female with a fox, a jaybird, and a nit, who all live together, and then afterwards with the chief's son.[9]

One older member of the Winnebago had said of the Trickster that he "roamed about his world and loved all things. He called them all brothers and yet they all abused him. Never could he get the better of anyone, everyone played tricks on him" (*TT*, 147). As a mythic expression in story, there seems to be a Native American comprehension of the sense that there is a level of reality, one that is even divine or sacred, in which we are all ensnared, animal and human. It can be frustrating if we want to maintain strict control, but it is potentially liberating in its chaotic intermixing of all creatures of the earth. It can be a source for overcoming seriousness and goal orientation in humor and vitality. In their particular gestures and games, animals seem to be inviting us back to this realm we both know, but animals seem more adept at teaching us to remember.

Even, in the more pranksterish or trickster-like aspect of play, there is a ubiquity of joke and humor to be savored that seems to run through the heart of the planet's energy fields. Certainly the trick and the humor has to be articulated by the animate creatures of the world, but nevertheless it is inherent in the structure of the world itself. We creatures bring out the luminosity or gracefulness or beauty of the world, but it is there like light or water that we then notice, name, and use. When shown the Winnebago Trickster tales, Karl Kerenyi, an expert on Greek mythology, expressed this idea: "There is much trickery at large in the world, all sorts of sly and cunning tricks among human beings, animals and even plants, which could no more remain hidden from the story-teller whose inner life was as much bound up with the world as his outer one" (*TT*, 174). If animals are essential to this both playful and humorous dimension of reality, that most delightful part of the dream, this augments their power as teachers. W. H. Auden, wrote several poems addressed to animals as our potential teachers in how to celebrate bodies and the senses, and how to approach all creatures with more compassion. In one of his poems to dogs, he states, "Humor and joy to your thinking are one, / so that you laugh with your whole body."[10] The Native American tales recognize this, as most of the lessons imparted to the humans come about through play and humor. As Archie Fire Lame Deer says of the trickster spirits infiltrating all realms of the animate and inanimate: "they are mostly harmless troublemakers and tricksters . . .

often helpful to us humans . . . to make us laugh at ourselves—even during hours of sadness and trouble. They teach us not to take ourselves and our problems too seriously" (*GP*, 181). In these states we are open-hearted and can take in lessons about ourselves and our ways with the world. While in a more serious state, we might feel more pain about these lessons, more threatened or assaulted. In the spirit of humor, we can learn more fluidly, shedding destructive behaviors without sinking, supported by the buoyancy of celebrating life.

If this book has been successful at giving us a sense of earthbodies, if Merleau-Ponty is right in his lectures about animals, if the Native Americans had mythic insight, if D. H. Lawrence, the Romantics, W. H. Auden, and the many other writers were right, the real test of recognizing our kinship with animals is not through finding behavioral or biological overlaps, but through the understanding that makes up our own bodies. As part of a planetary flow of energies and meaning through our earthbodies, we know inside our bodies, we know inside our imaginations, we know inside our dreams, we know among our many, many selves, and we know within our feelings that animals are there. If we take the deepest stirrings and layers that flow through our earthbodies, we realize we have felt and have communicated with all the animal brothers and sisters, as the Native Americans put it, and that their voices are inextricably woven into the energies of trees, moon, rocks, and the inanimate voices that sound through us.

The presence of these voices,—which are about delight in the earthly, which help the sensual import of matter be so richly ambiguous with so many possible meanings, which open us to a level of dream that is compelling and energizing; which open us to levels of feeling that all beings are bound together and thus become touched by compassion, that there are so many forms of beauty, and that there is an underlying gratitude embedded in the rhythms of kinship in being a part of this earthly round dance—speaks of a powerful kind of spirituality that is best called "biospirituality" (*SA*, 98). As James Hillman has been articulating for decades, if we look at soul not as a mystical substance, but as an activity (which fits with the sense of this book that our bodies, our persons, and the whole world, itself, is an unfolding process), then soul is about "soul-making." It is an ongoing task, a process, and something we have to keep doing every moment. Compassion or a sense of beauty or a feeling of love for others as some of the soulful qualities only exist by being brought into existence by each of us and exercised, practiced, rediscovered,—or we lose them.

Souls are not things, but a certain kind of rhythm with others, the world, and oneself, a certain kind of becoming attuned or being sensitive, and this happens only by entering these processes among beings which birth them through "timing." Hillman has also said for decades that this kind of soul-making is "dehumanizing" (*RP*, 180-1). To become soulful, we need to get *outside* human boundaries. The energies of soul-making are not self-generating. We pick up on them, join into them, by their presence in the world: "The world is as much the home of soul as is my breast and its emotions. Soul-making becomes more possible as it becomes less singly focused on the human" (*RP*, 181). Hillman says if we look beyond the human, "we will find soul more richly and widely." Animals are a large part of the presence of these energies and rhythms in the world. It deepens our own sense of loyalty to see the jackdaws as Lorenz did, or to experience the elephants as Cynthia Moss did. We need to be fed other and different images, rhythms, and presences that can then resonate with our own and enliven, expand, and deepen them. Animals provide this resonance.

In the effort to have soul and to be virtuous, then, we are asserting the exact opposite of much of the tradition of Western thought: not that we need to turn away from the earth, to isolate ourselves in some sort of "purification," but rather that we need help to feel these qualities of compassion, reverence, wonder, depths of meaning, love, gratitude, humor, and play, and find different concrete ways they are expressed on this planet that can touch us. All these values mean very little as abstract qualities. It is only in their concrete shape, in specific actions and ways of behaving, that they speak to our earthbodies in sensual richness, in particular emotions, and in varied images. In giving us these specific messages, animals are our helpers, teachers, and partners. We need to see cranes dance, swallows frolic, monkeys help each other, pelicans care for their blind family members, Koko grieve for her cat, or wild apes sob for each other. To become more humane we need animals.

These ideas about human and animal inseparability do not answer some of the tough questions we face: How can we stop the rampant extinction of species caused by the development of the world when complex questions of human needs are also involved? What are the ethically compassionate limits that should be put on animal experimentation? Where does cruelty to animals begin? But these ideas do cast into relief that what is at stake is also violating the part of ourselves that flows into us from animals and also the danger to the intrinsic value of the world in its beauty, truth, and goodness. This planet of dreaming can be torn apart, so that it becomes a functioning machine where this dimension—which is the source of feelings, passions, the imaginary, intuitions, and non-rational meanings of all sorts—can be damaged or destroyed. Animals are an integral part of this dimension of reality, and we must find ways to include their well-being with ours on an equally important basis. Life without animals will not be worth living in many ways, or will at least be very much impoverished. Remember the android nightmare world Philip Dick portrays. It is important at this point to turn to how we can see ethics in a new way, so that it is not a matter of either/or decision making, another destructive use of the diabolical logic that passes for the necessary tools of ethics. If we have to decide between us and the animals, as they did in *Silent Running*, then whatever the decision, it is a violation of the whole idea of earthbody ethics, to which we must now turn.

Traditional Western Ethics as a Perverse Reaction to the Planet

The ethical traditions that we rely upon to guide us—when we do in fact turn to ethics, whether the Judeo-Christian standards, utilitarianism, psychologically inspired notions of self-actualization, social contract theory, virtue ethics, or an appeal to rationally self-evident first principles—are all traditions that rely upon the diabolical logic with which we began this meditation. Many have worried, of course, that this in the age of "moral minimalism" we hardly turn to ethics at all in making most decisions, however, ethics itself may be at fault for some of this disregard. Certainly, all the consumerist, media saturated, and distractedly apathetic cultural institutions do contribute to the current moral black hole into which we've stumbled, but also a part of the reason is that, traditionally, ethics has been conceived and touted as coming from a black hole—as having a kind of supra-terrestrial immaculate or divine origin or as supposedly popping up from nowhere in the fabric of daily life as some "voice" to stop us in our tracks to tell us what to do.

Ethics understood this way is about what we "ought to do" in contrast to how we actually live, or, in other words, acting according to what opposes our natural inclinations. Kant, usually taken as the greatest moral philosopher, even goes so far as to say if we are not doing something from a sense of duty, if we are not legislating to ourselves or "ruling" over ourselves, but instead follow what seems our natural inclinations, then the act has no moral or ethical value whatsoever. In other words, if I give you food when you're starving or help a blind person across a crowded intersection, if I am doing this from the motivation of the pleasure it gives me to help, then that act embodies no ethical worth.

Although there are certainly times of crisis, misunderstanding, and conflict in which we must oppose our feelings and natural inclinations in order to do the right thing, that this opposition can be seen to be the basis of the ethical worth of an action is a deeply wrong principle. It is a wrong to the deeper natural rightness inherent in the unfolding of a miraculous planet and a wrong vision of the nature of goodness. *Pleasure should not be opposed to goodness in principle. It is wrong to consider that to be drawn to the joy of the planet cannot be the way to the good.* Again, as in other realms we've examined, the guiding operative logic is that of opposition, of disjunction, of either being "natural" or being "good." The major terms of ethics are all the results of chopping our relationships with others, creatures, and things to pieces, and placing barriers just where we should be opening more reciprocal communication.

Ethics, as we usually understand it, is about rules, decisions, being at fault, conflict situations, definite answers, standards to aspire towards, and a guide about how to do things the right way. All these ideas rely upon our seeing ourselves as static, or at least stable entities at odds with the world, with other people and creatures, and hoping to achieve some state of "goodness" or "satisfaction" or "rightness" that corresponds to something above or beyond or behind the earth as its reason, purpose, or ultimate meaning. They all assume that pain is either bad or something to minimize, that earthly or spiritual success is a goal to be achieved, that persons are the ultimate agents, the responsible ones of the planet, and the ones to whom some sort of special place is reserved in the larger scheme of things. So, the earth is a place of obstacles, pitfalls, or temptations, which we must rise above to achieve a worth higher than that endemic to this vale of suffering and evil. Humans are set apart and above.

The idea that ethics is about choosing between right and wrong courses of action, or deciding which party is right and which is wrong, or justifying abstractly the reasons for action against some defined standard, is diabolical. Not only does it separate different people's values and ways of life that need to go together for a sense of ethics or the good suited to our being earthbodies as part of this planet, but it also leads to violence. We become adversaries and are objectified by these judgments. It assumes that we are certain distinct persons, who stand at a distance from others and decide how to act towards these others according to abstracted principles. Instead, under earthbody logic, we are part of the flow and unfolding of others and the planet, and our actions should be a result not of "my" doing, but of an influx of meaning, energy, and motion which comes from the entire situation, including other people, non-human creatures, and even the things around us and the messages they hold for us. The "goodness" of such actions is from the harmony with the situation and the joining of a rhythm that dances towards overall expression of all partners on the planet. Ethical humans need not judge and separate from each other, but should allow themselves to overlap more. Humanity, as a whole, needs to find greater insertion in the planet's larger life. This is where ethics should begin.

Such a resonant approach to life allows a depth of meaning and reciprocal realization from the contribution of other beings adding to our own. The "should" in the preceding sentences recognizes the need for hearkening to others, if all need each other's contribution for full realization. Taking earthbodies seriously would mean that if we backed ourselves into a corner where we had to choose between two alternatives, and had to decide that one side or the other was wrong and one right, then somehow we had constricted the possible interchange and flow so that other possibilities of mutual care had not yet emerged or were driven underground. An ethical lapse, in a deeper sense, has occurred to allow things to get to this point at which we normally think ethics is first needed.

If we get to this constricted, oppositional point, we may be forced to make decisions, one against the other, or one part of myself against another part (for example, reason versus passion), but the point is that an *ethos*—a creative and responsive "way of life" (as *ethos*, the root word of ethics, meant) would not get into this position. The idea of an ethics would be one which concentrated on other ways to be such that we timed ourselves more gracefully with others. This assumes that conflicts may arise, but ultimately they always have possible resolutions which call for mutual transformations, instead of resorting to the one-sided imposition of force to impose an abstract judgment (although certainly, if and when people— such as violent criminals—adamantly refuse to enter into dialogue these judgments are essential). However, we are addressing how we could change our sense of being "good" in our everyday working with family, friends, co-workers, the environment, etc., that would move us from hiding behind feeling morally "justified" to feeling morally compelled to become sensitive, expressive, imaginative, flexible, support-ive, emotionally attuned, etc.

Carol Gilligan's feminist critique of the tradition of ethics, *In a Different Voice*, makes this point: that such rational decision making is a dead-end ethics in that it deflects attention from how we can find more inclusive, more ambiguous, long-term ways of negotiating and accommodating those whom we are to meet creatively in a way that enriches all. This is a good start to criticizing the tradition of ethics, that as Gilligan points out, has been dominated by the masculine voice.[11] She wishes it balanced by this other voice found more strikingly in female psychological development for a variety of historical, sociological, biological—and who knows what other—combined factors. What is important is not to blame the history of ethics, nor to throw it away entirely, but to broaden its scope with a whole new vocabulary and way of looking at people's lives within the planet. *The ethics we have to use when backed into a corner should not be our only guide to life.* We should find ways of transforming ourselves adaptively and resonantly with others that lead us to better situations from which to act together. Implied in this critique, too, is that ethics should be about *who we are*, as much as *what we choose to do* in a certain conflicted situation. If we existed in different ways, different futures would come about for us personally and as a community. With the exception of Aristotle's emphasis on becoming a virtuous person in the sense of developing certain emotional and expressive capacities or dispositions, very little of our traditional ethics directly helps us *become* more expressive, sensitive, and creative people who can time their lives out harmoniously with the rest of the planet.

It is the dynamics of earthbodies that could offer a powerful new set of images and terms to revamp ethics as a whole. Instead of legislating rules for ourselves or having the rules legislated for us, we would be responsible for becoming attuned to others, to the environment, to animals, and to the rhythms of the things that we help to create and how they enter into the pre-existing rhythms of the whole. If one is to be a dancer, there is a need to return to the body and to live that body as a potentially open-ended receiver of rhythm, embrace, and grace with others. Expressivity is not a personal preference, but a value that others within the dance are reliant upon.

Yet, to look at these characteristics for a moment—sensitivity, attunement, open-endedness of bodily reception, and emotional expression—we see that they are not even seen traditionally as "ethical terms," but as matters of "personal style" or aesthetic preference. At best, some modern psychologies might promote these as ways to be more "mentally healthful" or "self-fulfilling." It is absurd to say that keeping contracts or being honest is important ethically, and yet being emotionally open and sensitive to others is not.

Contracts are stopgap measures to be used when the other levels of communication have broken down, usually because they haven't really been pursued. They are psychically distant ways of acting with others, which may be important if there is no possibility of ongoing personal contact because of literal distance intervening, or for helping large numbers of people interact in an impersonal way, but again the contract is problematic as the ethical paradigm for relating to all people. If we could experience another person or parts of our environment with enough sensitivity and with a proclivity for responsive and open communication, we would see their side of things in a new way, and empathize with them in felt experiences that would make it unlikely (although not impossible) that we would do anything to hurt or violate them. Actually, we would be most likely to perform "spontaneous right action," as the Buddhists call the urge to help the well-being of others and ourselves that wells up from a sensitively compassionate engagement in situation. *Expressivity and sensitivity are ethical achievements, obligations of being human and an earthbody, not psychological characteristics.*

We often argue that these attributes are not ethical matters, because our emotional dispositions, our abilities to apprehend the feelings of others or to express our concerns to others are seen as "hard-wired" into us or a result of a conditioning that determines our makeup. On the other hand, keeping a contract or being honest is seen as based on a rational and willful decision. However, this is a reflection of the traditional philosophy that we have been critically examining throughout this book: that the human self is a disembodied self found within a power to reason that is "above" the body and the flow of energies that move the emotions; and its key self-relationship is one of will power, commanding the body to do as it decides is best and that the body, sensuality, emotion, imagination, and the earthly powers are obstinate forces "beneath" us. We are used to dealing with reason in opposition to passion, sensuality, imagination, etc., as first set up by Plato's philosophy, and therefore we feel we can work with reason and the will. Of course, our rational assessments, which are in opposition to the rest of us, often later prove to not really be rational— or even if they are, may not have been the best course of action for our well-being or the well-being of others—but it doesn't dampen our faith that this is the "spiritual" and ethical dimension towards which to aspire. Our will often fails us, or even when it doesn't, it sometimes proves to be hurtful to ourselves or others. We still feel it is our "higher" sense of control and dignity. Since these are the powers we have traditionally associated with our human excellence, we feel that our human freedom is expressed in reason and will, whether the results bear it out or not.

The emotions, the ability to apprehend others' feelings, to be more sensually acute, to be more emotionally expressive, are abilities which *can be heightened greatly* through attention and practice, once we befriend them as essential parts of ourselves. That is to say, analogously to the development of rational capacities, emotional capacities require our familiarity, practice, and effort in working towards their realization. They are not merely given to us as unchangeable attributes. We have often treated them that way, as if, being more "animal" faculties, we were not going to identify with them or develop the artistry with them that we devote to cultivating reason. With the appreciation for their power and excellence, and with any kind of comparable commitment of time and effort to their artful development as that we devote to learning greater reasoning ability, we would become more proficient in these emotional, imaginative, expressive dimensions. This would mean we would become more capable of ethical action as sensitive, empathetic, relational, and compassionate beings.

Our schools spend more than a decade helping us learn to use our reason, to inquire rationally, to accomplish logical assessments, and to express ourselves in a rational, coherent fashion. Reason can be compartmentalized into areas that seem to be mastered in discrete jumps, whether of logical reasoning, mathematical reasoning, kinds of induction, etc., and correlated with specific problem areas. Reason seems a tool that can be used from a distance, as we prefer to deal with the world in our diabolical logic (like Lestat, who fears the enmeshment in the pain and feelings of others). A judgment seems able to be made quickly. Its rules and techniques can be mastered efficiently. By contrast, emotional sensitivity or imaginative expressiveness seems to take time; one must gradually join into greater resonance with the whole. It never yields yes and no answers, but leads to ever-denser ambiguities, which can give increasingly rich insights with more depth and facets,—but these call for more ongoing involvement to appreciate. We want something that is instantaneous and doesn't take an ongoing relationship which we will have to maintain and which will overrun our carefully constructed boundaries.

To work with the emotional, imaginative, sensitive, and immediately empathetically responsive levels of our relations with others means to focus on the body, the body as way station to others. Yet we insist on viewing the body as a given, something we are stuck with as our lot in life or have hard-wired into us, taking our identity again from the machines we've created. This allows us to hold on to the prejudices we've examined, that the body is not even seen as truly "me" or the self. In this way, my anger at this petty offense by my child or my enraged jealousy at my spouse, which is totally unwarranted in the larger context of our relationship, doesn't have to be taken as my responsibility or as a "moral failing." *Yet, if we are earthbodies, such societal attitudes—that we are not responsible for opening our emotions more or for continually experiencing our bodily apprehension of sensory, emotive, and imaginative nuances in our environment—themselves are profoundly immoral and unethical.* It leads us to wall ourselves off from our redeeming capacities of creating a spontaneous flow of mutually reinforcing creative and responsive energies among us.

To look at ourselves as earthbodies, where the sense of reality comes though our senses lined with imaginative, emotional, and remembered levels of meaning, we see we are bodies first and foremost. As earthbodies, we can find ways to time ourselves with others and the richer apprehension of them in the environment. My body can become more sensitive to shades of color, to differing sounds and odors, if I concentrate on and practice such basic apprehensive abilities. Similarly, if I pay attention and care about, practice and welcome the opportunities for sensing the other person's feelings at the moment or sensing their relationships to parts of the environment or to other people around us, my body becomes more alert, more sensitive, and more aware of the energy flows, the feeling flows, and the meanings apprehensible in the surroundings in which we find ourselves with others.

Another way to think about this shift in ethics—from rules about adjudicating conflicts to cultivating and transforming oneself to become sensitive to and expressive with others such that these conflicts will not arise—is to think of the shift from intervention to prevention. The case for an earthbody ethics might be made in a parallel with medicine and other fields that have embraced the idea that preventing breakdown is more beneficial to the well-being of persons, as well as less costly in effort, time, resources, and distress to society, than intervening only when the person has arrived at a crisis. In our current cultural climate, we tend to think of ethics as we do of other crisis intervention techniques, rather than as a way of preventing breakdowns of relationships with others or with ourselves. The preventative approach in medicine is not geared toward the negative, the break-down, but rather is about facilitating a more robust quality of life that is a gain in itself whether it forestalls disease or not, because the quality of life is higher regard-less of the duration of health. Analogously, an ethics that would pull our lives together in a way in that augments the relational nature of our life with others and the natural world allows for a more robust life. This is what ethics started out to be: *ethos*—a "way of life" that was a good life. The parallel is even closer in that, for Aristotle, the idea of virtue and of ethos was not a moralistic one, but rather one which embodied "the fullest functioning of the organism." Morality and vitality are not opposites, as we have often thought by seeing morality as a check on the robustness of life in a planet-denying way of thinking of "goodness" as the restric-tion on earthly vitality. Rather morality and vitality should be thought of as syn-onymous, or at least as different facets of coming into the vibrancy of earthbodies.

The idea of ethics as a set of rules, standards, or decision-making proce-dures not only expresses the diabolical sense that we live in opposition to the world and others, but also furthers the alienated ideal of self-sufficiency. Morality or eth-ical action becomes something "I"—the isolated Cartesian self—achieves through its mind or intention or will. Just as the vampire wishes to gain nourishment with-out being touched by these others whose emotional experiences is drained with their blood or the aesthete who stays in the fortress of his or her mind while using others as occasions for entertainment, so this model of the ethical person is a model one who has "internalized" these rules and standards and can operate within them-selves, within their "integrity," to arrive at the proper decisions and course of con-duct. Such a person is not swayed by others, knows himself or herself, and is in control of his or her emotions and actions. The resistance to the pull of others, especially our emotional relatedness to them, is seen as the mark of a fully achieved "integrity," which is in some aspects a way of cutting our ties to others.

The roots of the word "integrity" are the same as for the word "integer," which designates a whole unit, and has the overtones of the original Latin sense of "untouched" and "undivided" as part of its connotation. Yet, perhaps, this is exactly what should not be esteemed in the ethical person. Consider the following situation: an irate husband, carrying a gun, bangs at the door of a friend who is sheltering his fleeing, frightened wife. Under Kantian principles the friend must tell the irate spouse that she is there. Yet, most people would see that steadfastly maintaining an abstract ethical principle—here, of honesty—and not being swayed to deviate by empathy for the irrational suffering and danger of the couple within this situation, is ethically shal-low and wrong. The underlying model of clinging to the principles with which one identifies regardless of the situation of those around one is flawed. Kant's idea is that, in articulating to itself through the faculty of reason the idea justifying the action, the individual should maintain a rational consistency and unswerving logic, such that the reason for the act would be valid for any rational being as the only logical alternative to pursue. One can't be dishonest in any situation, not even at this perilous moment between one's two best friends, or even between two emotionally distraught strangers, because the idea of telling a lie is illogical. All speech is only rationally possible if we assume people tell the truth. If it were all right for everyone to lie, then language wouldn't make sense in communicating anything. Since lying is wrong as a general principle, it is wrong in this specific situation, because situations are irrelevant. We generate from within the power of one's reason all the principles necessary to be a good person. Even if the husband should lose control and beat or kill the wife, Kant would feel that the correct ethical decision of revealing her presence was made by adhering to the principle of honesty.

Yes, there needs to be a certain steadfast self-completeness in arriving at choices of action in order not to be carried away by the mob mentality of certain stressful and ethically dangerous moments. However, that ethics envisions achieving this consistency as an unswerving cleaving to certain principles and to an unquestioned self-identity (as Kant declared was our ethical duty) through being *self-contained* and *self-propelled* may be the opposite of what we should expect in an ethical human being as an earthbody. For Kant, this was the mark of our human dignity that morality helped us to see and appreciate: that we are autonomous or can generate principles of goodness without any dependency on the specifics of a situation or the nature of any specific relations with other people, things, or nature.

If we look at emotional sensitivity and an ability to be bodily responsive to the shared rhythms of the situation as at the heart of augmenting others' well-being, then isn't being touched by and divided among oneself and others—and even the trees, waves, and birds—just what is needed to be an ethical earthbody? The idea that integrity, as self-sufficiency and as a rational shaping of one's will through reason in the "inner sanctum" of one's private conscience (the popular way of refer-ring to Kant's idea of self-legislation), is the way to be ethical and embody good-ness is a dangerous model of humanity as walled off into itself. *It may be that humans, in attempting to make themselves achieve integrity are being morally arrogant or deeply pessimistic about their abilities to really enter moral relationships.* The arro-gance is embodied in the sense that we can shape ourselves without an interde-pendence on others or on parts of the non-human world that contribute to our responsiveness in unique and sensitive ways given each situation, and that who we are may have to constantly change with the help of other energies entering us in order to stay "good." "Goodness" may be an interdependent ongoing process of allowing and promoting transformation of who we are in timing or resonance with those around us. The pessimism about the corrupting influence of others is a lack of faith in the world. It is a lack of faith that with other people and with the con-tributions of other energies of beauty, grace, sensitivity, energy, flexibility, etc., from the environment, we won't be sufficiently nourished and catalyzed in our chang-ing with the situation to do the right thing. It is also a fear that how one is shaped by others may turn one into another kind of self, someone other than the carefully constricted image of the self one has chosen as one's identity and security.

Under the guise of "duty" that is the heart of much traditional Western moral-ity to suppress the body and the emotions—as potentially swaying, through voices of the world, one's will to be fully self-determining through a "higher" reason and goodness—we may be pursuing a course that in its very mechanism is contrary to moral goodness. The sanctity of the will, of self-legislation through pure reason, and of self-sufficiency as vital to integrity is severely criticized in D. H. Lawrence's poem, "Two Ways of Living and Dying." Lawrence poetically explores how there is a difference among the three things we're considering here: (1) a full sense of self that is gained through the body's openness to streams of energy and meaning from the cosmos and others; (2) a contrasting kind of self-propulsion, self-determination, and self-sufficiency integral to a sense of self that places a barrier between the person and their world; and (3) a courage of resistance and a steadiness that comes from drawing upon the openness with the world to then provide a deeper and truer sense of individuality and sensitivity to others. D. H. Lawrence, like the Native Americans in the myths we examined at the beginning of this book or like Silko, Allen, Gilligan, Kowalski, Slater, and others we've discussed in the course of this book, articulates a sense of self that emerges from a more primal source of vitality, care, and self-respect that courses through the planet as a shared energy, as part of a flow of meaning, purpose, and creative intermeshment, which he then contrasts with a self of self-conscious self-direction and will power.

In the first stanza of "Two Ways of Living and Dying," Lawrence describes the body as a way-station of planetary energy and vitality:

> While people live the life
> they are open to the restless skies, and streams flow in and out
> darkly from the fecund cosmos, from the angry red sun, from the moon
> up from the bounding earth, strange pregnant streams, in and out of
> the flesh,
> and man is an iridescent fountain, rising up to flower
> for a moment godly, like Baal or Krishna, or Adonis and Balder, or
> Lucifer. (*DH*, 675)

Lawrence expresses here an understanding of humans as earthbodies: that our sense of purpose, of vitality, and of being something noble, touched by divinity, and expressing forth for others comes from our initial openness to the sources of energy and meaning that encircle the globe and run through the material and natural forces that can infuse people and their culture to become something more than they were by themselves. This gives a fullness to their lives which may be part of an ethos of care, both towards oneself and others.

In the second stanza there is a contrast with the kind of self-legislating existence that in the Kantian and other models are paradigmatic of the moral person:

> But when people are only self-conscious and self-willed
> they cannot die, their corpus still runs on,
> while nothing comes from the open heaven, from earth, from the sun
> and moon
> to them, nothing, nothing;
> only the mechanical power of self-directed energy
> drives them on and on, like machines,
> on and on, and their triumph in mere motion
> full of friction, full of grinding, full of danger to the gentle passengers

of growing life,
but on and on, on and on, till the friction wears them out.
(*DH*, p. 676).

In this contrasting way of living, Lawrence describes how persons who stake their lives on their sense of themselves as self-generating, as deciding who and what they are within themselves, and then using those values to propel themselves through life, are unable to feel the pulsings of energy and meaning from the world, since their design is to impose their will upon the world, not be transformed by it.

Lawrence describes how without streams flowing in, this self-propulsion empties them out, how it means they are really machines, in the nineteenth-century idea of machines as grinding forward in a set pattern (versus some of today's sophisticated machines set into feedback loops with the environment), and how they are dangerous to other people and the creatures of the earth. There is a friction, a grinding down of self and others through this lack of attunement with others, so these people just run through and over what stands in their way. Not only is this disastrous for the meaning of life, according to Lawrence, but this self-propulsion leads to "hideous shrieks of steely rage and frustration." This frustration is from the feelings of emptiness, and rage from experiencing others only as obstacles. This rage and frustration can easily be expressed in either overt or indirect acts of violence. We tend to think of this self-assertion in terms of commerce and consumption, people trying to succeed at their self-determined materialistic goals. We also use the same model for characterizing the pursuit of morality when morality has become the cleaving unswervingly to the internal sense of what is ethically right, no matter what else beckons to us to alter that sense of morality.

Life becomes just a means to these goals and death becomes just the cessation of this drive towards these goals. Lawrence calls it "the death of nothingness" that reflects the isolated emptiness of the preceding life of self-determination. He contrasts this with the different way of living, and therefore of dying, of those who let the energies of the earth enter through them, and appear through their distinctive shaping, so that their voices are added to these other voices:

> But when living people die in the ripeness of their time
> terrible and strange the god lies on the bed, wistful, coldly wonderful,
> beyond us, now beyond, departing with that purity
> that flickered forth in the best hours of life,
> when the man was himself, so a god in his singleness,
> and the woman was herself, never to be duplicated, a goddess there
> gleaming her hour in life as she now gleams in death
> and departing inviolate, nothing can lay hands on her,
> she who at her best hours was herself, warm, flickering,
> herself, therefore, a goddess
> and who now draws slowly away, cold, the wistful goddess receding. (*DH*, 676)

In contrast to the long tradition inaugurated by Plato and carried forth by European culture for two millennia, Lawrence is asserting that what is touched by divinity in human beings is this openness to the streams of the earth flowing in and out, and that by joining up with this community of beings one finds the uniqueness of each person and their dignity through how they can mesh with and add to this flow. When part of the circle of dancers, one is carried beyond oneself to new rhythms, capacities, gracefulness, and a sense of the meaning of the dance. In other words, one is transformed. However, we also discover through this process who we are and what unique contributions we brought to this joint effort that may have never been called forth before this engagement.

Lawrence is pointedly attacking the "either/or" or diabolical logic, that opposes a unique self vulnerable to the danger of being swallowed up by others. He is insisting that only by becoming open to the skies and all parts of the fecund cosmos does one have the energy, the vitality, the depth of meaning and purpose—which is the grace of life—that yields to each person a unique step. *Individuality is not the opposite of community, but rather is its other side.* When a person creatively, openly, and responsively engages with others and the world, then he or she also comes back to self as discovered and actualized through the interaction in new dimensions.

This has profound implications for ethics. Our ethics asserts the necessity to step back, to be in control, to judge others, to judge oneself, to assert one's will, to be rational, to decide, and be autonomous, and not how to harmonize, to be sensitive, relational, or open, or how to creatively synthesize. These latter attributes— if they, in opposition to the tradition, are the key to ethics, in the sense of being the heart of what it means to be good as a human and to work for the vitality and expressive potential of the whole—are not about rules or standards. Instead, these attributes are about who we are, and are achieved not through decision-making procedures, but rather by becoming transformed into nimble dancers with others. This means that ethics has to concern itself with the deeper ways of being or of living, as Lawrence puts it, that make this transformation possible and give birth to these attributes.

As we were saying, this means that the very approach of traditional ethics may be unethical. It leads us to aspire to a "higher" realm, a realm of "eternal" values, a realm beyond the earthly "frailties," and of certain answers, the "right" ones. If becoming ethical is about transforming oneself to be open to all these energies streaming in and out of the body, to hearkening to all these voices of creatures, objects, and other people, then it may be about a way of existing that makes the growth of these attributes possible. Instead of being about those aspects of transcendence listed above, ethics may be about entering time, becoming more fully embodied, getting beyond the will, abandoning the self-determining sense of "I", and becoming a many.

Chapter Six

Rejoining the Planet

An Earthbody Ethics of Achieving Presence and Co-presence

The old sense of ethics often called for a faith that transcended experience. The ethical person had to believe there was a higher being, a higher law, an inner self, or a reward elsewhere; correlatively in the opposite direction there was a threatening demonic dimension, or a punishment below. One had to believe in an essence of goodness and/or evil beyond time in eternity. This kind of belief must be adhered to in spite of doubts and contrary feelings or experiences, because it is faith in what can never be grasped or comprehended by mere mortal beings. Because we have no direct experience of these "higher" grounds, we must believe or have faith in them—both in their existence and their transcending value.

Earthbody ethics also calls for a faith, but it is one of a far different kind. Our culture, both in its common sense and intellectual tradition, has assumed that belief is not necessary to what we actually experience in an ongoing everyday way, because our ongoing bodily, perceptual, active, and interactive experience is obvious in its accessibility and value. Although this seems logical, it is wrong. The hardest thing for most contemporary Americans and for those of most modern cultures to believe in is the ongoing actual experience of each person. Of course, we all believe that the events of each day actually happened. However, this does not mean that we fully assent to them.

We tend to discount experience as merely "my impressions," but as we have seen if we give into the beckoning depths of experience, it is not "just mine." The experience is contributed to by birds, waterfalls, Native Americans centuries ago, settlers on the Plains, Siddhartha under the Bodhi-tree, the clouds overhead, etc. We see facts and figures—the abstracted fragments of experience—on the one hand, and supersensible causes, on the other, as more real. So, for example, as we discussed early in the book, we discount the different speeds of time, its different rhythms, its being empty or full, or its being disconnected or expansive as being merely our impression of it and that it is really this abstract entity "beyond us."

This belief in what is real of events in turn might mean that we do not in some sense "experience" them either. So then we come full circle to the point at which this disbelief has become correct, because in some sense, many people in our current cultures have no experience of phenomena such as a plurality of time senses. As things stand with most of us, experiences are not worthy of full belief.

Belief is not a mere cognitive function. Belief is an assent, a saying yes to something, a movement to affirm whatever it is that one believes in as having weight as existing—of being significant in some way, and perhaps, even of having some value. However, there is yet another dimension to belief that hasn't been properly appreciated: *belief makes certain levels of experience possible. Then having experienced certain dimensions of "timing oneself" with aspects of reality, a belief in the reality of these dimensions becomes possible.* In other words, we are dealing with a feedback loop, or what philosophers would call a "dialectical relationship"—where each term emerges as a function of the other term. The opposite is true: if we don't believe in certain dimensions of our experience, or don't trust in it as a whole, then these dimensions aren't available to us or our experience becomes thinner as a whole, therefore less worthy of our belief in its meaning and power.

Many books and movies of the twentieth century were about the hollowness of our experience, from high culture icons, such as Eliot's *The Waste Land*, to pop culture's mega-hits like *E.T.* Eliot's Madame Sosotris tells us of the doom of so many who continue to walk the death shuffle across London each with his eyes fixed on his feet. Spielberg's extraterrestrial showed us we don't know what life and death are about; we fail to supply the "heart life" that ET needs in order to revive from its coma and that only children in our culture seem to retain. The century was filled with a constant barrage of messages that, as Heidegger most tellingly puts it, the holocaust may have occurred.

How Heidegger can claim the ultimate holocaust might have occurred without our noticing it can be understood by seeing that life can be destroyed even though everything seems to stand and continue in a physically undamaged sort of way: "The devastation of the earth can easily go hand in hand with a guaranteed supreme standard of living for all men. Devastation can be the same as both, and can haunt us everywhere in the most unearthly way—by keeping itself hidden."[1] Heidegger states that this holocaust is about the high-speed expulsion from being rooted in a deeper sense of memory or becoming re-membered. We might say "becoming remembered" is about rejoining the body of earthbody existence and is about experiencing the emotional, sensual, embodied, and thought-provoking currents of meaning always present in the sensual depth of the earth's presence. Yet, if we don't understand this, then "woe, to him, who hides wastelands within"—the wasteland being our disconnection from these currents. In our own wasteland, we are not really experiencing our experience and all has been lost. This book is full of these images: Philip K. Dick's prophesy of a people who will be like their androids; Silko's warning about the "destroyers"; our description of the ghouls, vampires, and aesthetes; and the danger of pseudo–cyber-community. All these are images of a holocaust. The dance of life on the planet continues, but all we see is empty motion.

These images are about those who have lost faith in themselves as earth-bodies, in the depth, cogency, and spirituality of earthly experience. They have lost faith in the sense that experience can be what we called "ceremonial" in chapter one. Then, without this belief, experience gets constricted to what we believe is real, largely as it has been shaped by the dominant teachings of culture, (a sense of "brute physicality" or mere "objective stuff," what the scientific and rationalist revolutions called "mere matter in motion" or the quantifiable). This belief is a self-fulfilling prophecy. Those who adhere to it can't feel the life of the environment, of things, of animals, and in some sense, even of other humans. Nor certainly can they feel the power of dreams, of imaginary stories and images, of collective memories, and a host of other experiences that bring out other layers of meaning and reality in our shared dance with all the world. They enter a vicious cycle of impoverished experience that leads to some of the excesses we've examined (the vampire, the ghoul, the cyberspace abuser, and the violator of animals), but also to the mechanical type of existence Lawrence has articulated as "full of danger to the gentle passengers of this life."

Belief in one's experience,—that what I feel, what I sense, what I dream, what haunts me and calls out to my intuitions or stirs within my body viscerally is a gift to which I must hearken and open myself—is an ethical action, a virtuous action. Achieving this state of being comes from a deeper sense of ethical action as "ethos"—"way of life"—rather than any particular deed that emanates from it. It also doesn't follow, as the moralizing rationalist traditions of ethics have preached, that to open to earthbodies and these voices is to *abandon* the rational in their either/or formulations. Rather, to really be open as human is to allow our distinct ability to be rational to become added to these energies: that is the fully realized or healthy human response, and also the ethical one. Reason and emotion, human and animal, mind and matter, and morality and vitality are not at odds with each other or with goodness, as the either/or tradition of ethics dictates in an oppositional stance of the walled-in ego versus the larger world.

By pointing to famous modern Western cultural icons, we could mistakenly think this is a white male self-involved problem.[2] However, to consider *Ulysses*, *Beloved*, *Ceremony*, and *Surfacing*—novels of this century that have touched many deeply—is to think about tales that have had a great impact on Western culture, yet were told from four varying perspectives. All document a similar trajectory, and only one is about a white male. Whether it is Leopold in Dublin, Seth in the Midwest after the Civil War, Tayo after World War II in the Laguna Pueblo, or the narrator of *Surfacing* in post-Vietnam Canada, all these protagonists face a painful journey. They must move from some kind of living death or way of living in which their experience has become emptied of meaning and is dislocated in time, space, and place, to a way of life in which they can again truly believe in experience and thus become fully open to it.

All four of these novels show an the individual recovering the ability to be good and to become creative in their lives as the result of a psychic journey and a re-education about the reality of the world and the power of believing in experience.

Each learns this through listening to the body's deeper sense of energies and meanings present in their experience, in which they must encounter other humans and other voices in a larger swirl of historical, cultural, and natural forces and voices. After ten years of living in shock at the death of their child, Leopold and Molly in *Ulysses* have not really felt their feelings; they pass through the days, lying head to toe, not having intercourse, lost in a limbo life. The funeral of his friend and her taking a lover on this fateful day have suddenly awakened the pair to the possibility that they might re-enter their experience and find new meaning, and, perhaps, even love for each other. Joyce says of Leopold—that, at the end of this day of revelations and wrenching events, "he traveled," and so does Molly, to a new point where she can say repeatedly, "yes," as the book ends. They've suffered excruciating pain with the death of their son, Rudy, in a socially oppressive context in which Leopold is devalued in his talents and seen as a Jew, and of Molly, is seen as a fading beauty and talent. The resulting withdrawal of their faith in the richness and meaning of experience, has lead them to a paralysis where they no longer rejoin the rhythms and propulsive, unfolding sense of experience, until perhaps tomorrow, June, 17, 1904, when they have resolved to awaken more fully.

Seth and many of the characters in *Beloved* have been abused by being bought and sold, beaten, raped, and degraded. The smiles on their faces are masks, their hearts are like Paul D's—"locked in a tin"—and even the natural world is too painful in its vitality to experience, since to feel one emotion deeply brings all the others, interlaced in a rhythm, to the forefront. Here is another sense of the vicious cycle that we can enter ethically, if we ignore earthbody ethics: those who no longer experience the reality of their experience, who no longer let the waves of empathy, emotional apprehension, sensitivity move through them from others, can do horrible things to other humans beings, especially if the society's laws and current ethics condone this abuse, as did the institutions of slavery. This lack of connection, however, not only allows the ethical victimizers to become ethical monsters who rape, pillage, and destroy others with no sense of the other's torment, but it also *doubly victimizes* those who suffer from such treatment. They suffer not only from the immediate impact of violation, but also suffer from the long-term reverberations.

In some sense, we can all see ourselves in this latter role, since most have suffered some sort of injustice or cruelty from others, whether in personal incidents of child or spouse abuse, as the object of violence, or from less personal trauma of wartime violence, industrial exploitation, or inhumane treatment by so many of the institutional forms of oppression in modern society. The greater the hurt suffered, the more likely that the person will have to withdraw further from fully "being there," from fully living their experience, or from fully giving themselves over to the earthbody currents which flow through the environment into us in the depths of our senses. This dilemma is expressed eloquently in *Beloved* as Paul D struggles with his feelings during his five unsuccessful attempts to escape from slavery, the longest of which lasts for three years:

> And in all those escapes he could not help being astonished by the beauty of this land that was not his. He hid in its breast, fingered its earth for food, clung to its

banks to lap water and tried not to love it. On nights when the sky was personal, weak with the weight of its own stars, he made himself not love it. Its graveyards and low-lying rivers. Or just a house—solitary under a chinaberry tree; maybe a mule tethered and the light hitting its hide just so. Anything could stir him and he tried hard not to love it.[3]

Paul D, like other victims of extreme cruelty and oppression, has to block out the flow of energies as an earthbody, even though these are the energies that would bring him back into contact with vitality, feeling, and a responsiveness that would heal him. However, he would become transformed into a new being with new connections to the things, creatures, and people of the earth. He would be restored to vulnerability, which would be used against him by his tormentors. The plight for those who are objects of ongoing violence is that in order to survive, they cannot allow themselves to feel the pull of the open planet.

For someone in Paul D's circumstances, to feel the flow of these admittedly positive energies is to bring back *all* feelings, including the horrendous ones of being violating, of being hurt, and of being degraded. Instead of continually re-experiencing this pain, these people are forced to hide within the body as if it were an empty shell, or "tin box," as Paul D puts it. Secondly, there can be no question of opening oneself up to the flow of feeling and transformation when the same hostile environment still exists: the sensitivity and openness will be only become a weapon in the oppressor's hand for the victim to feel more intensely further annihilating emotions. The worst part of being a victim is the aftermath of living death. This is part of how we get a population of ghouls, vampires, aesthetes, cyberescapees, and people out of time and place.

Tayo, in *Ceremony*, physically survives much: he is part of the Bataan Death March, made more excruciating by having to carry his mortally wounded brother, Rocky, and he endures a lifetime of degradation and scorn by both whites and Native Americans for being a "half-breed." Tayo has come to feel that "for a long time he had been white smoke." Tayo explains that this white smoke doesn't really have sense of itself and experiences the world as outlines, even "outlines of the food they pushed into his mouth, which was only an outline too, like all the outlines he saw" (*C*, 14–15). He is amazed that others can't see beyond his outline, "but they did not realize it was hollow inside." Tayo is not here and the world is not here with him. This state is more obvious with Tayo, given his sensitivity, but it also true of all his friends, who hide from their own sense of unreality behind their drunkenness and anger.

Unlike most victims of violation, Tayo undertakes a long, painstaking search for healing, for a way to make his life ceremonial. He finds guidance from others, especially the non-traditional medicine man, Betonie. He listens to the myths and stories that inspire a different connection with the landscape, with others of the earth, where each people and each aspect of nature intertwine in emotional and imaginative significance that, if hearkened to, allows a "timing'" in which we meet up with the energy flows conveying purpose and meaning:

> Dragonflies came and hovered over the pool. They were colors of blue—powdery sky blue, dark night blue, shimmering with almost black iridescent light, and mountain blue. There were stories about the dragonflies too. He turned. Everywhere he looked, he saw a world made of stories, the long ago, time immemorial stories, as old Grandma called them. It was a world alive, always changing and moving; and if you knew where to look, you could see it, sometimes almost imperceptible, like the motion of the stars against the sky. (*C*, 95)

The stories that move us back into resonance with the world are moving through the world and are spoken by voices throughout the planet. The language of these stories and others like them does not "scientifically" or "objectively" describe the world, but rather is the repository of images, feelings, and intuitions shared among people and evoked in response to the earthy powers around them. Language is used here to return one to experience, to break one free from distance and to help one become open to the pulsing of the world. For Tayo, it is as though he had somehow re-entered time and space after a long absence, an absence of years. His re-entry is about feeling that always alive and changing world moving through his body, feelings, and mind. He is there now in a different way, part of the circle of dancers again.

Tayo's journey back to a moving space and time, experienced through a ceremonial life, is not just a psychological breakthrough: both he and his people recognize it as an ethical matter—a matter of the highest obligation. The elders have met to discuss his condition and the condition of his friends many times, and they feel that the fate of the people, the fate of the world or the goodness of the world, the "rightness" of the people, is at stake. There are different ways to see that this is an ethical dimension, not a psychological one, or rather that such a distinction is both wrong and itself unethical. On the most straightforward level, the victims of violence who don't realize they've retreated from their experience, who have lost their faith in life, in being open to feeling and the flow of meaning as earthbodies, often become further perpetrators of violence against themselves and others. After Tayo's friends return from the war and are again treated as second-class riffraff instead of conquering heroes, they turn their pain into an ongoing drunken haze and life of denial: "So, they tried to sink the loss in booze, and silence their grief with war stories about their courage, defending the land they had already lost" (*C*, 169). By the end of the novel they try to destroy Tayo, rather than have him wake up and make them see the truth and respond to it creatively. Finally, they destroy each other, through violence, torture, and drunken self-destructiveness. There is where ethics should enter, at the root cause of destructive and self-destructive behavior: for a society that has already "lost the land," and that is most of us at the beginning of the twenty-first century, we have to re-find ourselves in the power of being fully present in space and time as fluid and moving through our bodies, or fail our obligations to each other and the planet.

The other way in which this is an ethical matter is that Tayo and the village elders realize this is the only way to defeat "the destroyers" we spoke of at the beginning of chapter three—those who "see no life / When they look / they see only objects. / The world is a dead thing for them" (*C*, 135). The only way to fight those who fear the world as something antagonistic to them is to become fully present and part of the flow of energy on the planet. To be fully present and energized through the flow of the world's energies is infectious and powerful, although it can be denied:

> The dreams had been terror at loss, at something lost forever; but nothing was lost; all was retained between the sky and the earth, and within himself. . . . They logged the trees, they killed the deer, the bear, the mountain lions, they built their fences high; but the mountain was far greater than any or all of these things. The mountain outdistanced their destruction, just as love had outdistanced death. The mountain could not be lost to them, because it was in their bones . . . . This feeling was their life, vitality locked deep in blood memory. (*C*, 219–20)

No matter how much literal destruction and violence is wrought, to have a human body means to have this ability to be attuned to a deeper revitalizing energy that makes one sensitive to everything and everyone around. The only way to try to combat those who perpetrate acts of violation, in the long term, is not to combat them, but to help them rejoin the earth in a sensitive relationship by awakening them to the sensitivity granted to them by being earthbodies: "As far as he could see, in all directions, the world was alive. He could feel the motion pushing out of the damp earth into the sunshine—the yellow spotted snake the first to emerge, carrying this message on his back to the people." This is the heart of an ethos we share with all living creatures and all objects on the planet—not a human-centered "standard." It is a way of life that gradually times out a relatedness to others and all living things.

Finally, the protagonist of Margaret Atwood's novel *Surfacing* is the character who has to travel the furthest distance to rejoin her experience and find a way to believe in it, because she is unaware of how far she is from the reality of her life and the planet. Leopold, Molly, Seth, Paul D, Tayo, and the other Laguna men know something is wrong with their lives, even though they are lost. To Atwood's narrator, life makes sense and she thinks she is present and doing tolerably well as a modern woman with a career as an illustrator, even though she is actually, in ways unknown to her, utterly displaced in space, time, body, feeling, and thought. This is a frightening condition, because when we don't know something is lost, we don't look for it. If what is lost is our experience, our reality, then we see how the holocaust can occur when we feel like everything is all right. This is what Socrates recognized: ignorance is dangerous, but not nearly so dangerous as being ignorant that one is ignorant. Knowing this, Socrates tried to reveal this to the Athenians, so they could start to know they had to search for themselves.

The narrator of *Surfacing* doesn't realize that her past has been experienced as so violating to her, especially her abortion and the fact that she was discarded by her lover. She has remembered a past according to more acceptable societal images that have reconstructed her life according to more acceptable feelings and ideas. It has left her without a life with which she is really connected:

> It was all real enough, it was enough reality for ever, I couldn't accept it, that muti-
> lation, ruin that I'd made, I needed another version. I pieced it together the best
> way I could, flattening it, scrapbook, collage, pasting over all the wrong parts. A
> faked album, the memories as fraudulent as passports; but a paper house was bet-
> ter than none and I could almost live in it, I'd lived in it until now. (S, 168–169)

This slide towards reconfiguring experience according to society's dictates of what
is acceptable and to minimize both our personal pain and the need to go through
being shattered and coming out the other side happens more easily and gradually
than we realize. The shift in memories, the elision of feelings, and the comfort with
a constructed identity that goes through days like a drill passing through wood,
without being caught up in the currents, the eddies, the depths of ongoing experience, builds imperceptibly, reinforced by society's proliferating images of career,
consumption, and common sense. Traditional ethics does not disturb this condition and feeds into the holocaust, where people may decide by standards, but really
have no deeply felt sense of who is deciding or about what. *The prime effort of ethics
should be to awaken us.* To be fully awake every day is an achievement, an ethical
achievement of attaining an ethos as a *way* of *life*, of being alive! This is why the
Buddha, which means "the awakened one," claimed that to be jolted into full awareness, to become fully engaged in the ongoing reality of everyday life, and not to be
at a distance of ego worries, societal diversions, and general categories of existence
that substitute for actually experiencing the unique presence of life at every second
would bring each person to an immediate sense of compassion.

In *Surfacing*, the protagonist has returned to her childhood backwoods home
to search for her father, who is missing. What she discovers is that the reality of
her life has been far more complex and compelling than she had allowed herself to
experience, for in some way she had always been learning to distance and to not
believe what she felt, or not to dive into its depths. In searching for her father, she
discovers her parents were present to her in ways she had never allowed herself to
take in and even this backwoods was not what she had allowed it to be. Her mother
and father had both strengths and weaknesses she had not fathomed, as also this
countryside had treasures and horrors beyond her memories. Instead of the backward hospitalities and cruelties she had paid attention to, she realizes there are
deeper sinister societal forces, like the developers in this landscape who are violent
and destructive or the hunters who "mainline power." In the landscape, in the lake,
are also other dimensions, like the sacred spots marked by the painted figures of
an older native people with presences and mysteries of which she had not dreamed.

She realizes that her father was both more evil and more weak, as someone
who helped the developers; he also had deeper insight, daring, and feeling than she
had known, as she discovers when she finds all the evidence of his explorations of
the mysterious spirit sites of the lake. The scorned backward country of her youth,
in its lack of sophistication, also holds answers and powers that grab hold of her,
as she continues to explore the spirit spots her father had been trying to fathom.
She is forced to dive into the depths of the lake searching for her father's body, and

the depths of her past in seeing the repressed vision of a fetus at lake bottom, and her old identity drowns. She loses her wits and society's clothing, and lives naked and wild for days, becoming in tune with the currents of meaning and energy embedded here. She feels as though, "after the failure of logic" leads her to follow the hints of the native peoples to experience the spirituality of the landscape, it is like "stepping through a usual door and finding yourself in a different galaxy, purple trees and red moons and a green sun (*S*, 171)." However, it is just really experiencing the reality, the earthsense, of her world for the first time. This is how far we've distanced ourselves from our earthbodies and the energies around us.

Vowing to herself that the hurts she has suffered will no longer keep her at odds with experience, ("This above all, to refuse to be a victim,"), she decides to trust and let go. Now that she understands in a deeply felt way, in a visceral fashion, the complexity of her parents' sensibilities and feelings for her and their world, she also vows, "to prefer life, I also owe them that" (*S*, 220). Feeling her body in a new way, as if "a creature neither animal nor human," unearthing its openness and vitality from under layers of cosmetics, clothing, and societal niceties, she feels her world in a new way:

> The forest leaps upward, enormous, the way it was before they cut it, columns of sunlight frozen; the boulders float, melt, everything is made of water, even the rocks. In one of the languages there are nouns, only verbs held for a longer moment. The animals have no need for speech, why talk when you are a word. I lean against a tree, I am a tree leaning. (*S*, 212)

No longer distrusting the depth of experience and keeping a distance from her body, she feels her environment's presence in and through her in a new way and feels her belonging to that interplay of energies. The supposedly insubstantial parts of the world, like light and space, have substance and the supposedly solid world is fluid, moving through everything. What is most overpowering is that everything is meaning-laden, as if a word, and not that words and meaning come only from humans and their rationality. We are "reversible" with things, as Merleau-Ponty put it, intertwined within each other, tree and person leaning, seeing and speaking, for example, rather than confronting "dead matter" across an unbridgeable gap.

To enter our full presence with the world, to take up our earthbodies, is the prime ethical obligation and directive aimed at us by the rest of the planet and the cosmos. Atwood shows us what that means in a sense much different from its traditional interpretation. "Presence" is a word that has come to be denigrated within academic circles and within the larger postmodern culture in the past decades. The critique of the traditional sense of "presence" was well warranted. Traditionally, presence has been about something being utterly here, completely manifest, and impossible to deny, or in other words, something "absolute." To this absolute we owed reverence and duty, and we were somehow to become one with it. Whether the presence was the Absolute Spirit, the materialization of some purely rational idea, some Supersensible Spirit (like the New Age's "white light"), or some brutely physical monolith, it was a way of avoiding this world of ambiguity, of changing identity, and of being interdependent and mixed up with everything else. The kind of presence that flows though earthbodies is just the opposite: fleeting, richly ambiguous, and moving among boundaries in motion and rhythm, in which each being is incomplete in itself, yet taken up in an interplay among all. Throughout this book, we symbolized this swirling, changing, being caught up with all other beings on the planet, with the image of the circle of dancers.

No blinding light, no utter transparency, no absolute revelation, and no escape from the shifting cultural, historical, and natural energies in interchange and ongoing evolution awaits us as fully open to earthly experience. Rather, we can find ourselves shaping but caught up in energies beyond us by participating in an embodied, moving, linking, rhythmic gathering of depths of meaning. This brings us to a presence much more like that Shakespeare described in his declaration at the end of *The Tempest*: we "are but the stuff that dreams are made on." Like a dream, however, there is drama, meaning, and magic, if we are able to enter its play whole-heartedly. As *Surfacing's* narrator says in one of her final insights, "'I'" am not an animal or a tree, I am a thing in which the trees and animals move and grow, I am a place" (*S*, 213). Humans cannot just blot out their insecurities and limitations by melding with something behind the world as an absolute. Yet the world beckons us as it moves through us. So, neither can we distance ourselves from this circuit of meaning and pulsation that moves through earthbodies without rupturing a communing both needed and offered as a rich gift by the linked planetary ener-gies of humans, creatures, and things. We are more and less than mere physical entity or mechanism, less solid, but more open to a special magic because we are less solid. Instead, we are a place, a space, or a special opening in which humans can trace out the meanings flowing through and given to us by the world. It was this "in-between" state, when one becomes fully a body that communes with all parts of the world through its senses and feelings, that terrified Lestat. However, as human beings and not vampires, this is our special human ethos. It is the ethi-cal call addressed to us as a special kind of dancer whom the planet invites to par-ticipate in its dance and to witness in our human way of thought, speech, and expression of all kinds.

What Leopold, Seth, Paul D, Tayo, and *Surfacing's* narrator all discover is a secret that the Buddhists have known for two and a half millennia: that to return to the quiet presence of the body which then buzzes with all the voices of the planet is to feel compassion for all beings, living and non-living. To cease cloud-ing the channels of our earthbodies' abilities to carry through us all the sensibil-ities of all other beings on this planet—their energies, their meanings, and their worth—by silencing the ultimatums of the separate sense of "I" that wants to con-trol opens a sensitivity that is awesome. The kinship of all beings, how we are woven together, that swells up as a compassion allows us to see our reality in new ways and suddenly experience our actions as having a different significance in the need to serve the whole of the planet. Such openness doesn't give us rules or absolutes of a different kind, but rather brings us into a sensitivity that is respon-sive to the rest of the planet. From there is not a sure way, but it is an interactive way that seeks to find together long-term rhythms of mutual fulfillment that are also a beautiful and glorious sort of dance together.

Patterns of Perversity in Flight from Pain

Why have we, in the European-centered cultures persisted for thousands of years in thinking of ourselves, creatures, and the stuff of the world as substances, as hardened chunks of reality, as reducible to atoms or particles or pure spirit—or whatever else would simply be there, unchangeable—when life is so palpably about transformation, deep movement, and interfusion of objects and people and creatures? Why cut ourselves off from this unfolding process of vitality and meaning as a separate block of reality? The most obvious answer would be to repeat one of our cultural psychological truisms that to be so open to the input of other energies (as we would be by embracing our sense of being earthbodies) is to be open to the unknown and thus prey to insecurities. This is an obvious answer: we're scared. Although this is true, I don't think it is the most compelling reason. We humans are not as straightforward as we seem.

Another obvious and more current cultural response to this question would be the warning to avoid a "poor investment" in terms of time, energy, and emotion in causes that don't immediately "pay off." To "maximize investments" seems the new global commandment of free enterprise. To feel oneself caught up compassionately with the plight of others, whether starving children or caged chickens or acid rain damaged trees, is to lose the control over the self as having its own destiny, desires, and agenda, causing one to get sidetracked from productive self-fulfilling pursuits. Even love, as a truly open embrace of all the ambiguities of the depths and transformations of the other person, is becoming to be seen as a sentimental project that can be superseded by a more rational program of exchanging mates—get a newer, more compatible model. If this is more efficient in terms of time, energy, and financial resources, then why not pursue this program? If life is about materiality, considered to be just a collection of inert objects that can be possessed and manipulated, then it makes sense to keep trading at any moment for greater satisfaction. If we live facing a distant, solid, and menacing world, we should control it in order to secure for ourselves greater pleasure. Then the meaning that comes from pain and suffering in allowing ourselves to feel fully related to all other beings is one that can and should be avoided, at least to a manageable degree. To feel openly with others is just a personal preference or an idiosyncrasy, and one that is often counterproductive to the true "bottom line."

Although this reasoning seems eminently sensible, given the dominant world view, we may live the way we do for far less rational reasons. Edgar Allen Poe, who had a sensitivity to bizarre happenings in the world and those that we imagined might threaten us through the supernatural, also had a keen eye for the bizarre turns of our psyche. He described the power of what he called "the imp of the perverse" within all our psyches; he called our psyches a "radical, primitive impulse—elementary." He described how, dreading to make an error, we also feel drawn irresistibly to make a mistake; afraid of offending someone, we also desire to enrage them; and, at the last extreme, facing even death from falling from a precipice, thinking of the crushing and breaking of our bones:,". . . this fall—this rushing annihilation—for the very reason that it involves that one most ghastly and loathsome of all the most loathsome and ghastly images of death and suffering which have ever presented themselves to our imagination—for this very cause do we now most vividly desire it."[4] This desire to plunge into the worst suffering is part of us as beings who are called to the dance of life. There is an intensity here that is compelling, even more so as we construct existences which are flat and lifeless or don't ever touch us deeply. Nietzsche, too, pointed out this will to destruction, this revenge against ourselves, as a powerful force behind Western culture once it has denied the passion of the body and the senses, and is therefore starving for vitality. Nietzsche diagnosed dominant Western culture as having been in thrall to this desperate attempt to feel life by going against its very sources of life, of wanting to feel the pain of going counter to life rather than languish in the throes of a feeling of lifelessness we've endured for the past few thousand years, (especially since Platonic and Christian philosophy had gained ascendancy, then followed by science), in a denial of living openly the body and its passions. Freud, too, was more and more impressed, as he aged and fled to London in response to the threat of the Nazis, that Western culture as overly repressed was driven more by Thanatos, the desire for destruction and self-destruction than by the erotic desire to join with the world.

It is hard to acknowledge the self-destructive irrational pulls that have an even more fundamental purchase on our psyches. It is the worm wound around the core of the way we have constructed our sense of self. Given the distance we have put between ourselves and the energy flow of the planet, we feel empty and hopeless. We persist insanely, denying our earthbodies as interwoven, dynamic, and ever-changing flows of energy and meaning with the world. We create another loop in a vicious cycle. *We deny our larger, renewing selves as energy patterns, because we feel deep in our bodies that this way of life that cuts us off from life hurts. We are addicted to this self-hurting style.* Part of the payoff is the pain itself. It is vitality, a rush of energy in the face of nothingness, a hurt that tells us we are still alive. Paradoxically, a culture that flees pain of all sorts, from headaches to mourning, continually condemns itself to a deeper, more pervasive, pain as its addictive need.

This addictive need for pain is perhaps also what is most distinctive and dangerous about human beings. James Hillman once said in a lecture that each animal has a distinctive display that its life exhibits to the cosmos. The display is each creature's way of turning the overflow of life, of vitality, into something that is amazing and is shown to the rest of the world. So, in Hillman's example, the soaring, looping, and graceful flight of birds shines down on other creatures and infiltrates their being with its awesomeness. Hillman couldn't discern what the human display might be, but it immediately occurred to me that it was our ability to deny parts of ourselves. Only humans can turn against their very nature and destroy parts of the meaning of their own existence. The Greek chorus realized that, in witnessing the mythic Greek houses indulge in cycles of self-destructiveness, there was something uniquely human and awe-inspiring at work. We can create mighty, and even beautiful, things from this turning against ourselves, but sometimes the price is just too high, either for the individual, the culture, or the planet. The often portrayed artist who squeezes out creation from their life at the cost of great self-destruction is testimony to this addictive drive. Yet it is one that can be tempered.

There is a necessary pain to a full life. The unavoidable pains that we encounter in our interpersonal relationships, in our engagements with the world, and even within our flesh come as a direct result of being dynamically part of an interaction. Pain is a vital sensitivity to other energy forces in the larger pattern. One way to understand the traditional view of the body as a physical container divorced from the world, as well as the contemporary strategies of being vampires, ghouls, aesthetes, cyber-escapees, etc., is to see that it is a desperate attempt to save ourselves from the hurt of becoming openly part of these larger patterns. The roots of the word "hurt" mean literally "to be impacted upon." This is what hurt is about. Since our bodies are energy flows caught up with others, they are impacted upon and altered in this collision of forces. This hurts, it makes us feel the spots where we are enmeshed with other forces, whether it is something physical like a rock that slides down on us as we ascend a mountain, or it is our desire to have a person do something we would like while their desires bring them in some opposing direction.

Hurt can be appreciated as bringing ourselves back to this point of contact with others, registered in our flesh and emotion as this being torn apart. Hurt, if paid attention to and then embraced by letting it take us to the point in our psyches at which we have met this other opposing force, can usually bring transformation. The encounter of forces, if catalyzed in their potential interaction, will alter each force. Even hurts to the materiality of our bodies (let alone all the emotional hurts), as they register in our earthbodies with visceral feelings, are lined with emotions, images, memories, etc., into whose force flow we can enter.

As the Buddhists realized, the *worst pain* of even trauma like disease, or accidental damage to the organic body, is the pain in the psyche about the pain. Faced with a broken leg or cancer, it hurts in *tormenting ways* when we are racked with emotions and thoughts, often resentments, such as, why me? In other words, the initial pain of the impact upon psychological or fleshly boundaries within or without does not hurt with the same corrosive force as the anguish we *create* by attempting to fight the existence of the pain and by believing it is evil, rather than a way of discovering wrenching interrelations. A culture that is phobic about hurt and pain finds strategies to avoid these moments of contact. However, the avoidance is itself another sort of hurt that takes its toll on us and also deprives us of these moments of potential transformation. Pain is a map that directs our earthbody's energy flows to meeting with other forces that offers spiritual growth and changing, enriched identities through interaction.

The roots of the word "pain" come from the Greek work for "penalty," which originally meant "to be indebted." The hurt of pain shows us how who we are and what we may become is a debt to the other forces with whom we are interacting,

perhaps even colliding. There is the hurt and the pain of losing the accustomed trajectory of the way we have been unfolding as forces and patterns. There is no way
not to register in the body this wrenching, but this dimension of pain is bearable
and enlightening. It is a gift from the other beings of the world, allowing us to see
where our trajectories and theirs are in opposition and further movement and transformation is needed. This is the type of pain to which Oedipus refers, as portrayed
by Sophocles in *Oedipus at Colonus*. After twenty years of wandering as a blind beg-
gar, the former king seems different, more at peace, and a better man, and remarks:
"Suffering and time have been instructors in contentment."[5] Each torment taught
Oedipus about old relationships, values, and ways of being that had run counter to
the lives of others. He could then emotionally "see," despite his literal blindness. He
could find more intrinsically rewarding alternatives to his old behavior patterns,
such as facing difficulties instead of running from them, or being more humble
instead of imperious and arrogant. The pain gave blind Oedipus more vision and
insight than he had had previously as "far-seeing" hero and king, who avoided emotional challenge and pain in particular, always escaping through his wits. Pain is a
key path of openness to interconnectedness of the world as earthbodies.

The pain of denying the necessary pains earthbodies bring with them causes
the specific pain of *cutting all these threads* which weave us into the world, or at least
cutting as many as we can without making ourself into an utter zombie. It is the
ripping apart of the lines of meaning and energy that bind us with the world. It
hurts terribly, deep within our suppressed feelings, as the wrenching away, the ripping out from the midst of our larger bodies as energy patterns, the heart of vitality. Yet this deep searing pain at the root of our culture has become some sort of last
gasp feeling of something. It resembles the gesture of the Nazi scientist in the last
scene of Bergman's *The Serpent's Egg*, so frustrated at no longer feeling anything,
not even when he tortures his victims, he watches himself slit his own throat in the
mirror in the last ditch attempt to feel something. To take the body as a thing or
live it as a ghoul or vampire is to feel the same pain as while having the physical
heart ripped out from the physical body. Here, we rip out the heart of energy, movement, and meaning from a radiant, dynamic, and deep flow phenomenon. We do
this to avoid so many other pains that would make us grow, yet we mainline this
underlying self-destructive pain as our last gasp perverse proof that we are still alive.

However, it is obviously a self-defeating gesture: by attacking our spirits as
a last ditch effort to feel alive, we make ourselves feel disgusted with life. On some
level, we want this disappointment, this feeling like we can't win and that life is
merely a gradual expenditure of energies and passions that will never be fully rec-
ompensed and will erode gradually into nothingness. As Sartre put it in the famous
final sentence of *Being and Nothingness*, experiencing ourselves as seeking to get
from an adversarial world some sense of having "made it," we end by feeling that
"life is a vain passion." With this sense of desperation, that we are locked in a battle with a distant and threatening world and with competing fellow creatures for
a small piece of the pie of satisfaction, we stay hungry, driven, and able to be manipulated to keep buying, striving, and having to be entertained to forget it all. It is

our motivation. We seek to engage in the hopeless battle as a noble gesture. To be told that life itself, without buying anything, without achieving anything, and without having to conquer, offers itself as an infinite gift of energy, wonder, and meaning is ridiculed. It is ridiculed, because we feel that it is unthinkable, unimaginable. If we were to see the obvious, that this planet, this existence as earthbodies is magical and wondrous, then we would lose our way of life and our world as we know it. This life and this world answers a deep need in us, or else we wouldn't expend so much energy, so much belief, and work so hard to keep it as it is. The notion that fulfillment comes just by being, by letting go and becoming aware of ourselves as part of rich and deeply meaningful dancing energies, threatens us with a loss of everything we use to orient ourselves in this uphill struggle of life.

It is a scary thought that we are lost doing things as our stated goals that we know on a deeper level cut us away from the heart of life. We fear facing pain, so frantically pursue goals that insure a deeper pain. Towards the end of the nineteenth century Tolstoy captured this fear and abhorrence with incredible power and purity in the character of Ivan, in his novella *The Death of Ivan Ilyich*. Ivan had followed society's pathways of success and desire unquestioningly. He had used his contacts and manipulated the bureaucracy to rise to a secure and profitable job, which he performed with no real love, but as a diversion, so that he did not have to really deal with the complexities of his relationship to his wife, children, and friends. This way he could keep them at a comfortable distance. He avoided pain whenever possible, including his wife's depression after childbirth and then, later, the death of some of their children, because he thought life was about finding ways to have pleasure. There is much more that could be said about Ivan's life and its patterns in their similarities to those described in this book, but what is relevant here is that after his health fails at the height of his life, from an absurd, trivial accident, he goes through stages of despair and rage. At first he is furious about dying, but then he realizes his rage is really about how he has lived. The lack of real connection with others, their collective inability to deal honestly with their deeper feelings and with the emptiness of their lives as a series of diversions suddenly slaps him in the face. How could playing cards have been the central pleasure and focus of his life!

After passing through anger with society for providing him with a life pattern so superficial and disconnected, and with others for still being caught in these patterns, Ivan finally turns to his own disgust with himself. Before he dies, he realizes that in his world, in the relationships of people with each other, and in the entire way they experience, there is nothing that is real. It is all a way to distract themselves from the fact they are living, sentient, feeling, and potentially expressive human beings. As Ivan realizes that his life has been a lie, he begins to howl in rage. He howls for the next three days, "three days of incessant screaming, screaming so terrible that even two rooms away one could not hear it without trembling."[6] Ivan's first response is to feel terror in realizing he spent his life avoiding the feeling, open, and spontaneous life of the body as interwoven with others that Gerasim, his servant, is able to demonstrate in his nights of holding

Ivan. Gerasim's emotional spontaneity and compassion shows Ivan that he has been caught in a horror film, to anachronistically use an earlier image of this book, and that he and his friends and family are the monsters, the ghouls. Then, fury fuels his days of rage as he realizes the planet is in the possession of the ghouls and that he knows no other way to be.

To let go of the lie, the diversion, and the distance of this life is no less over-whelming for him than it was for Lestat to give up his invulnerable vampire body for a body that felt the pain of others. This is the terror: of being drawn out of the non-life, which is empty, in which one is always driven by an underlying craving for something that would satisfy, but never does, after a brief respite with each new conquest. However, at a deeper level, there is the rage at giving up the familiar pain and at abandoning the inner sense of going down to ultimate defeat that we feel we all deserve as mere mortals, and with it, the accustomed round of self-loathing and loathing of others that lies behind this distanced world of interactions. Let us starve ourselves, for that is all we get and all we deserve. We are addicted to this heroic role in face of defeat, as if we were all in a tear-jerking film. This gives us the rush—that surge of desperate energy it takes to fight impossible odds—and the poignancy of being not quite able to be up to the task, the tragic halo around our image of self surrounded by overwhelming forces. We are addicted to this underlying pain and will howl if some force threatens to take it away.

Nietzsche tried to point out that the cheerful industriousness and round of pleasures with which European culture had busied itself was a disguise for a disgust with life and a self-hatred. He has the townspeople of the town of Motley Cow (called this, because they patch together their diversions into a life of chewing their cud) say to Zarathustra: "One has one's little pleasure for the day and one's little pleasures for the night: but one has a regard for health. / 'We have invented happi-ness,' say the last men and they blink"(*TSZ*, 130). They have a regard for health in the sense that they never tax themselves or challenge themselves. They have invented happiness in the sense that it's a state of mind they've created for themselves that keeps them untouched by life's deeper problems and engagements, or, as they put it, "a fool whoever still stumbles over stones or human beings." They don't slow down or stumble, they speed ahead with life's tasks, like the jester who drives the tightrope walker to death by being behind him shouting, "forward lamefoot!" They blink, so as to avoid seeing the possibilities for new creation and openness that Nietzsche located in the figure of the "child" who is "a new beginning, a game, a self-propelled wheel, a first movement, a sacred 'Yes'." To reach this final stage of transformation, as Nietzsche articulated coming to affirm life in its imperfection, earthly sensuality, and creativity through a series of "metamorphoses" culminating in a final childlike stage requires " a sacred 'Yes.'" to our fate that we are interconnected with others as part of an "interplay of forces" and energies.

To be part of an "interplay of forces" in which "every atom of being affects all the rest," and is in turn affected by them, means we will hurt and we will fail at times, since we encounter many energies and forces that have their own trajecto-ries. It means that ultimately we are powerless before the grasp of death. For each failure to achieve our goal, for each time we are shown the emptiness of what we thought was our answer, and certainly by death, Nietzsche says we "go under," but for him this is a gift and an opportunity to be thrown into the game of self-creation with all these forces. It is the satisfaction of entering this creative process for which we must be grateful and which is the meaning of life of "this world," the world of the body, emotions, and constant transformation that Plato sought to leave behind, the world many religions have sought to abandon for a more "perfect place," and that in some sense our American culture drives us to try to conquer. However, for Nietzsche, this sense of pain, struggle, and necessity could be used as an appreciative sense that we are impacted upon by every atom in the universe as interconnected, and so included in the game of existence and potential creativity in response to this interplay. We could see that we are lucky to be earthbodies who are fragile enough in our flow patterns to be so affected by the world and thus invited to play within its game. Suffering pain is the price of openness to creative transformation.

To achieve this childlike openness means to be willing to affirm that we are changeable. If we take ourselves as mere substances, whether biochemical machines or pure spirits of a definite unchanging nature, then we remove ourselves from the interplay of forces with the world. Psychologically, we take our toys, go home, and shut the door. We have already seen that belief has the power to change our possibilities. We need to believe in the power of our experiences for them to gain their full potency. We can deny what we are and so reality appears to conform to this disbelief. We have the magical power to make life seem isolated and cut ourselves off from the planet's embracing energies in an open interactive way. To believe that we can be transformed is not to believe that we can just change ourselves. It is to see that learning, growth, and change are indirect paths. *We can't will ourselves to become anything, at least not directly.* Our will is potentially very powerful, when cleared out from being entangled within the images and desires that lock us further into ourselves. When our will moves us out into the world to find resonances, it can become empowered. As this book has hopefully shown, as "inner psyches" we are nothing. It is in allowing larger energies from other people, other kinds of people, natural phenomena, culturally diverse events, from animals, from differing historical understandings, etc., to flow through us that we gain meaning and energies. We can always allow change to happen, by opening ourselves to influences that have promise for us to become transformed in creative ways. It takes a steadfastness to remain open to new meanings and energies. However, it is not as if we can just change ourselves, like removing parts from a machine and putting in new ones. Rather, as humans we have to let ourselves go into new patterns that will return us to ourselves in new dimensions we couldn't merely open for ourselves.

Rhythm's Power, Changing Destructive Patterns, and Finding Place

Given our traditional prejudices, we think of our identities in terms of substances and their characteristics. However, we are both less and more changeable than a substance. A rock or a machine or a chemical compound has to be taken apart by direct, forceful, and invasive impact to be altered. It may be destroyed in the process. These alterations are brought about by frontal assault according to a plan, and take on an established and palpable nature. There are parts of us that can be reduced to or altered as such a biological substance. When a surgeon invades our bodies, removes organs or puts in organic or mechanical parts, we have agreed to be treated as a mere substance and functioning mechanism for this purpose. However, in our fuller reality, humans are more diffuse and multifaceted, given that their identities flow into and through them from all to which they are related. As Oliver Sacks' book, *A Leg to Stand On*, demonstrates, even while trying to reduce ourselves to biological machines and substance for medical purposes, if the other dimensions of our meaning and energies are totally suppressed, the "repair" to even the mechanical level of our body won't be successful. Sacks had suffered a serious compound fracture of his leg, and bone, muscle, and nerve tissue had been disconnected. Much intricate surgery was required for his leg's reconstruction. However, after his surgeries and recuperation, he still couldn't walk or move properly, because he didn't have the sense of this being his leg. His doctors became puzzled and frustrated, because mechanically, all was back in order. This feeling of it no longer being his leg was so extreme, that one night, Sacks became alarmed and tried to throw his leg out of bed. Of course, he was right. A biologically perfectly constructed leg was not Oliver Sacks' leg. His leg was part of the energy flow and context of significance that made up the life of Oliver Sacks. Sacks, an ardent music lover, discovered that when he began to listen to music, his leg began to twitch with some spark of vitality and interconnectedness. Sacks listened to increasingly more music, and gradually he "danced" his leg back into the flow of his body as an integrated part of the circulation of energy and meaning. As Sacks talked with other patients, he discovered that most of them reported being aware of some phase in their recovery where they had to find a way to take their bodies, as substances that felt alien to them as mere parts, and find a way to re-integrate them into the energy and meaning flow of their bodies as earthbodies.

Earthbodies are a field of forces that interact with all other forces in patterns. Patterns in dynamic phenomena are both very fragile, in the sense that well-timed and artfully applied small changes may alter them dramatically, but also amazingly durable, if the forces that feed into them stay in the same relation and rhythm. A vortex in the river flow may remain in the same spot for hours or days, weaving its dynamic way in the same area and with the same contour, or there may be some slight shift in some part of the river that upsets the forces of flow entering that stretch of the river which then alters the relationships and disperses the vortex. As earthbodies, we are vortices.

People are surprised that changes in their behavior, changes in their physical states, or changes in their feelings are so difficult to achieve; it is a long struggle against the re-emergence of patterns. It is this stubbornness of the past that fuels explanations of our makeup as substances and tempts us to disown responsibility for who we can be, rather than engage in the long and laborious process of transformation. If we are not substances, then why can't we just will away our insecurities or stop eating too much or stop responding to our spouses in a way that undermines our communication? Yet, patterns of flow as constellations of many forces involve a multiplicity of relations. It is not a matter of just changing "me." There is no simple "me." Who I am is this dynamic network of relations in unfolding events of all sorts. Each time I change the world is changed, and each change in the world of which I am part, if I allow it to be taken to heart, allows new selves to emerge in me.

Even the most simple behavior or understanding or way of coping may be a constellation of many, many forces in multiple relations. For example, when, in *Ceremony*, Tayo wants to halt his sense of helplessness and depression, he can't will them away. They are intertwined with Rocky's death, his long history with Rocky, his devaluation by his aunt, his relationship with his uncle, the lost horses, his degradation by the whites, the despoiling of the land, the toxicity of the uranium mine, his mother's upbringing of him in bars, his half-breed status with both the whites and the Pueblo people, his family traditions, his drinking in the service, his relationship with Night Swan, the rustling of the herd by the rich white rancher, the call of the mountain, the sense of the dragonflies, the power of the tribal myths of Bear and Trickster and others, the way in which he drove his stomach to nausea, the way in which he, too, found relief in drinking, the way in which he retreated to sleep, the way in which his body is now out of shape, the ways in which even he doesn't experience his senses as finely attuned to the land as he always did, and on and on. Betonie, the unorthodox medicine man, realizes that the complex ritual that Tayo will have to follow will take months or maybe years, or maybe the rest of Tayo's life. Tayo will have to address many of these personal events, cultural displacements, physiological upheavals, natural presences, other people, and myriad aspects within his environment, his cultural context, and history.

To change ourselves is to enter into new relationships with so many of the forces that flow through us. Multiple forces make us become who we are in how we greet and shape them. It is an exhaustive process of locating for each person what these specific interweavings are about and how to find the paths to meet up with them in resonant rhythms. In a society that wants a quick fix and no responsibility, this does not play well. We'd rather have it be a problem with a "thing" out there that can be replaced. If it is our problem, then we'd prefer it to be a matter of replacing some "thing" within us, as if it were a faulty part—like altering chemicals or some genes or something we can manipulate without entering into relation. Relation takes energy, sensitivity, exhaustive exploration, and ongoing attuning emotionally, behaviorally, intellectually, and expressively. In a society that promotes ever-more passive consumption, instead of individual exploration and expressivity, this search for ourselves in transformation not only seems undesirable, but even impossible to many.

To change patterns takes the patience and the painstaking effort to find all these myriad interconnection points and to find new ways of entering into them. This takes a level of introspection, analysis of situation and relations, and attention to the smallest details of how these relations are forged that most of us are not taught, and that is not promoted by the pace and focus of our present consumer culture. It also means this task, though partly reflective and intellectual in its process of careful self-discovery, is even more one that calls for bodily trust. We have to be able to give ourselves over to the viscerality of the body in order both to discover and to find indirect ways of modulating these patterned relations. This is the power of Gestalt therapy's attention to each part of the body, its energy, and its feeling tone, as reflecting a unique relationship, or set of relationships, to parts of the client's situation.

The body as unfolding dynamic patterns of interchange with the world flowing around and through it can be read viscerally, emotionally, and imaginatively to yield an understanding of these vectors. In Gestalt therapy, for example, the therapist might ask the client to become the knot in his or her stomach or the fluttering in his or her, arms and give voice to how those visceral energies are the embodiment of feelings in connection with parts of the world. In a therapy session while I was in graduate school, the therapist helped guide my attention to the ball of tension at the pit of my stomach. In giving myself over to the energies that seemed to be congregated in my abdomen, by trying to feel what these visceral feelings meant in an emotional and emblematic way about my life situation, I discovered they contained the emotions swirling around my inability to write freely at the time. The energies, as I explored what they felt like and what they seemed to be suggesting or to what they seemed connected, felt like they were the heavy stone weight of Yale University Graduate School pressing down on me. The centuries of Yale's austere and intimidating expectations seemed crushing to my excitement as a writer.

My felt relationship with that reputation and what it meant for me had become something I had to painfully digest in the writing process. After identifying that relationship as it flowed through my body at that moment, I was then able to find a more dancing energy in my feet and shoulders that flowed into me, once I had faced the fear and pain in my stomach. This more lively and playful energy led into a playful sense of space that betokened a dancing, fun relationship with other parts of the world that could then be linked to the work I was trying to write at the time. As I experienced this new playful energy as another part of the writing process that I had not noticed before (with my being riveted on the tension in my stomach), I was then able even to invite the old stuffiness of Yale to enter a jig with me. I danced around the floor with my imaginary thesis as my partner, opening up a flood of other emotions, memories, fantasies, and ideas. This helped me to start to find a way to enjoy writing my thesis and to think about it as my own particular dance, something that would reflect my own rhythm and not Yale's. In the depths of the energies that run through our earthbodies viscerally, the imagined, remembered, felt, thought, and intuited interweave in their flow, and by letting go into their sense within the body, we can enter into their shared current.

Patterns continue with force because they come to embody a certain rhythm, a rhythm that has been set up among many events, people, and places. Each facet woven into the network of relations adds more strength to the pattern and more energy to the rhythm. The relations are also reinforced, since we have entered them in a bodily way that is immediate and visceral, becoming vital to our own rhythmic way of relating to the rest of the world and our lives. Once we have unfolded in our relations with the world by continually moving in certain patterns, it seems unthinkable to really imagine other patterns, for reality itself in many of its facets would change its identity. For example, in *Ceremony*, Tayo's nausea is not a simple feeling. It has a certain rhythm of frenetically fleeing and rifling through his past and present, but never getting anywhere, like a tire spinning with no traction in the sand. This is the visceral sense of all the events and relationships with the world that his stomach experiences as upsetting and nauseating. His part of the pattern and rhythm is a frenzied seeking, but not finding a proper place, and the world's part is that of being cold and solid in its exclusion of him. Tayo's drinking embodies this sense of dizziness combined with a despairing letting it all go, sliding towards a black hole of oblivion, added to an angry jerking away from possible creative relations. This is part of the sense of increasing velocity as his life slips away. The rhythms are indefinite in their number and nuance given each person we confront and each relation we enter, but take on a similar energy as part of our unique way of directing and shaping energies. It takes a considerable trusting of the body just to begin to detect them and then even more trust to start to work with them in transformation.

Rhythm comes about from the synchronous movement and harmonizing or interweaving with other forces in the environment and within ourselves. Rhythm gives patterns an added dimension of coherence or felt belonging among its constituents. They are no longer just related by circumstances or by cause and effect, but instead parts come to echo each other, to resonate to each other, to enter into a vitalizing energy that is passed back and forth, and augmented. Rather than mere repetition, there is a stressing and moving that has a musical sense of progression, and with it an inclusive electricity, drawing other beings into its spell or field, like shavings drawn to a magnet. In his book, *Wild Hunger: The Primal Roots of Modern Addiction*, Bruce Wilshire describes the most basic level of the person's relationship to the world as rhythmic. Wilshire comes to this conclusion after exploring how the self is a "body-self," comprising a circulation of energies with the world, similar to the description in this book of earthbodies. As he struggles to understand what we crave in addiction, Wilshire sees that Emerson's idea of the Earth's "circular power returning into itself" through our body-selves is a circuit that can be broken. Once this circuit is broken, we crave some other sort of sense of power and connection in its stead, or we can find ways to enter this flow of energy and meaning more completely.

Rhythm, explains Wilshire, gives us access to the melodic aspect of the unfolding of energies and meaning that are at the heart of the way things, people, and creatures come to enter the dance of manifestation together. Wilshire notes how Emerson saw that there is a musical sense of things, the way each thing, person, and creature is distinct is as a melody. Rhythm is the way those melodies join into each other or, as Wilshire explains, how a person and a stream can come together rhythmically: "Each coils into and instantly confirms the other within the resounding world that feeds back into itself."[7] Rhythm is a centripetal force that joins us to things and others by a fleshly synchronizing with the musical quality of their flowing forth. This is not an intellectual identification, but rather is the way as earthbodies, as material beings in our concrete sensual connection to specific things, we hold together in our moving through them energetically. As Wilshire phrases this insight: "For stretching through time, the underlying rhythmic reciprocity of body and world, essentially musical, orders, arrays, and re-collects all things sensuously—meaningfully." We are drawn into the world through this matching and responsive moving in time in our bodies. This is the way we have the ongoing continuity that we attribute in our culture's philosophical misunderstanding to some underlying substance or thing-like aspect of ourselves.

In order to read this sentence well, for example, the reader must enter a certain rhythm. Similarly, in order to function like a team in any sport, a group of people must find a rhythm in their movements and actions. Even in order to perceive meaningfully an object, there must be a felt rhythm among the sensations we take in through whatever sensory modality. For a discussion to become responsive and to take on meaning, a rhythm must spring up between its participants. In order for two people to communicate erotically and sexually, a rhythm is born between them that carries them like a tide. Rhythm is vital to all happenings in which a person generates meaning, works toward a purpose, or augments sensitivity. The opposite is also true: sometimes a discussion just can't proceed, if mired in dissonances, or suddenly the basketball team and all its members lose their rhythm and each shot clanks away from the basket, a task which was building upon itself, whether writing or painting a fence, loses its beat and synchronicity. Immediately, miscues start erupting. Rhythm allows us to interplay with other aspects of our world and within ourselves. Rhythm gives us a continuity and a momentum.

Our rhythms, embodying our basic sense of directedness through the world, are not easy to alter. The body moves within rhythm's power as if being surrounded with a field of energy and attraction that helps focus and propel its unfolding relations with things. A rhythm has a momentum and draws upon the combined force of its constituents, so that it tends to keep going, even though it is fragile in requiring the coordinated input of all its members to remain in existence. To alter a rhythm that governs significant relations with the world would require a prolonged effort to find a new series of what is noticed, what is emphasized, and what is valued in different ways of moving with accustomed things, or in finding new sets of things with which to move. We would be forging a whole new kind of relation in movement with the things that matter to us. This doesn't mean it can't be done, but it does mean finding out all the ways we have attuned ourselves to the world in a certain rhythm in order to modulate ourselves into a new one. It is a complex task to undo deliberately what rhythm achieves automatically in drawing upon multiple influxes.

A recent novel that demonstrates through the stirring struggle of one of its two main characters, Ada, the dynamics and power of shifting the rhythms of one's life in forging new relations with the world around us is Charles Frazier's *Cold Mountain*. Ada had moved to the rural setting of the Blue Ridge Mountains from the comfort of Charleston with her father, Monroe, a preacher, in the hopes his consumption would improve. They find themselves at odds with the people, their ways, and the world in which they now are. Instead of the mountain air helping him, after six years Monroe dies. It is during the Civil War, and Ada is alone, without hired men available to help her, facing making a life in a setting to which she has never attuned herself. It was not only that she had been pampered by her father to never worry about work, nor that she knew nothing about farming nor living alone, but her psyche was forced to emerge from a kind of trance to find itself dislocated in time and space. In our own culture, many might find themselves in the same state, were they to suddenly awaken from their disconnection as ghouls, vampires, aesthetes, harried clock-driven workers, etc. Ada realizes that she not only knows nothing of the flowers, plants, trees, hills, and creatures around her, nor does she know what her own body can do, but also that she had been just as adrift previously in Charleston, and did not really know who she was or if there were any real purpose to her life. In Charleston, she had drifted with the rhythms of its life. Now, she had to find a rhythm within her that rang true and could make sense of her world.

With the help of a tough, self-sufficient country girl, Ruby, who has fended for herself since early childhood, Ada begins to learn how to apply herself to tasks, to discover how strong her body can be, the animals, plants, weather conditions, social customs, etc., are in her environs. However, each day Ada must stop her old rhythms of lying down in what she had assumed was tiredness, or giving in to supposedly feeling sad, or paying no attention to the changing plants on her acreage. Each day seems impossible to Ada. Ruby seems to bring to her attention detail after detail of farm life and of the exigencies of subsistence, and demand new movements from Ada's body and psyche that continually feel unavailable to her. Yet, gradually and painfully, with dogged attention and persistence, the whole rhythm of Ada's life gradually changes. Looking at the same fields she has looked at for years, she eventually can see plants or animals or implements she couldn't see before or she can see them in different aspects with a whole new set of values and appreciation in a relation that engages her deeply versus just moving by her and her walking by them.

At a key turning point in the novel, Ada has learned each night to watch with interest exactly where on the ridge the sun disappears behind the horizon. She muses:

> Were she to decide fully to live here in Black Cove unto death, she believed she would erect towers on the south and north points of the sun's annual swing. She owned the entire span or ridge where the sun set through the year, that was a thing to savor. One then just had to mark the points in December and June when the sun wrenched itself from its course and doubled back for another set of seasons. Though upon reflection, she decided a tower was not entirely needed. Only clear some trees to notch the ridge at the turning point. It would be a great pleasure year after year to watch with anticipation as the sun drew nigh to the notch and then on a specified day fell into it and then rose out of it and retraced its path. Over time, watching that happen again and again might make the years seem not such an awful linear progress but instead a looping and a return. Keeping track of

such a thing would place a person, would be a way of saying, You are here, in this one station, now. It would be an answer to the question: Where am I?[8]

Through days of "shucking walnuts out of their stinking pulpy husks" (*CM*, 326) (as she puts it in her letter to her Charleston cousin, Lucy), or swinging the scythe for hour after hour, or burning the brush pile, Ada has come to pay attention to the way the land moves and can move her, its details and messages to her, and has taken its rhythm into hers, although she too shapes it in her unique way. Now, she can even see the deeper, slower rhythms of the land around her that take years, season after season, to infiltrate the body and which could encompass her. To take up these rhythms, Ada realizes, is to come to "have" a "place" or, we might say, to become *emplaced*: to feel in the body and heart as if one were located in a space because one has felt its connectedness and connection to oneself. Ada also realizes that to belong to a space in relation, to *be somewhere* in a fully human or earthbody sense as aware and savoring of these interconnections, is also to have a sense of who we are in being somewhere on this earth. Having an identity, Ada discovers, is about this sense of directed, located, belonging to the environs, having found an ability to respond and shape oneself in order to enter larger rhythms that can resonate with a creative sense of self.

Rhythm doesn't just happen instantly. It takes time to unfold in its extended identity, to infiltrate our bodies, and for us to become sensitive to the emanations from the things with whom we meet in this connection. A rhythm builds and then suddenly "catches" among its participants. There is that awkward forced stretch of time while synchronization and catchy new beats are established. At first, connections seem awkward, tenuous, and unstable. There is some clashing and disequilibrium. Flow isn't immediate. Only gradually do we move, resonate, and join in melodically after working with resistances and dissonances. Like the pain of tearing away from connectedness, which is a measure of the way we seek to avoid changing our established ways of flowing in response to the changing world about us, the world, too, resists a smooth and harmonizing yielding to relationship. The things of the world "hold back" into themselves, as Heidegger puts it. They are self-enclosing, at least in the short stretch of time. Of course, it isn't a deliberate response on the part of the world, especially in its inanimate parts. Only other people and living creatures resist more knowingly such opening to others. However, whether people, creatures, or inert objects, all reality resists the immediate loss of boundaries afforded by the momentum of keeping its established rhythm of flowing back into itself. Only as we talk more will people melt somewhat and find a cadence of listening and speaking, of starting to understand and empathize, that starts to open possibilities for new rhythms together. However, even the most inert object, like a mountain or a rock, also has its own rhythm, and only gradually will it be taken up into the hand of the sculptor or by the legs of the hiker or by the eye of the painter. Cézanne painted Mount Saint Victoire for a decade, as Steiglitz shot photographs of the tree behind his house for decades. This resistance of rhythm is its reality: its depth, multiplicity of facets, and further levels to be explored.

A Dynamic Sense of the Depths of Surfaces

The goal of achieving depth, in our lives in works of art, or in other endeavors, had been assumed to be a worthy aim culturally until recent years. This goal, has come into disrepute in light of the current postmodern preference for surfaces. This reaction is a quite understandable and overdue response to the traditional emphasis on depth as more noteworthy and significant than what is present on the surface. The surface was merely "superficial," not just in the literal sense of that phrase, but as an assessment of meaning. The true meaning was seen to lie at a depth, rather than "on the surface" of things or people,—as if the two were opposed to each other. Depth was often presented as something "hidden," which only the expert, such as the scientist or psychoanalyst or intellectual, could locate. Others, lacking their training or talent just couldn't see into this dimension. This was part of the same Greek-through-modern-Europe cultural prejudice that we have critiqued throughout this work: against the senses, the emotions, and that which was experientially available to all as somehow not true knowledge. The truth was buried within things at their depths and had to be uncovered so its nature could be released, reflecting the power of the upper ethereal and eternal realm. One had to dig for this insight. All the commonly available experiences of the bodily emotional realm were condemned to being the "mere surface of life."

However understandable the current obsession with surfaces and the accompanying ridicule of depth, it is also unfortunate in its reinforcement of the same dichotomy between surface and depth. A recent popular television ad for Canon cameras asserts, "image is everything." It is meant to echo part of the current cultural wisdom, and if it is taken seriously as a sensibility or guide to significance in life, it is self-defeating in blocking access to other levels of meanings that have to be balanced with the sensual and emotional impacts of the surfaces of phenomena. Both dimensions, surface and depth, and the meanings they have to offer, are real, interdependent, and mutually enriching. However, to see this relationship and to derive the most meaning from both, it is necessary to have another model of meaning and depth based on another sense of the body.

Besides being oppositional (and thus excluding the devalued term), the traditional notions of surface and depth assume a *clarity of meaning* that needs to be questioned. In the most obvious reference, this distinction refers to things as if they were merely quantities of inert matter, and surface and depth were merely determined by their respective physical locations, though as the Mobius-like constructions of Escher make us aware, even this comparison is not so simple or clear-cut. However, all the other meanings of this dyad, whether referring to our superficial feelings versus deeper ones, or the superficial causes of a political event versus the deeper ones, etc., refer to a broader horizon of significance. Whether the surface meaning is assumed to be obvious, for all to see, or the meaning lying at the depths is hidden, and to be discovered only by the expert or through a journey of exploration, both references as commonly made assume a closure and univocality of discovery that belies the structure of earthbodies.

From the earliest tales of the "hero's quest," so insightfully brought to the public's attention by Joseph Campbell, going all the way to back to the tale of Gilgamesh and his labors, it has been the presumption that there is some answer, some transcendent meaning, or some special talisman to be gained to restore to us the proper sense of life's meaning. So, for example, in the myths surrounding Gilgamesh (the oldest recorded hero's tales), he seeks the secret of immortality when faced with the horror of death after his best friend has died. In one attempt to secure this secret, he ties rocks to his feet to weigh down his body and plunges down into the depths of the waters to secure a magical spiny plant that insures immortality. (It perhaps symbolizes a "growth" fraught with pain, a lesson he resists in trying to get a quick simple solution to aging and death.) Although he cuts his hands, he does get the plant, but that night a serpent seizes the plant and dives back into the depths of the waters with it. The secret of living life forever is indeed one that lies in the depths, but it is not to be gained by merely plunging down to a spot and returning with a quick, simple solution. Gilgamesh laments that the secret of everlasting life has eluded him on his quest: "For myself I have gained nothing; not I, but the beast of the earth has joy of it now."[9] That is right: the serpent, the longstanding symbol of the cycles of the earth, has the secret of everlasting life. It is enmeshed in the history and proliferation of intertwined lives within these earthy cycles of birth, death, and rebirth.

In the heroic mentality to which our culture often subscribes, the depths are to be found at the conclusion of a quest as a prize, or a solution to a vexing problem. The depths have kept hidden some definite formula. Our shared Western presumption, since Plato on, is that a question has an answer and success is achieved by seizing that answer. Capturing the prize constitutes knowledge and sometimes wisdom. However, as Roland Barthes expressed in a protesting counter to this notion, it may be more the case at many times for many issues of significance, that "the key to the treasure is the treasure itself"[10] (as he writes in *Chimera*.) There is no key, either lying self-evidently in front of our noses, nor hidden away to be discovered, but rather to keep asking questions is itself the answer, to stay open to searching, to be involved in the matter at hand such that there is a *flow of partial answers*, giving rise to new inquiries, to new stories. As we have seen, humans and the planet might be better described as flow phenomena—dynamic, multileveled, and ever-changing. Barthes' tale is a tale about tales, about where this book began, in the power of story and ceremony to keep life alive and moving, if it stays responsive to the larger whole and can keep evolving.

A better notion of depth, one that fits our experience as earthbodies and can encompass the end of the story of this book and its search for meaning, is the one proposed by Merleau-Ponty. Rather than being the "third dimension," as depth has been traditionally conceived in its literal representation as coming after point and length, Merleau-Ponty suggests that depth is the "dimension of dimensions"[12] out of which all the others emerge, as does meaning itself. In other words, in our immediate experience and its particular logic, wholes precede parts. Even in its basic perceptual meaning, Merleau-Ponty asserts that depth does not come "after"

establishing points in space, then connecting them into lengths, and then projecting these lengths into planes, giving rise to a sense of depth. Rather, Merleau-Ponty
shows that human bodies are not located at particular discrete points in space, as
if we were mere objects, like coffee cups or rocks. We are "inside space" in myriad
locations as being in relation with all the parts of the world.

Instead of starting from an isolated point and building up points to form
our space, and then from within this space proceeding to forge relations with things,
people, creatures, events, institutions, etc., Merleau-Ponty shows where our consciousness as bodies-within-a-world, as relational bodies or earthbodies, *emerges
from* a web of interconnections of implicit meaning. Humans are *immediately* "at
the depths" by being related to the world as a whole through flows of energy and
meaning. To be a human body is to be immersed within this web of relationships
that gives the so-called physical world its orientation and sense. We can be rational
creatures when we take a distance from things and consider them reflectively.
Equally unique, when we are caught up with things there is an immediate kind of
bodily understanding in which the echoes of that rationality have melded with the
new perceptual, emotional, memorial, imaginative, and other presences in this
immediately felt (although implicitly so) web of relationships. Furthermore, the
kind of relatedness to things, people, events is not just within this lived sense of
space but also within a web of temporal relations. The space-time relational field
of earthbodies to the world is inextricable.

Depth comes first, because it is the sense of being enmeshed at many distances in many situations, even when that seems predominately to be there "just
perceptually." When I look up at the blue sky, I don't have to project out towards
this expanse as if I had to build out from where I am stuck towards the measurable
physical distance located within a depth. Rather my vision is a kind of sensing in
which I "come back" to myself from my interconnection with the sky, a kind of visceral "flowing back" into myself from being at one with the sky's movement and
energy on this brilliant summer day. Vision and the other senses enter the other
being's rhythm in perceiving something meaningfully and fully. In really looking at
the sky, I am "skied" in some sense (we don't have words for these aspects of experience) that adds its sense to my sense of being on the ground. The being "grounded"
is in relation and interconnection with the expanse of sky, something a mere mechanical registering device wouldn't feel in its limbs and stomach. Such a device could-
n't be "under" the sky in the same sense, as we earthbodies who have the implicit
feeling and relational understanding of it as a "soarable space" that permeates our
bodies. Similarly, to add more emotion and imagination to the nuance of a similar
perception, as there is also usually present, when a bird flying overhead does capture our explicit attention and we watch its flight with some thrill, there is a visceral, emotional, imaginative, etc., sense of what that flight is like because there is
an echo of flight in my body that flows back into me while watching the bird.

Given we are these earthbodies, whose *bodies* are as different and unique
(although allied in kind with animals and even objects in this circulation of energy
and sense) as we have traditionally thought of our minds, our sense of depth (which

infuses our more complex experiences, such as those that are the subject of "depth psychology," for example), is unique as resulting from human perception and embodiment. We find ourselves being a creature of our personal and collective histories embedded in everything around us. As we walk down the street, for example, we are not only partially caught up in the store towards which the walk is to terminate and which gives the intervening steps their direction and purpose, but we are also caught up back at the house feeling emotions about our loved ones, are partially caught up at work with tasks unfinished yesterday, are pulled towards the locale hundreds of years ago where the event occurred that is celebrated in today's holiday, or may even be caught up in the energy and meaning of the moon or space station where our country's astronauts are performing an important mission. This sketch of how we walk through the world already contained in various depths, both spatial and temporal, is consistent with reality as painted throughout this book, taking our experience as earthbodies as, circulation of energies and meaning as our guide.

If we look, listen, and feel to observe how we actually experience the world, we would see that at any given instant we are pulled in many directions at once. These pulls and tugs have to do with how we have forged and intensified previous relationships, but are also about the new things that call out to us for involvement. Also, they are about the many different contexts in which we live and find meaning, many of which are quite different from each other. So, the garden to be pruned, the car to be waxed, or the mountain to be climbed may beckon to a worker at the desk and be part of the consciousness and felt sense of the body at any instant. He or she is not entirely confined to the chair at the desk, but somehow is still located within the contexts of family life at home with the kids or with the group of buddies at the pool table or with the sick relative in the hospital. All the energy and meaning flows which pass through our earthbodies gives each of us a distinctive way of being anywhere, which is not strictly locatable on a geometric grid. What is most significant is that these sorts of spatialized and temporalized currents of meaning also indicate something important about the identity we can have as earthbodies. We feel, we think, we dream, we strive, we suffer, we mourn for and believe in things, persons, creatures, and dimensions that take us on paths of meaning which are widely divergent and sometimes even contradictory. For a purely mental being that had to live in its head in a logical realm, this would be a problem, an impossible one. However, for a being which is a constantly transforming energy and meaning flow, which is in relation to all parts of its world through its bodily rhythms and extensions of circulating presence, it is a multidimensionality that makes us unique as earthbodies.

We often notice that a person who is called to many dimensions has a richness of involvement, personality, and meaning to their lives we might label as a "depth" versus someone else we might find "shallow." This accords with Merleau-Ponty's notion of depth as "the going together of what is incompossible" (*PP*, 264–5). In other words, what seems unrelated, or even contradictory or logically at odds, does co-exist, does cohere, for us in our experience and it is precisely this coming together within difference that makes up the more embracing sense of depth. Without a context, these feelings or ideas or senses would be exclusive of each other, but our bodies' relationship to these varying factors draws them into the context of our experience, within our distinctive rhythms. *The context becomes richer, not logically deficient,* through these oppositions or tensions or different vectors.

Our experience as perceiving bodies allows us entrance to a world that is temporally dynamic in its jostling structures. Our experience of time as we listen to a sentence or walk down the block may swing back and forth from moments of the past, future, and present, which intermingle and give each a different sense. At one point, the land around Ada's house may have been a forbidding, sterile landscape, home to ignorant people, yet simultaneously it was God's beautiful creation and a place to relax while her father composed his sermons, or a reading spot, etc. It still has all these meanings within its depths as she walks through it. Later it also becomes the place to trap turkeys, to shuck corn, or to grind flour. When Ada walks across her fields at the end, the intense labors with Ruby flow through her steps and make the field something different in the present with different possible futures like the one we examined, where the coming rhythmic swing of the sun's orbit will give her a sense of belonging to this land—which wouldn't have been possible without that recent past that has transformed the present. She has taken on depths explored at different times that are present to her as she has worked with the world around her.

Similarly, we experience spatiality with this same jostling sense that is dynamic, both immediately and also in what spaces come to mean in a more enduring way. This jostling, ever-changing sense is clearly highlighted in an experience shared by Ada and Ruby. In a dangerous wintry attempt to help Ruby's father, Ada and Ruby round the corners of a steep path. The path isn't laid out before them in that orderly fashion of clear and distinct perspectives, but rather things emerge with shifting meanings and appearances. Things appears first to be ice or water or just cold air, or a cave or a drop in the path or deep shadows of the trees as they try to move through the treacherous conditions. The path's identity as they actually experience it envelopes them and infiltrates them with deeply felt ambiguities that get resolved for the moment only to give way to new ones. Their immediate experience is indicative of the dynamic perceptual sense space has for our earthbodies, which becomes more evident in these heightened moments of danger, emotional intensity, and accelerated flux.

However, these immediate environmental perceptions of dynamic time and space are the basis for the way more enduring, complex, and abstract identities also form as a jostle of different meanings. For example, the man they are out to save, Ruby's father, is: a scoundrel; an abusive, derelict father; a ruthless schemer; an utterly transfixing, inspired violin player; a self-sacrificing creator of beauty; a source of good cheer; a cruel person, selfish thief, and manipulative user; a friend, and comrade; and an embodiment of many other contradictory dimensions. Ruby and Ada have the commitment, artistry, and patience to allow the different dimensions of his depth to emerge and can embrace the ambiguities of their relationship with him.

As we really live through our experiences, time "enjambs" or piles into itself, as does space, both of which are present all around us "in" the world and its beings, and not just "in" our heads. Rather, neither of these oppositions are true: meaning emerges from the dialogue of us *with* things, others, and creatures. In these ongoing meetings in which the incompossibles come together to give depth to our lives, the past, present, and future are all "now," at different layers of a "thickness" of time, space, and experience that does not fall into the neatly linear order into which rationality tries to force this richer and more wild sense of our experience. We find this depth of time not just in "our heads" and with our memories, but by being open to the way objects and their spaces encroach upon each other in the same wave of meaning and "hold" within themselves networks of events and experiences spanning different times and places. We can recover different depths in different places with different objects, because we are all part of a circulation of energy and meaning. The porch is the place where Ada read a momentous letter or sat with her late father, just as it is also the place of shucking corn with Ruby at this moment, a place which evokes in her different senses of loss and security, and has layers of different times held within its floorboards.

In the paintings of Cézanne, Merleau-Ponty found a better representation of the primary experience of depth in perception than in the traditional "vanishing point" perspective of Renaissance-Albertian inspired painting. Cézanne abandoned the progressive, rational sense of depth "building up" through planes used within traditional European painting. Instead, he depicted depth through a jostling of different outlines, different planes, different positions, and overlappings of objects. Merleau-Ponty found it represented how we actually experience perception and perceived objects, before we take rational distance from them. It is not logically possible that the table has five different edges or three different angles, yet as we walk by that table that well may be our experienced sense of it. This is the source of depth in perception as actually experienced: there is an openness to multiplicity that later gets more resolved and crystallized, only to become fluid again at the next moment.

As earthbodies, our loves, our ideals, our goals, and even our values and beliefs are always shifting, dynamic, and ambiguous—like the outlines of Cézanne's tabletop—if we listen to our bodies. We can feel a vitality and richness of meaning in our identities, values, and beliefs, if we keep ourselves open to the influx of energies and meaning from the world with which they are interrelated. If we were to see we are earthbodies and affirm this dimension of ourselves, we would dictate a cultural shift away from the social demand that our identities, values, and beliefs stay static and unchanging. The demand to remain constant and clearly identifiable fits the old Platonic sense that the true reality lies outside the embodied, material realm in the ether of pure, unchanging mental or spiritual ideals. *A spirituality or an ethics or a psychology that is earth-centered is one that stresses an openness to being enmeshed or com-pelled (having to act in concert with other forces, in response to them) by the dynamically changing world of which we are part, naturally and culturally (a blurred, evolving, and fluid boundary).*

This pregnant, given ambiguity means there is always a working out of what becomes possible on the basis of what has emerged from a past which keeps changing itself. Human freedom is not the freedom to soar above and just remake the earth or humans or the rest of creation, but rather is the ability to work with what the maximal sense of the situation has presented to us as a challenge. Unlike a god, we do not choose our choices, but rather they are given to us by history, culture, matter, and all sorts of factual givens that confront us in the faces of objects, landscapes, institutions, situations, etc., that make up the texture of our lives. This gives us the responsibility to enter that dialogue with these things, with people, with events to find out the depths of meaning they hold for us. Our cultural heritage from Plato onwards has looked for the factual, the mathematically precise, as being our way into the world, by mastering its tendencies and manipulating them for our declared purposes. Meaning has been seen to be a creation of humans opposed to such a factual dimension. We are the ones who think and speak. This book has suggested that both—fact and meaning—are sides of each other, interdependent when maximally expressive of both the world and ourselves. The world speaks and dreams and feels through our becoming rooted in it. The imagination disconnected from the factual reality around it is entertaining, but not liberating in the same way as the dreams that grow out of matter, the passions that respond to the uniqueness of our situation, the memories that resonate to specific qualities of the environment that need to be kept open for future articulation, etc. These are the challenges that confront us not just personally, but globally, in how we can listen to the environment to represent and articulate the voices of creatures, or rocks and waterways, as they surround us as interlocators. This sense of depth invites us to take in what unique properties and possibilities lie in new technological realms like cyberspace or wireless communication that can resonate with and celebrate the interplay of all forces at a depth of meaning in order to extend human creativity and depth. Depth in this sense is not the inaccessible. It is not what lies hidden beneath the surface. It is an enveloping, dynamic complexity which both plays across the surface of things, spans their temporal and spatial interconnectedness, and also does lie within. The voyage is not exclusively to far-off realms, but often takes only a return to where one already is with an openness to the tensions which simultaneously clash and compel.

Responsibility, Reverberating Resonance, and Joy

Decades ago, Gestalt therapists, existentialists, and others in various human potential movements began to point out that the word and idea of "responsibility" contains the notion that our obligations are always really about our "ability to respond." The ideas, the values, the goals, and the identities of our lives come not from above, but from all around us in the way everything touches everything as an interplay of energies and forces. It is up to us to allow the particular meanings of our lives and its particularly challenging ambiguities to emerge from the world; we must register their significance by entering into a dialogue, as we are uniquely able to do as earthbodies. If meaning is in the world around us, it requires a level of increasing awareness resulting from an ongoing attempt to become sensitive to detail, to rhythm, to overall moods, and to the shifting interplay of all beings. This takes a lot of work—there is no ready-made answer or quickly consumed sound-bite wisdom. A counter-cultural cry of the sixties and seventies was "be here now." However, that phrase, without an understanding of earthbodies, is utterly misleading. There is no simple way to "be" a human self, no given "here" that is simply there, no simple "now" that is disconnected from the interplay of temporal vectors in a depth dimension.

Aristotle, in the *Nicomachean Ethics*, likened the development of a human self with character to the creation of an artwork, except humans were both the artist and the artwork, and so had the task of continually creating or shaping themselves. In such passages, he is specifically taking to task his teacher Plato and his teaching that there are universal goods, eternal truths, and that our task is to rise above the earth. Instead, Aristotle, in this particular moment, is hearkening back to ideas that predate the Greek rationalists and returns to a sensibility that everything is dynamic and interlocking in trajectory and requires our sensitive care-taking to mesh fruitfully. In his non-moralistic sense of ethics, he espouses a full use of all our human excellences to achieve human "goodness," but says this is achieved by nurturing feelings neither insensitive nor exaggerated and "to feel them at the right times, with reference to the right objects, towards the right people, with the right motive, and in the right way"[12] which will be intuited within each unique situation. Aristotle's vision is one that calls for the whole person responding to all of the factors within their concrete situation and doing so emotionally, as well as rationally, imaginatively, etc., and staying with this project during a lifetime of evolutionary transformations of both the person and the world. This kind of tolerance for ambiguity, an attempt to be committed to a long process for the sake of the inherent worth of the process itself, and to the purpose of bringing forth the maximal actualization of self, community, and world—where the latter includes other creatures and nature—is very much an earthbody ethic and sensibility. This can only happen when we understand responsibility to encompass our emotional being, the imaginative, intuitive, rational, expressive, and other dimensions of who we are. This means part of responsibility is to focus continually on our awareness, responsiveness, openness to ambiguity, pain, and difficulty. This goes counter to a culture dedicated to self-gratification and "quick fixes."

Rather than seeking the simple sound-bite answer, we would have to become committed to complex answers that keep us exploring the nuances and diversity of our myriad relations with the world and others. Language can make possible other ways of understanding and openness to realms of experience. However, language can also keep us sealed off from such journeys of self-actualization. Rather than promoting speech that is easily consumed, thoughtlessly, we need to speak continually in a more exploratory use of language that keeps letting us know there is not a closure to taking in more meaning and evolving significance. At a time when this courage to break out of the everyday categories of language is needed to combat our mass consumer and entertainment culture, we retreat further and further linguistically into the conventional, the stylized, and the neatly packaged. Our children need to be taught to be imaginative, feelingful, bold, and expressive with words, not made into "slick communicators." Yet, real imagination is the last thing we devote time to in our schools' curricula. Poetry, the medium that most promotes this wondering and wandering through language, is seen as a marginal activity. Adults need even more to wander with their words to avenues of discovery, not stay in the distanced, prepackaged ways of expression.

Our advances in biotechnology offer the same danger as the advances in communication technology. Their stunning success in dealing with certain aspects of the body and physiology can easily lead us into an addictive reliance upon *them* to fashion our lives at times when we have the opportunity to meaningfully participate in our development. Rather than looking for pills or machines or other devices to do it for us, we should relish the ways in which we can shape and transform in meaning anything that our biology, our environment, and our culture confronts us with as a challenge. Rather than constantly trying to manipulate the world seen as mere objects, including our own bodies as mere physiological objects, we should respond to what is given to us in our situation as potential interlocutors, partners in a dialogue with whom we can enter into relation and shape our connection. This means having the painstaking commitment to slowly work with ourselves, others, and things, the way the artist stays with repainting, rewriting, and never just finally finishing the witnessing and expression. For example, our emotional expressions and responses can be altered quickly by medications that screen out our sensitivities to parts of the world whose meaning we find too daunting. In taking this route, we have lost some of the depth of our lives and the chance to be transformed through the dialogue with those challenging aspects of our experience. We may have succeeded in "controlling" unwanted anger or sadness or whatever feeling we found troublesome, yet this gain also masks a lost opportunity. Sometimes this may be necessary if we have wandered too far out of balance with our ways of relating to the world or in our biochemistry (each of which is a cause and an effect in cyclic ways as part of the same process, and eventually translate into each other as body/mind).

However, to rely solely on medications or on similar manipulations by exterior forces is to forfeit possibilities of meaning and self-transformation that come from working through the dialogue. One can easily imagine that if Ada had lived a century and a half later, she may have been given Prozac or another psychotropic medication to deal with the loss of her father and the sudden despair at having to make a living and find her way in this foreign backwoods setting. She would probably have been both medicated and shipped back to Charleston to her more familiar "support network." She never would have embarked on her long and at times heartbreaking path of discovering the myriad aspects of farming and surviving in the wild. Those different selves within her own psyche that she had no idea were there would never have been given a voice. As earthbodies and artists of our lives, we can also alter emotions very slowly and gradually, as part of a faithful and concentrated effort to work through and with a myriad of relations with different aspects of ourselves and the world. There is no traditional moral reason to prefer this latter course, but there is a practical one. The way we get to this new sense of balance leaves us with a different relationship to the world and self. We are enriched with the residue of different sorts of depths opened up for us and the world has been witnessed in its details, which does maximize an earthbody ethic of opening more potential fruitful relationships.

The key to this kind of work with oneself in relation to the world is in Ada's story, to which we should return one more time. Her decision to find out who she could become, given what she has been in her past, and what historical, cultural, and natural conditions she's found around her, follows Aristotle's or Nietzsche's sense of the artist of life slowly developing sensitivity to the senses, emotions, imagination, the depths of memory, intuition, and a thought which keeps coming back to these sources to shape and be furthered shaped by working with them. A large part of this task lies in developing an ever more focused awareness as part of the ability to become fully present. Much of this book, whether about our lack of ceremony, of myth, of meaningful story, of being vampires, ghouls, aesthetes, consumers, cyberspace escapees, or alienation from the animal dimension of human being, is about strategies that we use habitually in our current cultural milieu to achieve not really being here and becoming distracted. This book is largely about a pervasive sense of disconnection and absence that haunt the world at the beginning of this new millennium, the philosophies that helped cause this state, and a lack of day-to-day awareness about ourselves in relation to myriad beings around us. After Ada has gone through much of her hard labor and transformation, she thinks to herself:

> North, south, east, west. It would go a way toward ordering her mind congruent with where she was. Ruby always seemed to know the compass points and to find them significant, not just when she was giving directions but even in telling a story and indicating where an event had happened. West bank of the Little East Fork, east bank of the Little West Fork, that sort of thing. What was required to speak that language was a picture held in the mind of the land one occupied. Ada knew the ridges and coves and drainages were the frame of it, the skeleton. You learned them and where they stood in relation to each other, and then you filled in the details working from those known marks. General to particular. Everything had a name. To live fully in a place all your life, you kept aiming smaller and smaller in attention to detail. (*CM*, 388)

The responsibility to the world and working on shaping oneself to be more creatively open comes through this painstaking process of delving more and more finely into the landscape around one, where that landscape is understood as not just land, but also people, institutions, events, relationships of all sorts and even the sense of the physical materials around one. However, Ada is wrong in phrasing this to herself as primarily a mental task. It does require working to be mentally keen, striving to stay alert and probing, but it requires equally developing the bodily sense of what is around us kinesthetically, sensually, emotionally, imaginatively, etc. This gives us an underlying connection and direction in our situation to be plumbed in its rich but ambiguous depths. As Edward Casey writes in *Getting Back into Place*: "It is felt: felt bodily first of all. For we feel the presence of places by and in our bodies even more than we see or think or recollect them. Places are not so much the direct objects of sight or thought or recollection as what we feel *with* and *around, under* and *above, before* and *behind* our lived bodies."[13] The attunement to place is an attunement to the dynamic body informed by its surroundings in its inexhaustible detail.

This is where a notion like "self" enters. Throughout this work, there has been a critique of the sense of eternal, ethereal self, or enduring internal, substantial self, or against other models of self as an entity or state "given" to us. Rather we have tried to detail, from the Native American tales opening the book through the intervening descriptions to ending with the tale of *Cold Mountain*, how the most vital, richly meaningful, and ethically responsible sense of self emerges from a process of discovery of ourselves through entering relationships with the world around us and by allowing the self to be an ambiguous, ever-transforming "flow phenomena." This doesn't mean we are passive. To let things, forces, and events work through us, to impact us, and then respond to their sense is an active process of what Heidegger called "letting be" (*Gelassenheit*).

To shape, witness, and to articulate the meanings we encounter in our particular rhythm, according to our distinctive ideas, feelings, history, and values, is how a sense of self emerges within this ongoing and transforming process. We are both contributor and recipient, as the dancers who symbolize the idea of this book are swept up in a dance that they create, but are carried beyond themselves in finding new dimensions of who they can become. Merely being carried off in different directions would not add depth to our lives, just disruption and dislocation. However, taking to heart the various beckonings of the world that mean something to us, meeting them with responsiveness and engagement, and then allowing them to carry us in new directions in summoning up the creativity to work through their challenge, enlarges and deepens this flowing sense of self.

The ethics of authenticity have been misunderstood as a "being true" to an "inner self" in the face of social pressure to conform. The original sense of authenticity as used by Heidegger, Sartre, and others, was a verb form of a process. It was about "*making* oneself be one's own" as an ongoing task of responsive self-creation. Not creation from nothing, like God is supposed to do, but from an ongoing committed encounter with others and the world. Catherine Keller, a contemporary feminist theologian, has expressed this notion of self as a verb form: "selving." As Keller puts it, "Thus the self contains within its parameters everything that is not itself; yet the self is clearly distinguishable *as* itself. It *selves* its world. There is nothing that is not somewhere part of it; yet in a moment it parts with its own selfness."[14] If a sense of self only emerges in sensitive and responsive dialogue, it is not a private matter, nor is it a holding onto something previously achieved. It is about finding a way in which, when meeting others, we can all add what is distinctive about us, so each of us is reflected in the emerging process, as the dancers are in their dance. When Tayo listens to the wisdom of the elders, when he follows the advice of Betonie, and when he takes up the tasks left to him by his Uncle Josiah, his distinctive "way" emerges in this performance of the ceremony and tasks. Someone else following the same path would have a somewhat different journey, with results that were unique to him or her.

Yet, initially, Tayo was not "there" at all and had no sense of self, as he painfully discovered while being swallowed up in "the white cloud" in which he felt himself contained while he was in the veteran's hospital. He had retreated from any real encounters with others. He finds "himself" when the elders and medicine man put him on a path of encounter with his world. Similarly, Ada, at the beginning of her years on Cold Mountain, feels utterly empty and lost with no idea who she was or is or could become in her isolation. Relying on her own resources, she is at a loss. Often, when we look "inward" as individuals at odds with the world, what we find is nothing. When Ada takes a risk, out of desperation because she literally might not survive, to trust Ruby and join forces with her, she starts a process of painful give and take with Ruby and the strange natural and cultural world around her from which a growing sense of self emerges.

This sense of responsibility as the engaged and gradually learned ability to respond keenly and sensitively to the relationships that beckon to us from the surrounding world leads us into an increasing emotional delight. It differs from notions of responsibility and self that call for the self to deny itself or the richness of relationship with others and the world. However, such an emotional resonance only emerges from a long process of development and transformation. It is not the quick fun or elevated mood of entertainments that amuse without resonating with multiple aspects of self and its network of relationships.

It is at this moment, the moment that leads to joy, that the aestheticism, the distancing from the entangling interaction of earthbodies, and the constant distraction of our current culture shows its saddest face. When we considered the addictive power of the Internet, we discussed how Nietzsche had the vision, more than a century ago, that humankind might become a race of beings who had lost faith in themselves and the creative power of life, who announced with pleasure, intoxication, and self-satisfaction, "we have invented happiness!" and blinked. At a time when we seem happy, we may be most lost. At a time when we seem most happy, we may have given up on the kind of responsibility we uniquely have as earthbodies that leads to joy. If our consumer society aims to provide continual pleasures, experiences which amuse us because they appeal to the senses' momentary stimulation or with possessions that are valued, this cannot substitute for joy, as it is being used in this context. Joy emerges from a vitality, purpose, and belonging that come from honing our timing with the world: we have met other human beings or animals or inanimate beings in a way that drew out mutual value. The shining on the horizon that the girl, Umai, found in the Yurok tale that we considered is the sign of joy when one has been able to find the rhythm within oneself and the world that resonates in mutual recognition and wonder.

If self is a process that emerges from a painstaking care and creative engagement with as many facets of one's world as possible, it finds joy after a long and faithful struggle with pain, necessity, and challenge, since these experiences are intrinsic to forging ongoing relationships with diverse beings. It is by pursuing greater connection with the complexities of the world as a vital and varied process, and by fully immersing in its energy flows and currents of meaning, that the spiral of self comes round and branches into new directions of development and inspired spirits. This is the source of joy, which is akin to the delight we feel in hearing one of those Tibetan "singing bowls." The different metals that make up the bowl are imparted vibration through the sensitive motion around their perimeter—the rhythmic pressing and guiding of the wooden clapper around the edge, which is a kind of caress of steady focus and flow beyond boundaries as energy is expressed through the hand. The metals sing with a deep ringing resonance that seems as if the very matter of the metal has been given a voice of celebration and declaration. The smile that hearing one of these bowls sing inspires springs from feeling the different parts of the environment, and in some sense the world at large, vibrating together in a resonance that celebrates each part as precious, as adding to a beautiful sound, a song. Joy would be a similar sense, but one that comes not from the singing bowl but from deep within our earthbodies, as through its interactions with myriad parts of the world there is the same kind of reverberating resonance struck through the hand and heart circling its world of care.

Such joy is very different from the kind of happiness our culture promotes. A popular song of a number of years ago had the refrain, "Don't worry, be happy!." It expressed perhaps more blatantly than we often do a cultural desire to find continual occasions to experience the much hyped state of "happiness." This emotional state can be marketed and promoted, and is usually seen as a goal to be pursued. Yet a life of such happiness, does it ring hollow in its failure to bind us to the world, to direct us towards meaningful expression, and to just "pass time" pleasantly? If we were to substitute, "Don't worry, be joyous!," the refrain doesn't work. Why?

Nietzsche considered the direct pursuit of happiness not a human goal, but, as he put it, a bovine one. Cows chewing their cud were happy. Yet, certainly we all desire a happy life. The vital distinction here is whether happiness as an emotional state is desirable as a goal *in itself.* We can stimulate part of our brains with an electrode, take various chemicals, and can promote a feeling of happiness as an "inner mental state" by many other means. Here, the dualistic mind/body phrase is warranted, for such a feeling does come closer to the aesthete's vision as we discussed it earlier in the book (staying defended in one's mind as a fortress, and enjoying whatever happens in the world as a "mere occasion" from the vantage point of one's "inner psyche"). We can try to split our minds off from our bodies or emotions or other more immediate entanglements in the world. Like the drunk who severs his consciousness from the world and elevates it to a "high," such happiness is a way of avoiding our place in the world with its challenges, relationships, and opportunities for authentic expression. Just as a drink now and then, there is no harm in some occasions of escaping the call of the myriad relationships and commitments of our lives, but as a constant craving, as something which runs our lives, the pursuit of happiness is the pursuit of being diverted from who we are and how we can be creatively here together. It is a way of blocking out our earthbodies. It is a diversion and, at worst, a kind of dissociation with the world, savoring one's psychological states and finding ways to promote them as a way of staying entertained by life. *A life spent seeking to stay happy as a direct goal, to be stimulated by means at hand, becomes a trivialized and distant life.* It works by shutting out who we are, the currents that flow through our earthbodies. Since they beckon to us to transform ourselves in giving ourselves over to engagement and the effort to actualize the possibilities within our world, they would disrupt this pursuit of happiness.

There is an uplift of the spirits that comes from working creatively within relationships with others and with the world, where the feeling engendered emerges from within the process of an engaged interaction. The goal at those moments is to be involved in the interaction or the commitment of whatever sort we have with the world. The feeling state is an *indirect* outcome of the responsiveness, the expressiveness, and the satisfaction of creating something worthwhile with another or with the world, whether it be learning to harvest wheat, holding a stimulating conversation, making passionate love, or helping build a house.

Instead of "passing time," in responsive commitment we become, as we described at the beginning of this book, *capable of being time.* We have that experience where "things come together" or "fall into place" as having "timed" ourselves with others and with things, so that we have fed into each other. We are carried along within the current of flow that is the heart of time. There is both the erasure of boundaries *and* the simultaneous feeling of being most ourselves. As we have described it, at this moment we feel a new depth, an expansiveness, and impulsion of energy and meaning that is joyous. We have both "let go" in moving into the fluidity of intermingling transformation—in a way that struck terror into Lestat, as it does to all of us insofar as we have slipped into being vampires, ghouls, aesthetes, addictive consumers, entertainment junkies, etc.,—and also "let be" in the sense of truly witnessing, registering with acute senses, and feeling with sensitive emotion and imagination, something we can't when only partially or minimally present.

Happiness is often about the simple. To be enjoyed, to be consumed, and to be entertained simply can bring happiness: eating that ice cream cone, scoring that victory in pinball, or watching that fireworks displays. These experiences are mere events that do not require much of us and do not perplex or challenge us. They have a place in our lives. But as the goal of life, they speak of a lack of faith in ourselves as earthbodies. This was Ivan Ilyich's terrible discovery, when he realized he never *lived* with his life of happiness about card playing, fancy furniture, and the status of his job. The faith that is required for joy is to believe in the richness of our experience, to open to its depth and ambiguity, and respond to it or be responsible in the earthbody sense of that term. The belief is in the flexibility of bodily capacity and how it opens us to a reality of experience, based not on some outside foundation, but on its own vitality and depth that moves towards its enlargement through encounter and interchange. We won't experience these depths without a sense that mere happiness grows to joy through such an opening, the world has its own order, its own offering of meaning, and that by entering into its sway, its facets are highlighted, the world deepens, and we will expand.

Joy of this sort has a dimension of peace that is not from an imposed secure order, closure, or cessation of challenge. Rather, it is the peace of dynamism, of having let go into a process that has achieved rhythm, that is affirming in each contribution entering into the dance of constituents and calling forth further flowing change from all who are participating. This is the joy of vitality, of belonging, and of responsive capability. It is as though that childhood joy, the sense of well-being which seems so difficult to achieve the older we get, lurks within all things and all creatures. It will come out to play with us, or within us all so participating, if we move from being caught in time as an alienating force, a dimension outside us that relentlessly moves along towards our ending, to becoming time itself.

As time itself, the old is new as coming to exist again in the "coming together," the timing of which we are all part and can celebrate by making our lives ceremony. In the moment of encounter, fully entered in awareness and with all the dimensions of our earthbodies, sensual, perceptual, emotional, thoughtful, intuitive, imaginative, kinaesethetic, and recollective, we come into being as this particular meeting with tree, smile, roar, color, idea, operation, or whatever, and so does all that we greet in encounter. To bring into our awareness this sense of ever-springing-forth newness, means the person we love, the canyon we're in, or the house in which we dwell doesn't have to be abandoned for a literally new one. We have experienced in the fluidity of the world how it always flows out from itself back into itself in a renewal we need to witness, and it is this dynamic renewal which is the sheer joyousness of all the existences of which we humans are a part. We don't have to generate vitality, meaning, or depth. Through the indeterminacy of our earthbodies we are drawn into currents of the world's sense that in their interplay among themselves through us, enliven, illuminate, and deepen us.

We speak of the joys of entering into various relationships, whether the joys of parenting, of creating—whether art or a way for people to improve their neighborhood—or the joys of a commitment to an activity, like backpacking, wood crafting, or teaching. These joys emerge from working with factors that are given to us, that means we have to accept necessity—that what resists us or challenges us gives meaning to us as its particular gift. Without the force of gravity against us or the heat wearing on us, hiking up the hill has no meaning and fosters no deepening relationship with the path, the air, and sky. Without the difficulty of student's learning, teaching can't happen in its progress.

Also, the way in which some beings exist within processes that go at angles of collision to our own trajectories is what is meant by hurt or pain. We are continually hurt, "impacted upon." Whether this happens within the collectivity of forces that make up my body (and cells collide in trajectories in disease or muscle collides with bone in trauma or in effort), or whether among people (and there are those who want different policies or represent different ideas), or whether among humans and natural forces (such as the trajectories of weather forces and human activities), the impact that wrenches us in this experience of being hurt or pained can lead us back to these points of intersection and understanding our network of relationships. Our current cultural intolerance for pain robs us of connection with parts of the planet.

Pain and the world's necessities, sometimes quite unexpected in their emergence, can become interlocutors in working with them towards joy. Despite their difficulty, they can become part of the substance of our relationships and creative processes culminating in joy. For a culture that would only seek happiness in life, the earth's resistances are always to be conquered or managed or walled out of our lives. This narrows continually who we are and can become creatively. It leads us to not take care with parts of our planet, including each other. Happiness often is promoted as an escape from creatively dealing with the planet's complexities and from the task of understanding them. Joy is a kind of understanding that comes from working through relationships. It is not mindless. It is not bodiless. Rather, if earthbodies are affirmed in their myriad entanglements with the planet, sensitively using their capacities for discovery and expression in the process of a give and take in relationships, the felt sense we have of this working through challenges tends towards joy.

Afterword

A Poem

As a poet as well as a philosopher, I would like to end this book with a poem that I wrote that captures the heart of the message of this book (reprinted with permission of *Ellipsis*: Literature and Art 36 (Spring, 2000), pp. 32–33.).

Inexorably Marching Time and the Other Time of Encounter

The slivers of time's soul
are said by scientists to waft unmolested
from the guts of decaying particles,
yet the same scientist thinks of neutrinos
as his wife shudders beneath his touch
and looks aside as his dog's dying eyes
sink into glacial pools of milk.

For the rest of us, when we think of this
fugitive time, we would like to nail
its heart to the floor and give it some pain.
We know that right now it runs by our houses,
smirking in the windows, and feel the fingers close
on the back of our necks, below the ears,
where the pumping of blood drones,
and see its moments as several fingers
squeezing in a heavyweight grip
with all the cards and a sadistic mind.
We call it the cheap pimp of death,
and locked in this wrestling match,
we can't find the imp behind the machine,
or see flowers growing in the sidewalk's cracks.

Yet, when two suns crisscross on their way
across the sky and the rocks signal quiet joy

to the gulls, the clam that shatters
by the drop from soaring air to sea ledge,
not only yields its smashed flesh
but offers a twinned darker glow of another passing
from the shell of the sky answered by stone.
The gull laughs knowingly at the welcome
of this other time of encounter, the time we can hear
when we pause on deserted beaches.

The second type of vibration held within
the dusky interior of relentless time,
only emerges in shattering,
when air and rock and sky and flesh seem to collide
but each is lost in the others,
shifting outside themselves, like when
the beam of the child's eye caught by cerulean,
laughing at the sky
hits yours
and you splinter in the reflected gleam,
and find yourself within caverns
you thought lost long ago.

Whenever we feel the throb of the neck
we imagine the grip and time's night,
and dream ourselves pursuing as superspies
saving our families from the international terrorist
whose explosives are concealed in all things.
Instead, the fears we send out collide with everything
since clumsy and unseeing, they lunge ahead,
convinced time will collect them, so they must hit first.
But, if we are lucky in how they smack their heads,
it is the fears that die, shattered
against the sight of the spring green of leaves
or the softness of skin pressed,
or by smells of the vaporous thicket of fruit stalls
at market. If we're really lucky, the gulls spot them
and drop them for us onto the rocks.

Only then do we come to the doggy knowledge
outside the realm of science that was in the eyes
when the tail wagged in recognition
of greeting the time of encounter. Its story
is found within the shade of all real meeting
and the blurring of hand on hand,
when the particles cease the straight lines
of decay and begin the round dance
about the glow of shimmering

and the soft and the pungent
and all things become a gesture
of fingers clasped and folded back
with others within themselves.

Notes

Chapter One. The Earthly Dance of Interconnection

1. This is a parallel point to Carol Gilligan's point that there is an "ethics of care" that is needed to supplement the ethics of categorical rationality. See Carol Gilligan, *In a Different Voice* (Cambridge: Harvard University Press, 1982).

2. Philip K. Dick, *Do Androids Dream of Electric Sheep?* (New York: Ballantine, 1982). Any further references to this work will be in parentheses within the text with the page number preceded by *ES*.

3. The original passage is William Faulkner, *Light in August* (New York: Modern Library; 1950), p. 406, as cited by Jean-Paul Sartre, in *Being and Nothingness*, trans. by Hazel Barnes (New York. Washington Square Press, 1956), p. 526. Any further references to this work will be in parentheses within the text with the page number preceded by *BN*.

4. For example, if one knows that "Socrates is a man," and that "all men are mortal," then it logically follows that "Socrates is mortal."

5. Richard Rorty, *Contingency, Irony, and Solidarity* (New York: Cambridge University Press, 1991), p. 6.

6. Leslie Marmon Silko, *Ceremony* (New York: Penguin Books, 1986), p.229. Any further references to this work will be in parentheses within the text with the page number preceded by *C*.

7. Johan Huizinga, *Homo Ludens: A Study of the Play Element in Culture* (Boston: Beacon Press, 1955), p. 25. Any further references to this work will be in parentheses within the text with the page number preceded by *HL*.

8. Paula Gunn Allen, *The Sacred Hoop: Recovering the Feminine in American Indian Traditions* (Boston: Beacon Press, 1986), p. 62. Any further references to this work will be in parentheses within the text with the page number preceded by *SH*.

9. Thich Nhat Hahn, *The Miracle of Mindfulness*, trans. by Mobi Ho (Boston: Beacon Press, 1975), p. 12.

10. As Luce Irigaray has called it in her famous essay "When Our Lips Speak Together," in *This Sex Which Is Not One*, trans. by Catherine Porter (Ithaca: Cornell University Press, 1985).

Chapter Two. Earthbody Dimensions

1. Theodora Kroeber, *The Inland Whale: Nine Stories Retold from California Indian Legends* (Berkeley: University of California Press, 1959), p. 25. Any further references to this work will be in parentheses within the text with the page number preceded by *IW*.

2. Marcel Proust, *Remembrance of Things Past*, vol. 1, trans. by C. K. Scott Moncrieff and Terence Kilmartin (New York: Vintage/Random House, 1982), p. 150. Any further references to this work will be in parentheses within the text with the page number preceded by *RTP*.

3. Willa Cather, *Death Comes to the Archbishop* (New York: Vintage Books, 1990), p.43.

4. Plato, *Phaedo*, trans. by W. H. D. Rouse, in *Great Dialogues of Plato* (New York: Mentor, 1956), p. 487 [83B]. Any further references to Plato's works will be cited from this collection; they will be given in parentheses within the text with the page number preceded by *Pl* and followed in brackets with the standard reference subdivisions used in all Plato scholarship.

5. Rene Descartes, *The Philosophical Works of Descartes*, vol. 1, "Meditations on a First Philosophy," trans. by Elizabeth Haldane and G. R. T. Ross (London: Cambridge University Press, 1969), p. 153. Any further references to this work will be in parentheses within the text with the page number preceded by *WD*.

6. For a much longer discussion of these origins of the words and ideas embedded in the experience of hurt and pain, see the first chapter of my book *The Trickster, Magician, and Grieving Man: Returning Men to Earth* (Sante Fe: Bear and Co. Press, 1994), esp. pp. 5–21. This issue of avoiding pain is particularly relevant to masculine defensive postures and so is discussed at length here, but is also a wider cultural issue.

7. Loren Eiseley, *The Immense Journey* (New York: Vintage, 1959), pp. 19–20. Any further references to this work will be in parentheses within the text with the page number preceded by *IJ*.

8. Diane Wolkstein and Samuel Noah Kramer, editors and translator, *Inanna: Queen of Heaven and Earth* (New York: Harper and Row, 1983), p.40. Any further references to this work will be in parentheses within the text with the page number preceded by *IN*.

9. A wonderful discussion of these notions of going from what she calls the "separative" self to the "soluble" self is contained in the first chapter of Catherine Keller, *From a Broken Web*: *Separatism, Sexism, and Self* (Boston: Beacon Press, 1986).

Chapter Three. Discordant Contemporary Rhythms

1. James B. Twitchell, *The Living Dead* (Durham: Duke Univ. Press, 1981), p. 8. Any further references to this work will be in parentheses within the text with the page number preceded by *LD*.

2. Gregory A. Waller, *The Living and the Undead* (Urbana: University of Illinois Press, 1986), p. 289. Any further references to this work will be in parentheses within the text with the page number preceded by *LU*.

3. Philip Slater, *The Pursuit of Loneliness* (Boston: Beacon Press, 1970).

4. Three of the common explanations offered for the meaning and appeal of horror films offered by Waller in his introductory essay citing the work of Twitchell, Wood, and Giles; see Gregory Waller, *American Horrors: Essays on the American Horror Film* (Urbana: University of Illinois Press, 1987), p. 6. Any further references to this work will be in parentheses within the text with the page number preceded by *AH*.

5. Alain Silver and James Ursini, *The Vampire Film: From Nosferatu to Bram Stoker's Dracula* (New York: Limelight, 1993), pp. 23, 55. Any further references to this work will be in parentheses within the text with the page number preceded by *VF*.

6. Ann Rice, *The Tale of the Body Thief* (New York: Ballantine, 1992), p. 187. Any further references to this work will be in parentheses within the text with the page number preceded by *BT*.

7. These are the metaphors I use in the first half of my book, *The Trickster, Magician, and Grieving Man: Reconnecting Men with Earth* to examine the dynamics of "heroic masculinity" in Western tradition and in our current popular culture.

8. Sören Kierkegaard, *Either/Or*, vol. 1, trans. by David Swenson and Lillian Swenson (New York: Anchor Books, 1959), p. 37. Any further references to this work will be in parentheses within the text with the page number preceded by *EO*.

9. If it is not too abused by destructive adults—even though adult physical abuse or turning the world into a hell world with a war, for example, won't probably utterly annihilate this dimension in the child, except in rare cases.

10. Maurice Merleau-Ponty, "The Child's Relations with Others," in *The Primacy of Perception*, ed. by James Edie (Evanston: Northwestern University Press, 1964).

11. John Fowles, *The Magus*, (New York: Laurel, 1985), p. 20. Any further references to this work will be in parentheses within the text with the page number preceded by *TM*.

12. This idea is explained in depth in Jean-Paul Sartre's opus *Being and Nothingness* in the section "Doing and Having: Possession," trans. by Hazel Barnes (New York: Washington Square Press, 1956), pp. 734–64. It is explained even more clearly in Simone de Beauvoir's *Ethics of Ambiguity*.

13. Conrad Hyers, *The Laughing Buddha: Zen and the Comic Spirit*, (Montrose: Longwood Academic, 1989) p. 53. Any further references to this work will be in parentheses within the text with the page number preceded by *LB*.

Chapter Four. Cyberspace: Rootedness versus Being in Orbit

1. D. H. Lawrence, *The Complete Poems of D. H. Lawrence*, ed. by Vivian de Sola Pinto and E. Warren Roberts (New York: Viking Press, 1964), p. 525.

2. Stephen Talbott, *The Future Does Not Compute: Transcending the Machines in Our Midst* (Sebastapol: C. Reilly and Associates, 1995), p. 5.

3. Howard Rheingold, *The Virtual Community: Homesteading on the Electronic Frontier* (New York: Addison Wesley, 1993), p. 3.

4. Quoted by Leslie Miller in "Can the Internet Save Souls?," *USA Today* (September, 30, 1997), p. 14D.

5. Sherry Turkle, *Life on the Screen: Identity in the Age of the Internet* (New York: Touchstone, 1995), p. 22. Any further references to this work will be in parentheses within the text with the page number preceded by *LS*.

6. Maurice Merleau-Ponty, *The Visible and the Invisible*, trans. by Alphonso Lingis (Evanston: Northwestern University Press, 1968), pp. 139, 147. Any further references to this work will be in parentheses within the text with the page number preceded by *VI*.

7. Maurice Merleau-Ponty, *Phenomenology of Perception*, trans. by Colin Smith (New York: Humanities, 1962), p. 264. Any further references to this text will be indicated by *PP* within parentheses followed by the page number.

8. Richard Ellman,ed., *The Norton Anthology of Modern Poetry* (New York: W. W. Norton and Company, 1970), p. 742.

9. Edward Conze, *The Buddhist Scriptures* (New York: Penguin, 1959), p. 172. Any further references to this work will be in parentheses within the text with the page number preceded by *BS*.

10. See Riane Eisler's summary of much of the research and speculation on this idea that a longstanding tradition throughout Europe and the Mediterranean of spiritual and philo-sophical identification with natural cycles and kinship with animals, plants, and other humans was being usurped by the detached, rationalistic, patriarchal, and individualistic spirituality, society, and philosophy being articulated by Plato, Aristotle, Euripides, and others in Athens (*The Chalice and the Blade* [San Francisco: Harper, 1988]).

11. Friedrich Nietzsche, *Thus Spoke Zarathustra*, trans. by Walter Kaufmann, in *Portable Nietzsche* (New York: Viking, 1977), p. 227. Any further references to this work will be in parentheses within the text with the page number preceded by *TSZ*.

12. This notion of "perspectivism" is most concisely stated in *Will to Power* (New York: Random House, 1987), p. 339.

13. Carl Jung, *Collected Works*, vol. 9 (Princeton: Princeton University Press, 1981), pp. 37–38.

14. James Hillman, *Re-Visioning Psychology* (New York: Harper and Row, 1975), p. 32. Any further references to this work will be in parentheses within the text with the page number preceded by *RP*.

15. Donna J. Haraway, *Modest_Witness@Second Millennium. FemaleMan_Meets_Oncomouse: Feminism and Technoscience* (New York: Routledge, 1997), p. 51.

16. T. H. White, *The Once and Future King* (New York: Ace [Putnam], 1987), p. 195. Any further references to this work will be in parentheses within the text with the page number preceded by *FK*.

17. Alan Lightman, *Einstein's Dreams* (New York: Warner Books, 1994), pp. 25–26.

18. Much of the following discussion about the nature of sensitive emotion, sentiment, and emotional dangers draws on material from my book, *Emotion and Embodiment* (New York: Peter Lang, 1993).

19. D. H. Lawrence, *The Complete Poems of D. H. Lawrence*, ed. by Vivian de Sola Pinto and F. Warren Roberts (New York: Viking Press, 1964), p. 525. Further references to this work will be in parentheses within the text with the page number preceded by *DH*.

20. Ludwig Feuerbach, *The Essence of Christianity*, trans. by George Elliot (New York: Harper and Row, 1957), p. 140.

21. Margaret Atwood, *Surfacing* (New York: Simon and Shuster, 1976), p. 171. Any further references to this work will be in parentheses within the text with the page number preceded by *S*.

22. *The Random House Dictionary of the English Language* (New York: Random House, 1994), p. 1300.

23. Of course, the work which started to articulate this difference in emotional development between boys and girls was Carol Gilligan's *In a Different Voice* (Cambridge: Harvard University Press, 1982). She has continued to study these gender differences, and recently to look closely at boy's development. My own book, *Trickster, Magician, and Grieving Man: Reconnecting Men with Earth* examines how the masculine avoidance of experiencing pain, especially emotional pain, leads to violence and to living the male body as at "high altitude," trained to be "a tank body," with "missile sexuality," and speaking to others as "giving the briefing."

Chapter Five. Planetary Meaningfulness

1. These lectures at the Sorbonne from 1956-1958 and 1959 to 1960 have been published as *La Nature* (Paris: Gallimard, 1995).

2. Carl Jung, "The Spiritual Problem of Modern Man," collected in *The Portable Jung* (New York: Viking Press, 1971), p. 457.

3. Gaston Bachelard, *The Poetics of Reverie* (Boston: Beacon Press, 1969), p. 158. Any further references to this work will be in parentheses within the text with the page number preceded by *PR*. Bachelard wrote many fine explorations of how while awake we are dreamers dreaming our sense of home, our sense of love, our sense of vitality, our sense of what others mean to us, and even what the different sectors of time and space are to each of us. A good collection of excerpted pieces of his writing on this topic is *On Poetic Imagination and Reverie*, ed. by Colette Gaudin (New York: Bobbs-Merrill, 1971).

4. Richard Erdoes and Alfonso Ortiz, *American Indian Myths and Legends* (New York: Pantheon Books, 1984), p. 5.

5. Bruce Wilshire, *Wild Hunger* (Lanham: Rowman and Littlefield Publishers, 1998), pp. ix–x.

6. Gary Kowalski, *The Souls of Animals* (Walpole: Stillpoint, 1991) p. 3. Any further references to this work will be in parentheses within the text with the page number preceded by *SA*.

7. Archie Fire Lame Deer and Richard Erdoes, *Gift of Power: The Life and Teachings of a Lakota Medicine Man* (Santa Fe: Bear and Co., 1992), p. 152. Any further references to this work will be in parentheses within the text with the page number preceded by *GP*.

8. Frederick Turner, editor, *The Portable North American Indian Reader* (New York: Penguin, 1977), pp. 93–95.

9. Paul Radin, *The Trickster* (New York: Schocken, 1971), pp. 22–23. Any further references to this work will be in parentheses within the text with the page number preceded by *TT*.

10. W. H. Auden, *Collected Poems* (New York: Vintage, 1991), p. 868.

11. It is amazing that before Gilligan wrote *In a Different Voice,* no one had noticed that Lawrence Kohlberg's famous studies on moral development and its correlative definitions and markers had been based exclusively on male subjects.

Chapter Six. Rejoining the Planet

1. Martin Heidegger, *What Is Called Thinking?*, trans. by J. Glenn Gray (New York: Harper and Row, 1968), p. 30

2. Again, *The Trickster, Magician, and Grieving Man: Reconnecting Men with Earth* (Santa Fe: Bear and Co., 1994) explores in depth the heroic masculine gender identity's disconnection from the earth.

3. Toni Morrison, *Beloved* (New York: Alfred A. Knopf, 1987), p. 268.

4. Edgar Allan Poe, "The Imp of the Perverse," in *Great Short Works of Edgar Allan Poe* (New York: Harper and Row, 1970), p. 476.

5. Sophocles, *The Oedipus Cycle*, trans. by Dudley Fitts and Robert Fitzgerald (New York: Harcourt, Brace and World, Inc., 1969), p. 82.

6. Leo Tolstoy, *The Death of Ivan Ilyich*, trans. by Lynn Solotaroff (New York: Bantam, 1981), p. 131.

7. Bruce Wilshire, *Wild Hunger: The Primal Roots of Modern Addiction* (Lanham: Rowman and Littlefield, 1998), p. 185.

8. Charles Frazier, *Cold Mountain* (New York: Random House, Vintage, 1998), p. 330. Any further references to this work will be in parentheses within the text with the page number preceded by *CM*.

9. Harold Lubin, *Heroes and Anti-Heroes: A reader in Depth* (San Francisco: Chandler, 1968), p. 30. (Gilgamesh tale is on pp. 16–31.)

10. John Barthes, *Chimera* (New York: Fawcett, 1972), p. 19.

11. Maurice Merleau-Ponty, "Eye and Mind," in *The Primacy of Perception*, ed. by James Edie (Evanston: Northwestern University Press, 1964), p. 185. Any further references to this work will be in parentheses within the text with the page number preceded by *PP*.

12. Aristotle, *Nicomachean Ethics,* (book II), in *The Pocket Aristotle* (New York: Washington Square Press, 1958), p. 190.

13. Edward S. Casey, *Getting Back into Place: Toward a Renewed Understanding of the Place-World* (Bloomington: Indianan University Press, 1993), p. 313.

14. Catherine Keller, *From a Broken Web: Separation, Sexism, and Self* (Boston: Beacon Press, 1986), p. 195.

Index